THE PICTURE OF
ABJECTION: FILM,
FETISH, AND THE
NATURE OF
DIFFERENCE

THE
PICTURE
OF
ABJECTION

Film, Fetish,
and the Nature
of Difference

Tina Chanter

INDIANA UNIVERSITY PRESS

Bloomington and Indianapolis

This book is a publication of

Indiana University Press
601 North Morton Street
Bloomington, IN 47404-3797 USA

http://iupress.indiana.edu

Telephone orders 800-842-6796
Fax orders 812-855-7931
Orders by e-mail iuporder@indiana.edu

The paper used in this publication meets the minimum
requirements of American National Standard for Information
Sciences–Permanence of Paper for Printed Library
Materials, ANSI Z39.48-1984.

Manufactured in the United States of America

Library of Congress Cataloging-in-Publication Data

Chanter, Tina, 1960-
   The picture of abjection : film, fetish, and the nature of difference / Tina Chanter.
      p. cm.
   Includes bibliographical references and index.
   ISBN-13: 978-0-253-34917-0 (cloth)
   ISBN-13: 978-0-253-21918-3 (pbk.)
   1. Abjection in motion pictures. 2. Sex in motion pictures. I. Title.
   PN1995.9.A25C43 2007
   791. 43'6538—dc22   2007032952

1 2 3 4 5 13 12 11 10 09 08

Contents

THE PICTURE OF ABJECTION: FILM, FETISH, AND THE NATURE OF DIFFERENCE

INTRODUCTION

A CLOSE-UP MIRROR IMAGE of a child carefully applying lipstick seduces the audience into gendered assumptions that director Alain Berliner sets out to render unstable in *Ma vie en rose*. When Ludovic's parents dismiss his wearing his sister's "princess" dress as a "joke," their laughter deflects his deadly serious identification as a girl, yet not before both their new neighbors and the audience are offered the opportunity to be unwittingly complicit with Ludovic's desire to identify as a girl.[1] The heteronormative causal lines that are usually assumed to operate among bodies, gender, and desire are thereby momentarily suspended, before being reenacted. The parents of Ludovic's schoolmates petition to have him removed from school, and his house is daubed with the words "bent boys out." Forced out of their affluent, suburban neighborhood after Ludovic's father loses his job, his family discovers that the causality that requires male bodies to underlie masculine genders and female bodies to ground femininity is also constitutive of middle-class identity.

Identificatory regimes operate according to imaginaries that facilitate and support symbolic matrices in ways that remain inarticulate or invisible to dominant representations. By effecting a momentary disruption of such identificatory regimes, film can bring into relief alternative imaginaries, and in doing so can open up the possibility of transforming the terms in which dominant socio-symbolic representations construct identification as normative. At the same time, film can expose the complicity among dominant configurations of gender, sexuality, class, and race, such as the way in which middle-class identity relies upon the causal implication between a male body and masculinity. Gender assumptions are revealed to be constitutive of class identity. They are part of the fabric that helps to consolidate the image that the middle class projects of itself and imposes on those who fall short of it. When Ludovic fails to live up to these assumptions, he is effectively expelled from the community. Unable to tolerate the disorder that Ludovic represents, the community thus strives to maintain intact the continuity between male bodies and masculine gender that Ludovic's very existence challenges. Excluding Ludovic becomes a way of reasserting and consolidating the community's coherence on the basis of gendered norms that prove to be constitutive of its self-understanding.

The films with which this book is preoccupied enact the ways in which the social texts of gender, race, class, and sexuality constitute one another. The constitutive nature of social groupings is exposed through processes, acts, and states of abjection. In particular, the fluidity of abjection is revealed as the social fabric of hegemonic assumptions is torn and reconstituted. Subjects are abjected by identificatory regimes that preclude them or render them unintelligible. Striving to establish or maintain their integrity, subjects abandon others to abject states, often in an attempt to consolidate boundaries that are threatened. Yet abjection can also be taken up as a political strategy, given shape as a way of protesting and disrupting imaginaries that are sustained through the systematic exclusion of certain others. Subjects can be momentarily abjected by undergoing the disruption of hegemonic identificatory regimes that they typically take to be stable and beyond question. Abjection can render visible an imaginary that remains for the most part invisible to groups whose identity as subjects has been purchased in part at the cost of abjecting those whose excluded status prevents them from appearing as subjects. Abjection can shore up the identities of some subjects as privileged while effectively preventing other subjects from being able to constitute themselves as subjects or from having their attempts to do so recognized as such. Sometimes abjecting themselves in the service of ideologies, subjects strive to maintain symbolic systems of authority as cohesive. In the process, the legacy of exclusionary ideologies and practices is perpetuated and reinvigorated.

One does not, of course, approach film empty-handed. We bring certain assumptions to our cinematic viewing, assumptions that will sometimes be overturned in our viewing, in ways that might have more permanent effects if we are ready to theorize our assumptions, and reflect on them in a way that makes them available to challenge, rendering us capable of tracking the ways in which we are challenged aesthetically or politically. We bring with us assumptions about the desirability of realism, for example, or the need for verisimilitude or the political salience of film—or, conversely, its apolitical status. Film does not merely serve as an exemplification of theoretical insights, but rather as a medium that can sometimes reveal *signifiance* in excess of theory, just as theory can function, at times, in excess of film, indicating its lacunae, or helping us reflect critically on its trajectory. The relationship between film and theory is explored here as one that is not so much dialectical as mutually constitutive, wherein theory can illuminate film; yet, equally, film can open up, reorganize, challenge—reconstitute—theory, highlighting its blind spots, foregrounding its limitations, contributing to, or expanding, its insights. Sometimes an organizing moment in the narrative films explored here will confirm a theoretical stance, add substance or weight to it, and sometimes it will reach beyond theory, take theory further, add to it, or contest it.

Abjection renders problematic any assumption of the stability of boundaries separating objects and subjects. Its moral charge is neither inherently good nor inherently bad. While it is necessarily transgressive in the sense that it does not respect the fixity of boundaries between self and other, passive and active, private and public, or inside and outside, its transgressive character can be mobilized in the service of politically regressive or progressive forces. Abject moments can put into crisis imaginaries by exposing their instability. As such they can provide opportunities for reworking identificatory mechanisms. The deferral and production of abject moments in film can facilitate and disrupt identification in ways that make available for reflection and interrogation the imaginary operations that we usually take to be indicative of who we are, of our identities and the identity of others. Equally, abject moments can be used to shore up identities whose stability has been threatened in the wake of breaching boundaries that might have been assumed to be unassailable.

Any discourse that claims for itself a foundational status by exempting from its orbit those it designates as other at the same time as appropriating what it can from them conforms to the logic of abjection. Whether the language of appropriation is sexist, colonialist, or imperialist, meaning and value is established through absorbing what can be assimilated, and relegating to some unthinkable region that which does not conform to the dominant values. Whether the value to be tapped is reproductive capacity, labor resources, a market for consumer products, raw materials, energy sources, or land for cultivation, the logic of appropriation consigns to prehistory that which is discarded, and designates it as an inassimilable other. Women are rendered unthinkable by patriarchy except as reproductive vessels or maternal caretakers, while the humanity of workers cannot be registered within the logic of capitalism, which acknowledges them only as labor power or consumer power. The environment is reduced to the wasteland of slag heaps, while the natives of colonized lands either are not recognized as properly human, or only become so through forced practices of assimilation.[2] Thus, there is a systematic production of waste, of that which is useless, unproductive, of that which does not conform to the logic of patriarchy, capitalism, or colonialism. At the same time there is a usurpation, exploitation, and appropriation of precisely that which is only admitted insofar as it is capable of conforming to such logics. Theoretical discourses endorse, participate in, and reinvent such dynamics, creating their own logics of marginality.

Take psychoanalysis, for example, which has the dubious merit of constructing multiple marginal figures, on the basis of their gender, sexuality, class, and race, but whose primary other is figured in terms of femininity. In their attempt to legitimate themselves, psychoanalytic narratives produce sites of excess or irrationality that are posited as exterior and interior to their own coherence and logic. The feminine comes to stand for a mythical past, relegated to a time that predates the Oedipal narrative, the terms of which are formulated in a way that precludes the entry of the feminine, other than as masquerade. At the same time psychoanalytic constructions of femininity systematically appeal to raced others. The very possibility of representation is consonant with Oedipal identity, such that any claims to be heard outside Oedipal logic are condemned as illogical or nonsensical. The sole form of representation that is admitted as coherent is that condoned by the Oedipal narrative, which represents itself as universal only by foreclosing any interrogation of its historical and progressive privileging of masculinity, which it presents as a more advanced or civilized state than femininity, and which is therefore determinative of meaning. The Oedipal configuration thereby surreptitiously acknowledges what it repudiates. Phallic privilege comes to determine what constitutes value, the contingency of which is occluded through a conflation of the values that are instantiated by the ideal of masculinity and those that are taken as representative of humanity. A symbolic system of meaning and its values is established by way of a compensatory narrative that covers over its lack, finitude, or frailty, by positing this inadequacy as outside itself, an outside that is projected into a mythical past that comes to be associated with the feminine. Figured as a castrated—and castrating—other, femininity presides over "meanings" that, from the perspective of phallic logic, are inassimilable and can only ever appear to be fragmentary, incomplete, or momentarily incandescent. Lacking, by definition, the phallic principle of completion, which is achieved precisely through the fantasmatic and prosthetic production of wholeness in the face of its threat, the feminine becomes a constitutive outside of the very discourse it both enables and from which it is exempted.

The production of the feminine as a site of excess by a masculine imaginary allows for the inclusion of those aspects that prove useful for inclusion and incorporation by a masculinist and ostensibly universalist logic. The feminine is admitted only insofar as it constitutes the raw material to be worked over and made to conform to a logic that will not admit it as excessive or different, but that requires its otherness or alterity to subsist as inferior and contained. Thus, both at the material level of the reproduction of the species, and at the level of signification, the feminine is admitted only insofar as it can contribute productively to the society or the state, the ends of which are defined by an invisibly white, patriarchal capitalism. Anything that cannot be converted into assets from this point of view is discarded as incoherent, insane, nonsensical, outside the bounds of reason, as defined by a logic that is taken to be universal. To be admitted into the system as meaningful is to signify within its terms. To exceed its terms is to be dismissed as inferior or meaningless. Yet the site of conversion from non-meaning to meaning remains significant in a way that cannot be captured from the point of view of the categories in which meaning resides. How, then, can this significance be acknowledged without assuming the legitimacy of the meaning toward which the scales are tipped?

While this logic of marginality is replicated across various discourses—patriarchal, capitalist, colonialist—it is equally true that attempts to bring into question each of these discourses are liable to reproduce a similar logic internally. Feminist discourses produce their own internal others, variously marked in racial, sexual, or class terms. Whatever advances are made in the name of feminism must be balanced against the capacity of particular feminist discourses to remain critically alert to their own complicity with racist, heterosexist, and middle-class assumptions. Postcolonial discourses, unless they pay systematic attention to issues of gender, are liable to reinvent gender oppression in their efforts to formulate anticolonial, nationalist discourses. The internally differentiated logic of each metadiscourse—even apparently progressive discourses such as feminist and subaltern movements—militates against any attempt to render them completely homologous with one another. The tendency of radical politics to reproduce at another level and in a new guise the exclusionary gestures against which they are protesting, and thus to invent a new series of others in their attempt to combat the processes that have in turn hypostasized them as other, demands theoretical reflection.

Forms of self-expression are dictated according to the norms legitimated by commodity culture, so that in order to be recognized as such, even the available means of dissent have been anticipated, and conveniently packaged for consumption.[3] Needless to say, such control need not be overt or coercive; indeed, more often than not, consent is manufactured, and ideology functions in a way that assimilates potential rebels or transgressors through procedures of self-regulation.[4] Given the efficiency with which consumer-citizens produce themselves in accordance with dominant norms, subjecting themselves to and reproducing commonly recognized forms of expression, perhaps it is not surprising that even apparently progressive discourses such as feminist, antiracist, anticolonialist, anticapitalist, and lesbian, gay, and bisexual discourses tend to have recourse to available forms of discriminatory logic. In order to shore up their own claims to be recognized, such discourses resort, often unconsciously, to the same kind of divisive thought patterns to which they object, setting up their own internal others to be maligned, disparaged, or dehumanized. Subjects thereby replicate the structures according to which they have been marginalized, merely infusing them with new content.

In efforts to take seriously the fact that the construction of gender has relied upon an inarticulate, indeterminate notion of race, or that race has a repressed, gendered history, theorists have rendered determinate those racialized or gendered histories that have been left indeterminate. The very process of rendering determinate this indeterminacy leads to possibilities of reifying or fetishizing those marginal excluded others who have played a constitutive role in the configuration of gender or race discourses, but whose role has not been acknowledged as such, or has only been acknowledged in exclusionary ways.[5] Not only is there a danger of fetishizing previously excluded others, but in the process of bringing to light their abjection, in the process of giving shape to, or specifying the contours of their history and experience, as often as not new others are abjected.

Abjection, as Julia Kristeva puts it, "draws me toward the place where meaning collapses" (1982, 2). At the same time as threatening the current symbolic order, abjection provides the opportunity for its reworking, precisely insofar as it represents a crisis in meaning. By paying attention to abject moments, and to the moments that produce and follow them, moments in which identity appears to coagulate and cover over the fissures and cracks that help to produce it, we can contest the forces that tend to gain hegemonic power over us. The specific histories of particular individuals, and the political circumstances in terms of which identities have been shaped, together with the irreducibly singular ways in which we as individuals come to respond to what life presents to us, can be revealed in the fractures of the stories we tell, and are told, about others and about ourselves. Privileged moments of abjection can help to reveal the ways in which I have been unconsciously shaped by forces over which I am never in complete control. If intrinsic to the operation and elaboration of the symbolic is not only the necessity of abject positions, together with the impossibility of their complete articulation within the systems they maintain, but also the production of new abjects, it might be wise to pay attention to the logic of this operation. Abjection can figure as a site of dissolution or undoing of the categories fetishism works so hard to keep in place by bolstering up the symbolic meaning that is always already secured in advance by a masculine imaginary, subtended by a racial imaginary, the interrogation of which psychoanalysis has largely foreclosed. Abject moments can erupt, and can take effect variously. Abjection "is something rejected from which one does not part" (Kristeva 1982, 4). Whether it is a matter of subjects identifying their subjectivity, or communities cementing what binds them by way of expelling that which comes to be constituted as radically other, the movement of expulsion is constitutive of subjects and communities. It is not just that there is an outside constitutive of who I am, nor merely that in order to consolidate my identity there are various exclusions that I do not so much perform as discover myself as having always already benefited from, even as I challenge them and in doing so transform them. The point is to understand the inherent mobility of such constitutive gestures, the ways in which they can turn into something else, or become other than themselves—sometimes in creatively transformative ways and sometimes in regressively defensive ways.[6]

Abjection is constitutive of the coherence and integrity of subjects and communities, such that a movement of rejection or expulsion is foundational to the identity of subjects and communities. If central to the founding of subjectivity is an expulsion that is at the same time constitutive of the other as other and the subject as subject, then subjectivity is indebted to and contingent upon a defining of boundaries that establishes the distinction between subjectivity and otherness. In this sense, that which becomes other, that which is designated other, is constitutive of subjectivity precisely in its exclusion. The very possibility of being a subject, and of distinguishing other objects and subjects from oneself, owes itself to a preliminary and tentative positing of boundaries, a demarcation or discrimination of I from not-I that marks the moment of moving beyond primary narcissism. For Kristeva, at the level of the subject the separation of the infant from the mother is paradigmatic of abjection. It is a separation that is, for the infant, at the same time a provisional institution of subjectivity through the rejection of the mother as other. Kristeva's account of the abjection of the mother marks a departure from Freud, for whom the mother is the first object-choice. It marks a departure from Lacan insofar as it rewrites the mirror phase, situating the significance of the prematurity of the infant at an earlier point of development. The mirror stage, fetishism, and castration theory have taken center stage in Lacanian film theory. Abjection offers a way of developing a new direction in film theory. Of particular interest is the way in which abjection returns to haunt the symbolic that it both founds, and from which it is rejected. If the abjection of the mother's body is a founding moment of the symbolic/social order, it is only through the order that it founds that its movement comes to be articulated. That articulation occurs in political discourse, even purportedly liberatory discourses, in a way that establishes a metonymic chain of dejects—as raced, classed, or othered in ways that fall outside of the normative, idealized subjects that stand for the status quo.

Since for Lacan the entry into the symbolic is indissociable from castration, to be a desiring subject is to be a subject of castration. Built into castration theory, with its attendant theory of fetishism, and the transcendental role of the phallus as master signifier, is an understanding of sexual difference that positions the maternal-feminine as prior to language or pre-symbolic.[7] Freud attributes a lack to women, based on their failure to live up to the expectation that women, like men, have penises, a mythical castration that provokes castration anxiety. Fetishism is a defense against the threat that women thereby represent. Women are the occasion for fetishism, yet have little need of fetishism themselves, for women are always already subject to a mythical castration. This has not prevented film theory from having taken up fetishism as an interpretive strategy intended to shed light on the general experience of spectators.[8]

As a corollary of castration theory, in Freud there is a consistent, although problematic, distinction between identification as aligned with the father, and object-choice, which is aligned with the mother. In fact Freud's introduction of the phallic phase could be read as symptomatic of his repression of maternal identification. The consequences of this extend beyond Freud's well-established failure to elaborate a theory of maternal identification. For, although less pronounced than the discourse that reads it as a defense against women's mythical castration, the trope of fetishism is also implicated in a racialized discourse. If femininity is figured as lack—the horrific, abject, unthought ground of castration anxiety—its abject status is articulated in terms of an imaginary racing of subjectivity that subtends the more overtly thematic organization of psychoanalysis by sexual differentiation. In this sense one might say that race is the real, that which stages the psychoanalytic oedipal narrative, but which itself remains unvoiced or unrepresented by it. The impossibility of figuring the symbolic work of this racial discourse that breathes life into the psychoanalytic scenario, but which is itself strategically omitted from its theoretical recycling, is reflective of a cultural imaginary that has repudiated the necessity to think through the racial tropes that help to constitute the psychoanalytic corpus. While the theoretical work that race does for the trope of fetishism is usually ejected from the terms of textual analysis, it is recuperated at the level of cultural criticism. The fetish becomes applicable to racial marginalization, but in a way that repudiates its elaboration in terms of sexual difference. Without thinking through how race and gender are implicated in one another, race theorists transfer the fetish in an exchange that takes place between the discourses of feminist theory and race theory, so that it is reflective of a universal, monolithic value, albeit reborn.

The logic of fetishism, employed in different ways by psychoanalytic theory and Marxist theory, has found its way into feminist theory, race theory, film theory, and cultural theory. In questioning the continued theoretical commitment to recycling the logic of disavowal, even when this fetishistic trope is used as a critical resource, or even when its production is inadvertent, I suggest that Kristeva's notion of the abject can provide critical resources. Neither object nor subject, the abject designates a domain to which those unthought, excluded others are relegated, whose borderline (non)existence secures the identity of those who occupy authoritative positions in relation to dominant discourses. Kristeva says, "there are lives not sustained by *desire,* as desire is always for objects. Such lives are based on *exclusion*" (1982, 6). Abjection designates the problem of the constitutive outside, or the always improperly excluded other, that which is excluded for the sake of establishing identity as coherent. Mothers, daughters, and wives whose unpaid physical and psychic labor could not be recognized by Marxist class theory were abjected by a theory that is incapable of acknowledging the contribution of women due to its exclusive concentration on class relations and the categories of paid labor. In turn, those shadowy figures who people the imaginary of the official story that mainstream, white, middle-class, Western feminism tells itself function as abject. African American domestic workers, or South Asian immigrant homeworkers, render precarious the public/private distinction that has been so central to formulating mainstream feminist theory.[9] The very existence of racialized minorities who perform paid labor within the home is ignored by the representation of home as domestic space out of which (privileged, white, Western) women must migrate, and the public realm as a space of freedom and work that must be accessed. Far from being a space of liberation, as it is typically construed within Western feminist frameworks, the public realm operates in oppressive and imperialist ways for colonized peoples. The forced inclusion and incorporation of Native American women by United States governmental systems, and the imposition of U.S. citizenship on these (non)subjects, whose land and ways of life were appropriated, cannot be accounted for by the categories of mainstream feminist categories (Guerrero 1997). Peripheral yet facilitating, the zones that these figures occupy are ambiguous border zones that straddle the neat dichotomy between public and private, and complicate the legacy of civil rights as unambiguously liberatory.[10]

The ignorance that has allowed mainstream feminist theory to proceed in ways that are oblivious to the racialized exploitation of certain others has been explored in a variety of ways. Yet these corrective analyses systematically encounter the problem of reinventing new forms of marginalization in the very attempt to redress hegemonic relations. The invention of new others can be specified as a problem of omission—where the interests or concerns of certain marginalized groups are simply neglected or overlooked. Or it can be construed as structurally produced by the ongoing specification or inclusion of previously marginalized groups as no longer marginalized, or not-to-be-marginalized. A dynamic is set up whereby new forms of fetishization spawn new subjects who are placed in relation to abjection, new dejects. To take just one example, the imperative that South Asian women should not be marginalized by white, Western, feminist discourse is issued with the self-consciousness that even the category "South Asian" functions hegemonically, reinventing the terms of imperialism, and privileging the experiences and reflections of some South Asians over others (see Bhattacharjee 1997).

The language of fetishism has gained currency, and with it the concept of disavowal has begun to circulate, often in contexts that remain ignorant of, or disown, the ideological commitments to which the purveyors of this term thereby commit themselves.[11] It is recycled with varying degrees of success, but the economic laws governing its recirculation are not in question. They are governed by masculinist and racist assumptions, the measure of which has apparently not yet been taken, given the prevalence of the language of fetishism, which takes on a universal, homogenizing symbolic value, much like the monetary value decried by Marx under the commodity form of production. An unreflective commitment to a universally fetishizing discourse recycles in a subtle but pervasive way the priority of white, heterosexist, masculinist, capitalist values, a tendency to be guarded against, especially in work that takes itself to be feminist, or presents itself as asserting the importance of race in the face of white feminists' and psychoanalytic neglect of it.

Is the univocal register in terms of which theories of fetishism establish themselves as the cultural currency of theory accidental, or does it reflect something internal to the theory itself? If the universality with which gender or race or class assert themselves as the privileged, authoritative, and autonomous terms of radical discourses mimetically reflects the dominance assumed by the discourses of patriarchy, white supremacy, or bourgeois ideology against which they are mobilized, can the tendency to produce new dominant narratives of gender, class, race, or sexuality guard against new forms of abjection? Must each of these discourses retain a discrete, impervious focus that reinvents the hegemonic terms of the very discourses under protest in order to achieve success? Is there too much anxiety associated with confronting multiple forms of oppression at once? What could help prevent the all too frequent relapse into a false universalism that undercuts the radical intentions of apparently progressive discourses?

By casting fetishism as only a moment of an ongoing process that is implicated in the fluidity of imaginary, amorphous, invisible, excluded, unthought others, we can draw attention to the logic of abjection that grounds fetishistic discourses, a logic that such discourses utilize more or less consciously. There is an ambivalent inclusion of subjects, who are on the one hand situated outside of representation, in a mythical, indeterminate past that is mythologized as prior to civilized society, and on the other hand granted access to forms of representation that are nevertheless shaped and informed by their exclusion. Access is granted to these forms of representation only if those who are excluded acquiesce to their representation as subjects who conform to the imaginaries of dominant narratives. Articulating this logic of abjection clarifies how discourses of racism, sexism, classism, heterosexism, and nationalism are implicated in each other in ways that play off one another to produce their own internal others. At the same time, the prevalence of the trope of fetishism, a trope that has asserted itself in different ways within the discourses of Marxism and psychoanalysis, and has been imported into the discourses of feminist and race theory to create new, dominant narratives, depends upon the erection and celebration of a univocal, monolithic value. While the value of fetishistic theory—whether in commodity fetishism or its psychoanalytic variant—resides in its capacity for transference across discourses, its reassertion of an apparently universal standard of value in every case marks the limits of its interpretive capacity. What needs to be problematized is the tendency of discourses that take themselves to be progressive to reinvent the universal appeal of fetishistic values, without heeding their own production of the abject. From the beginning of her work, Kristeva has been concerned with demystifying the fetish that either commodities or signs become in the processes of economic or symbolic exchange characteristic of capitalism. As Joan Brandt puts it in her exploration of Kristeva's affiliation with the journal *Tel Quel*, "Productive labor . . . is essentially denied by the capitalist system, concealed by society's fetishization of the product and of the money that serves as its sign in the system of exchange. Kristeva's emphasis on textual productivity and her attempt to uncover the multiple, pre-linguistic processes that both constitute but also undermine the unity of meaning are . . . central to her own and *Tel Quel*'s critique of traditional notions of language" (Brandt 2005, 26). If critics have successfully mapped the continuity in Kristeva's work between her earlier critique of fetishism from a Maoist point of view, to her later critique of consumer society (Brandt 2005, 34), they have focused less on the critical distance Kristeva takes on the version of fetishism Freud embraces and Lacan inherits. Kristeva turns to Freud in *Revolution in Poetic Language* for a theory of subjectivity that she finds missing in Marxism, but in what way does she rework Freudian fetishism? How are multiple sites of meaning opened up in the imaginary or semiotic processes that Freud and Lacan recuperate in the form of primary processes under the name of the paternal signifier, and in terms of fetishistic theory? Specifically, how might abjection refigure the univocal meaning enshrined in the trope of fetishism?

If in one sense the import of the trope of fetishism for Freud admits of proliferating references, in another sense these meanings are controlled by the overarching structure of the Oedipal father. Any object (or word, or condensation of the two) can stand in for the missing penis of the mother, and thus play the role of the fetish, but this material and verbal diversity is undercut by its highly restrictive symbolic meaning. Symbolically, the role of the fetish is always and only to represent a penis that never existed. Or rather, it only ever exists as conforming to the *expectation* fostered in the masculine imaginary that organizes Freudian and Lacanian psychoanalysis, namely that women *should* have a penis. The trope of fetishism, then, operates as subordinate to phallic discourse, which is organized according to a logic of castration that confers a univocal value on the phallus, in relation to which not only ontological or proprietary meanings are bestowed, but the fundamental distinction of sexual difference is determined. Either one has the phallus, or one is the phallus. From this point of view, the theory of fetishism constitutes a defense against the proliferation of meanings, of which women become symbolic. It is women's morphological difference from men that challenges the masculine expectation that women's pleasure should be essentially the same as men's, and that it should be defined according to a narcissistic investment in a penis (or penis substitute). The fetish is produced in an attempt to ward off the threat that this difference presents, and to rein in its significance not by canceling it out, but by allowing it to co-exist: I know that women are castrated, but by producing a fetish I can deny it. Of course this "knowledge" itself proceeds from an imaginary expectation that women resemble men, and in this sense, the fetish serves to reestablish the legitimacy and coherence of that mythical expectation, and to cover up the fear both that such an expectation might be thwarted, and that it not be thwarted. That is, castration anxiety amounts to the fear that boys might after all resemble girls in the sense that they might lose the penis and become, like the girl, in the masculinist psychoanalytic imaginary, castrated.

To be sure, within this highly restrictive economy, and as distinct from the mechanisms of foreclosure and repudiation, the trope of fetishism admits of a limited ambivalence. As Kelly Oliver says, "the male child both accepts and denies that his mother is castrated by substituting a fetish for her missing penis. In this way, the child accepts external prohibitions and satisfies his internal drive forces at the same time. This ambivalent relation to reality—both accepting and denying—is more flexible than any foreclosure" (2001, 63). It is more flexible, but its flexibility is only effective within the confining discourse of phallocentrism. Outside of that closed field, as the sign of that which effects its closure, is the real of sexual difference, including women's capacity to give birth, a capacity that is unspoken, unsymbolized except insofar as it provokes horror: the excluded real of Lacan and Freud, that which can only be represented by the fear of women's genitals. In Lacanian terms, having been excluded from the realm of the symbolic, as unrepresentable within its terms, the series of separations that occur before castration confers its ambivalent law of similitude can only signify within the Oedipal logic of the name of the father. As Ewa Ziarek puts it, "Because narcissistic and erotic investment is intertwined with a threat of castration, the phallus subsumes all the prior experiences of loss from birth trauma, oral deprivation of the breast, anal separation, to castration, and in doing so becomes a signifier of lack" (2005, 69).

If Lacan extends castration retroactively so that it incorporates pre-oedipal losses, so that castration functions metonymically to name previous instances of loss associated with separation from the maternal body, Freud is more cautious. In a footnote written in 1923 to the case history of Little Hans—the same year in which "The Ego and the Id" (1953e) and "The Infantile Genital Organization" (1953i) were published—Freud considers, and rejects, the advisability of extending the reference of the "castration complex" to other instances of loss.

It has been urged that every time his mother's breast is withdrawn from a baby he is bound to feel it as castration (that is to say, as the loss of what he regards as an important part of his own body); that, further, he cannot fail to be similarly affected by the regular loss of his faeces; and, finally, that the act of birth itself (consisting as it does in the separation of the child from his mother, with whom he has hitherto been united) is the prototype of all castration. While recognizing all of these roots of the complex, I have

nevertheless put forward the view that the term "castration complex"
ought to be confined to those excitations and consequences which are
bound up with the loss of the *penis*. (1953a, 8, n. 2)[12]

Kaja Silverman also quotes this passage, commenting that Freud's
"refusal to identify castration with any of the divisions which occur prior
to the registration of sexual difference reveals Freud's desire to place a
maximum distance between the male subject and the notion of lack. To
admit that the loss of the object is also a castration would be to acknowledge that the male subject is already structured by absence prior to the
moment at which he registers woman's anatomical difference—to concede that he, like the female subject, has already been deprived of being,
and already been marked by the language and desires of the Other"
(1988, 15). Not only is Freud reluctant to admit, as Silverman suggests,
that the male subject, like the female subject, is marked by lack before the
registering of sexual difference, before castration anxiety sets in. Perhaps
still more significantly, the passage signifies Freud's attempt to recuperate the notion of lack in such a way that woman, as castrated, becomes
its sole representative for a subject who becomes the sole representative of subjectivity—the male subject. In this sense, there is a masculine
imaginary at work that precludes women from a productive relation to
the law: the production of fetishes is restricted to male subjects, who
represent female subjects in relation to a fetish, in order to cover their
lack. The fetish represents the law of similitude, and is underwritten by
phallic monism.

We are all subjects of the law. We are brought into being as desiring subjects in accordance with a set of norms or codes that are shaped
by certain familial and societal prohibitions, such that even when we
transgress those prohibitions, even when desire consists in transgressing
the law, our desires are still intelligible in the light of the law. The possibility of transgressing the law nonetheless signals a discrepancy that
can be specified in terms of a lack of fit between the imaginary and the
symbolic. So long as the symbolic exchange of signifiers adheres to the
imaginary law of sameness, the material reality of women's morphology—their actual sex—functions as excluded, its meaning foreclosed as
horrific, and hence as abject. It is the unthought, abject ground that
has been rejected by phallic theory. At the same time, castration, which
signifies the entry into language in Lacanian theory, becomes not just
the mark of sexual difference, but also the mark of cultural intelligibility as dictated by the heteronormative and mutually exclusive gender
norms that it founds. This is why Judith Butler is right to elaborate a
critical distance on the "normalization of (hetero)sexuality" (1993, 92)

that organizes Lacan's formulation of the symbolic. She is also right to mobilize the term "abjection" as a way of figuring those who are "inarticulate yet organizing figures within the Lacanian symbolic" (1993, 103).

Criticizing Butler, Oliver says, "Those who are foreclosed by social norms that constitute the subject are excluded as unintelligible, invisible, and nonexistent. To exist is to be intelligible and to be intelligible is to exist" (2001, 62). Regimes of intelligibility are multiple and competing, so that to suffer abjection as a raced subject can be understood as falling outside the norms of intelligibility, while gendered norms of intelligibility might render the same subject intelligible. In a sense, then, Oliver is right, to say that Butler (at least in 1997) "prevents any effective distinction between types of alienation or subordination" (2001, 65), although I understand Butler's use of the logics of repudiation, foreclosure, and abjection to yield results that go beyond the "patriarchal imaginary" (Oliver 2001, 68) of psychoanalysis.[13] Butler demonstrates the ways in which Lacan's formulation of the law forecloses certain identifications as viable while at the same time using abjection in a way that reaps the benefits of an imaginary rewriting of the psychoanalytic scenario that is indebted to Irigaray's feminine imaginary.

On my reading, Butler is not using abjection as a political category, as Beardsworth suggests, so much as commenting on how society functions according to taboos that situate homosexuality as unclean or improper.[14] Psychoanalysis replicates and reproduces a hegemonic imaginary that situates heterosexuality as central, and homosexuality as deviant. While psychoanalysis inscribes a genealogy in which certain forms of sexuality are admitted into its theoretical apparatus in the form of case histories that document psychic aberrations, its normative force resides in delineating the pathological as deviating from the norm. That norm is provided by the Oedipal myth that forms the architecture of psychoanalytic theory, which stipulates a heterosexual destiny and assumes idealized sexual positions are exclusive of one another. Various dejects populate the pages of psychoanalytic theory, not as instances of viable sexuality, but precisely as unviable. It is thus society and psychoanalysis (which is far from immune from recycling, legitimating, and reconstituting heteronormative mythology, and in fact has been one of its primary mythmakers) that politicizes homosexuality in qualifying its deviance, and in doing so constitutes it as a political and moral aberration, which transgresses the law. Butler's intervention is one that resignifies what already constitutes a political category, and uses the language of abjection to do so. Normative identity is thus constituted according to a logic that would set up heterosexuality as original (natural), and yet, according to a binary logic on which Butler draws, in doing so it has always already referred to homosexuality even if to distinguish itself from it. The "originality" of heterosexuality is thus displaced, as it is in fact established through a socially induced prohibition that discards homosexuality as an improper mode of sexuality. The symbolic authority of heterosexuality therefore accrues from a discrimination that has deposed homosexuality as inferior to itself, while at the same time using it as a counterbalance to itself, precisely as other. Castration theory relies on the positioning of women as phallic representatives, as "being" the phallus, while men are figured as always inadequately "having" the phallus. According to Butler there is an anxious need to reiterate the mutually exclusive sexual positions of male and female, in order to ward off the ambiguity that would otherwise set in. "Identifications are never fully and finally made; they are incessantly reconstituted and, as such, are subject to the volatile logic of iterability" (1993, 105). In this sense, she reads the heteronormative order as a defense against sexual ambiguity. Society designates as abject those who threaten the cultural order it ordains when it insists that there are only two sexes, male and female, and only two genders, masculinity and femininity. The causal lines of heteronormative desire require that unambiguously male bodies underlie masculine gender and construe themselves as desiring subjects in relation to unambiguously female bodies that underlie feminine bodies. By asking whether the "undelineated figures" of "feminized 'fag' and the phallicized 'dyke' " are "structuring absences of symbolic demand" (1993, 103), Butler points to the way in which the psychoanalytic imaginary conforms to a heteronormative law that it institutes as normative precisely through "the exclusion and abjection of a domain of relations in which all the wrong identifications are pursued" (103). Butler reads the performative resignification of the symbolic by certain figures whom it typically marginalizes as creatively transforming symbolic authority.

Butler's critique is aimed at the "political inadequacy" of Lacan's conception of the law, which "suggests that the law . . . cannot itself be reworked" (1993, 105). While Beardsworth is right to criticize Butler's earlier work for suggesting that the effect of Kristeva's imaginary or semiotic can only be "temporary" or "futile" (232), in *Bodies that Matter,* far from relegating any transformation of the imaginary to a realm that is temporary and futile, Butler is fully cognizant of the force of the imaginary.[15] She makes this clear when she understands identifications as imaginary, as "never fully and finally made" (1993, 105), as always performed in relationship to the threat of the law. "To identify with a sex is to stand in some relation to an imaginary threat, imaginary and forceful, *forceful precisely because it is imaginary*" (1993, 100; my italics). Perhaps it would be helpful to distinguish between two different senses of abjection in order to understand that Butler is using abjection to make an intervention into the sexualized imaginary of psychoanalysis. Insofar as Kristeva's use of abjection remains internal to the mechanics of Oedipal theory, it functions more or less analogously to the Lacanian real, but insofar as it interrupts and refigures that theory, it participates in a regeneration of the psychoanalytic imaginary. In this sense abjection stipulates not only the Lacanian real, but also reworks it. While Butler herself does not make a thematic distinction between the functioning of the abject at the registers of the real and the imaginary, I think she strategically exploits the notion of abjection in a way that participates in and extends Kristeva's rewriting of the psychoanalytic imaginary. In this sense Butler takes up Kristeva's notion of the abject and applies it more critically to Lacanian psychoanalytic theory than Kristeva does, by taking a distance on its heteronormative contours.

While critics have recognized that abjection is a defensive mechanism and that it also constitutes a reworking of the mirror stage, the full implications of this have not been worked through for film theory.[16] I read abjection as a staging of a defensive dynamic that has the potential to significantly rework the imaginary commitments of Oedipal theory, specifically its privileging of masculinity and fetishism. At the same time, the abject signals that which is excluded from the system of meaningful signification, as excessive to its logic, intolerable to its terms, an impossibility. It is the refuse or waste product—the real of phallic thought that threatens to contaminate it, always only provisionally excluded. Kristeva develops the notion of abjection in a framework whose allegiance to Lacanian psychoanalysis does not allow a radical departure from its phallic commitments, with the result that she adheres to the basic premise of the primacy of sexual difference, a premise that I think needs to be put in question.[17] Butler has taken up Kristeva's notion of abjection and put it to work in contexts that resist the binary, heteronormative assumptions of Freudian and Lacanian psychoanalysis (Butler 1993), and Iris Marion Young has extended its application beyond sexual difference. "Racism, sexism, homophobia, ageism, and ableism, are partly structured by abjection, an involuntary, unconscious judgment of ugliness and loathing" (1990, 145). Oliver and Trigo have not only shown how abjection can be used to elaborate how various defenses are produced in an attempt to secure the "blurred boundaries of racial, sexual, and national identity" (2003, xv), but have also done so in the context of film theory. Their enquiry focuses on film noir, however, while mine deals with contemporary film. Barbara Creed (1993) has also used the motif of abjection to explore film, limiting herself, however, to horror film. This book argues that Kristeva's notion of abjection, and the ways

in which it has been extended by other critical analyses, can be taken
up as a productive intervention into film theory. It does so by interrogating the relationship between abjection and fetishism, interrogating the
apparent universality that theories of fetishism have attained in cultural theory, and challenging the monolithic values thereby upheld.
Abjection can help us think about the ways in which the imaginaries of
imperialism, nationalism, racism, sexism, and homophobia appeal to
exclusionary logics in ways that often play off one another. It can help
us think about the ways in which psychoanalytic, feminist, and race theories participate in, co-construct, and benefit from such exclusionary
logics. It can also help us think about how sexualized, racialized, and
classed others function as abject within certain theoretical discourses,
such as psychoanalytic and film theory. That is, they facilitate and enable
theories of identification and fetishism to stabilize themselves around
privileged tropes such as the phallus, without requiring that those tropes
remain accountable for the ways in which they benefit from homophobic, masculinist, nationalist, or racist condensations and displacements
that help to construct that privilege. In Kristeva's work, abjection functions
in a way that privileges the maternal body as a site of abjection that
facilitates the child's separation from the other by instituting an initial
and unstable boundary between subjects and objects. It works to set up
a tentative subjectivity for the infant, who sets itself up as an I through
rejecting what comes to be figured as the abject maternal body, while
remaining beholden to, desirous of, and fascinated by the pleasure and
gratification provided by the maternal body. At the same time abjection
participates in and facilitates the imaginary logics in terms of which
societies understand themselves. These logics enable nations to distinguish themselves from one another, drawing not only on racist, colonialist, and imperialist myths, but also articulating these myths by
relying on sexist, homophobic, and classist ideologies. Young comments
on the interchangeability of these myths, which suggests both that these
mythologies constitute systems of exchange in and of themselves, and
that they communicate with one another in ways that legitimate and
shore up one another.[18] These logics not only often draw on one another
in ways that are mutually supporting in that they serve to confirm the
invisible authority of whiteness, masculinity, heterosexism, and middle-
class identity but also produce their own internal abject casualties in order
to reassert their authority.

    Kristeva has mapped out the logic of abjection by showing how the
mother's body becomes the site of a defensive maneuver on the part of
the child, such that all that is displeasing comes to be posited as outside
the body, while all that is pleasurable comes to be contained in the body,

and thus a clean and proper body is instituted as the imaginary body. This reworks Freud's understanding of the bodily ego, the boundaries of which are instituted by a defensive mechanism that does not yet conform to the phallic, fetishistic logic that sets up sexual differentiation.[19] If imaginary bodies come into being on the basis of what pleases me, and what displeases me (or disgusts me), and if that pleasure is not yet calibrated in terms that privilege sexual difference, it is possible to think about the ways in which racist, classist, or nationalist imaginaries inform what, in the language of Freud's essay "Negation" (1953o), I would like to be inside me, and what I would like to remain outside me. That the delineation of inside and outside remains, initially, fantasmatic, in the developmental chronology Melanie Klein maps out, and on which Kristeva draws, only serves to highlight the usefulness of the trope of abjection as having explanatory force in the sphere of political imaginaries. Abject figures become the repositories of a world in which shifting boundaries allow various dejects to mark the limits of socially acceptable, purified, civilized imaginary norms.

Everything from conventions and rituals of cleanliness and ideologies of child-rearing, to variations in ethnic cuisines, will impact what is available to be taken into the body and what is construed as that which must be kept outside the body. Tastes and dislikes will be constructed according to cultural variation. What can be taken into the body and what must be kept out, what I separate myself from, and what I identify with, will be organized according to strictures that organize the world according to religious, cultural, and social prohibitions and taboos. This opens up the possibility of understanding how subjects construct, from infancy, a sense of themselves that draws on, for example, racist imaginaries, such as that which informs the child who, in Frantz Fanon's famous description, abjects (we could say) him with the words "Look, a Negro! . . . I'm frightened!" (Fanon 1967a, 112). As such, it potentially expands the compass of psychoanalytic thinking, making it possible to think the primal mapping of the body in terms of racial geographies, such as Fanon's account of the corporeal fragmentation he experiences under the gaze of the child. Critical attention has tended to focus on the fragmentation and dislocation of the body image experienced by Fanon, yet equally important is the power of the mythology that has impacted the white child's way of seeing Fanon's black skin. If a nascent theory of abjection is born in Fanon's phenomenological reworking of the mirror-stage, it remains subordinate to an overarching commitment to a fetishistic narrative by which Fanon confirms rather than displaces the normative theories of sexual difference that pervade Freudian and Lacanian psychoanalysis.[20]

Drawing on Mary Douglas, Kristeva has shown how rituals of purification help to delineate the identity of communities, and how such rituals separate what comes to be understood as human, as distinct from
the animal and the spiritual. The sacred and the profane are thus distinguished according to communal frameworks that endorse a culturally and historically specific understanding of what is acceptable and
what is unacceptable. The boundaries of cleanliness and uncleanliness,
the boundaries of the pure and the impure, the boundaries of decorum
are set up in line with culturally generated taboos. Thus *Powers of Horror*
is concerned, first, with the provisional boundaries the infant sets up in
abjecting the mother and becoming a subject, henceforth capable of formulating a desire for objects that are now understood in contradistinction
from itself as subject. It is equally concerned with the ways in which
social and cultural boundaries are put in place as a defense against what
henceforth is figured as defilement and impurity: dirt, menstrual taboos,
excrement, sites that are constructed as disgusting and unclean. Since
parental codes are constituted in the light of culturally specific norms
that specify what counts as unclean and impure, the ways in which infants
abject the maternal body will also be informed by cultural codes that
discriminate, in Klein's language, the fantasmatic good object from the
bad object.

Even the construction of the maternal body as abject might be read as
inseparable from the devaluation of motherhood that pervades the
postindustrialist capitalist logics of modernity. In this sense, we should not
take for granted that Kristeva's privileging of the maternal body as abject
is innocent of the pervasive sexism that infects psychoanalytic theory, any
more than we should read as neutral the taboos and cultural constructs
that Douglas analyzes, including those which posit menstruation as
taboo, as innocent of sexist assumptions.[21] Having said this, the import
of Kristeva's reading of abjection in *Powers of Horror*—even if it derives
in part from a logic that sometimes participates in, or is complicit with,
the abjection of the feminine—resides in the opportunity it opens up to
go beyond the privileging of the incestual and parricidal taboos of oedipal logic, replete with the patriarchal heterosexism constitutive of that
logic.

In chapter 1 I argue that a racialized discourse of primitivism subtends
Freud's discourse of fetishism and sexual difference. Film theorists such as
Christian Metz have focused on Lacan's mirror stage, elaborating fetishism as the principal mechanism for film criticism. Kristeva's notion of
abjection rewrites the mirror stage in a way that has implications for
the concepts of identification that inform Metz's argument. Articulating
the relation between abjection and fetishism facilitates reflection on the

relationship—and dissonance—between the imaginary and the symbolic and thus allows for a consideration of how identification can be disrupted and transformed.

In chapter 2 I situate Kristeva's notion of abjection in relation to Freud and Klein. I suggest that we read the notion of abjection in the context of Freud's essay on "Negation," an essay to which Kristeva turns in a number of her texts, and one on which Jean Hyppolite has commented at Lacan's invitation. The essay has also proved to be a focal point for Klein and her followers, especially Susan Isaacs and Paula Heimann. Kristeva's notion of abjection is indebted to Klein's notion of projective identification—this much is clear from Kristeva's own acknowledgments as early as *Tales of Love*. It also becomes clear in Kristeva's intellectual biography of Melanie Klein that Kristeva's notion of the imaginary father, which is allied to abjection, is closely related to Klein's "combined parent figure."[22] Focusing on *Powers of Horror, Tales of Love*, and *Melanie Klein*, and also referring to *Sense and Non-Sense of Revolt*, I take my cue from Cynthia Chase and Mary Jacobus, both of whom have argued that in mapping the infant's rejection of the mother, Kristeva inscribes a primary identification with the mother. This primary or maternal identification can be traced back to Klein's projective identification, in which the child sketches in a provisional, fantasmatic fashion a primary myth of inside and outside—to borrow Hyppolite's phrase in his description of Freud. It is just such a myth that Freud will harmonize in his essay on "Negation" with an account of judgment and the emergence of repression and the symbol. I suggest that abjection be understood as an inscription of negativity that functions as a precondition of fetishistic disavowal, and I read abjection as Kristeva's interrogation of the absolute status of the phallus. As Sarah Ahmed (2005) has shown, the fantasmatic or hallucinatory sketching of a border between inside and outside can be applied beyond the infant's attempt to separate from the mother. The imaginary symbolics fueling racialized, nationalist myths can also be thought in terms of the defensive maneuvers of abjection. As a protection against emptiness, narcissism is elaborated as a defense against abjection, one that precedes the mirror stage, and is elaborated by Kristeva in a sensorial register, not limited to the scopic drive that fuels either the mirror stage or fetishistic disavowal. As such, the fantasmatic narcissistic defenses that political imaginaries articulate in order to ward off abjection can be read in the registers of racism, and not restricted to that of a primary sexual difference.

Recent engagements with aesthetics, psychoanalysis, and politics have gravitated toward the question of mourning and melancholia. In chapter 3, I argue, with reference to the Canadian film, *Margaret's Museum,* that abjection provides a more fruitful political engagement with art and psychoanalysis in some ways. Issues of purification have long characterized the relationship between art and philosophy, both in the sense that theorists have tried to discriminate amongst the arts, establishing a hierarchy among them, and in the attempt to establish the true function of art. Modernism, then, for some critics, becomes the truth of art. While I want to resist the drive to purify art, as if art had only one legitimate form or function, and to remain skeptical about the privileging of one art over all the others, I also want to take seriously the importance of the specular in conferring unity on the bodily ego, to which Lacan has drawn attention. At the same time, I follow Kristeva's insistence that the priority accorded to the visual is a belated phenomenon, occurring only in the wake of a corporeal mapping of the sensory body, over which the maternal or caregiving function presides, and which includes the vocalic, as well as touch.

For Kristeva, the attempt to purify oneself, and one's society, and hence the impulse of abjection, is constitutive of identity. As that which shows us what we normally attempt to thrust aside, the corpse is a privileged site of abjection. *Margaret's Museum* (Canada, 1995) concerns the taking up and transformation of a woman's abjection, a resignifying of that which a capitalist economy has rejected as its waste product. By introducing the abject into the context of a museum, Margaret issues a challenge to the economy that has laid waste to her family, while the film issues a challenge to the traditional contents and function of museums. At the same time, it raises questions about the form of art as political protest. Conventional distinctions between form and content are thrown into disarray, as that which is excluded from an economic system that produces death without signifying loss, except in the shape of requiring women to mourn effectively, is reintroduced as signifying differently.

Chapter 4 continues to develop an account of how abjection functions in relation to film, referring to some of Kristeva's lesser-known texts on film. For Kristeva film exercises fascination over us because of the trace of unrepresentable aggression it bears within it. In certain instances, film refers to fantasies even as they fascinate us. This reference to fantasy as such Kristeva calls the thought specular. Like abjection, the thought specular precedes the mirror stage. I take up the attention Kristeva pays to those instances in which film takes up fantasy as fantasy, and in doing so distances spectators from fantasy even as it continues to exercise a certain fascination. While taking up her focus on films in which fantasy is referred to as such, I move beyond Kristeva's adherence to the oedipal narrative and her tendency to focus on avant-garde art, and on horror films. I explore the opportunities that abjection opens up for the potential reorganization of identification by referring to the foundational fantasies that orchestrate social subjects in two Dogme 95 films, Lars von Trier's *Breaking the Waves* (Denmark, 1996) and Thomas Vinterberg's *The Celebration* (Denmark, 1998).

Lévi-Strauss appeals to women as objects of exchange in a system of communication that essentially excludes women from an active or creative relation to meaning. By relegating women to the role of bearers of meaning, the ultimate arbiter of which is instantiated by the phallus, Lacan appealed to the logic of gift-giving as that which cements the boundaries between social groups, a logic that expresses itself in its ultimate form in the exchange of women in marriage. In chapter 5 I suggest why feminist theorists need to distance themselves not only from Lacan's formulation of the symbolic—which is heavily indebted to Lévi-Strauss's understanding of women as signs of social exchange that sediments familial taboos—but also from the trope of fetishism. This chapter elaborates on the problematic of fetishism, both in its Marxian and psychoanalytic register, in relation to Canadian (although of Armenian extraction) director Atom Egoyan's *Exotica* (Canada, 1994), commenting on the limitations of Lacan's notion of the symbolic, which remains entrenched in Lévi-Strauss's theory of society as predicated on the exchange of women. A film that explores the conditions under which the white, male, heterosexist gaze fetishizes women, *Exotica* can be read as elaborating a critique of fetishism and the sexual commodification of women. *Exotica* is a film that uses the trope of fetishism even as it destabilizes it, at the same time as it reworks the mirror stage that has been a mainstay of film theory.

An opening scene of *Exotica* interrogates the dominant heterosexual, white gaze, replacing it with what bell hooks has called an "oppositional gaze."[23] As we witness a black customs officer being trained to scrutinize potential offenders of the law, an officer we later discover is gay, the power of the gaze is redistributed in a way that disrupts dominant regimes of vision. Later, when the officer confiscates the exotic eggs that Thomas has smuggled across national boundaries, having just satisfied his desire by transgressing the sexual borders of the heterosexist norm, we understand that the sites of power are differential and malleable. Disrupting social and political boundaries is a theme with which Egoyan is preoccupied. By having a black, gay man represent the law protecting national boundaries in the interests of capitalism, one whose gaze comes to restructure Thomas's relation to his own sexuality as well as to the law, Egoyan might be said to rework the paternal metaphor, usually taken to be invisibly white. He evokes the body of work that has organized itself in film theory around Lacan's mirror stage, a motif to which he refers throughout the film. Club Exotica, for which the film is named, is carefully delineated as a space for the indulgence of pleasure, gratifying the desires of middle-class men whose hard work has earned them the right to relax. Francis is chastised for attempting to work through the effects of trauma in a place that is not designed for therapeutic ends. The separation of therapy from pleasure that Zoe (Arsinée Khanjian), the club's female manager, attempts to maintain suggests that Francis is mixing up categories that capitalism maintains as discrete. Christina (Mia Kirshner) does not respect the boundaries of commodity fetishism any more than Francis (Bruce Greenwood) does. In her role as exotic dancer, she defends herself against the neglect she suffered as a child at the same time as allowing herself to exploit, even as she subjects herself to, the sexual commodification of women's bodies. By combining a working-through of childhood trauma with the role of an exotic dancer she complicates any simple analysis of such roles as signifying women's victimization by commodity fetishism. Christina's fetishization constitutes a complex condensation of racial and sexual forces, a trope that Egoyan uses at the same time as he interrogates it, exposing the abject excluded ground on which racial and sexual taboos are erected.

Hegemonic influences make themselves felt in cultural practices that organize education in ways that participate in imaginary formations that replicate the fetishization of disciplines, both in formal and institutional ways, producing "heteroclite" islands (Kristeva 1984, 13) that tend to hermetically seal themselves from influences that are constituted as "outside."[24] That educators and primary caregivers reproduce these hegemonic practices in relation to children, who are inculcated according to modes of interaction that reinvent socially, culturally, and politically exclusionary boundaries, should not surprise us, but it should foster critical thinking. Subjects separate from their mothers in ways that are structured by conventions that already participate in racist, sexist, homophobic, classist, and nationalist imaginaries. I follow up abjection in a way that might serve as a revolutionary impulse to move beyond the relentless celebration of phallic, fetishistic, paternalistic logic of oedipal theory, which privileges sexual differences over other socially salient differences.[25]

I suggest such a reworking in chapter 6 by exploring how the taboo of miscegenation is constitutive of nationalist imaginaries that are played out it in D. W. Griffith's notorious *The Birth of a Nation* (United States, 1915), Michael Curtiz's *Casablanca* (United States, 1942), and Tony Kaye's *American History X* (United States, 1998). These three films can be seen as significant landmarks in the representation of race relations in American film history. (Although director Tony Kaye is British, *American History X*, a study of neo-Nazi ideology and race relations in America, is set in California's Venice Beach.) Embedded in *Casablanca*, heralded by some critics as a decisive advance over overtly racist representations such as those of *The Birth of a Nation*, is a Euro-American myth prohibiting homosexuality and miscegenation, but which passes for the Ur-American myth of heroic, masculine, benevolence. Sam has been read in terms of the trope of fetishism in the critical literature on *Casablanca*, yet such readings tend to stabilize rather than destabilize the hegemonic forces of masculinity, racism, and nationalism that constitute its imaginary. Even sophisticated readings that interpret Sam's role as fetishistic neglect the national imaginary that *Casablanca* sketches out for the United States. Robert Gooding-Williams, whose reading might be said to reap the benefits of Freud's understanding of fetishism as a defense against homosexuality, reads Sam as the musical go-between, whose song "As Time Goes By" brings Rick and Ilsa together. This analysis of Sam, while highly suggestive, does not go as far as it might, inasmuch as it recycles the trope of fetishism in a way that condenses in the figure of Sam its hermeneutical valence for sexual difference and racial difference without accounting for the fantasmatic role that each of these tropes play as part of a nationalist imaginary. By mobilizing the trope of abjection to uncover the forces that subtend Sam's fetishistic role, I attempt to shed light on the sexual, racial, and national imaginaries that help to construct one another. I situate *Casablanca* in the context of *The Birth of a Nation*, a film whose aesthetic achievements cannot be divorced from its overt racism, and the more recent *American History X*, in which the formation and deformation of a white, racist imaginary is explored in the context of class and immigration.

Chapter 7 is devoted to a reading of Irish director Neil Jordan's *The Crying Game* (Ireland, 1992), a film that participates in a postcolonial narrative, in a way that self-consciously interrogates the metaphorical and metonymical relations of gender, race, and class to one another. Refusing to privilege one imaginary over another, *The Crying Game* uses the motif of transgender to disrupt the binary relationship of feminine and masculine, and the binary logic by which genders are typically understood to map onto underlying female and male bodies within heterosexist regimes. Exploring the racial oppositions of black and white, and Anglo and Irish, and the ways in which racial taboos can function to mask gender ambiguity, the film does not allow us to treat gender, sexual, or racial boundaries as stable. It thereby suggests how abject responses are elicited as defenses in subjects when crises erupt that call into question the boundaries with which they typically protect themselves. In the context of a narrative within which Dil's comparatively light skin color renders Fergus's desire for her less taboo than that of his homoerotic relationship with the darker-skinned Jody, race functions to facilitate Dil's passing as a woman. It functions in a way that facilitates, and is constitutive of, sexual desire. On discovering Dil's penis, Fergus hits out at her, and then vomits. The moment can be described as one of abjection, the impact of which encompasses not only Dil and Fergus, but potentially also the audience. Dil's abjection occurs as the sexual identity Fergus thought he had established for himself is thrown into question, and as those in the audience who had identified with what they (and he) took to be Fergus's heterosexual desire for Dil are, along with Fergus, abjected. Yet by asking the audience to reread Fergus's desire for Dil through his identification with Jody, Jordan interrogates the abjection of Dil, relocating it in a perspective that does not assume the fixity of boundaries and that serves as the imperative to abject transgendered identity. At the same time Jordan allows the figure of Dil to present a challenge to the logic of fetishism. In Jody's eyes Dil is not the monstrous phallic woman—a woman on whose body the fetish gives way to the imaginary, mythical penis. Dil demystifies the veiled problematic of fetishism, the success of which depends precisely on the lack of conformity of the fetish to the penis, at the same time as she highlights the heterosexist and homophobic assumptions of fetishistic theory. The critical reception of *The Crying Game* reveals that critics have had difficulty juggling Jordan's multiple concerns without giving way to the tendency to claim that one is foundational, in the process abjecting the others. I explore the way in which abjection structures the relations in the film at a number of levels, but I am also interested in how abjection unfolds itself as a practice of reading in the critical literature on *The Crying Game*, even, perhaps especially, in readings that present themselves to be, and which have been read as, progressive.

In chapter 8, moving away from a tendency to assume Europe, or the West, as the default point of reference, I examine the way in which fetishistic logics reassert themselves in race and postcolonial contexts. Drawing on postcolonial theorist David Lloyd (1999), I suggest that Homi Bhabha (1994) and Frantz Fanon (1967a) are limited by their adherence to a theory of fetishism, which has infiltrated itself into the political rhetoric of nationalism, a rhetoric that continues to trade in abjection without acknowledging it. I consider Uma Narayan's exploration of how Third World feminists are construed by masculinist postcolonial narratives by suggesting that such narratives articulate themselves according to mythologies that, on the one hand, involve a regressive throwback to a mythical precolonial past, and on the other hand require that women protect an imagined spiritual purity that becomes representative of this mythic past. In Deepa Mehta's *Fire* (Canada/India, 1996), Radha and Sita contest such constructions by instituting an economy of desire as an alternative to the restrictive demands of a postcolonial nationalist imaginary constituted at the confluence of Indian, Hindu, and patriarchal beliefs and a defensive yet exploitative posture toward the imaginary of the capitalist, materialist West. I suggest that both Fanon and Bhabha participate in discourses of fetishism that are displaced by Narayan and by Deepa Metha's *Fire*.

The concluding chapter situates Kristeva's account of abjection in relation to the problem of fetishism, clarifying how abjection pushes beyond Freudian and Lacanian oedipal and symbolic theories, in particular, how its fantasmatics read a different lesson into the Fort/Da game that Lacan takes up from Freud's "Beyond the Pleasure Principle" (1953b). I refer to Mike Leigh's *Secrets and Lies* (England, 1996) in order to point to the difference between a Lacanian and a Kristevan reading. While Seshadri-Crooks's Lacanian reading of the film emphasizes the role of the absent father, I suggest, through a reading that engages the trope of abjection, the metaphorical work that racialized relations perform in the condensation of racial and sexual tropes performed by an insult Roxanne hurls at Cynthia, her mother. In response to Cynthia's revelation that black-skinned Hortense is in fact Cynthia's child, Roxanne calls her mother a "slag," thereby condemning her not only for conceiving Hortense out of wedlock but also at the same time reasserting the boundaries prohibiting miscegenation.

In addressing the ways in which the notions of race, class, sexuality, and nationalism need to be thought as constitutive of one another, I am suggesting that it is not enough to see these as factors, vectors, or axes of discrimination that can be thought of as overlapping, intersecting, or operating in hybrid conjunction with one another. Rather than presuppose the coherence of these categories in and of themselves, I propose to advance the critical project of uncovering how they are always already shaped and informed by, implicated in, one another. A good deal of feminist theory is in the process of attempting to formulate more adequately than has been done in the past the relationships among race, class, gender, and sexuality. Current terms of analysis are dominated by a model of intersectionality, in which these categories are construed as interconnecting, overlapping, or intersecting with one another. While feminist theorists have put such models to productive use, this way of envisaging the relationships inscribed in the complex field that now constitutes the terrain of feminist theory can be problematic, depending on how carefully the notion of intersectionality or interlocking oppressions are articulated. The tendency to attribute an analytic equivalence to the concepts of class, gender, race, and sexuality, or to assume that these concepts are transparent, that they have integrity in and of themselves, needs to be avoided. Otherwise we fall short of conceptualizing the ways in which these categories have in fact been historically formative of one another, although the constituting role that, for example, race has played in configuring gender, has remained invisible in (white) feminist formulations of gender.

One of the theoretical stakes of resisting the language of "interlocking" axes of oppression is gestured toward in Jean-François Lyotard's insight that even genuinely transformative or revolutionary gestures are not just liable but bound to produce new oversights.[26] To entrench ourselves in the language of gender or race—even to inhabit those discourses in ways that are intended to be liberatory—is to endorse a reification of such concepts that is bound to overlook the abjection of other subject positions that are relegated to background phenomena, and rendered insignificant by the very elucidation or critical deployment of one concept rather than another.

In fact, the "categories" of race and gender are always already indelibly shaped by one another, and their emergence at specific points in history is tied to a convoluted interdependence, in which they take on a particular historical configuration specific to a historical epoch. Race, as a modern concept, emerges at a particular time (industrial, capitalist, colonialist). As such, its legibility inheres in discourses that have been constructed around the production of surplus value and organized not only around class tensions and competing myths of nationalism, but also around ideologies of gender and sexuality. Gender, as a category mobilized by Western feminists, takes shape initially as a white, middle-class, heterosexist concept, but its emergence as a political category intended to specify all women renders invisible its race, class, and heterosexist biases. To take seriously this history of indebtedness is also to see that categories of identity based on the signifiers of race, gender, class, or sexuality are far from self-evident. Not only does any knowledge claimed on the basis of identifying with such categories have to be achieved as the product of critical self-reflection, the categories themselves are historically and politically implicated in one another in ways that render them contestable.

Precisely as invisible, race has functioned in ways that have shaped, informed, and produced the discourse of gender, but its role has remained undertheorized, inarticulate. It has been included in covert ways, as an ambiguous ground. There is a compacted and sedimented history that cannot be parsed out without confronting the ways in which one category has served as constitutive of another in a particular historical epoch. If feminist theory fails to pay attention to the constitutive but invisible role that race, class, and sexuality, in different moments, have played in the configuration of gender, the apparently foundational and universal valence of gender will reassert itself. Race, sexuality, and class will only be permitted to take second place in relation to gender, which will continue to operate as if it were neutral with regard to these secondary, derivative differences while in fact it retains the middle-class privilege of white heteronormativity.

The problem I am pointing to is not limited to feminist theory, but finds itself replicated in race theory. Race theorists who privilege the trope of fetishism have fallen prey to a similar theoretical impasse. In attempting to contest the hegemonic privilege of whiteness, race theorists contest this racial privilege by rendering visible those who have been both historically and theoretically marginalized according to the invisibly normative standard of whiteness. In doing so, race theory has tended to draw attention to whiteness as the hidden privilege in terms of which the dynamic of racialization has played itself out. In order to maintain itself as the dominant narrative, whiteness has constructed for itself the racialized other, which has functioned as an excluded ground. Just as feminist theory has allowed the concept of gender to dictate its liberatory agenda, so race theory has allowed the concept of race to remain at the center of its analyses. Feminist theory thereby continues to marginalize the experiences of its racialized others, just as race theory continues to marginalize its gendered others. This process is replicated between various competing discourses, each of which makes an implicit appeal to the proper placement of boundaries, as if those boundaries were sacred, and any disruption of them would lead to disorder. Is it necessary to oversimplify multifaceted oppression in order to focus concentrated attention on invisible mechanisms that have structured our imaginary, communal life in ways that render difficult any attempt to articulate them?

1

Abjection as the Unthought Ground of Fetishism

It is hopeless to attempt to isolate the three elements of mimetic desire: identification, choice of object, and rivalry . . . whenever any one of them appears, the other two are sure to follow.

—Girard, *Violence and the Sacred*

ACCORDING TO FREUDO-LACANIAN psychoanalysis, identification is reserved for the father, the law, the symbolic, while object-relations are aligned with the maternal, or with the relation that develops following on from the auto-eroticism of the mother-child dyad. Feminist theorists have good reason to point to the problematic set of assumptions informing this distribution, assumptions that construe the mother-child relation in terms of need, as one primarily concerned with self-preservation, that is, with animality, or the biological. By contrast, adhering to Hegel's distinction between need, demand, and desire, the symbolic realm of language is construed as the specifically human, as opposed to the merely animal, domain. It does not seem to have occurred to Lacan (or if it did, it was of little consequence) that the application of Hegelian triplicity to early infantile development might be a product of a Western imaginary, rather than a universal state of affairs. If Oedipal triangulation amounts to a naturalization of the modern, postindustrial familial relations unique to the nuclear, Western family, what would it mean to rethink the imperative of separation, individuation, or realization of autonomy in a way that no longer aligns biology, need, and self-preservative instincts with the mother, and humanity, desire, and orientation to the Other with the father? Lacan's appropriation of the Hegelian tripartite structure extends not only to the distinction between need, demand, and desire, and its rebirth as the real, imaginary, and symbolic, but also to the abiding importance of Freud's Oedipal triangle. What informs the association of the father with the law, desire, and prohibition, and the mother with the provider of biological needs? Isn't there a heterosexist, reproductive teleology that requires the mother to assume the limited and singular function of biological provider, and the father to assume that of disciplinarian?

The conceptual importance of separation on the psychoanalytic account is bound up with the child's self-reflective comprehension of maternal love as meaningful, that is, as directed toward the child in its particularity, to employ Hegelian terminology—the child as having its own, clean, and proper body, to use Kristeva's language from *Powers of Horror*. Hence the insistence of the dramatic importance of the child's realization that it is not the sole object of the mother's desire, the child's inculcation of the phallus as a sign that signifies that the mother's desire lies elsewhere. It is, says Kristeva, with respect to the father that the mother is proud of, and loves, the child (see Kristeva 1987). For love to be distinct from that which satisfies need (food, warmth, clothing—the bare necessities), for it to figure as significant—as abstracted from the oceanic universe in which the child is immersed—the child must be differentiated from the mother, and from the world of necessity she traditionally provides. Without such differentiation, no object can exist for the child. Ironically, in the assumption that the child's relation with the father must be the site of this differentiation, one can discern a characteristic failure of the psychoanalytic narrative to separate the mother from the background of all that she offers and makes available to the child. In this sense, psychoanalytic theory itself might be said to have separation issues. We find here too resonances with Hegel's deification of Antigone on the one hand for her pure ethical intuition, and his denigration of her on the other hand for her failure of self-consciousness: she is, in Klein's language, the good and the bad mother, rolled into one. So too, parallels with Levinas's elemental and those shadowy, feminine figures that inhabit the dwelling, making it a home, do not fail to impose themselves.

The need for the child to individuate itself from the mother is conflated, in the psychoanalytic narrative, with the assumption that individuation must be a function of a paternal third. Kristeva's refusal of the question of the origin of identification—is it with the father or the mother?—is symptomatic of her refusal to question as rigorously as she might the Hegelian legacy of Lacan, and the heteronormative imaginary that fuels the psychoanalytic scenario (see Kristeva 1987). She does, however, challenge the habitual association of the mother with object relations and the father with identification (see 1982, 32), in order to focus attention on the instability of the object relation, thereby highlighting the formative, preoedipal period, in which the child's ego is not yet fully formed—the period prior to the mirror stage, prior to the visual synthesis that enables the child to confer stability on the object relation through naming. For Kristeva, influenced by Klein, fantasmatic, pseudo-object relations—the good or bad object—exist prior to the child's initiation into language.[1] Fantasmatic objects do not adhere to the stable contours of the imaginary body or corporeal schema that results from the bodily projection of the ego, but they do operate according to the still-unstable borders of what will be inside, and what will be outside, to adopt the language of Freud's important essay, "Negation."

The instability of the object relation is characteristic of early infantile, fantasmatic attempts to order the world according to what is good and what is bad, in terms of likes and dislikes, pleasure and displeasure, taste and repulsion. Symbolic language brings stability to the early mapping of inside and outside, facilitating meaningful communication, while at the same time inviting the risks of reification, burdened as it is with all the normative injunctions a given political community entails. Among these normative injunctions is the importance of separating out the specifically human from the merely animal, a moral and philosophical imperative that has found its way into aesthetic judgments. Accordingly, there is not only a denigration of biological need and a concomitant devaluation of the domestic sphere, which is historically marked as feminine; but also a denigration of everything that is useful and an association of usefulness and need with ugliness.[2] Such a denigration finds its corollary in the formalist conception of art, originating from the eighteenth century, for which, as Arthur Danto puts it, "art, taste, beauty and pleasure" are bound together in a "tight, conceptual package."[3]

One wonders how much the horror that Freud associated with female genitalia was derivative of the aesthetic proclivities of the eighteenth century. Is the horror of castration anxiety provoked not only by the "nothing to see," but also by the associations of female genitals with birth, need, biology, usefulness—self-preservation of the human species? Against the context of an aesthetics of taste, in which, as Keats famously said, "Beauty is truth, truth beauty,—that is all / Ye know on earth, and all ye need to know," the effort of artists to bring back in ugliness, to point to the horrific underside of all that formalist aesthetics considers beautiful, is also an attempt to ask at what cost is the Kantian analogy between beauty and moral goodness sustained.[4] Who is relegated to the outer reaches of ugliness, primitivism, and bestiality in order for the "civilized" world to celebrate it own mimetic and perspectival art as great? Abject art points to the hypocrisy that is evident in the wielding of the criteria according to which that which is rejected by civilized society—as animal/feminine/primitive-need, usefulness, ugliness—is precisely necessary in order for the pursuit of ideals of freedom, goodness, and beauty that transcend the merely animal and qualify as specifically human traits. The latter come to be marked as white, as masculinist, but their flourishing depends upon keeping hidden or under wraps the realm of biological need—marked as the feminine/primitive. The suggestion that sublime terror expands the soul, while horror contracts the body, might be read along similar lines.[5]

The psychoanalytic terms that are taken up by film theory constitute a highly contested terrain. The status of reality and its relation to fantasy, the meaning of identification, the importance of castration theory, and the significance of each of these for the Oedipus complex and sexual difference—none of these can be presupposed. Christian Metz has been criticized for the way in which he took over Freud's problematic theory of identification, and for failing to address the question of sexual difference, difficulties that were then recycled throughout film theory. In attempting to solve these difficulties, even critics of psychoanalytic theory have held fast to a theory of castration and its attendant Oedipus complex, without confronting the ways in which Freud's Oedipal account of castration is fraught with an unacknowledged tension over the relative importance, and precise function of, the mother and father. Identification, and in particular, Freud's inability to sustain a coherent distinction between paternal identification and maternal object-choice, has become a notoriously problematic site.[6] This problem can be addressed by establishing the connection between Freud's failure to sustain a coherent distinction between object-choice as maternal and identification as paternal with his "discovery" of the phallic phase and the concomitant development of the logic of fetishism. In this sense the introduction of the phallic phase can be read as symptomatic of Freud's repression of maternal identification, while Kristeva's theory of abjection figures as a response to the dominant logic of fetishism, a logic that governs Freud's texts and film theory as well. I draw on the discourse of abjection to open up a way of questioning that requires that psychoanalysis be answerable for its exclusion not only of feminized others but also of "other" others—those who are subject to racialized, classed, and sexualized regimes. In doing so, I both locate in Freud the problem Kristeva designates abjection, and go beyond Kristeva's own elaboration of abjection.

In its attempt to understand the cinematic experience, spectator gaze or apparatus theory, as it has come to be known, has privileged Lacan's mirror stage. The audience is said to identify with the images with which they are presented in a way that is similar to the child's recognition of itself in the mirror. The language of the cinematic screen thus functions analogously to the mirror, its vocabulary consisting of a range of codes that take the place of signs. In both cases, there is a relatively inhibited motor activity on the part of the spectator/infant, and an illusory and idealized quality in the apparent perfection, completion, and mastery of the projected screen/mirror image. Like the prisoners in Plato's cave, cinema spectators are in a dark, womblike environment, enthralled by the images that pass before their eyes, images that seem to emit sounds, phantoms that are taken for reality. If not in literal chains, the audience is subjected to a powerful fascination exerted by the screen image, which encourages the immobility, isolation, gullibility, and passivity of the spectator. The protagonists onscreen appear to drive the action of the narrative that unfolds before the spectators, yet behind the scenes and before the screening of the film an absent director presides over that vision. By means of actors and the narrative in which their characters are embedded, idealized versions of the spectators are thereby represented to themselves. The typical action hero survives the dangers he confronts, gets the girl he pursues, or conquers the mystery he investigates. What might be unattainable in real life, is attainable through identification with the larger-than-life characters onscreen. The symbolic goals of the rich, the famous, and the beautiful are enacted in a way that both renders them accessible to us, and reminds us of the distance that separates us from the perfectible, illusory world of Hollywood.[7]

Like Lacan's infant, we are both captivated, enchanted by the image confronting us, and at the same time alienated by it. We are not, after all, the hero who gets the girl, conquers the world, or lives a life of luxury and leisure—but we could be. Lacan's mirror image presents the child with an image of himself not as he is—for he is still submerged in nursling dependence, still unstable, still unable to stand by himself—but as he will become: stable, whole, autonomous. Modeled on the lack of motor coordination of the infant, film theory reads the split between the passivity of the spectator, and the idealized mastery of the characters onscreen, in terms of the ideological processes by which the audience understands the message of the cinematic images with which it is presented. The subject thus constitutes the meaning of the film by taking over the perfection of the image, at the same time becoming (potential) master of his own fate. Hollywood holds out to us the possibility of realizing the American dream. Presenting us with a salutary image of what the future might hold, the film text offers us a vision of what we hope to achieve, just as the mirror presents the child with an anticipatory grasp of what he could become. Although he has not yet achieved it, the child can attain the mastery and independence that his image reflects back to him. In the same way, the cinematic screen offers us a glimpse of the dreams we could realize. We are able to temporarily lose ourselves in the world opened up by the screen, a fantasy world of possibilities that goes beyond the restrictions of our everyday life. In psychoanalytic terms at issue is how narcissism is structured in relation to the other, how the (symbolic) ego ideal is related to the (imaginary) ideal ego, and how their relationship plays out in terms of identification. The ego ideal or superego is associated with the law of the father, while the ideal ego is associated with maternal omnipotence, which for Freud and Lacan is interpreted as the phallic mother.

If "film is like the mirror" it is, as Christian Metz says, a "strange mirror" (1982, 45–49). It is "very like that of childhood, and very different. Very like, as Jean-Louis Baudry has emphasized, because during the showing we are, like the child, in a sub-motor and hyper-perceptive state; because, like the child again, we are prey to the imaginary, the double, and are so paradoxically through a real perception. Very different, because this mirror returns us everything but ourselves" (49). The "one thing . . . that is never reflected," Metz maintains, is "the spectator's own body" (45). On the contrary, I would say that there is an important sense in which mainstream film does reflect, again and again, imaginary bodies that, while not empirically the spectator's "own" body, certainly serve to render that body symbolically intelligible precisely through depicting bodies that operate according to sanctioned regimes of sexuality, race, and class. In this sense, it is not at all clear that because "the spectator has already known the experience of the mirror" he is "thus able to constitute a world of objects without having first to recognize himself within it" (46). Rather, our recognition of ourselves in a world of objects is one that is accomplished only through a series of repetitive operations that signify and resignify identity in a temporal dialectic that cannot be contained by Metz's suggestion that the spectator already "knows himself and he knows his like" (46), as if identity were completed once and for all after the child has gone through the experience of the mirror stage. In fact, film functions in a way that participates in, endorses, reifies, and sometimes challenges the codes by which we become recognizable even to ourselves, such that it can sometimes show us that what we thought we knew about ourselves is open to question. To say that "the spectator knows that objects exist, that he himself exists as a subject, that he becomes an object for others" (46) is to assume too much about the knowing subject, the assumption of which Lacan's mirror stage served to put into question. Lacan's subject was precisely not the knowing Cartesian subject, but one who in confronting the image in the mirror experiences recognition as misrecognition—alienation (see Lacan 1977a, 22). Whatever mastery is achieved through identifying with an image, whatever self-unity must be assumed in order to construct an image as meaningful, when an image confounds or challenges the meanings we bring to it, that mastery is displaced. Through the deformation of meaning the subject reconstitutes itself.[8]

Along with the mirror stage, castration theory and fetishism have taken center stage in the transcription that Freudian and Lacanian ideas have undergone in film theory. Thus disavowal, the operation put in play by fetishism, has also played a leading role. It has done so at two levels, first in terms of the spectator's disavowal of reality: the spectator knows that the images unfolding onscreen are fantasy, but nonetheless suspends this knowledge, and believes in their reality. Second, the model of fetishism operates at the level of diegetic identification: the spectator knows that women are castrated, but nonetheless attributes to them a phallus, or a fetish, a phallus substitute. Just as psychoanalytic theory tends to assume as normative a male subject by default, a subject whose masculinity and heterosexual desire operates invisibly, so the cinematic viewing subject is taken to be neutral, while in fact fetishistic theory marks it as anything but. It becomes clear that the implied spectator of film theory is not some disembodied subject, but the subject of castration. Since the inception of language is bound up for Lacan with the recognition of sexual difference, and since the castration complex is construed by Freud as a resolution (albeit incomplete) of the Oedipus complex, castration theory becomes an indelible part of the story that film theory tells itself about the cinematic experience. At the same time, its partiality is made unavailable for interrogation, precisely because any and all meaning is understood to derive from a subject that has always already taken a position in relation to castration.

To insist, as psychoanalytic theory does, that all subjects (irrespective of sex/gender) are subjects of castration is to fail to engage the work that castration theory does at the level of metatheory. Insofar as this narrative assumes the experience of the male subject as paradigmatic, one might have expected the status of castration to become a focal point for feminist critiques. Curiously, while Kristeva herself responds to this predicament by casting women's role as "ironic" in the mode of Hegel's Antigone, feminist critiques have been driven by a dynamic that has remained, for the most part, within the confines of masculinist film theory discourse, in that fetishism—one of the defenses exhibited by the (usually) masculine/male subject against castration anxiety—has remained a centerpiece.[9] This puts feminist film theory in a somewhat awkward position vis-à-vis the masculinist discourse it seeks to contest. On the one hand, the assumption that the spectator is male/masculinist needs to be upset, but on the other hand the privileged role that castration theory has accorded to fetishism has gone unquestioned. The explanation for the apparently ubiquitous legacy of fetishism for film theory lies in its having inherited from psychoanalytic theory the apparent inseparability of the acquisition of language from the recognition of sexual difference. The inseparability of the subject's entry into language from the acceptance of sexual difference concerns the role of the phallus, as symbolic of the penis *and of its lack*. It also derives from an attachment to the Hegelian tendency to think difference in terms of self-recognition through the other, such that one's particularity is bound up with a process of conceptual differentiation between myself and others, predicated not on my sensuous sense of self but on the comprehension that I am not other. The status of symbolic lack in relation to the recognition of sexual difference therefore needs to be parsed out carefully. The phallus, under the auspices of castration theory, has been understood as the emblem of language, as the very possibility of representation. An interrogation of the precise ways in which the phallus has come to stand in for the conditions under which it is possible to conceive of a speaking subject reveals a repression not only of feminized, but also of racialized identification.

The mechanism that distinguishes disavowal (*Verleugnung*)—as the operation of fetishism—on the one hand from repression (*Verdrängung*) and on the other hand from negation (*Verneinung*) is developed by Freud hand in hand with his theories about the castration complex, which in turn is implicated in the Oedipus complex.[10] Permeating these theories is a discourse about femininity and a narrative about "primitives." This discourse about femininity and this narrative about primitivism turn out to be decisive in gauging the psychoanalytic significance of fetishism, castration theory, and the status of the phallus.

Freud elaborates the prehistory of the Oedipus complex according to an analogy that needs to be problematized. His analyses of psychic development rely on a set of psychic states that he takes to be analogous—those of childhood, neuroses, and "primitives" or "savages." Because of the obscurity in which Freud surrounds his account of femininity and maternity, it is far from clear how his account of psychic development is subtended by this analogy between the psychic life of children, neurotics, and "primitives." By drawing attention to the impasses with which Freud's investigations into femininity frequently meet, and by reading these alongside Freud's claims about the origins and development of psychic and social life, we can reflect on the implications of psychoanalysis not only for femininity and maternity but also for discourses of racism and nationalism—and we can do so more productively than Kristeva is perhaps either able or willing to do.

Even the texts of psychoanalysis—and certainly the social texts of polities—reveal the fact that subjects set themselves up as subjects not only by separating from the breast, or through birthing, but also by means of a process of fracturing, dividing, or classification that refers, among other mechanisms of division, to racialization. Kristeva opens the door for such an acknowledgment in *Powers of Horror*, with her reading of Mary Douglas, but closes it off in her situating of abjection within an Oedipal narrative in which the phallic order is "traversable," yet that very traversability still testifies to privileging sanctioned forms of hegemonic authority such as sexism and racism.[11] As Cynthia Chase puts it, "For Lacan, signification is determined, and language is a system of pre-existent positions in which gendered subjects find their assigned place" (1989, 77). Even if Elizabeth Cowie is correct to point out that identification is to be thought "not as identity but as taking up a position" (1997, 73) for Lacan identification as a position is thought "in relation to the other of identification" and as such it is "not just a content, the father as super-ego, but the taking up of a position, ultimately of the father in *his* acceptance of castration" (Cowie 1997, 74). Cowie emphasizes that "The stake of identification for the hysteric is not the trait or symptom it utilises (the cough etc.) but the position—ultimately in relation to desire—which is involved. Identification is not produced through imitation but through fantasy" (1997, 77). The question that remains is how far fantasies are circumscribed in advance by Lacan's and Freud's adherence to the Oedipal myth. Kristeva's return, effected through a Kleinian lens, to the question of fantasy allows a relaxation of the strictness with which fantasies must comply to those that play a foundational role for Lacan and Freud.[12] In particular, Kristeva's elaboration of the dynamic of abjection as the projection of the mother's body as that which must be rejected in order for a love relation to be conceptualized as such—which is to say, initially, in order for any relationship at all to be figured—admits the significance of fantasies that do not always already adhere to the phallic contours of Oedipus, fantasies that are not always destined to be, for example, castration fantasies. Rather it is precisely in moving away from the mother, creating a gap—rather than in the conceptual operation that understands conceptually the difference between infant and mother as a logical function, in which I am I because I am not-other—that the process of abjection opens up the imaginary terrain of mapping the body.

Taking up the Kleinian recognition of the central importance of Freud's essay on "Negation" (1953o), Kristeva articulates the dynamics of abjection in a way that substantiates Freud's etching out of a primary myth of inside and outside. Going beyond both Freud and Kristeva, one can also pose the question of how the demarcation of territories, including the imaginary boundaries of racialized nation-states, is mapped out according to myths specifying which subjects are allowed to remain inside national boundaries, and which subjects must be expelled outside these boundaries. Who may move about freely within the imaginary boundaries of a nation, and who risks deportation, or death at the hands of a police force whose actions are authorized by a paranoid racist imaginary that equates dark skin color with the threat of terrorism? How might the primary myth of an inside and an outside inform the projective identifications that authorize the most deep-seated psychoanalytic commitments, such as the idea that race is outside the scope of psychoanalysis? Freud says in "Group Psychology" that he is not concerned with race (1953h, 75, n. 1). True to form, the distance that Freud seeks to establish between psychoanalysis and the idea of a racial unconscious is severely compromised by his own explicit testimony. His disclaimer occurs in an essay that begins by establishing the continuity between "individual" and "social or group" psychology (69), and by stipulating that group psychology is "concerned with the individual man as a member of a race, of a nation, of a caste, of a profession, of an institution, or as component part of a crowd of people who have been organized into a group" (70).[13] Psychoanalysis, then, would seem to be very much concerned with race and nation, as Freud attests further when he comments, "We are no longer astonished that grea[t] differences should lead to an almost insuperable repugnance, such as the Gallic people feel for the German, the Aryan for the Semite, and the white races for the coloured" (101). It is worth underlining that what is said to hold such races apart is their lack of similarity, and that it is an overwhelming feeling, the affect of repugnance, that distinguishes these racial groups. What repels us is our differences from others. Elsewhere, in his description of the superego, Freud acknowledges that among the influences that constitute the ideals to which the ego tries to match up, are included that of the nation (1953p, 146). Kristeva has suggested that the nation and the subject should be thought as analogous to one another. Yet as Sarah Ahmed argues, drawing on Kristeva's discussion of abjection and disgust in *Powers of Horror,* the ways in which subjects move toward and away from one another, and the orchestration of such movements according to affects and emotions, are constitutive of how national collectivities configure themselves. Ahmed suggests that, rather than follow the model of a nation as an abstraction, which Kristeva puts forward, drawing on Montesquieu, we pursue a metonynmical understanding of bodies and nations (2005). To think of the relation between societies and subjects as corresponding to one another is to foreclose the possibility of a serious interrogation of the dynamics of power that are implicated in the formation of boundaries between nations and communities.

As Mary Ann Doane says, "If certain races (associated with the 'primitive') are constituted as outside or beyond the territory of the psychoanalytic endeavor—insofar as they lack repression or neurosis (perhaps even the unconscious)—the solution cannot be simply to take this system which posits their exclusion and apply it to them. . . . Psychoanalysis, unshaken in its premises, cannot be *applied* to issues of racial difference but must be radically destabilized by them" (Doane 1991, 216). If the issue needs to be framed not so much in terms of how psychoanalysis might be applied to its racialized others, but rather in terms of how psychoanalysis might be destabilized by the others that it has racialized as other, abjection can be mobilized as a resource. In other words, the question of how psychoanalysis has unwittingly benefited from its systematic exclusion of certain feminized and racialized others, is a matter of delineating what might be called not so much the unconscious of psychoanalysis as its excluded other.[14] What imaginary formations have remained indeterminate, but also indispensable for, the formulation of the central tenets of psychoanalytic theory, and in what ways is the imaginary structured by collective fantasies that require the exclusion of some subjects for the benefit of others? When these imaginary registers are parsed out in symbolic terms, how does psychoanalysis become accountable for its exclusions? If the collective exclusions reflected by psychoanalysis collaborates with and is unthinkingly complicit in racist, colonialist, and sexist constructions, we need to ask how fetishism has served as the cultural capital of the psychoanalytic imaginary. As Doane has pointed out, Freud's evocation of femininity as a "dark continent" participates in a racist construction that it does not own, at the same time as it situates certain subjects, on the basis of their sex or the color of their skin, as beyond the pale of psychoanalytic inquiry (1999, 210).[15] Inasmuch as women are seen as incapable of sublimation, or at least inhibited in their capacity to sublimate, and insofar as Freud understands primitivism as unrepressed sexuality, females and non-white races are made to stand for a stunted phase of psychic development. In Doane's words, "A metonymic chain is constructed which links infantile sexuality, female sexuality, and racial otherness" (210). Civilization is assumed to be masculine, white, and heterosexual, but in ways that are unmarked by psychoanalytic discourse. It is worth noting that although Doane acknowledges at a theoretical level that "It is dangerous and very misleading to claim that the position of white women is analogous to that of blacks simply because both take on the role of Other in relation to

the white man" and that "What is lost in the process is the situation of
the black woman" (231), she does not explicitly repudiate the analogical work that fetishism has done for race theory. In fact, she applies
the discourse of fetishism—developed in the context of sexual difference—to the racialized other. Even as she recognizes the unarticulated
ways in which the mythology of white patriarchy has borrowed from
black pathologies, she formulates race in a way that implicitly reproduces the trope of fetishism: "Blackness functions . . . not so much as a
term of comparison (as with the Hottentot and the prostitute), but as
an erotic accessory to whiteness" (215). The formulation of blackness
as accessory to whiteness, while suggestive, remains inadequate in its
continued adherence to the fetishistic trope. It fails to acknowledge
both that the abjection of women remains a model for the abjection of
racialized others, and that the accessory status that blackness accrues in
relation to whiteness is fashioned by a deeply embedded and institu-
tionally endemic racism that is in fact constitutive of whiteness. The
exclusion and denigration of blackness has helped to make both sexuality and whiteness what they are. Marked as superior to its black
other, whiteness has profited from blackness in a way that is not just
contingent but at the heart of what whiteness has become, and in a
way that it fails to acknowledge, while at the same time continuing to
exploit. This dynamic, by which whiteness capitalizes on blackness
without admitting it, can only be construed as a dynamic of disavowal
by means of a continued adherence to the discourse of fetishism, which
itself is facilitated by a continued privileging of a white, masculinist psychoanalytic discourse that remains unmarked as such. It is a dynamic
that relies on a repudiation of the humanity of blacks, but at the same
time elevates blackness to a mythical, godlike status, which it then appropriates to itself in a way that demonstrates the impossibility that whiteness stands alone.

Fetishism is taken up as a model for the cinematic experience in
the sense that the spectator knows that the film represents fantasy, but
takes it for reality: Je sais "mais quand même."[16] I know very well that
what unfolds onscreen is not real, but all the same I allow myself to react
to it as if it is. In taking illusion for reality, through identification, I feel
the surprise, pity, or joy that the fictional onscreen characters feel. Their
emotions become mine. If the avant-garde disruption of fantasy is an
exposure of the fetishistic theory of film, it is also a repudiation of the
idea of film as an art for the masses, with revolutionary potential. At
every moment I am reminded of my knowledge that the film is not "reality": I am not allowed to forget its illusory dependence on increasingly
sophisticated technology. Yet even as such reminders debunk the

fetishistic strategy, they confirm its authority. Pleasure can either conform to the fetishistic model, or it can be interrupted, dislocated—there is, apparently, no way of understanding filmic pleasure differently.

Walter Benjamin's understanding of film as breaking with an elitist tradition of auratic artwork, as an invitation to the general public to become critics in their own right, all but demands of directors that they call attention to the filmic apparatus. Precisely insofar as Benjamin considered film to present "a pure aspect freed from the foreign substance of equipment," an "equipment-free aspect" that is the "height of artifice" (1968b, 233) he calls for the subversion of the very breakthrough he articulates. Directors did not disappoint. A good deal of effort has been spent in reminding film audiences that they are watching something contrived, that their being sutured into the film is the result of a grand, carefully orchestrated technical illusion, that the filmic apparatus makes possible their immersion in the fantasy of narrative. This effort to recall self-consciousness at every moment follows in the tradition of Brechtian distanciation, and is intended to break up the pleasure of getting lost, for a while, in what unfolds onscreen. It has spawned an academic industry of its own. The film connoisseur, who can catalog the virtuosity of technical innovations, has reinvented the mantle of the art historian.

There is an important sense in which the fetishistic model, and the exposure of its logic, fail to acknowledge precisely the extent to which identification operates according to a logic that assumes as already in place socially cohesive communities, whose collective, imaginary body images are indeed reflected back to them as invisibly similar—or as noticeably dissimilar. The fetishistic disavowal that consists of bracketing the fact that I know the fantasy unfolding onscreen is not real (but I suspend this knowledge for the duration of the film) is thereby undercut by a communal recognition that allows spectators to read filmic images in terms of a shared imaginary that is coded as always already familiar—or marked as unfamiliar, different, exotic. By rendering unfamiliar the familiar, or by rendering familiar the unfamiliar, film can produce identifications against the grain of familiarity. It can do so by engaging in abject maneuvers, bordering on the uncanny.[17] Film can invoke different communities of knowers, as when Neil Jordan provides his audience certain visual codes that clue some of us in to the transgender identity of the Metro's clientele, providing clues in such a way that they will not be read—will not be seen, or recognized—by all film viewers. Jordan thereby appeals to socially inculcated differences in viewing practices in a way that draws attention to these differences. He allows us to situate our own fantasies within the fantasy he unravels for us, and invites us to hollow them out.

By using the abject to rework the fetishistic discourses that have come to dominate film theory, and which have been extended to encompass a good deal of race theory, I suggest an alternate route for film theory, one that takes account of the ways in which the imaginary dynamics of projective identification shape the symbolic. I draw attention to the way in which the famous enigma of woman in Freud is secured at key points by means of another enigma. Sexual difference founders on the rock of racial difference. It is as if Freud encounters certain blockages in his effort to think through sexual difference, which turn out to be shored up by a subterranean series of exclusions that are still more inaccessible to thematization than the feminine has revealed itself to be. This is not to endorse the idea that in general race goes deeper than gender—which would merely be to reverse the mistake that psychoanalytic film theory usually makes, in assuming sexual difference as the bedrock of identity and deriving all other socially salient differences, such as race, from this founding difference. For one thing, this is not a one-way relationship. Sometimes the feminine is marshaled as a means of blocking further inquiry into primitivism, and sometimes primitivism is appealed to as a means of avoiding further explanation of femininity. My point is rather that in attending to the textual details of Freud's corpus it emerges that the difficulty he had in thinking through the enigma of woman is exegetically and structurally bound up with a sometimes even more enigmatic series of gestures. This series is often more enigmatic because it is rendered less available for interrogation in terms of the overt themes of psychoanalysis, which privilege sexual difference.[18]

Jacqueline Rose has criticized Metz for, among other things, assuming that the body of the child is represented in the mirror, and Joan Copjec has criticized the fact that film theory tends to elide the proprietary relationship to otherness that is so central to Lacan.[19] I would add that through the operation of abjection film can unsettle the boundaries of subjects and objects, as subjects experience a disruption of the identificatory models that have served to consolidate the knowledge that allows Metz to say of his prototypical male subject that "he knows himself and he knows his like." In this sense, "the practice of cinema" does not so much "presuppos[e] that the primitive undifferentiation of the ego and the non-ego has been overcome" (Metz 1982, 46) but rather puts into play the identificatory regimes according to which such delineations are made, and thereby opens up the possibility for their redefinition. Precisely because film has the capacity to initiate such a reworking, the power of identification can unsettle identities, so that film is not merely "already on the side of the symbolic" (46) but also implicates the imaginary.

While much has been made in film theory of the parallel between the motor incapacitation of the infant, who is transfixed by its image in Lacan's mirror stage, and the relative immobility of the cinema spectator, who is fascinated by the screen image, the insistent reference to the mother's body in both Jean-Louis Baudry and Christian Metz has been, if not neglected, at least played down.[20] In part this is due to the influence of Lacan on film theory, whose emphasis of the symbolic rather than the imaginary register also had the effect of upholding the authority of the father rather than the semiotic authority of the maternal.[21] By recasting these references to the maternal body in the context of Kristeva's notion of abjection it will be possible to establish how Kristeva's notion of the abject can provide an alternative route for film theory.[22] Let me say immediately that while I claim that the erasure of the maternal corpus as a privileged site in the standard psychoanalytic accounts is significant, I also resist the typical Lacanian riposte that to insist on the significance of the breast, or the maternal body, necessarily amounts to a failure to understand the role that the phallus plays in Lacan's work.[23] Nor does this insistence foreclose the development of the desiring subject. Abjection does not operate by ignoring or forestalling the intricate relationship that Parveen Adams points to when she says that the "concept of the phallus puts in play all three orders of the Imaginary, the Symbolic and the Real" (1996, 55). My argument is rather that it is precisely by a rethinking of the phallic economy and its implication in the registers of the Imaginary, the Symbolic, and the Real that abjection reorders the phallic scene. Not by contesting the organizing role that the phallus plays in the production of symbolic meaning as such, but by displacing the centrality of castration theory, abjection offers a new way of thinking how an object comes to be an object for a subject.[24] It reworks Lacan's account of the subject's entry into language, offering an alternative account of the production of meaning, which no longer relies exclusively on the child's mastery of the play of presence and absence in the way that Freud's rendition of the Fort/Da game would have it. Rather than restrict her attention to the language and representation that is established by the abstract and syntactical function of signs standing in for the lost maternal object, the significance of which can only be recuperated through a master signifier, and underwritten by the paternal phallus, Kristeva opens up the question of meaning to ask how signs become productive of meaning in the first place. As Mary Jacobus says, "Probing beyond Lacan's question ('how does the imaginary give rise to the symbolic'), Kristeva asks instead: 'what are the conditions for the emergence of the imaginary?' "[25] Without "waiving the phallus"—to adopt the felicitous phrase of Parveen Adams—or adhering to its mastery completely, Kristeva is able to rethink the space of representation in a way that admits the possibility that meanings can emerge that are not decided in advance by the phallus. She does so by introducing the loving father as a site of primary identification into the preoedipal, semiotic, or imaginary register, as a loving support for the child in its rejection of the abject mother.[26] The imaginary father signals to the child that the mother's desire is elsewhere, and in this sense "he is simple virtuality, a potential presence" (Kristeva 1987, 43). He is also a site of immediate (rather than mediated) identification, a gift from the mother that the child need not elaborate for itself.[27]

In understanding this third as a father (albeit loving, rather than the strict father who inculcates the law and sets up the superego), Kristeva can be criticized for not distancing herself enough from the heteronormative assumptions of Western, oedipal psychoanalysis. Of course, one can argue that Kristeva is merely reflecting the patriarchal forms of authority that are operative in society, yet the question remains why this third is figured in these terms rather than any other, and how her interpretation consolidates rather than interrogates traditional forms of authority. Furthermore, how does Kristeva's imaginary father replicate or at least leave in place other forms of authority, such as those exhibited in patterns of racism?

Remaining close to Lacan in her acceptance of the status of castration, Kristeva does not allow her questions to culminate in the disruption of symbolic authority to the point of questioning the metatheoretical mimetic work that authorizes its equation with castration theory. Freud's association of identification with the father is evidence of his covering over or suppression of other types of possible identification, a suppression that is itself bound up with a repressed discourse not only of maternal but also of racial, class, and heterosexually normative identifications. The notion that has become so important for Kristeva's interpretation, what she calls the imaginary, archaic, or loving father—the "father of the individual's prehistory"—is, according to Kristeva "not yet a symbolic agency but already the beginning of the thirdness prefigured by the mother's desire for someone other than the child (her father? the child's father? an extrafamilial or symbolic agency?)."[28] Contrary to Kristeva's suggestions as to how this prefigured third must be thought, I suggest that we extrapolate from Kristeva's tentative suggestion that this third be understood as an "extrafamilial or symbolic agency" and understand it as, variously, the loving and symbolic agency of race, sexual difference, or class, or any other socially sanctioned script endowed with the capacity to render some individuals inferior to others, by extending loving support in ways not immune from unconscious forces. In this reworked scenario, what functions as the equivalent of the "imaginary" or "archaic" or "loving" father are social texts that typically privilege whiteness, male heterosexuality, or the middle class, but which need not do so. It is in moving away from, or abjecting, certain bodies, and moving toward others—whether the privileged trope of these bodies be materialized as raced, classed, sexed, or gendered—that the immediacy of identification needs to be understood. What mediates such identification are the social processes that construct who is likely to be nearby, and who is not, processes dictated by structural features of economic social life, infused with divisions of poverty, racialized hierarchy, and gender/sex taboos.

In "An Outline of Psycho-analysis," Freud says, "when the breast has to be separated from the body and shifted to the '*outside*' because the child so often finds it absent, it carries with it as an '*object*' a part of the original narcissistic libidinal cathexis" (1953p, 188).[29] Freud, I suggest, had stumbled across what Kristeva would designate abjection—the locus of which is the separation between the mother's breast and the infant, and at the same time the tentative institution of the infant's subjectivity. Thus, Kristeva's notion of abjection would be strategically located in the impossibility of maintaining a rigorous Freudian distinction between identification (marked as paternal by Freud) and object-choice (marked by Freud as maternal). This has radical implications both for Freud's theory of the phallic phase, and for the status of the phallus which is so decisive for theories of fetishism, including those that have found their way into film theory. The symptomatic confusion or undecidability that inhabits Freud's texts when it comes to distinguishing identification from object-choice is played out on the ground of a discourse of primitivism, as documented in the following instance.

In "Group Psychology" (1953h) Freud had underlined the "typically masculine" behavior of little boys, who "exhibit a special interest" in the father: the boy "would like to grow like him and be like him, and take his place everywhere. We may say simply that he takes his father as his ideal" (1953h, 105). Freud used the term "identification" to designate this behavior, claiming that it is "the earliest expression of an emotional tie with another person" and that it "helps to prepare the way for the Oedipus complex" (1953h, 105). Although Freud specifies that "This behaviour has nothing to do with a passive or feminine attitude towards his father" (1953h, 105), he goes on to say that "Identification . . . is ambivalent from the very first; it can turn into an expression of tenderness as easily as into a wish for someone's removal" (1953h, 105). Situating the boy's "attachment" of the anaclitic type, which he introduced in the essay on narcissism "towards his mother" as occurring "at the same time . . . or a little later," Freud designates this attachment "a true object-cathexis" (1953h, 105).[30] Freud sees the "sexual object-cathexis towards his mother" and the "identification with his father which takes him as a model" as "distinct ties," which "subsist side by side for a time without any mutual influence or interference" (1953h, 105). This does not prevent him from claiming—in a gesture that immediately muddles their apparent distinctness—that identification "behaves like a derivative of the first, *oral* phase of the organization of the libido" (1953h, 105).[31] To say that identification "behaves *like* . . . a derivative of the first oral phase . . . of the libido" is not the same thing as saying that it is a derivative—but it does suggest that the oral phase is a model for identification in some way. Since the oral phase concerns the infant's attachment to the mother's breast, which Freud claims to be the prototype of all love relations (see Freud 1953r, 222 and 1953p, 188), the question arises as to whether Freud has changed his mind on this point.

Has identification with the father, as "the earliest expression of an emotional tie with another person," taken the place of the prototypical "sucking at his mother's breast" (1953r, 222)? If identification is the earliest expression of an emotional tie with another person, and it is with the father, how does this stand with Freud's claim that the mother is the first love-object, and that the child's relation with the mother is the prototype of all love relations? Surely love is an emotional tie? Or is the point—as suggested by the account in "Outline"—that the first object is not yet a person (see 1953p, 188)?[32] Freud avoids confronting the question by taking up the oral phase not in terms of the prehistory of the individual but in terms of phylogenetic prehistory. There is therefore a slippage between the individual and the collective, one that is crucial for my argument, and one that is colored by two different aspects of the attempt to think about origins, which come to be symbolized respectively by femininity and primitivism. On the one hand Freud alludes to the love relation to the mother, yet on the other hand, as if he reaches an impasse that is symptomatic of his ultimate inability to think through the relation between identification with the father and love of the mother, he slips into a discourse about primitive, social configurations. It is not the mother's breast to which he refers, but cannibalism, in which "the object that we long for and prize is assimilated by eating and is in that way annihilated as such" (1953h, 105). By thus shifting registers, Freud resorts to a nebulous discourse concerning a primitive state of human development in order to evoke a less nebulous—but still highly underdeveloped—discourse concerning femininity. The reason this gesture is of particular interest, and seems to be symptomatic of Freud's having come across the limitations that his cultural prejudices produce for his theoretical investigation, is that rather than confronting the unresolved relationship between paternal identification and the maternal as love-object, rather than establishing one as originary, Freud injects another layer of discourse about origins into his ruminations. He appeals to a raced discourse, which is not really marked as such, but which lies subjacent to Freud's discourse about femininity, and in some way facilitates the obscurity within which that account is allowed to be shrouded. The fact that Freud has recourse to his highly speculative elaborations about the origins of culture, just at the point that his thought butts against the enigma of woman, is of more than passing interest.[33] It relegates the role of the maternal-feminine to the realm of the primitive by relying on a discourse of primitivism replete with racial connotations that are left unexplored. This repressed discourse reemerges in the privileged motif of fetishism, with its logic of disavowal and its reference to "savages." Race, in a sense, already plays the role of the third.

By rewriting the mirror stage in terms of the trope of abjection, and positing the imaginary or loving father as the corollary of the abject mother, and as a site of primary identification, Kristeva retains the idea that identification must be paternal. The loss of the mother is compensated for by language, which is still inaugurated by the father, although this father is now figured as imaginary, not symbolic. Freud's "discovery" of the phallic phase in his 1923 essay "The Infantile Genital Organization" (1953i), and the theory of the phallic mother, is itself fetishistic.[34] For Kristeva, the mother is abject before being phallic, but her figuring of the third as paternal reinstates, to a certain extent, phallic logic.

According to Freud's account in "Female Sexuality," the narcissism invested in the penis is what allows boys to overcome the Oedipus complex (see 1953g, 229). The boy would rather ward off the threat of castration than jeopardize the highly valued penis. He thus obeys the prohibition against masturbation, and either gives up his mother as a love object, or—in a move that foreshadows fetishism—attributes to her a penis, so that he does not have to take seriously the threat that her lack of a penis would otherwise represent. Yet, if, as Freud "discovers" in 1923, the mother is phallic, the little boy has no need of fetishism. Or rather, the *idea* of the mother as phallic comes to stand in for, to take the place of, to *substitute* for fetishism. It becomes clear that the status of the mother as phallic—and the significance of the phallus more generally for Freud—is in fact an extension of the fetishistic principle: the reign of the phallus is thoroughly fetishistic. As Charles Bernheimer puts it, the "wish to impose a theory of sexual sameness is the idealizing gesture that subtends the psychoanalytic theory of sexual difference. . . . the function of the castration fantasy is not to discredit the childhood story of universal maleness but to support it. Thus, insofar as castration explains sexual difference in terms of a theory that excludes difference, it is fetishistic in terms of Freud's own theory of the fetish" (1992, 123). By oscillating between the point of view of the little boy who attributes to the mother a phallus and the point of view of Freud the theorist, who is also Freud the adult, Freud develops in effect a fetishistic attitude to women which he then reifies, conceptualizing it into his discovery of the phallus.

It is worth pausing to reflect here that Freud's insistence upon reserving the castration complex to designate the penis—in contrast to Lacan's tendency to apply the concept of castration to all instances of loss—has the curious effect of opening up a space in which Kristeva and others can revisit the Freudian corpus and find it more, rather than less, congenial to a sustained consideration of femininity. Or perhaps this is not so curious, since Lacan's idealization of the phallus as transcendental signifier has the effect of putting out of bounds any direct reference to its material signified. To quote Bernheimer again, "Lacan's refusal to contextualize the phallus is part of his strategy to detach the unconscious from history," a strategy that extends as much to his distorted extrapolation of metonymy from Freud's notion of displacement as to his taking up of the paternal metaphor, which "voids that name of physical reference in precisely the same way that he detaches the phallus from its penile embodiment" (1992, 124–127). Lacan's return to Freud is effected by glossing over the differences between the oral, anal-sadistic, and phallic stages, in that castration becomes retrospectively symbolic of all instances of loss. Thus castration theory becomes inseparable from the symbolic in Lacan in a way that renders it schematically and structurally futile to parse out the differences between the act of birth, the loss of the breast, and the (imagined) loss of the penis. This also naturalizes the maternal role, by eliding the difference between the capacity to give birth and the need to care for infants, as if there were no possibility of parental or caring roles being performed by anyone, male or female, other than the biological mother. By the same token, given Lacan's extraordinary emphasis on language, and his famous pronouncement that the unconscious is structured like language, the difference between the preoedipal and oedipal phases is lost sight of. Since the castration complex and the oedipal complex go hand in hand (at least for the boy), and since the onset of castration anxiety is also the site of the subject's entry into language, the difference between the preoedipal and the oedipal phases becomes relatively insignificant for Lacan. Or rather the difference becomes inexpressible, insofar as language comes to be our only means of access to the prelinguistic, preoedipal realm. For Freud on the other hand, it becomes progressively more important as his corpus develops, and the differentiation between the preoedipal and the oedipal comes to bear a crucial mark of differentiation between the development of girls and boys. Not incidentally, Freud's increased sensitivity to this differentiation owes a good deal to female analysts such as Helene Deutsch and Melanie Klein. It also provides a foothold for Kristeva to rework what remained in Freud tentative and undeveloped suggestions into a much more elaborate developmental schema. While Freud contents himself with a footnote in "The Ego and the Id," which begins by suggesting that we should understand by father "parents," only to end by confining his research to the father, or with the skeletal suggestion that perhaps we should see the Oedipal complex as a "secondary formation" (1953e, 251), Kristeva will take up these sparse suggestions, fuse them with her generative semiotic account of the production of language, and come up with an affirmation of "phallic monism," which admits that while "phallic organization" plays a "structuring" role it is also "traversable" and "can be challenged."[35] The question remains as to whether, having done so, Kristeva does not exacerbate the hegemony of the phallus.

On Kristeva's account, the infant initiates itself as what will eventually become a desiring subject, as one who will become capable of bearing discourse, of distinguishing subject from object, by separating from, abjecting, the mother. What the infant took itself to be prior to this abjection is an issue only capable of being posed after the fact, only after the infant takes itself to be a subject—an impossibility before distinctions start to proliferate. This issue is complex not only because the question of representation is at the heart of what it means to be a subject but also because of the retroactive movement by which subjects posit their subjectivity. A necessary loss is incurred by the very language that is called for to translate the moment of abjection into a discourse about subjects, but without such loss, meaning would be impossible. Whatever loss occurs is constitutive of whatever meaning emerges. The process by which the infant separates from the mother, and in doing so situates itself, produces subjectivity precisely by rejecting a part of what it took itself to be—the mother's body, a part of the amorphous maternal corpus. The problem with such a formulation, of course, is that there was no self-conscious infantile subject, there was only the mother, and in this sense the infant could not take itself to be anything. Here is the difficulty of accounting for anything prior to the differentiated subject, since, strictly speaking, the infant only takes itself to be anything at all after it has become, however tentatively, a subject for itself (Hegel's self-consciousness). Heimann argues that the sense of "me-ness" derives primarily from sensations (and images of sensations), while Kristeva takes up a similar idea in terms of the corporeal mapping of the body. At issue is the organization of the sensuous body as that which is experienced, remembered, recollected, organized around a core body-memory. The very process of instituting subjectivity, the very possibility of making distinctions, is founded by the abjection of the mother, through which the infant begins to initiate itself as a desiring, that is unified, subject, a me as distinct from you. The decision to account for this initiatory process is typically made from a point of view that has decided in favor of certain privileged subjectivities, namely those whose systems of meaning—for economic, political, and social reasons—have risen to favor. Such systems tend to endorse and institutionalize, rather than bring into question, the abjection of the mother. Thus the mother is figured as a constitutive loss that is necessary for the production of meaning and the institution of subjectivities, and subjectivity is figured, by default, as replete with the privileges that characterize the systems of representation that prevail. Of course, none of these systems is determinate, all of them are contestable, and some are better than others at defensively recuperating the transgressions that they facilitate, more or less consciously, and with more or less cynicism. This means that their meaning is up for question even as they appear to constitute the condition of possibility for all meaning. Meaning is already inflected in certain ways, but is capable of being reworked, and able to sustain novelty. Abjection offers a new way of rethinking what is at issue in the Lacanian mirror stage, by pushing back the question in a way that doesn't foreclose the maternal body as a locus of the inception of meaning. Without presupposing that meaningful distinctions must be ideal or conceptual, it opens up the question of identification and in doing so, it allows for the possibility that signification does not necessarily endorse the current patriarchal, racist, classist, heterosexist social and political systems of meaning that dominate and facilitate, in vastly different ways, nationalist imaginaries.

I have suggested that the implications of Freud's introduction of the phallic phase should be read back into some of his earlier claims, especially concerning the relationship between identification and object-choice. By reading Freud's development of a theory of fetishism as symptomatic of his repression of maternal identification, we can see that not only is the mother-child relation relegated to the sidelines by the phallic phase and its fetishistic logic, but also that one of the key strategies by which Freud effects this repression is the appeal to primitivism. Freud's theories of fetishism and castration are interwoven with one another, indeed, inseparable from one another; and in addition, castration theory reflects, or anticipates, the divided attitude of the fetishist, irrespective of whether or not the strategy of fetishism is taken up. The mythical "castration" of women is taken as a fact, such that even though Freud "knows" that women do not have, and never had, penises, he acts as if they do. He treats the myth of castration as if it were a fact, and he even reads this myth back into anatomy, so that even anatomy appears to verify the myth that castration has some biological basis—the clitoris is a truncated penis.

Rather than tethering itself to a fantasy that derives its energy from an economy that privileges phallic predominance and that deals in a logic of equivalence, which presupposes a highly specific masculine norm, one that interprets individual development according to a pre-conception of likeness and similitude, abjection bequeaths to us an inheritance, namely, the need to think through what it might mean to let others be other, the need for me to be an I. What does it mean to take our cue from the undeniable material and ethical dictum, that there is a need for an individual to separate from its caregiver, a need for a child to envisage itself as not-the-mother, and a need for the mother to let the child go? What emerges as crucial is not merely the inherent dependence of the infant on the mother, not even the necessity that the child come into conflict with the mother in order to realize its own subjectivity, but the dual requirement that the mother both care for the child and let the child go, and that the child both allow itself to be cared for by a maternal figure and agree to separate from the figure(s) who bestow such care. The Kojèvian reading of the Hegelian dialectic of the master-slave relationship, in terms of which Lacan's return to Freud via the mirror stage tends to be taken up, is thereby complicated. It is not just that both facilitation and alienation is at stake in the child's self-recognition, it is not merely a matter of narcissism combined with a dehiscence, of love of self shot through with the splitting or fracturing of subjectivity that will be parsed out in terms of the difference between consciousness and unconsciousness. It is also a question of the maternal figure both maintaining a caring relationship, and letting go, abandoning the object of her care to the vicissitudes of the world. There is a dual requirement that needs to be thought through, namely, that the infant both be attached to itself and split from itself, and that the mother both be caring and capable of letting the child separate. The dynamic that gets played out between these conflicting aspects of both the mother and the child is one that has been short-circuited by Freud and Lacan, one that Kristeva's notion of abjection has enabled us to return to. The need for the infant to separate from, repudiate, and love—all at the same time—the mother is counterbalanced by the need for the mother to love the child, to facilitate its separation from her, and to deal with the trauma that will be associated with that separation. The complexity of this requirement consists in its balancing of love and discipline, a disciplining that begins in the care that delineates the body from the world, the infant from the mother, and is practiced through ingestion of food and production of waste. It secures corporeal boundaries through an excremental logic of what cleanliness means and how one's relation to oneself is established through an ability to detach not only from the breast but also from the world and the material objects that the body comes to produce. Whatever morality is at stake here, it is not yet that inculcated by the logic of paternal identification, through the superego. It is much more messy, much more halting, much more bound up with the need to distinguish figure from ground, me from you, my body from the world, the borders of where I start and where I stop, the need to care and to be cared for.

2

Abjection as the Failure of Protection against Emptiness: Narcissism, Negation, and Klein's Projective Identification

ALTHOUGH KRISTEVA does not cast her critique in terms of fetishism as such, she does suggest that the absolute status of the phallus/superego and the idealization associated with it is put into question by abjection.[1] Given that the transcendental status of the phallus is inevitably bound up for Freud and Lacan with the fantasy of castration and the trope of fetishism that is elaborated in order to defend against this fantasy, the implications of Kristeva's critique should be extended to fetishism. The task of this chapter then is to explore abjection not so much as an alternative to fetishism as the condition of the emergence of fetishism, a condition that could have been—and could still be—elaborated otherwise. I take up the notion of primary identification that Kristeva explores under the heading of the imaginary father, a first identification that constitutes that "most archaic unity" which is "the phallus desired by the mother."[2] This primary identification is, says Kristeva, "correlative to the establishment of the other as 'ab-jetted'" (1987, 41–42); it is the infant's rejection of the mother and identification with the desire of the mother for the father.[3] We will see that one of the major inspirations behind Kristeva's notion of abjection is Melanie Klein's notion of "projective identification."[4] Another important source is Freud's 1925 essay, "Negation" (Die Verneinung), which, along with Freud's famous discussion of the "Fort/Da" game in *Beyond the Pleasure Principle*, was central to Klein and her followers.[5]

I take Hyppolite's claim that Freud's discussion of the genesis of the symbol of negation must be read in the light of a primary myth of outside and inside to be a crucial one, which sheds light on Kristeva's notion of abjection.[6] Recall that in abjection, it is "As if the fundamental opposition were between I and Other or, in more archaic fashion, between Inside and Outside" (1982, 7). Narcissism is a chaotic attempt to preserve the integrity of boundaries separating inside from outside; it etches out and protects the unstable borders of the emerging subject. The ego develops only through sustaining loss: the primordial loss or absence of the mother is necessary for the birth or self-realization of the subject. Far from requiring that an ego capable of mastering absence and loss preexists before loss, both Klein and Kristeva embrace a theoretical position that construes the development of the ego precisely through encounters of loss.[7] In this respect, they echo Freud, for whom the ego cannot be assumed from the start, but which develops, through processes of incorporation, in which the subject comes to identify with a lost object.[8] The "abjection of self," says Kristeva, reveals that "all its objects" are based on "the inaugural *loss*" that laid the foundations of its own being" (1982, 5). "The abject is the violence of mourning for an 'object' that has always already been lost" (15). A loss, then, that is inscribed in the very inauguration of the subject, an event whose genealogy can only be sketched *for the subject* in the wake of its advent. Before recognizing the absence of the mother—before accepting that the mother's body is separate from the infant (that is, before having developed a defeasible ego)—a series of defensive maneuvers are put in play, protective maneuvers that inscribe the subject as capable of weathering the "comings and goings" of pleasurable satisfactions and painful deprivations.[9] Such maneuvers sketch out an inside and an outside, the contours of which do not yet adhere to the empirical borders of the infant's body, do not yet abide by a fixed or stable differentiation of "inner" or "outer" and hence do not yet attribute permanence or stability to an external reality outside the hallucinatory grasp of an apparently omnipotent imagination. The processes of introjection and projection that describe the infant's attempt to protect itself from the vicissitudes of the world are at the same time its initial defenses against loss. As such, they prepare for the object-relation proper, which culminates in the self-recognition of the mirror stage, in which the subject takes itself as an object of reflection through the intermediary discourse of the Other. Abjection can be understood as a defense mechanism that protects the emerging ego against difference, loss, or absence in an attempt to keep outside all that is bad—all that threatens to disrupt satisfaction—while keeping inside all that is good. In the attempt to withstand initial losses, in the shape of what will come to be figured as the absence of the breast, the developing ego fantasizes that it is under attack by a "bad breast," and in the attempt to protect itself against such attacks, it imagines that it has swallowed the "good breast"—that the breast or mother is inside it. Fears of retaliation on the part of the "bad breast," which figures as having been eaten up, or bitten, and feelings of reparation for such destructive fantasies, in which the child wants to compensate for having incorporated the breast, develop. Abjection, then, rejects all that is bad, without yet figuring it as absence.[10] It does not yet partake of the fetishistic maneuver, which reacts to difference by covering it over, such that the site of difference does not have to be recognized as threatening, since it takes on the appearance of sameness. Fetishism operates at the level of a disavowal of an imaginary idea, whereas abjection sketches out the possibility of objects, consisting of an affective exchange in which the boundaries between an external world of reality and the fantasy life are not yet fully operative (indeed, are they ever?). Fetishism operates by substituting an object for a fantasized idea, whereas abjection operates at the level of denial and omnipotence, in the currency of fantasies or hallucinations. In abjection the fantasmatic splitting that takes place does not conform to the delineation of an inner psychic reality and an outer external world. As for Klein, "frustration and persecution" are denied through the splitting of the object "into a good and a bad part."[11] This territorializing, or sketching out of boundaries, does not yet correspond to a stable distinction between the inner world and the outer world—its objects are fantasmatic, and they figure as preliminary to a rigid subject/object distinction. As a response to anxiety, abjection is produced as an attempt to ward off all that is unpleasurable, bad, or threatening, an attempt to safeguard all that is pleasurable, good, or enjoyable. Prior to the distinction between I and other, conscious or unconscious, it patrols the shifting borders of inside and outside without having lined up those borders with the contours of the body vis-à-vis permanent, external objects or fixed ideas.

Castration anxiety is operative for a subject who has already grasped the distinction between subject and object, has computed values in phallic terms, and who is confronted with the perplexity of the enigma of difference in the shape of female sexuality. It both renders indeterminacy determinate (figuring it as lack), and withholds the specificity of that determinacy as unavailable for interrogation, by presenting it as the only meaning available. As the indeterminate background against which male sexuality is covertly valued, female sexuality can henceforth only be cast as a threat to that value. The girl lacks a penis, or must have had one in the past, or has an inadequate one, or will grow a bigger one in the future. The lack of temporal specificity testifies not merely to the fact that the unconscious respects no temporal distinction, but to the eternal mythic presence of a masculine psychoanalytic imaginary that fuels the construction of female sexuality as falling short. In fact, however, the "perception" of "lack" is driven by a male, narcissistic fantasy of completion that assumes, without articulating it, that to be human is to be like a male, and that values masturbatory penile pleasure, and therefore finds it inadmissible that girls might lack such a highly valued organ as the penis. Having fabricated the lack by adhering to an implicit standard of comparison against which female sexuality is found wanting, the masculine imaginary provides the female with a substitute penis, a fetish, in order to avoid confronting the void of castration, and the threat of loss that this implies for the phallic fantasy of narcissistic completion. The production of the fetish thus covers over the indeterminacy that female sexuality represents, having converted indeterminacy into lack, a lack that is in its turn covered over by a determinate product that proceeds precisely from the anxiety of confronting the threat provoked by indeterminacy. Presenting itself as universal, castration theory preempts any alternative interpretations, and in doing so defuses in advance as meaningless any challenge to its hegemony. Holding at bay "the dark continent of femininity" in the replication of the phallus by the fetish is a way of privileging not only masculinity but also whiteness. The shadow of the racist assumptions of the eighteenth and nineteenth centuries does not fail to inflect Freud's use of the phrase "the dark continent of femininity," apparently unaware of its racial connotations. That these implicit assumptions are used to uphold not only Freud's observations about femininity but also psychoanalytic theories of meaning, which maintain the Oedipus complex and castration theory as central, exhibits the structural dependence of the privileged excluded other of psychoanalysis, namely the feminine other, on racialized others. An unacknowledged imaginary situates certain subjects, according to how they are raced, sexed, or classed, beyond the scope of psychoanalytic purchase, even while their deviance informs psychoanalytic theory.

The fetishistic solution is to invest libidinal energies in a particular site, to allow a symbolic representation of the phallus to cathect otherwise dispersed energies, to reify and harness (and thereby control and tame) the libido, to channel it away from the negativity that women's sexuality as lack has come to represent. At the same time, an apparently amorphous female sexuality is in fact configured in racialized terms, in terms that are not however admitted into the sexualized, masculinized, overdetermined discourse of fetishized production. Within the symbolic system that women's ostensible (but imaginary) lack founds, the only values that can circulate are phallic. Any other values are excluded—including those that challenge the legitimacy of phallic value as both partial and founded on a logic of substitution that only trades in values already constituted by a symbolic system that has come to represent itself not just as a local, culturally specific set of meanings, but as meaning per se. As if these problems—the contingency of the symbolic interpreted as phallic, the unacknowledged role that femininity plays as imaginary castration, and the foreclosure of the metaphorical work that race already does for this model—did not exist, race theory transposes the logic of fetishism into its own explanatory mechanisms. In place of an imaginary castration, the white imaginary reads the racialized other as lacking whiteness, as falling short of some unarticulated imperative, an implicit universal norm of whiteness. In response to this alleged inferiority or lack, there is an attribution of an emblem of whiteness that covers over the threat that the racialized other would pose without this cultural recognition. This is the dynamic that Frantz Fanon recognizes when he parodies the white man who says "I had a Senegalese buddy in the army who was really clever" or "We have a Senegalese history teacher. He is quite bright. . . . Our doctor is colored. He is very gentle" (1967a, 113–17). Being bright, or clever, or gentle are taken to be civilized, white characteristics, which are then extended to the racialized other, as if to clothe him in attributes that humanize him by making him like "us." The logic of compensation operates by holding blackness as abject, as indeterminate, a quality that is not an attribute, not a value, but is there without being thematized, that somehow defines the non-subject to whom it attaches. The invisible white standard that is being superimposed on the abject, racialized other constitutes the social space as white.[12] To be recognized, acknowledged, accepted, one has to take on the accoutrements of sameness, which are defined by one's ability to successfully mimic whiteness.

The transcription of the fetishistic model by race theory fails to theorize not only how race is the unacknowledged, imaginary, metaphorical backdrop of castration theory but also how fetishistic models developed in a psychoanalytic context that privileges sexual difference thereby foreclose any interrogation of race. What we find in race theory is the analogical displacement of fetishistic logic from the arena of a symbolic that is taken to be universal—but that is in fact a culturally specific psychoanalytic interpretation of a social contract (inherited via Lévi-Strauss and Lacan)—one that posits women's imaginary lack (castration) as calling for the phallus. By installing race in place of sexual difference, by substituting the foundational discourse of race for that of sexual difference, Fanon does not so much confront the mutual implication of race and sex in one another as reassert the founding status of masculinity and inflect it in the direction of racial visibility rather than invisibility. Masculinity can no longer be assumed to be white. Or at least its whiteness becomes a theme for interrogation.

In the psychoanalytic narrative imaginary, castration is itself a response to the horror inspired by female genitalia, a horror that is contrived of the expectation that women be essentially the same as men—a horror that is nothing more and nothing less than the confrontation with difference in the face of the expectation of sameness. In this sense the fetish that covers over the trauma of castration is a memorial to the shock of difference, an attempt to veil it behind a fabrication that perpetuates an imaginary sameness. Abjection can be read, in this context, as an archaic mapping out of the dread that is covered over by the invention of fetishistic discourse. Or fetishism can be read as rendering determinate the threat of loss by cashing it out in phallic terms. The fabricated fetish—whether its production is motivated by a trauma defined as the horrific wound of gender, or the infirmity that cripples the racialized other—is then passed around. The fetish, whether a prosthetic object, cultural artifact, or educational attribute, is made to stand in for the absolute value that after all produced it in the first place—the phallus as the gold standard. The unifying valence of fetishism smooths over and renders uniform fissures that are organized around a cultural landscape that presents itself as uncontestable, as if set in stone. When feminist theory ignores the question of race it reconstitutes the social space as white, putting the fetish (and not so much the phallus) back into circulation, and reproducing its laws of exchange. When race theory replaces the founding narrative of sexual difference with racial difference, it reconstitutes the symbolic as masculine, making race a fetish that assumes the priority of masculine morphology. And so the logic of substitution and denial continues.

Not only are Freud's theories of fetishism and castration interwoven with one another, indeed inseparable from one another. Castration theory reflects, or anticipates, the divided attitude of the fetishist, irrespective of whether or not the strategy of fetishism is taken up. The mythical "castration" of women is taken as a fact, such that even though Freud "knows" that women do not have, and never had, penises, he acts as if they do. He treats the myth of castration as if it were a fact and he even reads this myth back into anatomy, so that anatomy appears to verify the myth that castration has some biological basis. The past is thereby made uniform with the present, taking on the function of a kind of bedrock, an imaginary grounding for a symbolic that celebrates a particular model of splitting that henceforth becomes normative for the subject construed by psychoanalysis, capable of bearing discourse, withstanding and compensating for losses, and signifying loss in ways that not only make it tolerable but also become constitutive of subjectivity.

Klein's work takes up the Freudian notion of fantasy and refigures loss, introjection, and identification as the fantasmatic etching out of subjects not yet settled by fixed paths of identification, but operating in terms of metaphors that precede the Lacanian symbolic. Taking up the fantasy life of the pre-verbal infant that Klein explores under the heading of projective identification, Kristeva develops the notion of abjection and identification with the imaginary father. On Kristeva's account, abjection plays the role of a preliminary demarcation, whereby the infant begins to separate itself from a mother, a process in which neither the infant itself nor the mother have attained (for the infant) the status of subjects.[13] The infant does not yet constitute itself as a subject, but neither does it constitute the mother as its object of desire, rather the mother is precisely abject, as is the infant. As Jacobus puts it, with reference to Klein's case study of Dick, "For Kristeva, abjecting the mother is the condition for self-differentiation on the part of a not-yet-subject or 'abject'—the 'abject' being at once little Dick himself and the body of a maternal stand-in, the Kleinian not-yet-object" (1995, 144). Kristeva says, "Even before being *like*, 'I' am not but do *separate, reject, ab-ject*" (1982, 13). That is, prior to identification—prior to likeness (and thus prior to the unlikeness against which castration anxiety reacts)—the infant rejects the mother, separating from her, abjecting her, in a movement that does not cognize but *enacts* her separateness. In fact, since the boundary between subject and object is not yet fixed in place, there is an abjection of self. "I expel *myself*, I spit *myself* out, I abject *myself* within the same motion through which 'I' claim to establish myself" (1982, 3). Establishing in a bodily way that the mother is not everything, the infant positions itself without thinking itself as not-the-mother. Kristeva will say in *Tales of Love* that "The Imaginary Father" is "the indication that the mother is not complete but that she wants . . . Who? What? 'At any rate, not I.' . . . And it is out of this 'not I' . . . that an Ego painfully attempts to come into being" (1987, 41). One might as well say here, insofar as subject and object, I and other, and, most fundamentally, inside and outside are concepts that are in the process of being inaugurated, that the infant positions itself as not all. It is the mother's desire for the phallus that comprises the "unity of the imaginary father, a coagulation of the mother and her desire" (1987, 41). Such a unity does not yet characterize abjection in *Powers of Horror*, where the processes of dividing occur "Without *one* division, *one* separation, *one* subject/object having been constituted" (1982, 12).[14] In *Tales of Love*, citing Melanie Klein's notion of "projective identification" as a precursor to the amalgam abject-mother/imaginary-father by which the unstable narcissistic subject tries to stabilize itself, Kristeva underlines the importance of introducing a "third party" to usher in the signs that facilitate speech.[15] It is in this context that Kristeva suggests her own elaboration be taken as a modification of "the fantasy of a phallic mother" (1987, 44).[16] As Jacobus says, "The problem that troubles some feminist readers of Kristeva . . . how does [the] appeal to the 'father of individual pre-history' differ from Lacan's Name of the father?—is a nonissue for Kristeva herself; as she poses it, the problem is rather to avoid the regressive fantasy (or rather, the Kleinian 'phantasy') of a phallic mother" (1995, 148). Taking up Kristeva's suggestion and applying it beyond its intended target, we could inflect Kristeva's inscription of the imaginary father/abject mother so that it is not so much an indictment of Klein as a response to the pervasive phallic logic of fetishistic disavowal that structures Freudian and Lacanian psychoanalytic fantasies. Indeed, Kristeva points in such a direction when she questions the Lacanian "absolute of the reference to the Phallus" and warns against the risk of analysis "becoming set within the tyranny of idealization. . . . Of the Phallus or of the super-ego? A word to wise Lacanians should be enough!" (1987, 30).

In suggesting that abjection be taken up as a logic that precedes and foreshadows the logic of fetishism but also returns to haunt the fixity of castration logic, I am both taking my cue from Kristeva's critical questioning of the absolute status of the Lacanian phallus and the "always-already-there of language" (1987, 44), and moving beyond her insofar as Kristeva situates her account of abjection in a perspective that does not question as radically as I do the parameters of castration theory. I read abjection, which Kristeva associates with Klein's "projective identification" again in her study of Melanie Klein, as a defensive maneuver that reacts against difference, absence, separation, or lack, not as performed in a scenario that equates meaning with always already phallic subjects, but rather in the key of *Powers of Horror,* in which no single division or splitting is privileged, and no single unity (such as the imaginary father) is marshaled to ward off abjection and to herald primary identification.[17] Abjection describes a state that precedes the emergence of discrete subjects, but it also returns in a way that allows a questioning of the systematic circulation of phallic values, the economy according to which subjects recognize themselves and their desires as meaningful. Kristeva hypothesizes that "the totality of fantasy functioning, the birth of secondary symbolization, particularly that of language, and psychoanalytic interpretation are all concerned with projective identification—which, incidentally, is at the heart of the interpretive process itself" (2001, 72). Following through this hypothesis, we might cast the foundational fantasy of castration, the horror of the "nothing to see" and its disavowal by the fetish, which reinvents the mythical sameness of the masculine imaginary (woman is nothing but his mirror-image after all), in terms of the projective identification, or abject maneuvers, of psychoanalytic interpretation.[18] What is at stake here, in Jacqueline Rose's words, is the "psychoanalytic institution" coming up against "the fantasy of its own origins."[19] The absence that castration theory reads onto the girl's difference, her "lack" of a penis, would be compensated for by the fetish. Female genitalia are thus cast out of the Freudian/Lacanian systems as the impossible, inarticulate real, as that which falls out of an account sustainable within their symbolic terms, not yet thinkable as particularity, irrecuperable by the dialectic of desire, a beyond that is spat out of the system. At the level of nationalist imaginaries, the difference signaled by racialized subjects is projected outside Western, white imaginaries that support specific nationalist symbolic. Nations come to be figured as collectivities that cannot tolerate anyone who does not agree to represent themselves as partaking in a political body that imagines all its citizens to submit in the same way to the same ideal, an ideal fantasized as a neutral ground of sameness, but in fact drawn from the particular characteristics of socially privileged bodies. As Ahmed shows, it is on the basis of such grounds that Kristeva argues for elimination of the veil, which is read as a sign of difference marking out the Muslim woman as falling outside the nationalist imaginary of France (2005). I agree with Ahmed that Kristeva's account of abjection in *Powers of Horror* has the potential of offering a more productive account of the "strangers to ourselves" whom Kristeva considers in the later works she explicitly devotes to the problem of nationalism.[20] I think that the logic of sameness Kristeva invokes here in her model of citizenship, inspired by Montesquieu, can be read as a hangover of the trope of universalizing fetishistic disavowals.

It is already clear in *Tales of Love* that Kristeva's notion of abjection is heavily indebted to Melanie Klein's notion of projective identification. What also becomes clear in Kristeva's study of Klein is that Kristeva's notion of the imaginary father is a reworking of Klein's combined parental figure.[21] Indeed, it is Klein who first draws attention to the sexual ambiguity Freud installs in the father of individual prehistory, when he suggests, in the footnote to "The Ego and the Id," which becomes so important for Kristeva's notion of the imaginary father, that this father be understood as both "parents."[22] For both Kristeva and Klein a distinction that owes a great deal to Freud's essay on "Negation" proves dominant, that is, the emergent, prevailing, but unstable distinction between an inside and an outside. Let me emphasize what Hyppolite says has to be understood about Freud's essay, namely that it articulates "a primary myth of the outside and the inside"; "What is in question here is the genesis 'of the external and of the internal.'"[23] Since Lacan invited Hyppolite, the renowned Hegelian scholar, to present a commentary on this short but crucial essay by Freud, which was subsequently published as an appendix to Lacan's seminar on *Freud's Papers*

on Technique, the essay is of special importance in weighing Lacan's negotiation of Hegel in his reading of Freud, and thus also in gauging where
and how Kristeva departs from Lacan. At the same time, given Lacan's
discussion of Klein in the same seminar, the way in which Lacan positions himself toward Hyppolite's Hegelian reading of Freud, and Klein's
account of symbol formation, proves fascinating.

Lacan finds Klein's brutal, literal approach "revolting" (1991, 68),
but in his attribution to Klein of an automatic Oedipalization of Dick,
Jacobus reads not only a (Kleinian) symbolic equation of Dick and
Klein—both of them lack theoretical sophistication—but also a kind of
"projective identification" (1995, 139). Lacan rejects what he fears,
finding himself mirrored in Klein, projecting his self-recognition onto
her—in a rejection of the mother. Is it after all Lacan's own brutalization
that makes him fearful, his failure to pick up on the nuances of the
imaginary, his insistence on language, on the symbolic, on the Oedipus
complex? Lacan, then, abjects Klein—she "slams the symbolism" on
Dick "with complete brutality" (1991, 68), has "neither a theory of the
imaginary nor a theory of the ego" (82), but "animal instinct" (69);
Klein lacks the "category of the signifier," according to Lacan—who sup-
presses what he finds revolting, crass, abject in her crude theorization,
while raising up, sublating, what he finds to be of value in it.[24] Lacan
reminds us, at the beginning of his discussion of Klein, that *Aufhebung*
"signifies at once to deny, suppress, and also to preserve through suppression, to raise up" (62). Accordingly, while he denies any identification
between his own invocation of Oedipus, and Klein's crude verbalization
of it, he also strives to preserve what he finds essential in it, according
to the Hegelian paradigm just invoked: "if, in the human world, objects
become variegated, develop, with the luxuriance that makes for its originality, it is to the extent that they make their appearance within a process
of expulsion linked to the instinct of primitive destruction" (68). In
effect, Lacan mediates (purifies?) Klein's crudity by reading her through
Hyppolite's Hegelian reading of Freud on "Negation," in which Hyppolite
identifies "the operation of expulsion" as the "primordial operation upon
which the judgement of attribution is founded" (1991, 295).

Having paid close attention to Freud's essay "Negation" as early as
Revolution in Poetic Language, Kristeva returns to it repeatedly, most
notably in the context of her study on Klein, so that her readings of it
can serve as a useful guideline for the development of Kristeva's own
reflections, particularly her theory of abjection.[25] As Hyppolite comments, in this essay Freud makes "a truly profound discovery" (1991,
292). Hyppolite thinks that there is something "truly extraordinary"
(291) in Freud's analysis, and that its "implications" are "of prodigious

philosophical importance" (291). Since Freud's essay has proved so important for Klein and her followers, Hyppolite's acknowledgement should at least give pause to those who too readily follow Lacan's dismissal of object-relations theory. It is, then, hardly surprising that psychoanalytic critics have picked up on the central importance of Freud's essay.[26] Freud's discovery in this text can be seen as marking out the territory that Kristeva came to explore under the title "abjection."

Kristeva observes about Klein that she was seeking "her patients' aggressiveness—their restrained death drive—because it was by freeing up the death drive that she believed she could free up thought. Klein applied here the lesson Freud taught us in his writings contemporaneous with his discovery of what lies beyond the pleasure principle, in particular in his 'Negation' (1925)—or, more precisely, she subjected them to her own original development" (2001, 50). This freeing up of thought, which, as we will see in a moment, is related to what Hyppolite also discovers in Freud's text, is accomplished by the analyst naming the fantasies that the child plays out in games, which constitute for Klein a kind of *"primary symbolism* of the drives that is rudimentary but that already obeys the logic of 'equations'" (2001, 161). The analyst thus helps the child to negate the anxiety of separation and to move beyond the defensive maneuvers, including (and primarily), the splitting of the breast into "good" and "bad," and the concomitant splitting of the universe into "inside" and "outside."[27] The cursory logic of this process both serves to protect the child and introduces new problems.[28] It is not until the child can get beyond the fantasmatic splitting of the breast into good and bad, which is elaborated into the fear of being attacked by the bad breast and a need to protect (through separation) the good breast, that symbolism proper ensues. The fear of the destruction from the bad breast follows from a projection of all that is bad to the outside, in an attempt to retain all that is good on the inside. This preliminary demarcation of territories is what Kristeva will describe in the language of abjection. As Kristeva says in *Tales of Love*, "the bodily exchange of maternal fondness may take on the imaginary burden of representing love in its most characteristic form. Nevertheless, without the maternal 'diversion' toward a Third Party, the bodily exchange is abjection or devouring" (1987, 34). For Klein, since the child cannot yet experience absence—has not yet begun to speak in accordance with the signified/signifier structure—"he will experience the absence of the good object as an attack by the bad object. The infant will then proceed to split the object into a good part and a bad part while denying both frustration and persecution" (Kristeva 2001, 67–68). Projective identification is crucial to understanding the paranoid-schizoid position, replete with sadism.[29]

Only once the depressive position is reached can a true object relation be formed, according to Klein.[30] For Klein, then, projective identification is "manifested as the projection of the parts of the self onto an object in order to possess that very object: the mother's breast and the father's penis contain the violence of the attack and the split that project them outside the world as bad objects" (2001, 70).

Kristeva's reading of this Kleinian conglomerate breast/penis, or the combined parent, embodies a tension. On the one hand Klein mounts a challenge to Freudian orthodoxy, in the sense that penis-envy only follows on and emerges out of a primary breast envy.[31] Yet on the other hand, in response to Freud's excessive emphasis of the father, Klein emphasizes—to Kristeva's mind also excessively—the mother, while neglecting the role of the father, which, according to Kristeva, Klein "always underestimated" (2001, 177).[32] Kristeva, then, reads Klein's emphasis on matricide as the birth of thought as dogmatic, while at the same time reaping the benefits of the combined parent figure, as that which figures the penis as somehow inside the breast (mother)—as signaling the mother's desire not for the child but for another, typically (in Klein's and Kristeva's views) the father.[33] Klein says, "According to the child's earliest phantasies (or 'sexual theories') of parental coitus, the father's penis (or his whole body) becomes incorporated in the mother during the act. Thus the child's sadistic attacks have for their object both father and mother."[34] The importance of the combined parental figure, or the "united parents," for Klein is not only the child's preliminary understanding that it is not everything to the mother, that the mother has desires that are not restricted to the child—accompanied by an initial ability to begin to discriminate between I and not I, my body as distinct from the world.[35] It is also that *as combined,* the parental figure is representative of that toward which the child experiences affects (want/desire, jealousy, fear, even—perhaps especially— love) without having yet either made the discovery of sexual difference or learned the permanence of socially regulated distinctions—without, in other words, having become subject to the phallic law of the father, without being able to speak. The child is inculcated into a fully linguistic world, and as such is exposed to (we should not say yet "experiences") the vicissitudes of the powers that hold sway there, but is as yet unable to creatively master its meanings, or to "graft" language onto things, indeed is not yet able to patrol the borders of its own body in very precise ways.[36]

As premature, the infant lacks motor coordination, as Lacan emphasized, or does not have what Klein would term a "bodily presence." In short, the child has language (*langue*) but not speech (*parole*).[37] According to Hyppolite, what is at stake in Freud's text "Negation" is the birth of thought itself (see 1991, 292), or in a formulation that begins to measure the difficulty of the task that Freud sets himself, perhaps not so much of thinking as registering, "the origin of judgement and of thought itself (in the form of thought as such, since thought is already there before, in the primal, but it does not figure as thought there)" (297). One of the things at work in Freud's text is the separation—but never a complete one—between the intellectual and the affective (see 1991, 292–93), or as Hyppolite puts it, the possibility of generating "a margin of thought" (297).[38] Such a margin of thought is also at stake in Kristeva's inter-pretation of Klein, in which she says the analyst allows the analysand to *"think about* his truths rather than merge with them" (2001, 156). For Kristeva it is precisely the analyst's ability to tap into the metaphor-ical equations that Klein maps out in relation to children's fantasies, the projective identifications that Kristeva parses out in terms of abjec-tion, which allows the free space of associations necessary for the child's apprenticeship into the symbolic, and thus facilitates a rebirth. As Kristeva puts it:

> The maternal archaic—the archaic of her own relationship to the mater-nal *ab-ject* and the archaic of the motherly role she plays for her child—allows her to access the complexity of psychic life as well as the space between drives and words, between thought and the [*sic*] sense. When a woman so constructed listens to or "thinks about" her patient, she is nei-ther applying a system nor making a calculation. The logical process behind what has emerged as a phallic and symbolic computer, with its 0/1 grid, does not dominate here; instead, a striking imaginary coloring permeates our knowledge of transference and countertransference. Only then can the analyst be reborn and enable her analysand to be reborn. (2001, 156–57)

Before locking oneself into a system of symbolic values, and despite Klein's adherence to an Oedipal narrative, a space is hereby opened up in which no system is yet applicable. In such a space, the authority of Oedipus can be put on hold. Klein's work is sensitive to any abuse of authority, whether maternal or paternal, and directed toward a "free-dom" (2001, 238) achieved through the demystification of all forms of authority (see 2001, 236–37).[39] A space is thereby opened up in which, among other things, the racialization of the unconscious can be explored.

Freud, says Hyppolite, "deepens" the "relation between represen-tation and perception" when he shows that " 'in the beginning,' it is of no importance to know whether something exists or doesn't exist. . . . the question is <not> one of knowing whether this presentation still preserves its state in reality but if it can or cannot be refound. Such is the relation which Freud stresses: he founds [the testing] of the presentation by reality in the possibility of its object being refound once again" (1991, 295).

Freud situates the faculty of judgment in relation to the two instincts of eros and death. He construes judgment as on a continuum with the pleasure principle: "Judging is a continuation, along lines of expediency, of the original process by which the ego took things into itself or expelled them from itself, according to the pleasure principle" (1953o, 239). If, in one sense, judgment is a "continuation" of the pleasure principle, in another sense it can only arise once the ego is no longer completely governed by the pleasure principle. That is, it is only through the institution of a boundary that is representable—however unstable and permeable—between the ego and the world, between the subject and object, between inside and outside, that the function of judgment can be realized. To put it another way, inflected by Lacan, for Freud, it is only once the subject has been initiated into the order of symbols, only after the I is able to represent to itself what gives it pleasure (and what does not), that it can be said to make judgments. Still more specifically, it is the "symbol of negation" that makes judgment possible, since it frees thinking from "the compulsion of the pleasure principle" (239).

Freud distinguishes two functions of judgment, that of attribution, and that of existence. Judgments of attribution concern whether or not a given thing possesses an attribute. In the language of the pleasure principle, at issue is whether or not a particular thing is pleasurable. Whatever is judged to be good I want to introject, or take inside me, while whatever is judged as bad, I want to eject. "Expressed in the language of the oldest—the oral—instinctual impulses, the judgement is," says Freud, on the one hand " 'I should like to eat this,' " " 'I should like to take this into myself,' " or " 'It shall be inside me,' " and on the other hand, I should like " 'to spit it out,' " I should like to " 'keep that out,' " or " 'it shall be outside me' " (1953o, 237). Everything bad is initially outside me, while everything good is inside me. Judgments of attribution delineate, then, a provisional sense of inside and outside.

Judgments of existence also distinguish the internal from the external. "What is unreal, merely a presentation and subjective, is only internal; what is real is also there *outside*" (237). Yet what is also of concern in this aspect of judgment—that is clearly not in judgments of attribution—is the reality or lack of reality of a thing. "It is no longer a question of whether what has been perceived (a thing) shall be taken into the ego or not, but of whether something which is in the ego as a presentation can be rediscovered in perception (reality) as well" (237). Note that Freud says "rediscovered" because he believes that "all presentations originate

from perceptions and are repetitions of them" (237), although he qualifies this when he adds that we do not necessarily reproduce our perceptions faithfully, but rather introduce distortion through "omissions"
or "the merging of various elements" (238).[40] The fact remains however
that what is at issue is "not to *find* an object in real perception which
corresponds to the one presented, but to *refind* such an object" (237),
or that "objects shall have been lost which once brought real satisfaction" (239). In question is "whether it is there in the external world, so
that he can get hold of it whenever he needs it" (237). Freud aligns affirmation—the judgment of attribution that says, in effect, it shall be inside
me—with eros, and associates it with "uniting" (239), while he aligns
"negation—the successor to expulsion" with "the instinct of destruction"
or the death drive. Abjection becomes one of the primary ways in which
Kristeva takes up and elaborates Freudian drive theory.

In *Powers of Horror* the account of abjection presupposes a desiring
subject, who is "sickened" (1982, 1) by abjection at the same time as
tempted by it. The subject has forged relations with objects, has been
settled "within the fragile texture of a desire for meaning, which as a
matter of fact makes me ceaselessly and infinitely homologous to it"
(1–2). Disruptive of this meaning, this homology, the abject "draws me
toward the place where meaning collapses" (2). A "suffering" that "I
endure" since "I imagine it to be the desire of the other" (2), the father.
I exist only in the desire of the parents (see 3). There is in abjection an
"elsewhere as tempting as it is condemned" (1), a "vortex of summons
and repulsion" (1). The abject is a "jettisoned object" that has been
"radically excluded," "driven away" by a "superego" that has overwhelmed the ego (the "ego" has "merged with its master") (2). Yet, as
banished, the abject challenges the superego. The subject (such as it is)
is situated as "loathsome" (2) yet tries to separate from its designation as
such: "not me. Not that . . . a weight of meaningless . . . crushes me . . .
a reality that, if I acknowledge it, annihilates me" (2). Abjection is a protection against a threat that is "exorbitant" but whose provenance is
uncertain: does it come from inside or outside? (1).

In nausea, I protect myself, through the spasms of vomiting, from the
repugnant. This is a rejection of what I have become, a subject who exists
only in their desire (their laws, their symbols) and a birth of myself
through expulsion: I am not this. A refusal, a redrawing of boundaries.
Refuse, a corpse, shit, threaten the integrity of the "clean and proper" (8)
body, since they have been "thrust aside in order to live" (3) so that when
they encroach on me, they cross the border, disturbing "identity, order,
system" (4). Abjection "takes the ego back to its source on the abominable
limits from which, in order to be, the ego has broken away—it assigns it a

source in the non-ego, drives and death" (15). It is "a resurrection that has gone through death (of the ego). It is an alchemy that transforms death drive into a start of life, of new signifiance" (15).

In *Powers of Horror* the processes of dividing and separating are already situated in relation to the symbolic, already a function of the superego, although the relation is a perverse one. The law takes effect (without yet formalizing its effect in the permanence of signs).[41] Kristeva refers to abjection as a *"precondition of narcissism"* (1982, 13), yet at the same time considers it a "narcissistic crisis" (14–15). In *Tales of Love* she will clarify the relationship between narcissism and abjection. In order to see the significance of this clarification it will be helpful to first recall that Freud's paper "On Narcissism" (1914) is an important reference for Lacan's mirror-stage.[42] As is well known, Freud says that "a unity comparable to the ego cannot exist from the start; the ego has to be developed. The auto-erotic instincts, however, are there from the very first" and that "a new psychical action" is required "in order to bring about narcissism" (1953n, 77).[43] Commenting on this passage, Lacan reads the idea that the ego is not there from the start, but has to develop, as confirmation of his "conception of the mirror-stage. The *Urbild*, which is a unity comparable to the ego, is constituted at a specific moment in the history of the subject, at which point the ego begins to take on its functions. This means that the human ego is founded on the basis of the imaginary relation" (1991, 115). Jacqueline Rose explains the trajectory that Lacan's interpretation follows: "As a result of identifying itself with a discrete image, the child will be able to postulate a series of equivalencies between the objects of the surrounding world, based on the conviction that each has a recognizable permanence. Identification of an object world is therefore grounded in the moment when the child's image was alienated from itself as an imaginary object and sent back to it the message of its own subjecthood. It is the process of enumeration and exchange which sets off from this point that will inform Lacan's later concept of linguistic insistence, defined as a process which starts off from this position of a signifier which was primarily evicted from its own place" (1986, 173). Yet it is the prehistory of the process of signification with which Kristeva is preoccupied. Kristeva's return to, and rejuvenation of, Klein's notion of projective identification in her recasting of it as the abjection of the mother and transference love for the imaginary father represents a delicate balancing act between Klein's and Lacan's rereading of Freud. As Mary Jacobus puts it, there is a "difficult crossover between, on one hand, a Kristevan account of signification that is necessarily post-Lacanian, even in its divergence from Lacan, in its insistence on the missing, unsuspected category of the signifier as a necessary condition for the emergence of the subject, and, on the other hand, what Lacan himself views as regressive, a Kleinian account of eating (cannibalism, even), incorporation, and primary identification, or what Klein herself . . . calls 'projective identification,' which is ambiguously posed on the borderline of instinct and ego" (1995, 131). Kristeva registers this difficulty in *Sense and Non-Sense of Revolt*, when she says, "The emphasis placed on language as the organizer of psychical life, though judicious, has too often prevented us from fully appreciating the sensory (prelinguistic or translinguistic) experience."[44] Kristeva introduces this observation in the context of following up the divergent ramifications of the castration complex for girls and boys, arguing that, while girls accede to the phallic symbolic, they cultivate an ironic position in relation to it. The "[i]llusory" character that the "phallic-symbolic order" (2000, 100) maintains is due to a "dissociation" that is "structurally inscribed between the sensory and the signifying in the phallicism of the girl" (99). The "phallus as signifier of lack as well as of the law . . . is immediately perceived/thought of as extraneous, radically other" (99), since the "real and imaginary basis of phallic pleasure in the girl (the clitoris) immediately dissociates the female subject from the phallus in the sense of a privileged signifier" (99). The girl experiences disappointment as a result of being less valorized than boys by her family and due to "psychosocial configuration" (100). This unfavorable perception—"she is not the phallus" (100)—"reactivates the hallucination of earlier sensorial experiences (satisfaction and/or frustration in the daughter-mother" (100) relation. The "gap" between the phallic order, which undervalues the girl, and the "earlier perception/hallucination" dominated by a sensorial relation to the mother, which precedes or is "concealed from the appearance of language" (100), impacts "the female subject with a negation ('I am not what is,' 'I am nevertheless, because of *not*')"—a kind of "doubled negativity" (100).[45] Kristeva associates the ironic stance that women thereby adopt toward the symbolic order, which is both "illusory and indispensable" (100), with Antigone, whose ironic relation to the community Hegel famously articulated (see 102). The threat of castration, along with the extraneousness to the phallus, renders clitoral masturbation *disgusting:* the girl "rejects it" (102). Bernheimer also notes the "revulsion" experienced by the girl (123). Though Kristeva herself does not make the connection explicit, we could read the girl's horror at castration in terms of abjection.

If Freud's suggestion that the ego is not there from the start but has to be developed has had a vital legacy, another of the important contributions of the essay "On Narcissism" is the emergence of the ego-ideal, the concept that Freud would later designate the superego, that agent of repression, which does not however repress narcissism but rather accommodates it. Freud says, "As always where the libido is concerned, man has here again shown himself incapable of giving up a satisfaction he had once enjoyed. He is not willing to forgo the narcissistic perfection of his childhood; and when, as he grows up, he is disturbed by the admonitions of others and by the awakening of his own critical judgment, so that he can no longer retain that perfection, he seeks to recover it in the new form of an ego ideal. What he projects before him as his idea is the substitute for the lost narcissism of his childhood in which he was his own ideal" (Freud 1953n, 94). Or, as Freud elaborates it in "Group Psychology," the ego ideal is "heir to the original narcissism in which the childish ego enjoyed self-sufficiency; it gradually gathers up from the influences of the environment the demands which that environment makes upon the ego and which the ego cannot always rise to; so that a man, when he cannot be satisfied with his ego itself, may nevertheless be able to find satisfaction in the ego ideal which has been differentiated out of the ego" (1953h, 110). In *Tales of Love,* Kristeva emphasizes the supplementary character of narcissism, which, despite its "uneasy, ubiquity, and inconsistency" (1987, 24) in Freud, is "far from being originary" (22). Returning to the passage that Lacan had read as confirmation of his understanding of imaginary or primary identification in the mirror stage, Kristeva focuses on the supplementary character of narcissism, reading it as "a supplement . . . the product of a 'new action,' which we should understand as that of a third realm supplementing the autoeroticism of the mother-child dyad" (1987, 22). She goes on to elaborate that the status of narcissism is "intrasymbolic" or "dependent upon a third party" (1987, 22)—a point with which Lacan would agree, since not only primary (imaginary) identification but also secondary (symbolic) identification is at stake in the mirror stage.[46] Focusing on the supplementary character of narcissism, Kristeva suggests that this intrasymbolic status of narcissism in fact takes place within a ternary preoedipal structure, a disposition that is prior to the mirror stage, that of the imaginary father. It is "within a disposition that chronologically and logically precedes that of the Oedipal Ego. It prompts one to conceive of an archaic disposition of the paternal function, preceding the Name, the Symbolic, but also preceding the 'mirror stage' whose logical potentiality it would harbor—a disposition that one might call that of the Imaginary Father" (1987, 22). Accordingly, Kristeva asks, "Does the 'mirror stage' emerge out of nowhere? What are the conditions of its emergence? A whole *complex structuration* can seemingly be conceived . . . 'narcissism' . . . is an already ternary structuration with a different articulation from the Ego-object-Other triangle that is put together in the shadow of the Oedipus complex" (1987, 22–23). For Kristeva, narcissism is a protection of the *"emptiness* that is intrinsic to the beginnings of the symbolic function [which] appears as the first separation between what is not yet an *Ego* and what is not yet an *object"* (1987, 24). As Chase says, Kristeva casts primary narcissism "as an inaugural act of signification. . . . She locates the condition of signification—the condition that sustains the structure of the sign, the gap between the signifier and the signified—in the modality of 'primary narcissism'" (1989, 68–78). Narcissism is a kind of defense that protects emptiness against chaos, against the dissolution of borders. In other words, it is a defense of emptiness against abjection.

We could interpret the "doubled negativity" that Kristeva reads in the ironic stance towards the phallus, initiated by the gap between a reactivation of the girl's pre-linguistic sensory relation to the mother, and her extraneousness to the phallus, as an echo of the earlier inscription of the gap between the signifier and the signified. Just as Kristeva reads Klein as effecting the Hegelian "negation of the negation" (2001, 173) when she raises negativism "to a higher level in which it denies its own status as negativism and transforms itself into a form of self-knowledge" (2001, 168), so Kristeva herself elaborates a similar rewriting of determinate negation in the ironic stance of women toward the phallic order. Such irony is only always already recuperated by a Hegelian dialectic if the terms of that dialectic are accepted as decisive; thus, the figuring of Antigone as the eternal irony of the community is not defused in advance—it figures precisely as that which is spat out of the system, irrecuperable within its terms, intolerable to it.

In her study of Klein, Kristeva returns once more to the passage in Freud's "On Narcissism" that has become a touchstone in Lacan's understanding of the mirror stage, where Freud invokes a "new psychical action" known as "narcissism" (2001, 58). Again Kristeva underlines the supplementary character of narcissism: "When Freud began to develop his concept of narcissism in 'On Narcissism: An Introduction' (1914), he described an 'autoeroticism' that emerges early in life, an instinctual and, even more important, archaic, self-gratification for the baby that precedes a 'new psychical action' known as 'narcissism' in which the ego as a totality is deemed an object of love" (2001, 58). Where Lacan extrapolates the imaginary from the figure of Narcissus, who peers into the "maternal watery element" (1987, 42), by highlighting "the scopic function . . . in structuring the ego and the object" and the "symbolic function of the father," Klein's notion of the internal object is more "heterogeneous" (2001, 64). In turn, Kristeva will emphasize the vocal, auditory aspects rather than the strictly visual register. Like Klein, Kristeva's understanding of the imaginary is not restricted to a single sensory dimension. As Kristeva says, Klein's

> notion of the internal object is entirely distinct from Lacan's *imaginary,* for Lacan believed that narcissism takes hold through the intermediary of the object as a function of the subject's absorption into his mirror image—into the very place where he realizes he is an Other who is sustained by the alterity of a mother already placed under the rubric of a third-party phallus. . . . Klein's thinking here evokes a cornucopia of images, sensations and substances whose theoretical "impurity" is superseded by the clinical advances she proposes: the complexity of the internal object, in Klein's view, is indispensable for tracking the specifics of the fantasy in childhood as well as in borderline states or psychosis. (2001, 64)

While the logic of fetishistic disavowal privileges the scopic drive, as does Lacan's mirror stage, the sensorial fantasmatics in which the infant partakes in Klein's projective identification, and Kristeva's abjection are sketched out, as Susan Isaacs puts it, in terms of "oral impulses, bound up with taste, smell, touch (of the lips and mouth), kinaesthetic, visceral, and other somatic sensations. . . . images are scarcely if at all distinguishable from actual sensations and external perceptions. The skin is not yet felt to be a boundary between inner and outer reality."[47]

Taking up the model of abjection, as a preliminary marking out of what can be inside the body, and what must be kept outside, one can see how the imaginary political body of the nation-state is sketched out in a metonymical relation that is also delineated in terms of the need to keep out certain "others" in order to protect the sanctity of those envisaged as properly contained within its borders. In order to substantiate this suggestion, let me return to Ahmed, who suggests that "the skin of the community" is effected in exclusionary ways. Ahmed argues that "Rather than considering the stories of subject and nation as corresponding to each other" (2005, 95), we need a metonymical understanding of the relation between bodies and nations, one that capitalizes on how "the contiguity between signs . . . is affective or even dependent on emotional forms of attachment" (2005, 100). In arguing for a metonymical understanding of how the imaginary body of a nation takes certain bodies to stand for the nation as a whole, Ahmed in effect takes up Lacan's emphasis on metonymy, while inflecting it in a Kleinian and Kristevan direction, so that it impacts the preverbal realm of fantasy. The bodies that we move toward and away from sketch out the imaginary according to which the symbolic structures such movements at the level of the nation.

Ahmed suggests that the transformation of borders into objects is "an effect of disgust" and that "borders need to be threatened in order to be maintained" (2005, 102). Drawing on Kristeva's account of abjection as making and remaking "the border between self and other" (2005, 102), Ahmed shows how nationalist imaginaries function through "the separation of others into bodies that can be loved and hated" and that the "nation is a concrete effect of how some bodies have moved towards and away from other bodies" (2005, 108). Ahmed's call is to "acknowledge how others have already been recognized as stranger than other others, as border objects that have been incorporated and then expelled from the ideal of the community" (2005, 109). Such a "call" can be read as an intervention in the imaginary organizing the symbolic authority of the nation.[48] Yet, unlike Dick's call to Klein, this call is not addressed to the father, does not invoke the symbolic of the Oedipus complex. Rather it is a call that proceeds from an anxiety borne precisely out of the worry that Kristeva's reading of nationalist politics is inadequate to the dynamic of racism. In this sense it accords with my own "object of anxiety," namely that Kristeva adheres too closely to the Lacanian, oedipal symbolic, with its presupposition of the foundational status of sexual difference, to be able to sustain the impulse of tracing abjection beyond its resolution in the primary oedipal fantasy.

Let me return for a moment to Lacan's disgust at Klein—to her crudity, her lack of theoretical sophistication. What, precisely, is it that sickens him, what does he find so "revolting"? Jacobus implies that in Lacan's abjection of Klein we can read the defensive maneuvers of projective identification, a rejection and projection outside himself of the fear that his own analysis is heavy-handed. Jacobus discerns Lacan's own anxiety at the basis of his abject response to Klein, which is to refract Klein's case-study through a Hegelian lens, allowing him to recuperate it in the name of Freudian expulsion, while lending it an air of theoretical respectability, thereby keeping at bay that which he finds most disturbing in it. Projecting his own anxiety about his relation to theory onto Klein, he refuses to recognize it, or work through it.[49] Kristeva's response is more nuanced. On the one hand she seeks to avoid what she reads as the "regressive fantasy" (Jacobus 1995, 148) of the Kleinian phallic mother, all alone, "playing at the phallus game all by herself . . . in the back room of Kleinism and post-Kleinism" (1987, 44). She seeks to mediate this fantasy, with the "Third Party," the "archaic inscription of the father" (1987, 44). On the other hand, Kristeva wants to avoid the Lacanian "always-already-there of language," to subvert the "absolute reference" to the phallus. Does Lacan's defensive attack on Klein signal his premature identification with her, a too hasty application of the castration complex? Has anxiety "backfired" (Jacobus 1995, 132), just as it did for Dick, in his premature genital identification with the mother as object of attack? The threat that Klein would pose to Lacan would have to be mitigated through the fetishistic maneuver that recognizes Klein is lacking theoretically, while at the same time covering over that lack by substituting it with a Hegelian respectability. Kristeva, by contrast, identifies with Klein, "incorporating and introjecting her language" (1987, 26)—the combined or united parents, the abject or defensive maneuver of projective identification—in a "nonobjectal" or "metaphoric identification" (Jacobus 1995, 146) that adopts Lacanian theory as the third party. Kristeva rewrites Klein in a post-Lacanian register, transforming Lacan's abjection of her into an identification with a theoretical mother, rewriting Klein's legacy.[50] Kristeva neither adopts a position of blind, uncritical adherence, nor defensively rejects Klein, by abjecting her on the one hand and usurping her work on the other hand.[51] Her candid, appreciative, critical assessment does Klein the credit of taking her seriously, assessing her contribution, recognizing her originality, marking out her place in a tradition of psychoanalytic interpretation. It thereby writes her into a different history than one of abject mothers.

Maternal identification is strictly precluded on the Freudian/Lacanian schema insofar as the maternal function of satisfying hunger and thirst is considered on the level of need, rather than at the level of demand or desire. The mother has no particularity or determinacy before having undergone negation—a negation that occurs through an absence symbolized in language, under the auspices of the paternal third, in the light of whom the child rediscovers its relation to maternity. Finding again the object that has been lost, the infant also discovers itself as loved by the mother in relation to the father (isn't he beautiful?).[52] On this model, before the child's inauguration into language, the mother is not registered or recognized as a subject, and therefore there can be no identification with her. As far as the infant is concerned, as long as its biological or survival needs are met, it is of little importance who meets them. Yet Klein's projective identification and Kristeva's reworking of it as abjection elaborates identification as prior to language, sketched out in the presymbolic world of fantasy and pleasure. Unstable to be sure, a world of shifting boundaries, but the beginning of an ordering of what will be inside, and what will be outside. At the same time, there is a fantasmatic sketching out of what is good, and what is bad, or what must be attacked and what must be preserved. This imaginary identification might later be coded in terms of the Oedipal triangle, but it is also susceptible of other social configurations, such as race and class relations. These too are formulated in terms of that for which I acquire a taste—as opposed to that which I find distasteful, or more dramatically, that which disgusts or revolts me, and from which I seek to part in order to become myself. Alternatively I might resort to identifying with or in some sense becoming the abject.

3

Abject Art: Destabilizing the Drive for Purification, and Unmasking the Foundational Fantasy of Castration

Instability has long been at the heart of the negotiations that have played out between art and philosophy. The enacting of boundaries discriminating the pure from the impure, and the establishing of boundaries between the harmonic and the disturbing, have figured writ large. Whether it is a question of Plato's exile of Homer from the ideal city, Aristotelian catharsis, Burke's purging of terror from the sublime, or Kant's elimination of pain from pleasure in the experience of the sublime, purification has been pivotal to the relationship enacted between art and philosophy. More recently, attention has focused on art as the event of the inexpressible, where it falls to philosophy to recognize that its task is not to establish or reestablish its interpretive mastery over the unsettling disturbance of the work of art, but rather to allow the work itself to bear witness to its own disruptive impact. It falls to us, then, to react to the reverberations effected by the work of art, to tremble in its wake. Philosophy encounters its own limits, while art heightens our awareness of human finitude. Death and the impossibility of its transcendence figure prominently in this latest chapter of the fragility that characterizes our encounter of the event that is art.

The demands of realism have been brought into question by modernism, such that the impetus driving aesthetic enquiry is decisively removed from the question of how successfully and for what pedagogical or cultural ends action is imitated. Marking the transition from premodern to modernist art is the shift from a mimetic model to a *self-critical one*.[1] The emphasis on finitude brings with it a rethinking of the rationale of modernism, which is no longer calibrated so much in terms of a subjective or inward turn, a Cartesian meditation or Kantian reflection on how our knowing access to the world is structured. The recent pre-occupation with death, finitude, and the failure of transcendence gives the self-critical turn one more twist, so that the relevant question becomes: in what ways does art bring us face to face with the unrepresentable? Whether, with Clement Greenberg, one considers Kant to be the preeminent modernist philosopher, or identifies, with Arthur Danto, Descartes as the exemplary modernist philosopher, whether one sees Manet as the first modernist painter, or recognizes Van Gogh and Gauguin as worthy of that accolade, and finally, whether one construes the flatness of painting to be essential, or the consciousness of brushstroke, shape, surface, and pigment, there is substantial agreement that, as Danto puts it, "With modernism, the conditions of representation themselves become central, so that art in a way becomes its own subject" (Danto 1997, 7).[2]

Narratives of modernism as the failure of transcendence issue in accounts of postmodernism as the inevitable confrontation with finitude, where questions about representation remain central, but the limits of representation are emphasized above all. There is a break with the progressive understanding of history accompanying the belief that the history of art is the history of the ongoing discovery of truth, a history that finds its fulfillment in proper art. Thus understood, modernism ushers in the era in which art discovers its true essence, which implies that any art that does not conform to this essence must be degenerate. For Danto, "Modernism, overall, was the Age of Manifestos. . . . A manifesto singles out the art it justifies as the true and only art, as if the movement it expresses had made the philosophical discovery of what art essentially is" (1997, 29–34). Greenberg's idea of art, according to Danto, is essentially consonant with the modernist creed of manifesto art.[3] Inherent in Greenberg's celebration of Kant as the "first real modernist" (1997, 67) was the belief in the purity not only of art but also, concomitantly, of the arts. The truth, or essence, of each art must be identified and distinguished from that of every other art.

The assumptions embedded in Greenberg's Kantian view of modernism bear reflection, demonstrating, as they do, a concern with purity, erecting boundaries in order to distinguish the proper with the improper, and carrying the implication that everything that does not belong to true art must be purged. Art is construed not merely as a mode of knowing, but as one that must be, a priori, uncontaminated with any empiricism. On such a view, which presupposes the traditional relationship between cognition and aesthesis, not only must art have an essence, but so too must each art have its own essence, one that is unalloyed with materiality.[4] In order to remain true to its own proper spirit or essence, each art must reflect its own true mission, or ideal. Unsurprisingly, the philosophical attempt to determine the essence of each art has resulted in a hierarchy of arts. Thus, historical epochs can be differentiated from one another according to the function each epoch attributes to art, and according to which art it identifies as privileged. The idea that tragic dramatic poetry was considered to have been the highest art for the Greeks—and that poetry retained its privilege for Heidegger's appropriation of German idealism—cannot be divorced from the fact that the imitation of heroic action and the cathartic renewal it afforded served a propaedeutic purpose. Embedded in the history that tracks the purpose of art and argues the priority of one art over others, there is of course an association of the temporal unfolding of action taken to be characteristic of poetry with masculinity, and a corresponding feminization of the spatial dynamics considered to be at the heart of painting.[5] In this sense Merleau-Ponty's (1993) contestation of the privileged role of poetry, in the centrality he accords to the visual arts, and to painting in particular (in essays such as "Cézanne's Doubt") has been greeted as radical. It might succeed in reaping the benefits of Heidegger's decisive overturning of mimesis's authority in favor of art as epochal event, yet if the claim for painting over poetry only reinstalls one art over another as preeminent, it fails to move beyond the idea that discovering the essence of art is bound up with establishing the true priority of one art over all the others.[6]

To establish its legitimacy as an art, defenders of film inevitably found themselves waylaid by arguments concerning the nature and function of better established arts. In the effort to lay claim to its own domain—rather than, for example, that of theater or poetry—film as an art form has been characterized in ways that are not always sensitive to the assumptions being made about time and space, their relationship to one another, and the ways in which this relationship defines and is defined by the longstanding privilege accorded to poetry over painting. Concomitantly, neither have the respective associations of time with masculinity and space with femininity always been thought through. Proving the exception to the rule in this regard, Kristeva observes: "'Father's time, mother's species,' as Joyce puts it; and indeed, when evoking the name and destiny of women, one thinks more of the *space* generating and forming the human species than of *time,* becoming or history" (1986b, 190). Embedded in Kristeva's suggestion that today Hitchcock plays the role for us that Sophocles played for the Greeks is the assumption of a certain consonance between dramatic poetry—the highest form or art for the Greeks—and film.[7] Just as the cathartic unfolding of action in time, by means of character and plot, was integral to

Aristotle's understanding of tragic poetry (as the truth as revealed through kairos), so the "poetry" of horror film would lie in its capacity to purge us, and in doing so, to educate us out of a blind following of our drives.

Yet to assimilate film to poetry is, by default, to assume that film, like poetry, follows the action of its heroes, and to ignore the fact that film does not abide by the same rules of signification; it introduces another signifying system, the meaning of which is read off the sign as image, rather than as linguistic signifier. The understanding of film as a language on the model of poetry has tended to assume that film can be understood as text, assimilated to the temporal unfolding of action in terms of which poetry has typically been understood, eschewing the specific visual register of film. Rather than construing film as a visual art, akin to painting, which has typically been interpreted in terms of spatiality, films are read as narratives of action. Indeed one of the strengths of Gilles Deleuze's approach to cinema is his understanding of early film in *Cinema I* as a cinema of action, together with his insight that this characteristic of film—which aligns film with poetry—gives way to new characteristics, as the art of film comes into its own.

Deleuze construes the shift to modern film as a shift away from a cinema of action and movement, and toward a cinema of seeing, in which a direct time-image comes to the fore (rather than the indirect image of time of the movement-image found in early cinema), in which the dynamics of identification are complicated. Film's relationship to its own visuality becomes a principal problematic. We will see shortly how what Kristeva calls the "thought specular" and Deleuze analyzes as the image that is thought function in similar ways. Let me note for now that, while the exact contours of his argument might not remain applicable, Lessing's differentiation of the artificial from the natural sign as bound up with the synchrony of painting, and the diachrony of poetry (1984), anticipates a key move that both Deleuze and Kristeva make in attending to the meaning of film not solely in terms of the linguistic signifier (so central to Lacan's Saussurean rereading of Freud) but in terms of a semiotics (in the case of Kristeva), which opens up the question of the materiality of film in a new way and (in the case of Deleuze) refuses to subordinate the sign to a signifying system that assumes the priority of linguistics.[8]

Deleuze turns to Charles Pierce, rather than Ferdinand de Saussure, for a theory of signs that can be applied to cinema, since Pierce does not assume that the sign is inherently linguistic.[9] For Kristeva the semiotic is taken up by the symbolic, but not without remainder. The residue of affect cannot be fully appropriated by the sign for which it calls. The charge of energy that constitutes the primary processes or drives comes to be represented, to be sure, but its representation is always inadequate to its affective dimension. In this sense, fetishism, as the attempt not so much to cancel out as to accommodate difference, is heir to abjection. The point is not to outlaw fetishism so much as to think through the condition it refuses, or maintains only as enigmatic.

As we have begun to see, not only have the limits of representation come to the fore in the latest twist of the modernist turn to the conditions of representation, so too have the limits of a discourse of masterful subjectivity. In the effort to confront the limitations of theory to articulate the residual materiality of the work of art, or the ways in which the work of art constitutes an enigma that exceeds theory, resisting articulation, mourning as a central site of aesthetic interrogation has been inflected in the direction of trauma discourse, inspired in no small part by Cathy Caruth's authoritative *Unclaimed Experience*.[10] Fueled by Foucault's understanding of the modern period as a confrontation with human finitude, in the wake of Heidegger's emphasis on finitude as being-toward-death—filtered through Lacan's and Derrida's re-readings of Freud—recent interventions in the area of psychoanalysis and aesthetics have focused upon mourning.[11] So too, the impact of World War II leaves its mark on the effect wrought on us by the work of art, definitively putting to rest any lingering commitment to the notion that aesthetic judgment is universal and ahistorical. Auschwitz figures prominently in the attempt to understand this effect, as an event that exceeds comprehension, an event that tests the limits of representation, an event that barely qualifies as an event, in the sense that its traumatic effect is to contest the subject's capacity to experience it as such—the subject of trauma is displaced, decentered, or put into question. Without casting doubt on the relevance and importance of such investigations, I wonder whether the focus on loss has been articulated in a way that leaves intact some myths in need of interrogation. Remaining uncontested, the foundational fantasy of castration continues to organize psychoanalytic enquiries of the aesthetic.[12]

Death is figured as unavoidable, and we are called on to recognize it as ineluctable. The authority that philosophy has traditionally assumed over art is thereby either renewed in the guise of a demand for authentic mourning, or else it is decisively put into question, but at the cost of a reversal that leaves philosophy with nothing much to say. To authorize an authentic mode of mourning—one that is articulated as marginal to the allegedly inauthentic negotiations with the past that belong to mainstream postmodernist engagements, where the society of the spectacle rules—is to risk renewing the distinction between high and low culture, even as it is reworked around the notion of how successfully works of art negotiate the failure of transcendence. Such responses rework the criteria for differentiating between good and bad art, even as they dispense with the traditional formulation of those criteria, implicitly claiming, for example, that while discrete arts must no longer adhere to discrete essences, hybrid art can perform mourning either well or badly. Alternatively, art is read as the site in which philosophy must suffer this loss, where the residue of the past that we inherit cannot be fully recuperated or digested. The refusal to endorse an authentic or normative approach to death, a refusal to embrace any particular approach to that which remains unthinkable, is also a quasi-Heideggerian insistence on the openness of a stance whose meaning derives from philosophy's confrontation with its own limits. Philosophy cedes its authority to art, with the risk, perhaps, of turning philosophy's privilege over art into art's privilege over philosophy. Art is what it is, it carries with it a historical mandate, issuing the truth of its epoch, and designating to the philosopher the expository task of reflecting that truth, articulating it with humility, theoretically, and forever inadequately. Through the reversal that has taken place, whereby art is no longer the handmaiden of philosophy, philosophy waits on and mulls over the enigma art presents.

Endings, the spectral, the traumatic kernel, the unrepresentable residue—such have been the preoccupations motivating various returns to modernism, forays into the history of postmodernism. Accomplished as such interpretations are, their emphasis on the traumatic real leaves untroubled the myth of castration, which comes to function transcendentally, as a hidden but enabling condition, resting upon the enigmatic status of woman. Unspoken, the horror of women's genitalia—or to utilize an Irigarayan register, the horror of the nothing to see—becomes the dirty little secret, the unspeakable, veiled truth, around which the tenets of psychoanalytic theory are built. The very possibility of meaning is thus bound up with the riddle of women's lack—understood in terms of the lack of a signifier—and the disgust this elicits, figuring as the impenetrable *sine qua non* of the conceptual apparatus driving aesthetic theory. Theory knows without knowing the original traumatic scene. Metonymically displaced from its original signifier, trauma discourse reiterates itself across different registers, which come to substitute for the trauma of castration. The phallus arrogates to itself the creative capacity, traditionally the preserve of maternity, now co-opted under the guise of the paternal metaphor. Various cover-up operations are perpetrated in the name of this service—just so many fetishistic displacements. It is not castration as such, we learn from Lacan, but the *objet petit a* that looks back at me. The metonymically receding object of desire is caught up in a logic of substitution that only serves to barricade the originary enigmatic trauma behind further disguises, its inaccessibility adding to the apparent transcendental status of the phallus, and justifying the fetishistic ministrations enacted in its name. Remaining in its place, untouched by these ramifications, echoing through the discourse of trauma, the mythological horror of women's castrated sex is left unresolved, its reverberations unaccountably reborn in phallic shape. The abject feminine thus spawns new monsters, while the maternal abject retains its enigmatic status: unfathomable, inscrutable, unrepresentable, yet indispensable for everything that gets erected in the name of its impossibility. Through such translations, disavowal is appropriated as the mechanism of race, whereby the monstrosity of the feminine is transferred onto that of the racialized other, all the while confirming, rather than challenging, the originary, unspeakable horror of women's lack, the impossibility of signification. If some theorists have cast doubt on the efficacy of castration theory to kick-start the Oedipal machine, a detailed tracking of the effects of the unexamined yet ubiquitous appeal to castration theory has yet to be undertaken.[13] It is on this terrain that I situate my own investigation into the possibilities opened up by the abject.

By grounding my reading of Kristeva in *Powers of Horror*, rather than *Black Sun*, the book in which Kristeva confronts most explicitly the thematics of mourning and melancholia, I emphasize abjection. Focusing on abjection also gives us access to the repetitive stories of loss around which we marshal the defenses of our egos, as we endeavor to defend ourselves against the inevitable blows of what we call "life," as preparation for the new losses that we will unquestioningly sustain. Yet the recuperative move of mourning/melancholia (and for the moment I preserve the ambivalence in deference to Freud, and to Butler's readings, although it will shortly be necessary to parse these terms separately) is in a different register than that of abjection. In focusing on abjection I attend to Kristeva's Kleinian roots over and above her Lacanian frame of reference. Mourning/melancholia on the one hand and abjection on the other hand are situated in a differential relationship to Lacan's peremptory dismissal of object relations theorists as misconstruing the psychoanalytic endeavor.

A thorough understanding of abjection (and by extension, Kristeva's project in its entirety) can only be properly undertaken in the light of the enormous debt her notion of the abject owes to Melanie Klein. Accordingly, I read Kristeva as challenging Lacan's brute dismissal of object relations theorists as practitioners who mistakenly focus on the ego's defenses, as if the point were to shore up or strengthen the ego, rather than to explore, and to recognize as such, the apparently infinite variety of ways in which our defensive attempts to protect our narcissism spawn

new problems. Kristeva's notion of abjection takes a much more interesting tack in relation to Klein's work than Lacan, not arguing that there
is an indiscriminate and misplaced attempt to preserve the ego at all
costs, but rather following through the intricate mechanism by which
abjection throws up defenses, which themselves become threatening,
in order to ward off the greater anxiety of maternal loss or absence—the
loss that has, for the symbolic, always already occurred. An attempt, then,
to perpetuate the omnipotence of infantile narcissism, abjection is also
a refusal to accept loss, a response that hallucinates an object in reaction to the threat of loss. In this sense, abjection is precisely a manifestation of the prevalence in modernity of a situation that Beardsworth
has described in terms of the "loss of loss" (2004). Rejecting loss, the
deject devises territories, creates divisions, parcels out the world according to a refusal of loss, attempting to establish control from a fantasmat-
ically creative position that preserves the not yet I from absence, yet at
the same time ceaselessly differentiates between this and that, good
and bad, pure and impure, and thereby begins to institute a tentative
subjectivity even in the refusal of loss, or separation.

Discussions of the abject in the field of aesthetics tend to be limited
to the arts of photography, painting, and sculpture, rather than film.
While Barbara Creed has focused on horror film (1993) and Oliver and
Trigo (2003) have focused, more recently, on *film noir*, I share with
Rosalind Krauss an interest in moving beyond the emphasis on horror
as thematic, and recognize with Mulvey the need to move toward a
theory of art in which abjection displaces the centrality of the phallus
as transcendental signifier and that of the discourse of castration that
backs it up. Abjection provides not so much an alternative to the governing trope of fetishism in interpreting the cinematic apparatus, as it
does an acknowledgement of the remainder that is disavowed: an
attempt, then, to remobilize the remnant posited as outside the phallic
system of representation. As an intervention into feminist film theory,
I use abjection in order to negotiate between spectator studies and gaze
theory. Hal Foster (1996), Rosalind Krauss (1996), and Laura Mulvey
(1996) have discussed the work of photographer Cindy Sherman, and
other artists, in relation to the abject, with reference to Bataille and
Kristeva.[14] Krauss argues that Kristeva's notion of abjection should be
separated from Bataille's notion of *informe,* even while she acknowledges
that Bataille himself employs the term abjection (Krauss 1996). Krauss
suggests that abjection has been invoked in a way that insists on "themes
and substances" (1996, 103), and that abject art tends to thematize "the
marginalized, the traumatized, the wounded, as an essence that is feminine by nature, and deliquescent by substance" (98). According to

Krauss, Mulvey's reading of Sherman's work as abject capitulates to the semantic truth of woman as castrated, so that "the wound as woman" functions as a privileged signifier (98).[15] Rather than a "thematics of essences and substances," Krauss discerns in Sherman's work a "strong countercurrent to the constellation form/meaning," arguing for an "operational understanding of her work" (98).

While I agree with Krauss that Sherman's art works to undermine a rigid separation of form and meaning, I think that Mulvey's interpretation of it as abject is sensitive to this complication, and that, far from reinstalling in the place of the privileged signifier the truth of woman as castrated, Mulvey contests that privilege.[16] Sherman's work lends itself to an analysis of the abject not least because it complicates, and renders unstable, the relationship between subject and object. In *Untitled Film Stills*, for example, Sherman poses for a series of black and white photographs that evoke films from the fifties, and which draw attention to the trope of woman as masquerade. As Mulvey puts it, "Sherman, the model, dresses up into character while Sherman, the artist, reveals her character's masquerade" (1996, 68). There is thus an uncanny doubling, but one that, rather than confirm the myth of castration, unsettles it. Mulvey again: "The lure of voyeurism turns around like a trap, and the viewer ends up aware that Sherman, the artist, has set up a machine for making the gaze materialize uncomfortably in alliance with Sherman, the model" so that "just as she is artist and model, voyeur and looked at, active and passive, subject and object, the photographs set up a comparable variety of positions and responses for the viewer," for whom "there is no stable subject position" (1996, 68–69). Basing her reading on *Still #3*, which she interprets as a representation of a "good enough vamp," Kaja Silverman suggests that the *Untitled Film Stills* allow us to recognize "as our own something we would normally abject as 'other.' "[17] In this still, "the woman offers herself to be 'photographed' as 'vamp,' as sexual tease, but the mundane objects in her immediate vicinity contradict this self-definition, and proclaim her instead to be a '*Hausfrau*' " (1996, 210). In a 1981 series of color photographs, Sherman, again both the model and artist, parodies the supine poses of soft porn, evoking boredom, anxiety, restlessness, and fear in poses that replicate, but at a distance, the sexual availability of pornography. Here "the use of color and light and shade merges the female figure and her surroundings into a continuum, without hard edges. . . . the poses are soft and limp, polar opposites of a popular idea of fetishised femininity (high-heeled and corseted, erect, flamboyant and exhibitionist" (1996, 69–70). At the same time, the photos retain a reference to fetishism in their "glossy, high-quality finish" (70). The parody of fetishism is heightened in the

1983 series *Untitleds* (and the indistinct titles undermine their efficacy, in a refusal to signal how the images should be understood or differentiated from one another—a refusal to package them as consumer accessible). The grotesque and the monstrous begin to come to the fore, as Sherman explores the undoing of feminine masquerade and its ugly underside. By 1984 the female form gives way to fantastical figures, hallucinatory dread and terror, the stuff of nightmares. In a further exploration of the disintegration and breakdown of fetishized femininity, formlessness emerges in 1985. As Mulvey says, "nothing is left but disgust; the disgust of sexual detritus, decaying food, vomit, slime, menstrual blood, hair" (1996, 71). Mulvey thus reads Sherman's work along the trajectory of an increasingly intensive questioning of, and challenge to, the "regime of castration anxiety":

> A cosmetic, artificial surface covers, like a carapace, the wound or void left in the male psyche when it perceives the mark of sexual difference on the female body as an absence, a void, a castration. In this sense, the topography of the feminine masquerade echoes the topography of the fetish itself. . . . Sherman has slowly stripped the symptom away from its disavowal mechanisms, at the same time revealing the mechanisms for what they are. Sherman's ironic "unveiling'" also "unveils" the use of the female body as a metaphor for the division between surface allure and concealed decay, as though the stuff that has been projected for so long into a mythic space "behind" the mask of femininity had suddenly broken through the delicately painted veil. (1996, 72)

In her critique of Mulvey's reading of Sherman, Krauss assumes that the signifier/signified distinction organizes the discourse of abjection, drawing on Derrida's critique of Lacan. In fact, however, Kristeva's distinction between the symbolic and the semiotic contests the privilege Lacan accords to Saussure's central distinction, and thereby contests the privilege accorded to the logical, syntactical meaning of language. At the same time, Kristeva explicitly invokes Derrida's notion of the trace in her explication of the semiotic as functioning in excess of signification.[18] Far from falling prey to Derrida's critique of the Lacanian symbolic, the abject, as one articulation of the semiotic, displaces the authority of the phallus as transcendental, and the discourse of fetishism surrounding it, thereby providing resources for contesting the truth of woman as castrated, rather than confirming it. The operation of the signifying process on which Kristeva focuses is in fact that by which semiotic energies are transferred into the symbolic realm, transferred, then, to the account of the symbolic, precisely by means of the semiotic being taken up by the signifier. This is the movement according to which meaning accrues, and becomes solidified around the distinction between signifier and signified, a movement that proceeds by way of the production of sense, and then comes to be represented not only as conventional but also as sanctioned, as if theologically produced, *ex nihilo*. The thetic break, read in reference to the mirror stage and the discovery of castration, marks the boundary between the generative process of emergent meanings, and the permanence endowed by the setting up of a relationship between signifier and signified, the inception of a system of signs, the designation of which is symbolized by means of a symbol.

As Kristeva presents it, while on the one hand the thetic break is strictly necessary, on the other hand it is susceptible to transgression. Rather than presenting it as absolute, Kristeva understands the thetic break as a boundary to be crossed. The function of art is to mimic not a detached, settled, or preconceived object, but the movement according to which the symbolic economy is instituted. In miming not only this founding moment, but also pointing to, referring us to, what it excludes, art reenacts the founding moment of the symbolic, and at the same time opens up symbolic formations to interrogation. As such, art can rework that which theory buries as too difficult, too traumatic, or too unbearable to confront.

Under the burden of a history that has become too much to bear, in reaction to the event that cannot be thought, which resists assimilation (Auschwitz, Hiroshima), art takes on a different form. Kristeva's understanding of the role of art attends to the traumatic (non)events of the twentieth century, and their impact on the subject. In a similar vein, Deleuze points out that in the wake of the trauma of Auschwitz—the metonym of the non-event that is too much to bear, whose excess undoes us, rendering history unassimilable—film no longer depicts characters reacting to situations, but characters incapable of action. It no longer follows the movement of objects or characters, but focuses on what the characters see, thus bringing us to the specific visuality of film. The function of identification is no longer restricted to what takes place between the audience and the characters, as if a story unfolded onscreen that bequeaths a task of understanding its unity to an audience, who passively absorbs its meaning. Identification is now taken up as a relationship that directs but does not inhere in the movement of the images, such that seeing is not merely spectatorial, not just "for us,"the audience. Seeing becomes thematic for the characters themselves. Thus, in *Margaret's Museum* (Canada, 1995) we witness Margaret seeing, identifying with the fate of workers who are about to be carried down to the pit of the mine. The camera does not follow them, as it might have done in earlier film, the history of which is punctuated with innovative ways in which to enlist the ability of the camera to move and be moved, including an exploration of a moving elevator. The camera stays aboveground, with Margaret, who, like us, can only imagine what goes on below. Or rather, we confront the limits of our imagination, the limits of our capacity to know. The narrative explores the impact of the unrepresentable on a woman left behind to mourn those she loves, in a mining community that functions on the basis of her successful mourning. Without the work of mourning, on which the profits of the mine depend, the accumulation of profit could not be accomplished. Margaret will disrupt this dependence.

Heeding the logic of the drive for the accumulation of capital exposed by the film, it would be perfectly possible to read the film in terms of fetishism—both in terms of Marxist commodity fetishism and in terms of the psychoanalytic trope of fetishistic disavowal. Such readings would certainly capture central aspects of the film, yet would also render unreadable the demands made on Margaret by the capitalist system. Without the psychic work of mourning, which remains invisible both to the analysis of capital, and to interpretations driven by unquestioning adherence to the myth of castration, the reproduction of workers on which capitalism depends would not occur. The work of mourning is not like housework, not just another facet of uncompensated work that has traditionally been reserved for women, one which could potentially be incorporated into the analysis of paid labor. Its value resists such recuperation, going beyond any possible cashing out in terms of the logic of surplus value, or that of the reassuring fetish. Moreover, its excess to these mutually confirming signifying systems cannot be represented by those systems—the law that dictates that profit must be made at any cost, or the law that dictates that the trauma of castration must be veiled—except through the punishment of those who do not perform the work of mourning properly. The failure to perform the work of mourning according to the law results in abjection, which takes the form here of incarceration in an asylum, but which Margaret also subjects to re-signification. Not content to live by the rules of the game enshrined in the signifying systems of capitalism or fetishism, Margaret takes up the abjection to which the system subjects her, and re-signifies it, displaying its status as internal to the system that refuses it and her recognition.

An onlooker, an outsider, on the periphery of the mine, Margaret reads in the faces of the miners the horror of the machine of capitalism, the dehumanization of the workers, the emptiness in their eyes. What she sees is too much, unbearable—and we witness this too much. In this excess we confront the unrepresentable, the intolerable, the incapacity to react, which Deleuze reads as the legacy of World War II, a legacy that film inherits, and in this inheritance develops a new relationship to itself. A virtual image comes into play, as Margaret/the viewer hallucinate a horrific scene, which remains absent from the screen, but nonetheless comes into play. Inscribed in the image of the immobile, hardened expressions on the miners' faces in the moment before the elevator—the steel doors of which cage them in—drops, is a reference to Auschwitz. The reference is cemented by the next shot: showerheads from which not gas, but life-affirming water, flows in abundance, under which Margaret experiences, for the first time in her life, the pleasure of taking a shower. One might say that her pleasure becomes *jouissance*, as Neil's sexual embrace enfolds her, as the water that routinely flows to wash clean the skin of workers' bodies—a cleansing that only goes skin-deep—cannot dislodge the coal dust from the miners' lungs. Seduced by the flowing water, Margaret compromises with the intolerable, reconciles with her husband's decision to return to the mine, a reconciliation that heralds his death. Margaret won't have children she can't feed, and Neil won't have sex with a condom. As Margaret and Neil embrace, the layers of time separating us from Auschwitz become visible, condensed, crystallized in the image of free-flowing water that might as well be gas, as it turns out, since far from purifying the bodies of the workers it washes, it can only reach the surfaces of their bodies. The insides of the miners' bodies will be poisoned by black lung. The faces of the miners call up the horror of prisoners in a concentration camp.

The shot of the showerheads rebounds, constructing retroactively the significance of the image in which Margaret sees the faces of the miners heading down to the pit, in whose eyes we read the history of Auschwitz. Margaret becomes a seer, a viewer, even a visionary, inverting the usual regimes of identification, whereby the viewer identifies with the characters onscreen, confronting the "intolerable," which is "too unjust" (Deleuze 1989, 18).[19] A relationship is established between Auschwitz and the mine; not a relationship of identity, resemblance, or equivalence, but one of indiscernibility. Clearly it is not a question of reducing the dangers of working in a mine to the conditions of Nazi victims, as if imitation were at stake. It is rather a question of seeing the past in the future, as a repetition of the same, not such that one event comes to mimic another, but in the sense that the repetitive compulsion of the death drive reemerges as ruling capitalism, blinding it to the claim of any value other than that of exchange value, in its unremitting quest for surplus value. The virtual image that is called up from the past is the image of holocaust victims, an image seared in our collective memory, indiscernible from the image of the miners Margaret sees—and we see through her eyes—inexorably awaiting their fate as they are carried to the underground mine. The fact that identification is performed by the protagonist, in this case Margaret, and not only by the film viewer, becomes the hallmark of modern cinema for Deleuze. This is a "cinema of seeing" (Deleuze 1989, 9) and no longer a cinema of action. The motor-sensory action of classic cinema has given way to "motor helplessness" (3)—reminiscent of that of Lacan's *infans* in the mirror stage. Margaret is childlike in her capacity to see, yet not passive. She is, in fact, clair-voyant. The scene she witnesses undoes her, because she reads in it the future that is still to come—the mine will be the death of Neil, the unassimilable, undigested horror of the past has come back to haunt the present in which she reads a future yet to come. The hallucinatory quality of the men's faces, behind bars, about to go toward their inevitable fate, lies in the "indiscernibility" of the real and the imaginary, "as if the real and the imaginary were running after each other, as if each was being reflected in the other" (7).

The tension of the scene is relieved when it is juxtaposed to Margaret's delight, as not gas, but hot water, flows onto her body. The water flows not to wash away the coal dust that has penetrated her grandfather's lungs to incapacitate him, but for Margaret's gratuitous pleasure. The lovemaking that follows is an apparently joyful scene of rec-onciliation between Margaret and Neil, but its foreshadowing by shots of the wire perimeter surrounding the mine, the elevator, and the show-erheads, symbolizes the inhumanity of the oppressive and dangerous work conditions of the mine, by evoking the ultimate, unrepresentable atrocity. It is as if the dynamic of abjection is unfolded in reverse for us.

The horror of Auschwitz comes to haunt Margaret, placing the mine under its shadow. In this association lies an indication of the future to come, a world in which there is no possibility of distinguishing the value of human life from the drive for profit, a world in which one ideal replaces another, the ideal of surplus value substitutes for the Aryan ideal, a world in which there is no space to mark the value of life with-out mourning it. This possible future, haunted by the past, presents a danger from which Margaret recoils. The threat, which is communal, is one she wards off by creating a visual display, which she calls a museum. The horror evoked for the unintentional tourist, who happens upon Margaret's museum of coal mining, and whose scream frames the film, registers the contents of the museum as obscene. If the emptiness of horror lingers, unexplained, in the scream that opens the film, the second time we hear the scream, which also closes the film, its echo resounds to elicit our reflections on the function of museums. We re-read the scream in the light of the intolerable with which Margaret has been confronted, and her refusal to assimilate it.

After the mining accident that kills her husband and young brother—which follows the death of her father and older brother, and which is all but inevitable in the wake of the foreshadowing just outlined—Margaret takes the corpses of Neil and Jimmy to her mother's house, and cuts them up in order to put them on display in a museum. By pickling the lungs of her husband, who played the bagpipes and refused to return to the mine until Margaret declared she wouldn't have children she couldn't afford to feed, Margaret wants to show what healthy lungs should look like. By pickling the lungs of her grandfather, whose death coincides with the siren warning of another mine disaster, and whose black lungs reflect a lifetime of working as a coal miner, she wants to show what the work conditions have done to them. By pickling the penis of her fifteen-year-old brother, in a whimsical touch that I want to resist reading merely in terms of a reference to castration, Margaret puts on display the body part that was most important to him at his age. What she cannot tolerate is the total disregard that the mining company has for the value of human life in its imposition of apparently all-encompassing constraints on the community. If her reaction is unconventional, it is not for all that irrational—not unless rationality is determined by the measure of capitalist values. Notwithstanding, Margaret is put in an insane asylum for her trouble, resonating with a long history in which women have been trivialized, manipulated, and punished through their alleged association with madness. The wordless scream of horror of an unknown woman becomes meaningful once it is reconstituted in a symbolic framework that operates not at the level of disgust for pickled body parts, but as disgust for a capitalist system that fragments humans into corpses for the sake of profit, and requires women to pay the psychic cost of the all too inevitable death of miners through their successful performance of mourning. At the moment in which we hear the tourists' scream of horror we do not see the object of her horror. Instead, what gets repeated is the same piercing scream, the exact sound as heard at the beginning of the film—which could be read as drawing attention to the film's artifice, to the mechanics of its production or to the filmic apparatus.[20] I prefer to focus on its double signification. What is horrific for the tourist is not horrific for us, and in marking that difference the film provides a context that allows not just the re-signification of horror but a political demand. It is not that we, the audience, never see the jars of pickled body parts, but rather that when we see them, they fail to signify as horrific—for us, but not for the tourist. Her abjection—which remains unseen by us, represented only by her piercing scream—acknowledges the horror of mutilated bodies. If the jars become phobic objects for her, their threat is tied to the frailty of the symbolic order, the impossibility of mastering death. They signify metaphorically for that which is unnamable and unrepresentable: they localize the fear of nothingness. Their proximity brings close that which we try to keep at bay—our susceptibility to mortality, the contingency and materiality of life. The fragility of life is what we strive to keep under wraps, to sanitize and render anodyne. Anxiety, which might otherwise permeate and paralyze us, is provided with a focus, made into an object. If only the tourist can escape the threat presented in a pickling jar, the object of her horror, she might be safe.

If the same object fails to signify as horrific for us, it is because the context in which it is presented constitutes a narrative in which it signifies otherwise, registering Margaret's protest of a system that does not heed death as horrific, so long as it is the death of replaceable workers. Again the pickled contents of the jar function metaphorically, but this time signifying the cruel inhumanity of the ethic governing a mining company that is content to permanently thrust aside corpses in the blind, compulsive, repetitive drive for profit. In this sense, the logic of the pharmakon that Derrida has explored is applicable: the very token of horror also carries with it a curative potential, on being reintroduced into a system from which it has been expelled.[21] As it is presented to the characters in the film, a pickling jar signifies as horrific, or as a sign of Margaret's instability, yet for the viewer it functions as a warning sign to disrupt public complacency about, and governmental neglect of, safety standards in mines. Margaret's response to the horror around which the ethic of the mine circulates—routine death—is to expose it as abject. She puts on display for an unwitting public various body parts of her dead male relatives. A privileged site of abjection, the corpse is that from which the living extricate themselves in order to purify themselves of the threat of defilement it presents. Margaret turns her own abjection by the capitalist system into a political refusal of that system. Far from a refusal to honor the dead, her refusal to bury the bodies of her brother, her husband, and grandfather—whose lungs finally expire after his long and incapacitating struggle with black lung, as the siren warning of yet another mining accident sounds his death knell—her insistence on putting their body parts on display is a way of exposing the dishonor to which the mining company has subjected them. By subjecting the public to this display of abject body parts, Margaret transforms her abject status into a demand for change, and in doing so she abjects others. The meaning of abjection is thereby transformed, as Margaret takes on and reworks the abject status to which the mine has reduced her by miming this reduction, reproducing not children—new workers for the mine—but bottled, lifeless body parts.

These bodily, material fragments, to be preserved in Margaret's idiosyncratic museum, mimic the disarticulation of human lives wrought by the mine's disregard for the safety of its workers. In their dismemberment, they materialize the idealization of the law of profit. They render this fragmentation in the form of a curiosity, to be displayed for anyone to see. The bottled body parts can be read as an artistic intervention, which makes visible and tangible the fragmented bodies that the mining economy produces as routinely as it hides them. Margaret reintroduces that which the system rejects and conceals. She thereby brings into representation the abject processes that the economy does all it can to sustain as invisible, unreadable.[22] She makes the body parts into a sign that signifies abjection. At the same time, director Mort Ransen recalls the fate of Saarjite Baartman, who became known as the "Hottentot Venus," and whose genitalia were preserved in formalin and put on display in a bell jar by the Musée de l'Homme, Paris, for a curious public to view.[23] He thus contests the racist assumptions of a viewing public who turned Baartman into a monstrosity, transforming the method used to display parts of her body into a challenge to the routine production of death by unsafe, capitalist mining practices. In so doing, he reveals as monstrous the exploitation of the capitalist system in a way that also points out the racism that justified the display of Baartman's body parts in a museum.

That Margaret's response is to create a museum, to aestheticize the political, exemplifies the way in which art has become a substitute for more traditional forms of political protest, a site in which the political is sublimated. At the same time the museum Margaret creates contests the usual function of museums, provoking us to think about the facility with which we, as a consumer society, dispense with the lives of workers who produce the goods we consume. The contents of the museum, jars of pickled body parts, fly in the face of the Kantian definition of art as concerned with beauty. They are not what we have been trained to expect we might find in a museum of art. In fact, far from being considered beautiful, or instructive, they might qualify as obscene. Hence the response emanating from the unsuspecting female tourist looking for a restroom, whose scream of horror frames the narrative. The rationale of the unintentional tourist's visit is ironically underscored by the fact that a lavatory had been installed only belatedly in the oddly shaped house, built of timber discarded at a dump by the environmentally unsound mining company—waste that Neil has put to good use. It might not be going too far to read in this rationale a reference to Marcel Duchamp's *Fountain* (1917), which has been interpreted in various and conflicting ways. Seen as emblematic of modernism insofar as it is was a ready-made object, which tells us art can be anything, and does not have to be beautiful, thereby also refuting the idea of the artist as genius, the urinal has been on the other hand appreciated for its beauty.[24] The urinal was also enlisted in a 1993 exhibition at New York's Whitney Museum of Modern American Art devoted to abject art, titled "Abject art: Repulsion and Desire in American Art." In a publication based on the exhibit, Simon Taylor notes that the reception of the piece demonstrates "a remarkable ability to sublimate the object's sexual and psychological impact," an observation that he would no doubt see as applicable to both the suggestion that Duchamp was telling us art need not be beautiful, and the idea that its gleaming whiteness qualified it as such.[25] Innocent in her need to relieve herself, the tourist in *Margaret's Museum*, no doubt touring Nova Scotia on account of its natural beauty, is confronted with the waste of human life, around which the mining community of Glace Bay revolves, but which the mining company prefers to keep under wraps.

Overlooking the sea, the house that becomes Margaret's museum has a stunning vista of sea cliffs that might well qualify as sublime in the sense with which Kant invests the term "aesthetic," applicable no less to natural beauty than to works of art. Juxtaposed with the windows that would frame the austere grandeur of Nova Scotia's seascapes, are pickled body parts. If the museum is created as a memorial for the dead, its commemorative role functions as a protest against the ongoing exploitation of capitalist mining companies (as I put the finishing touches to this, a mining accident killed eleven miners in West Virginia), raising the question of what kind of intervention Margaret is effecting in putting the body parts of her dead male relatives on display. By creating a space that she calls a museum, by inviting members of a presumably unknowing and uncaring public to witness the horror of the system that produces death with regularity, she is asking the public not to forget, but also inciting responsibility. The director, Mort Ransen, is at the same time asking us to reflect on the function of museums, and the purpose of the works of art they house. In creating a museum that challenges the role that museums have typically played, as productive of imperial, colonial knowledge, or as confirming what Mohanty refers to as the triumphal role of the capitalist march of progress, Margaret's act provokes us to think about the political impact of art.[26] It thereby follows in the tradition of museums that function as memorials to a past that is never to be forgotten, not in order to celebrate that past as honorable, but to prevent its repetition. The abject contents of the museum are solicited in order to interrupt the repetitive compulsion of the death drive that propels the insatiable capitalist desire to accumulate wealth. In this way it recalls the holocaust museum, in Washington, D.C., which commemorates an event that in some sense exceeds the bounds of representation, an event conjured up in a virtual image to which the film refers implicitly, as we have seen. At the same time, the film thematizes in a narrative form the question it asks at a more formal level, namely what will be the political effects of films such as *Margaret's Museum*? It remains completely unclear, within the narrative of the film, what, if any, political effect, Margaret's museum will have. Perhaps it will have none. *Margaret's Museum,* without instructing its audience, bequeaths us the task of thinking about the function of abject art, putting the question of its political impact to us. Abjection can be a response to the failure of politics, but it can also re-instigate the political. The process by which sublimation of the political takes place needs to be elaborated. Such elaboration is the function of critical discourse.

There is of course a sense in which the very idea of creating a museum of body parts exceeds any recuperation of meaning, disgusting us in its macabre mimicking of a production system that trades in death as the guarantor of its profits, which circulate around dejects. Excess is produced by a signifying system that cannot contain or neutralize it, a system of representation that fails to represent its condition, which falls outside the circuit of signs we exchange as meaningful. This miming procedure is not a gratuitous citation of horror, although it might also succeed in offending certain commitments to the aesthetic domain as a realm conceived in terms of its purity from the muck, waste, and fragility of humdrum working-class life. If there is a sense in which the film operates on an affective level that eludes any attempt to draw the disgust it elicits back into a circuit of meaning, we could equally say that it gestures toward a society in which the abject is not put off-limits, or rendered unrepresentable by prevailing signifying systems. By demanding that we attend to the abject, not to think it through in the sense of transforming it absolutely into meaning, but rather to work it through in a way that does not cancel out its affect, what is gestured toward is not the harmonious vision of Kant's *sensus communis* but rather a society in which we can afford—psychologically and politically—to confront the ways in which we systematically ask certain of our members to bear burdens that are unbearable (and in doing so acknowledge our differential relationships to the boundary distinguishing aesthetics and politics). The film allows the abject to exceed its frame, by not insisting on a particular interpretation of its political significance, or suggesting a particular path of action, or taming the excess, the horror of abjection. The future toward which the film gestures, one in which there is a mapping out of the logic of abjection, rather than a disavowal, remains uncertain.

Even as the abject is re-signified, in the sense that its production as internal to the mechanisms of a capitalism that refuses to acknowledge it except by casting it out, comes to be represented, it remains exorbitant.

Deleuze would call the image of the showerheads, which reverberates with the close-up of the miners' faces in *Margaret's Museum*, an opsign, a purely optical sign. Discussing Rossellini's *Europa 51*, Deleuze says, "pure optical and sound situations can have two poles—objective and subjective, real and imaginary, physical and mental. But they give rise to opsigns and sonsigns, which bring the poles into continual contact, and which, in one direction or the other, guarantee passages and conversions, tending towards a point of indiscernibility (and not of confusion). . . . You do not have the image of a prison following one of a school: that would simply be pointing out a resemblance, a confused relation between two clear images. On the contrary, it is necessary to discover the separate elements and relations that elude us at the heart of an unclear image: to show how and in what sense school is a prison, housing estates are examples of prostitution" (1989, 9; 20–21).[27] The image from *Margaret's Museum* is particularly appropriate to Deleuze's analysis, which accords a privilege to World War II, after which film becomes modern: characters no longer react. They see, they identify. The indiscernibility of the real and the imaginary defines the image. This is not just a representation of time, but a thinking of time. "Image becomes thought, is able to catch the mechanisms of thought" (1995, 52). In the image, time passes. Layers of time become legible. Time no longer follows movement, but becomes traumatic, the real emerges. It does not pass along a line that links up all the nows. Time stops, crystallizes for a moment, rebounds on itself, before it gets taken up again in a new way, according to a different measure/movement. Time is out of joint.

Abject art affects us (through its artifice) at the same time as it makes us aware of that affect, making us self-conscious of it, but in a way that does not sublate its impact, in a way that does not negate the semiotic. The self-consciousness of the avant-garde does not evaporate into mere distanciation. This is the thought Kristeva names the "thought-specular" (2002).[28] In certain images, fantasies are referred to as such; they exercise their power of fascination while at the same time mocking their fascinating specular. Drawn back into the death trap of the mine by the mere attempt to sustain life, the dead miners of *Margaret's Museum* expose the ideology of capitalism, a mythology that endures through capitalism's routine expulsion of its casualties. Despite Neil's attempts to find alternative employment, the only way to make a living, to support a family, is to work in the mine. Neil's efforts to keep alive his Gaelic culture are neatly contained by the capitalist economy of the mine. The dismemberment, the horror, displayed in pickling jars, is capitalism's disavowed residue, internal to a system of values that cannot recognize its waste product as anything but formless and unrepresentable: cast out, these body parts are bottled up by Margaret, and re-signified as abject. Margaret introduces the abject back into the system that expels it as unsignifiable, marking that expulsion, and signifying the abject not as dispensable but on the contrary as that by which meaning is conditioned. The abject thereby enters into the circuit of meaning that cast it out on different terms, and the terms of its reentry constitute an endeavor to change the system of signification.

The fantasy that Margaret entertains, and with which we identify, is a fantasy that proves untenable under the prevailing regime of signification. Her fantasy is to have a family that will not always already have been lost to the mine, to live a life the meaning of which does not revolve around irrecuperable, intolerable loss. It is a fantasy in which we might share, with which we can identify, regardless of our gender or sexuality. At one level, what is at stake in identification is not whether we are women, whether or not we want or are able to have children, or whether or not our lives are governed by the wish to have children. Anyone, female or male, heterosexual or homosexual, can identify with Margaret. The point is not so much that we identify with the particular desire that fuels Margaret's particular fantasy (to have children)—although we might—but rather that we identify with her desire to desire, that is, with her desire to be a subject, a subject whose desire is not thwarted in advance by a system that operates according to an impossible demand. At stake here, then, is an understanding of the desiring subject that does not require women to foreclose their desire for the sake of taking on an idea of desire that is modeled on the masculinity of a male subject traumatized by castration anxiety—which seems to be demanded by psychoanalytic claims that present desire as if it were neutral. Such a model of desire installs women in a place of irrecuperable abjection, rendering women's bodies as the traumatic real of castration, without recognizing any position from which women's desire can be legitimated except as disruptive of the system. Capitalism, bolstered by and infused with patriarchy, requires Margaret to want children—and even makes this requirement into a qualification for normative femininity—while at the same time treating human life as just so much fodder for its machine, fodder that it feeds into the system, and passes out of the system in the shape of corpses, waste. It thus holds out a prize of recognition for achieving normative femininity, for being a good and loving mother, who dutifully raises sons to become laborers, in accordance with the capitalist law of production and accumulation. That prize is the dead bodies of sons and husbands, and the task of successfully achieving nonpathological mourning, cleaning up the mess, a cleansing that enables the system to continue, unheeding of its victims. A melancholic response to the system would interrupt or forestall its efficiency. Capitalism requires docile, obedient mothers, capable of taking on the task of mourning in a way that doesn't jam up the works.

I said above that we identify not with the particular desire that fuels Margaret's particular fantasy, but with her desire to desire. Yet the issue of fantasy as it has been played out in feminist film theory is a complex one, not least because castration theory, dear to classic psychoanalytic assumptions, puts women in the position of wanting to be desired rather than wanting to desire, wanting to be desirable, rather than wanting to be desiring subjects, wanting to assuage the anxiety of the nothing-to-see of castration trauma, by acquiescing to the logic of the fetish. Precisely what it means to identify with fantasy will differ according to how closely we adhere to the parameters of Freudo-Lacanian psychoanalytic assumptions. Informed by Laplanche and Pontalis (1986), film is understood by analogy to fantasy. In some quarters we are reminded that to reduce the film to its representative contents—including, for example, whether its character depictions might be racist or sexist—is to go awry on several different counts.[29] It is to assume that the function of film is representative, that identity is given, and that what makes film art is essentially its capacity to imitate realistic characters. By contrast, psychoanalytic gaze theories have tended to understand the film as text, assimilating meaning to a Saussurean linguistic model that privileges language (often ignoring the specificity of film technique), while importing oedipal assumptions about the structure of the unconscious.

While I do not want to take back the suggestion that our identification with Margaret is an identification with her desiring subjectivity, with her desire to have her desire (whatever the content of that desire) realized, rather than thwarted, neither do I accept the implication that the meaning of fantasies is given, that the recognition of desire happens on a level playing field, or that the content of desires is fabricated irrespective of ideologies. I bring into question the legitimacy of the foundational fantasy that guides psychoanalytic theory (including a good deal of psychoanalytically inspired feminist film theory), the fantasy of castration, in terms of which meaning is granted, recognition is provided, and desires are legitimated. To put the point another way, I do not want to accept the implication that in order to understand the issues of identification and fantasy "properly" we have to agree to suspend the legitimacy of taking into account social factors informing diverse audience positions. I sketch out a ground on the basis of which we can both regard as important identification with Margaret's desire to desire, her desire to be a subject capable of recognition outside the terms of the capitalist mining monopoly, and regard as significant the fact that some subjects will identify with the particularity of Margaret's desire (understood as her desire not merely to have children, but to have children whose future will not have been determined as lost to the mine) more fully than others. The desire to be a subject capable of recognition outside the terms of the mining company is both a desire to want children who have a chance of living full, healthy lives without the shadow of the mine standing over them, and a desire to change the terms of recognition offered by the mining company, and the capitalist economy it represents. Perhaps it is likely that some women will identify with the fantasy of having children more than others, and more, on the whole, than men, but it is also likely that some women (and some men) will identify with the fantasy of having children who will not have been lost to the death drive of capitalism (whether literally or figuratively) more than others.

Attempting to allow a space for such considerations, spectator studies have tended to proceed by way of content-driven analyses, often precluding formal analyses of film. Spectator studies, which focuses on the importance of the regimes of race, gender, class, and sexuality informing viewers' identification, has been looked on askance by gaze theory due to its alleged implication in a realism that is considered out of vogue. Gaze theory effectively refuses the importance of the idea that one's position as viewer informs one's identification with, and understanding of, film. Concerned that a commitment to such a position can be fueled only by a naive identity politics, this suspicion of spectator studies has been expressed with reference to the idea of fantasy, the mechanisms of which are taken to preclude the idea that gender, race, class, or sexuality are given, that there is a one to one correspondence between, for example, a gendered spectator-subject, and a gendered character onscreen. Understood on the basis of Saussure's foundational distinction between the signifier and the signified, sexuality, according to Lacanian film theory, is a structuralist affair; identity is not given, all that can be said with certainty is that there are various positions on the Lacanian sexuation graphs, positions which are understood to be available to any subject, and not determined according to biological sex. Prominent among theorists to have expressed skepticism of the concerns voiced in spectator studies on the basis of such theoretical commitments is Elizabeth Cowie, who has addressed the issue in terms of Freudian and Lacanian notions of fantasy. Cowie takes up Freud's notion of hysterical identification, about which I will say more shortly, as emblematic of the kind of identification that occurs in cinematic viewing.

First however, there are two issues in need of separation, issues that have been conflated with one another in efforts to discount the salience of race, sexuality, gender, and class. The first question is whether we can retain the salience of race, sexuality, gender, and class without assuming that identification occurs by means of a one to one, necessary correspondence between audience and character, such that racial, sexual, and class regimes are taken to be given and stable. If the naive identity politics that underlies some versions of spectator studies has been rightly challenged, it is often only at the cost of an appeal to psychoanalytic accounts that do not cease to invoke, without always articulating, the authority of the phallus as transcendental condition, informed by the myth of castration—a myth that either assumes the abject position of women, or constitutes the abject in a new way, finding an alternative deject with which to replace women. The status of the phallus might be veiled, fetishized, and inarticulate, but it is nonetheless productive of meaning. Fantasy provides the structure according to which film must be interpreted, yet, perhaps in the interests of preserving the pretense of a certain formalism, as if its intellectual and political commitments were disinterested, the precise nature of this fantasy is kept hidden from view, off limits, out of bounds.

Content driven analyses—and this is the second issue—have been criticized for failing to take account of the fantasy in terms of which film should be analyzed. Again, the difficulty is that psychoanalytically inspired film criticism tends to proceed by adhering unquestioningly to a set of theoretical commitments that assume the authority of the phallus. Castration theory operates as a privileged fantasy behind the scenes in the authorized versions of psychoanalysis, in a way that renders off-limits any enquiry into the representationalist commitments of the fantasy driving the psychoanalytic scene itself. To be meaningful, or intelligible, is to employ phallic discourse, to exchange phallic values. Any questioning of the unspoken tenet that intelligibility equals phallic meaning is outlawed. An analysis of abjection answers to this implicit taboo, not by offering abjection as an alternative grand narrative by which to displace the foundational castration fantasy that orchestrates the scene of fantasy behind the scenes. Rather, the logic of abjection exposes the gaps, holes, and fissures that emerge in that fantasy, and attends to the personages drawn in to block up or fill in those holes, on whose bodies abjection is inscribed. At the same time, the logic of abjection, a discourse of instability and an interrogation of the rite of purification, disrupts facile assumptions about the ease with which "content" can be separated from "form," or fantasy can be divorced from ideology, avoiding the stance sometimes adopted by formalist theories that eschew any sustained critical consideration of the political implications of narrative, by understanding narrative as a function of the montage form, and montage as a function of the oedipal narrative—and ignoring the ability of that form to put itself into question.

Kristeva locates the impact of art neither in materiality as such, nor in ideology, but precisely in "an explicit confrontation between jouissance and the thetic" (1984, 81). By reading two "events" as "counterparts" (1984, 74) to the thetic moment, namely sacrifice (see 1984, 75) and artistic practice (see 1984, 79), and by insisting on the possibilities of transgression opening up poetic language, Kristeva does not accept the implication in Lévi-Strauss that any splitting of the "symbolic chain is relegated outside" the field of enquiry, or that there can be no questioning of or challenge to the thetic (1984, 74). In other words, she accepts neither the theologization of sacrifice, the conferring of a theological status upon certain rituals of sacrifice and celebrated by religion, nor the transcendentalization of the discovery of castration, a transcendental status conferred by psychoanalysis. Kristeva understands the ritual dances or artistic performances that accompany sacrifice as " '*mime*' in the full sense of the term: it repeats not a detached object but the movement of the symbolic economy" itself (1984, 79).[30] Thus, the "subordination" of the signifying process "to the social relations between subjects caught in kinship relations" (1984, 78) can be put in question. The "exchange of women" as a means of society's "self-regulation" (1984, 72) is a prime example of such subordination. Consequently, for Kristeva, the discovery of castration does not amount to an understanding of the phallic function in which "a symbolic function" is equivalent to '*the* symbolic function" (1984, 47). Meaning is not set in stone (or represented by the phallus) once and for all, but is precisely capable of contestation: of revolution, renewal, rejuvenation, or rebirth.

By miming the movement of the symbolic economy, and thereby attending to the transition from animality to the human/social order, poetic language questions not only discrete ideologies but the "very principle of ideology," unfolding "the *unicity* of thetic (the precondition for meaning and signification)" (1984, 61). It does so by pointing to the excess, or materiality, that which is cast out of meaningful systems of exchange, based, as they are for Kristeva (influenced by Freud), on a founding sacrifice. Hence Kristeva associates artistic practice with Bataille's notion of expenditure (see 1984, 79), and poetry with the body that is expelled: "poetry confronts different 'soma' that are sacrificed—plants, animals, kinsmen, and finally man-god" (1984, 80). As a problematizing of the border to which sacrifice refers, art opens up meaning to "the motility where all meaning is erased" (1984, 79). Art "takes on murder and moves through it" (1984, 70), so that "death becomes interiorized by the subject" and the subject makes "himself the bearer of death" (1984, 70). The Hegelian resonance is clear: Antigone takes on the death of Polynices and thereby reconciles him with universality, rather than allowing him to founder in the particularity of nature, where his body is reduced to matter to be picked over by carrion birds. For Hegel, too, *Antigone* enacts a confrontation with, and working through of, the incest taboo. The famous lines in which Antigone proclaims her allegiance to her brother in a way that sets this relation apart from any relation she might have to a husband or a father—which has been construed as inexplicable and even spurious by authoritative commentators from Aristotle on—are in fact integral to Hegel's understanding of the play. Along with her burial of Polynices, Antigone also buries the legacy of the incestuous union that gave rise to both her own life and that of her brother's. In this sense, *Antigone* can be read as an encomium to the incest taboo, as a taking on of the jouissance it contains and orders, and as a confirmation of the symbolic order heralded by its containment in the form of an incest taboo. Yet, if Kristeva confirms that art functions as a taking on of death, thereby recalling Hegel's reading of *Antigone,* her emphasis is ultimately different, if only because she is less inclined to insist on the purity of the signifier that drives the dialectic of thought, and more inclined to point to the expulsions committed in the name of its purification.[31] Her analysis points us not toward death as such, but rather to death *as the founding moment of culture.* It points us toward the boundary between nature and culture and, most fundamentally, toward the possibility of rethinking that border as permeable.

As the site in which foundational taboos and prohibitions are taken on, art can also disrupt the conventions that have informed prohibitions, and have been confirmed in their wake. The unconscious associations women have acquired in the trauma of castration thereby become available for reworking, for rethinking. The space that art opens up extends to the imaginary within which women function as a threat to the symbolic order, a threat to be contained—it extends, in other words to the semiotic. Cut off from that realm, the idea in the service of which art proceeds for Hegel, for whom art is the sensible presentation of the idea, absolves itself from being answerable to the materiality that it relegates to the unthinkable. It does not open itself up to a challenging of the unspoken logic that lines up nature, family, woman on one side of an impermeable divide, and culture, civilization, man on the other. At stake for Kristeva is precisely the way in which such borders are permeable, susceptible to transgression, a transgression that extends as far as disrupting the imaginary equations that assert (without rendering themselves liable to contestation) woman is equal to nature, or man is the equivalent of culture, thereby effecting a series of equivalences that constitute an economy, the contours of which are considered to be off limits for enquiry. Any interrogation of the rules of exchange informing this economy is suspended. It as if the rules were inscribed in nature, rather than produced by culture.

Kristeva distances herself from the fixity of meaning enshrined in representation, where the authority of symbolic meaning is presented as unalterable, from the idea of poetry as a "fetishistic guardian of meaning and the subject"—where meanings are settled, fixed, and closed to transformation. At the same time she rejects the idea of poetry as "the lie of unspeakable delirium" (1984, 84), as if invoking the semiotic as an autonomous realm could succeed in meaningful discourse, rather than leaving us mired in meaninglessness, abandoned to psychosis. Kristeva identifies the poetic function with "rhythmic, lexical and even syntactic charges" that "disturb the transparency of the signifying chain and open it up to the material crucible of its production" (1984, 101), thereby making clear that art's reference to materiality is precisely the "reenacting of the signifying path taken from the symbolic [which] unfolds the symbolic itself" (1984, 79). Thus, the confrontation with materiality can at the same time function as a confrontation with ideology: "Going through the experience of this crucible exposes the subject to impossible dangers: relinquishing his identity in rhythm, dissolving the buffer of reality in a mobile discontinuity, leaving the shelter of the family, the state, or religion. The commotion the practice creates spares nothing: it destroys all constancy" (1984, 104). Kristeva points to Rothko and Giotto (1984, 103), but one might also relate Fergus's experience in *The Crying Game* to such a loss of identity (see chapter 7). By putting into question, making available for interrogation, the unconscious associations that play into symbolic distinctions that come to be enshrined as sacred, Kristeva does not confine the work of identification to the prevailing social order. Rather she works to uncover those unstable processes that are stabilized once they enter the symbolic, yet whose mythical, fantastical status is not for all that undone. "Since the violence of drive charges is not halted, blocked, or repressed, what takes the place of the bodily, natural, or social objects these charges pass through is not just a representation, a memory, or a sign. The instinctual *chora* in its very displacement, transgresses representation, memory, the sign. . . . this process breaks up the totality of the envisioned object and invests it with fragments (colors, lines, forms). . . . which the process rearranges in a new combination.

This combinatory moment, which accompanies the destructive process and makes it a *practice,* is always produced with reference to a moment of stasis, a boundary, a symbolic barrier" (1984, 102). If even syntax and form can be invested with semiotic charges, if what emerges is not just a new combination of established distinctions, but a questioning of these distinctions themselves, it becomes clear that received wisdom about how to draw distinctions between form and meaning or form and content cannot be taken for granted, as if it were settled once and for all and in advance of artworks that might contest their previous configurations.

For Kristeva, art is the "semiotization of the symbolic," it represents "the flow of jouissance into language" (1984, 79). While sacrifice is thus seen as the "prohibition of jouissance" (1984, 80) and religion as celebrating the thetic, Kristeva understands art as the "introduction of jouissance into and through language"—"art accepts the thetic break" but "through this break, art takes from ritual space what theology conceals: trans-symbolic jouissance, the irruption of the motility threatening the unity of the social realm and the subject" (1984, 80). The "founding break of the symbolic order" might be "represented by murder" or by "crime" but the function of art is the confrontation with this break, which sets up the border between the semiotic and symbolic. It is through taking on this border that art renders the thetic break "permeable" (1984, 63) or pervious—as that which can be transgressed.[32] Putting into question the language of totalization, the transcendental, the absolute, or the theological, Kristeva suggests that the Lacanian "phallus totalizes the effects of signifieds as having been produced by the signifier" (1984, 47), asking whether Lacan "transcendentalizes semiotic motility, setting it up as a transcendental Signifier?" (1984, 48). At the same time as putting into question the totalizing effects of the phallus, Kristeva also recognizes the necessity of "a completion [finition], a structuration, a kind of totalization of semiotic motility" (1984, 51). For Kristeva, however, rather than the repression of the semiotic in the setting up of a pure signifier, the thetic must be "taken on or undergone" as a "position" (1984, 51). "Castration must have been a . . . trauma . . . so that the semiotic can return through the symbolic position it brings about" (1984, 51). Not only must there be a "completion of the Oedipus complex" but also its "reactivation in puberty" (1984, 51), a " 'second-degree thetic,' i.e. a resumption of the functioning characteristic of the semiotic chora within the signifying device of language," that is, artistic practices, specifically poetic language (1984, 50). For Kristeva then, it is not a matter of a refusal, evasion or repression of "imaginary castration," but of the thetic as a "traversable boundary" (1984, 51). If castration cannot be evaded, neither is it a matter of "a castration imposed once and for all, perpetuating the well-ordered signifier and positing it as sacred and unalterable within the enclosure of the Other" (1984, 51). In fact, for Kristeva, it is precisely the mobility of the process of signification that should capture our attention, a process that only comes to be stabilized in a final stage, which is preceded by a period of language acquisition that Kristeva takes to be of paramount importance, the instability of which can never entirely be put to rest, and which returns as a "disturbance of language and/or of the order of the signifier" and even "destroys the symbolic" (1984, 50). That is, it is capable of effecting revolution, renewal, rejuvenation.

This is the significance of Kristeva's critique of formal linguistics as preoccupied with surface phenomena, and neglectful of the deep, diachronic structures that prepare the subject for language. The object of formal linguistics, according to this point of view, is sclerotic, fetishized; its procedures are necrophiliac, treating language as a system of signs already set in place, as if meanings were fixed or unassailable, as if thoughts were static, as if the study of signs were an archival or archaeological affair (see 1984, 13)—in short, as if language were dead, instead of living and capable of transgression. As part of the community of language-users, the task of theorists—including theorists of the semiotic—is inevitably to broach an analysis from the point of view of the symbolic. The task of analyzing the semiotic will therefore necessarily be a reconstructive, retroactive task, one that presupposes a certain fixity of terms, the stability conferred by the permanence that language confers on ideas. To put this another way is to acknowledge the "liminary" (1984, 30) or "boundary" (1984, 48) character of language considered from the point of view of syntactical, linguistic signs, where according to the conventions of language usage, certain representations have acquired a permanence, certain values have stabilized and become fixed; yet beneath the fixity of language, a dynamic, unstable domain (the topology of which is defined according to drives, primary processes (condensation and displacement, metaphor and metonymy, needs and demands) is in process. The fixity language endows on concepts, including concepts that have become defining categories for feminist theory, such as race, sexuality, class, and gender, renders these objects of enquiry as if their meaning were self-evident, heteroclite islands sufficient to themselves (see 1984, 13). In fact, however, subjects are produced under the sign of "an intersection," not as the obvious meeting places of such regimes, but precisely as "an impossible unity" (1984, 118), which refuses the logic of progressive linearity. To confront adequately the process that have produced a subject who has been situated (and is capable of re-situating) herself in relation to such regimes, we must be prepared to take on the retroactive temporality according to which these terms have accumulated the self-evidence with which we tend to represent them in feminist theories. We must read the unconscious associations according to which our energies are already set in motion before meanings become settled and prescribed. Hence, as Colette Guillaumin puts it, it is not enough to combat racism at the conscious, rational level of attempts to negate it; we must read race as a residue.[33]

Presided over by maternal regulation, the semiotic or preoedipal is characterized by stases and discontinuities, waves of activity and passivity, charges of energy, absences and presences, but there are as yet no firm distinctions between subject and object (or world), me and you, inner and outer. Thus, even though we designate the function to which needs and wants are harnessed "maternal," it is crucial to remember that such designations proceed according to the symbolic realm, or the paternal law, which has already decided in favor of certain privileges, not the least of which is the importance of symbolic castration, as marking the entry into language. That is, even though the preoedipal or semiotic is specified with regard to the maternal function, such a function is operational *for the child* in a way that precedes the discovery of castration, and as such precedes the discovery of sexual difference. Sexual difference, that is to say, is assigned retroactively. The specification of the semiotic as regulated by the maternal body is a specification that proceeds from the symbolic, from the point of view of the subject who has passed through the thetic phase, or who has entered into the symbolic, a subject who has taken on the discovery of castration, who has submitted to the law of sexual difference. For the child, however (just as for naive consciousness in Hegel), no such thematic distinction is possible, prior to the entry into the symbolic. This does not prevent certain associations being put in place with regularity. In this sense, one could also maintain that negative and positive associations are set in motion around racial presentations, associations that are not thought as racial distinctions, but yet which nevertheless come to inform these distinctions. The logic of some bodies moving away from others according to socially inculcated barriers that Ahmed traces can be followed out along these lines.

In Ahmed's interpretation, Audre Lorde's hallucination of a phobic object of the roach protects her from the traumatic truth her six-year-old consciousness has not yet assimilated—a truth that will always remain indigestible, but with which society will demand her compromise. The truth is that of racism, from which Lorde's hallucination, by imagining a roach, protects her, in an attempt to render comprehensible why a woman sitting next to her on a train would feel the need to pull away from her. Lorde can thus attribute the white woman's disgust not to the color of her own black skin, but to a roach that crawls between them: it is what must be untouchable, defending Lorde from the thought: I am untouchable because of the color of my skin.

In the light of abjection's refusal to allow us to settle into rigid assumptions about how to draw the line between form and content, the effects of thinking through abjection impact both interpretations of the formal, conceptual apparatus that have informed psychoanalytic film theory—the idea of fantasy that film theory takes over, and applies to the cinematic apparatus, replete with its commitments to castration theory—and the contents (including sexist or racist elements) that film is taken to represent. As already mentioned, the sense in which we identify with onscreen characters in film has been read through Freud's understanding of hysterical identification.[34] The importance of this reference to hysterical identification lies in its refusal of a one to one correspondence on the basis of gender, sexuality, or any other socially salient designator; the fact that we share a certain gender with a character onscreen need not dictate that our foremost identification will be with that character, rather than others. As Freud suggests in *The Interpretation of Dreams*, each of us can play all the parts, as it were.[35] Freud observes that "hysterical identification" enables "patients to express in their symptoms not only their own experiences but those of a large number of other people; it enables them, as it were, to suffer on behalf of a whole crowd of people and to act all the parts in a play single-handed" (1953j, 149). Based on "sympathy" (150) the hysteric draws an unconscious inference, which, if it entered consciousness, might give rise to fear, but which does not "penetrate into consciousness" (150), expressing itself, rather, as a symptom. Freud gives the example of hospital patients, having discovered the cause of a spasm suffered by one patient, developing hysterical attacks in the form of similar spasms, out of sympathy for a patient. The cause might be "a letter from home, the revival of some unhappy love-affair, or some such thing" (150). Thus, concludes Freud, "identification is not simple imitation but *assimilation* on the basis of a similar aetiological pretension; it expresses a resemblance and is derived from a common element which remains in the unconscious" (150). Freud applies this lesson to a dream, in which, he claims, a patient develops a symptom through which she identifies with her friend in the renunciation of a wish.

Freud recounts the dream, which was offered him as an example that contradicted his theory that dreams are wish-fulfillments, and proceeds to show in his interpretation that the dream is entirely consonant with his theory. The patient, dubbed by Freud as the "witty hysteric" and by Lacan the "butcher's wife," presents her dream as proof of "a dream in which one of my wishes was not fulfilled" (146).[36] Here is the dream:

> I wanted to give a supper-party, but I had nothing in the house but a lit-tle smoked salmon. I thought I would go out and buy something, but remembered that it was Sunday afternoon and all the shops would be shut. Next I tried to ring up some caterers, but the telephone was out of order. So I had to abandon my wish to give a supper-party. (147)

Reminding us that dreams have "more than one meaning" (149), Freud produces two interpretations of the dream that are not "mutually contra-dictory but both cover the same ground" (149), both of which indicate that, contrary to first appearances, the dream does indeed meet the con-dition of the fulfillment of a wish. The witty hysteric had a friend, of whom she was jealous, because her husband was "constantly singing [her friend's] praises" (148). "Fortunately," says Freud, "this friend of hers is very skinny and thin and her husband admires a plumper figure" (148). The thin friend, who wanted "to grow a little stouter," had expressed to the witty hysteric her wish to be invited to dinner since "You always feed one so well" (148). Freud accordingly interprets the dream as fulfilling his patient's wish "not to help [her] friend grow plumper" (148) so that her husband would not find the thin friend attractive. A second, "subtler" interpretation rests on the patient's identification with her friend, an interpretation in which Freud enlists anecdotal evidence provided by the patient concerning her wish for caviar, a wish that she nonetheless wanted to maintain as unfulfilled. The witty hysteric, who was very fond of caviar, and would have liked to be able to eat caviar sandwiches for breakfast every morning, nonetheless asks her husband not to grant her this wish, on account of the high cost of caviar. Due to the expense, the witty hysteric renounces her wish for caviar, a renunciation that echoes her dream, in which she "had put herself in her friend's place" (149) by renouncing smoked salmon, which was her friend's "favourite dish" (148). Freud thus interprets the renunciation of caviar as a hysterical symptom. Just as the witty hysteric creates the conditions in her dream to ensure that her thin friend will not grow plumper, and so will remain unattractive to her husband—thereby renouncing on behalf of her friend the wish to be invited to dinner—so she also renounces her own wish for caviar, thereby imitating her friend's symptom (the renounced wish).

Of particular interest to us is the fact that Freud's two (but not mutually exclusive) interpretations of the dream position the witty hysteric in two different roles. In the first interpretation, the witty hys-teric plays, as it were, herself (not wanting to help her friend put on weight), but in the second interpretation, she identifies with her friend (reproducing a hysterical symptom: in this case, the renunciation of a wish). On the basis of such flexibility, the conclusion is drawn, by analogy with the dream scenario, that identification between audience and film protagonist is equally multiple and shifting. Just as a dream can be peopled with characters with whom the dreamer can identify variously, so different personages can represent different elements of a single dreamer's desire, so a film viewer can identify with various characters in a film, characters who need not conform to one's gender, sexuality, class, or race.[37]

So far, so good. At this point, however, an unjustified leap is often made in the reasoning of film theorists at pains to defend the psychoanalytic view, based on a reading of Freud's notion of hysterical identification as a model for understanding film as a variation of fantasy scenarios. The idea that identification is not circumscribed by race, class, sexuality, or gender is taken to indicate that the identificatory regimes sanctioned by a given society have no bearing whatsoever on practices of identification. In one fell swoop, theorists thereby excuse themselves from having to account for the socially sanctioned regimes informing both spectator studies and Freud's and Lacan's analyses—including the political implications driving their commitment to castration theory, which provides the touchstone of dream interpretation and the form of fantasy. Important corrective responses to Laura Mulvey's "Visual Pleasure and Narrative Cinema," such as bell hooks's "The Oppositional Gaze," are thereby dismissed.[38] Pointing out that Mulvey's assumption of the universal valence of the male gaze, in this early, canonical article (the fetishistic assumptions of which Mulvey's more recent work brings into question), neglects the racial and class regimes that orchestrate viewing practices, hooks drives home the point that it is problematic to assume that all female viewers are situated in a similar relationship to the male gaze, as if that gaze were uniform in its white, hegemonic effects.

To say that one can identify across the lines of gender, and so on— that one *need not* identify with a character of the same gender—should not be taken as a denial of the compulsory identifications which conform, to a greater or lesser extent, to how one understands and performs one's own gender. Of course it is perfectly possible for a woman to identify with the male hero of a film, or vice versa, or for an African American to identify with a white character, but this does not evacuate the power of idealized and obligatory fictions informing gender and racial norms.[39] We might, and perhaps often do, identify with different characters within a narrative at different times, across gender, race, and class lines. None of this negates the impact of ideological and mythical gender ideals that continue to inform our viewing positions. The positions from which we identify remain differentially informed by those norms. Race, class, and heterosexist regimes impel, without requiring, subjects to identify in certain, qualified ways, and not in others. This implies, at the very least, that identifications will occur, the deep roots of which we might not always be fully conscious, identifications formed through habitual associations, on the basis of social bonds in the lived world, bonds that will be tainted by and constructed in terms of assumptions that are racist, sexist, classist, and heterosexist—regardless of our race, gender, class, and sexual identifications. In short, we should not fall into the trap of isolating the particular fantasy that fuels psychoanalytic theory, in an attempt to render it unimpeachable, as if it transcended the social and political realm, as if we can assume the legitimacy of this particular myth over any other, any more than we should assume that socially constructed regimes of identification circumscribe the possibilities of viewer identification in a determinate fashion.

In a reading of the dream of Freud's witty hysteric, Lacan suggests a third interpretation. The desire with which the dreamer identifies is neither her own, nor her friend's, but rather that of her husband; or, more accurately, it is an identification with the phallus. The woman seeks to take the place of her friend, to identify with her friend, in order to be that which is desirable to her husband. The question that Kristeva encourages us to ask is how far an identification with the phallus is a foregone conclusion for Lacan, and how far its predictability relies upon a suppression of semiotic motility, a repression of any tendency, that is, that would claim authority to speak against it. This question opens up, for example, differential ways of responding to the sexual division imposed by castration— so that the law according to which we must all choose to enter either the door that says "women" or the one that says "men" when we want to go to the bathroom no longer functions theologically. The foundational status of sexual difference assumed by psychoanalytic theory can be contested, by opening up the question of how racial and class regimes sanction and are sanctioned by this foundational status when they agree to occupy a secondary, inferior position. Through abjection, the risk of castration can be avoided, which is to say that there can be a working back to a situation that precedes castration, which puts the subject as such at risk, and a working forward from such a collapse of meaning to a point where meaning can be rebuilt in a way that transforms the meaning of castration. By thinking art as a site in which abjection is confronted, Kristeva provides an alternative to film theory that has taken up hysterical identification as its model. In doing so, she opens up the possibility of interrogating the primal fantasies that ground hysteria, including the fantasy of castration/fetishism, which drives the classic psychoanalytic scenario.

My aim is not to claim that abject art is true art, that it is necessarily better than other art, or that the most authentic abject art is that which is political. Neither am I committed to producing a grand narrative of art's development, which reads abject art as the fulfillment of modernism, as if abjection, rather than mourning, could take up that mantle. In fact the discourse of abjection attends to that which falls through the cracks of fetishistic theories, to that which is remaindered by discourses of mourning insofar as they leave fetishistic assumptions undisturbed; the abject is produced by a system that requires it, depends upon it, and yet which lacks, or perhaps refuses to develop, the means to represent it. In this sense, abjection is internal to a system that fails, by definition, to represent it. Rather, the signs that circulate, which constitute the system as meaningful, the meanings that count as valuable, combine to create a closed referential circuit, which precisely spits out the dejects it produces as meaningless nonsense, as unintelligible, in order to continue to establish its own hegemony. To develop a discourse of abjection is to re-signify that which is cast out of a system that finds its representation impossible, intolerable, too much. It is not possible for those who promulgate theories of fetishism to acknowledge their dejects, without rendering such theories radically unstable, without agreeing to call into question their fundamental tenets. Certain films both lend themselves to analysis in terms of abjection and help to advance an understanding of abjection. If it is true that art exceeds the philosophical attempt to establish intellectual mastery over it, then we should expect that excess to be capable, in some cases, of challenging received wisdom, including ideas about gender, race, class, and sexuality on the one hand and theories of fetishism on the other hand, without being resolvable into lessons—political or otherwise—that can be drawn from that excess.

This is not to say that all art is politically radical in its effect, only that it harbors potentially transformative effects, precisely in so far as it revisits the founding moment of culture. Art can equally well be a site of complicity with the cultural codes in operation, a means of supporting hegemonic codes. When art aligns itself with the prevailing modes of authority in a given culture, far from demonstrating that these particular symbolic codes (patriarchal, sexist, heterosexist) are not the only codes available, it puts its weight behind them, and conceals the revolutionary potential that the artist's confrontation with the founding moment of culture harbors within it. It plays a role equivalent to, or in service of, religion or ideology. When art opens up culture to the energies that are typically closed off, or repressed, by an unquestioning allegiance to the taboos that a particular society sanctions—such as the taboo on homosexuality—its revolutionary force is unleashed.

The abject retains a certain slipperiness with regard to disgust, repulsion, revolt on the one hand, and fascination, attraction, desire on the other hand. The political import of films of abjection must not be clearly resolvable as a call to specific actions, even if some films fulfill the role of cultural and political commentary more effectively than others, by making an intervention at the level of foundational fantasies, and in doing so, opening up a political space in which there is room for debate, in which not only dominant identificatory regimes can be contested but also the fantasies that legitimate them can be unearthed, and critically addressed.

4

Fantasy at a Distance: The Revolt
of Abjection

IN 1975 KRISTEVA PUBLISHED a short essay that was then translated in *Wide Angle* (1979) as "Ellipsis on Dread and the Specular Seduction."[1] It was later anthologized by Philip Rosen—along with key essays by Jean-Louis Baudry, Christian Metz, Laura Mulvey, and others—in *Narrative, Apparatus, Ideology*.[2] While the essays by Baudry, Metz, and Mulvey have played a formative role in the field of film theory, Kristeva's essay, although occasionally mentioned (see Cowie, 1997, 292 and Rose, 1986, 141), has hardly been pivotal.[3] By contrast, Baudry's essays, which include as important reference points not only Plato, Jacques Derrida, and Jacques Lacan, but also Melanie Klein, have, along with the work of Metz and Mulvey, set the agenda for the way in which psychoanalytic theory has been taken up by film theorists. By the 1980s, the mirror stage, fetishism, and castration theory had taken center stage in film theory and literary theory, and by the 1990s had been imported into race theory, a process facilitated by a selective borrowing from Mulvey and other feminist theorists. The primacy of the phallus thus reasserted itself, apparently oblivious to the possibilities opened up by Kristeva around the semiotic and the imaginary.[4] The exclusive priority of the specular, of which Kristeva is critical, is implicated in the role played by Lacan's mirror phase, precisely the aspect of his work that has proved so productive for film theory—and precisely the aspect of Lacan's work that Kristeva reinterprets, by providing an account of abjection which amounts to a rewriting of the mirror-stage, an inscription of a proto–mirror stage.[5] As Kaja Silverman puts it, "Lacanian psychoanalysis, with its emphasis on the ego as a product of specular relations has made it extremely difficult to theorize the role played there by bodily sensations."[6] Kristeva's insistence that both symbolic language and the specular are belated developments, preceded by echolalia, is an attempt to theorize just that role.

Clearly Kristeva's project is not to develop a theory of film—in fact she explicitly distances herself from such a project.[7] She also exhibits a consistent suspicion of the image, consonant with her acquiescence to Guy Debord's critique of the society of the spectacle. Yet in 1996 she returns to her 1975 essay, "Ellipsis on Dread and the Specular Seduction," reworking it in the context of a discussion of cinema and fantasy. In the lecture course published under the heading of *The Intimate Revolt,* in which she discusses the work of the imagination in the texts of Barthes and Sartre, among others, the newly worked essay suggests that perhaps Hitchcock's horror films constitute the spectacular *par excellence.* The second volume of *The Powers and Limits of Psychoanalysis,* following on from *The Sense and Non-sense of Revolt, The Intimate Revolt* is concerned with the imaginary rather than cinema per se. In these two volumes Kristeva returns explicitly to what had been the organizing thematic of *Revolution in Poetic Language,* and had remained an underlying and structuring theme of the intervening works. As the domain of the imaginary has commanded a good deal of critical attention among film theorists, despite the correct insistence of some theorists that one cannot attend adequately to the imaginary without situating it within the context of the symbolic and the real, Kristeva's work offers the opportunity of renewing the question of how film might be revolutionary. I focus this question by asking how the imaginary configures that aspect of the Lacanian real that Kristeva theorizes under the heading of abjection.[8] How does the symbolic tend to consolidate itself according to rather traditional forms of representation, leaving aside as abject that which cannot be readily assimilated by the available congruence of the symbolic and imaginary? And how does the abject come back to haunt the symbolic, by pointing out the misalignment of the symbolic and the imaginary, and thereby facilitating not only their transformation, but also that of their relationship?

We have seen that feminist psychoanalytic interpretations in film theory have appealed to hysterical identification and that this appeal has played out in the form of a resistance to the issues raised by spectator studies.[9] If identification is multiple, so the argument goes, sex, gender, race, and class cannot determine one's response to film. Such logic fails to acknowledge that spectator studies is not committed to the view that the social salience of these identifiers determines audience response, only to the fact that a reflective relationship to sex, gender, race, and class (irrespective of one's actual identifications) will have an impact on a viewer's reception of film. At the same time, the appeal to hysterical identification as a model for film theory tends to accompany an acceptance or endorsement of primal fantasies (see Foster 1991, 20) that are taken to fuel not only interpretations of film, but also the psychoanalytic scenario itself.[10] Certain equations are drawn, on the basis of an imaginary committed to a logic in which the father is the law, and the mother is the prototype of the object. Such a logic implicitly assumes a symbolic that appeals to a metaphoric relation as always already in play, and exempts itself from having to go back behind the scenes, in order to interrogate how such a relation comes to be set up in the first place, and what unspoken assumptions deriving from an object relation facilitate it. In elaborating abjection, Kristeva taps into a primal fear that does not operate at the level of repression, or according to the division between consciousness and the unconscious, which does not share in the etiology of hysteria. Negation is not yet at stake: symbols are not yet in play. Prior to the object relation that is repressed in hysteria, abjection functions by mapping out the very possibility of meaningful discourse, or distinguishable objects. A "primal" or "corporeal mapping" takes place, which is presided over by maternal authority that comes to be repressed by the phallic order (1982, 72). This mapping of the body proper is a preliminary distinguishing of the body's territory through touch and sensation, without yet being a Hegelian, mediated form of particularity, or "thisness," over and against that which must be rejected in order to sustain its borders.[11] The maternal function of sphincter training, for example, involves a separation of excrement from what thereby becomes the clean and proper body. At the same time, since the child and its relation to others always takes place within a social milieu, certain bodies are in close proximity with the child's body, while others are not. Those bodies will be classed, raced, and sexed in ways that are shot through with power regimes, in ways that will impinge upon the ordering of the child's relation to its own body and to those of others. Certain symbolic relations will be fostered, supported, and sustained by the presence of some bodies and the absence of others. The return of abjection in the symbolic—a return of the real, rather than of the repressed—includes the possibility of rearranging the symbolic, in a way that does not necessarily conform to the repetition compulsion.

Kristeva returns to the semiotic, to the initial, imaginary grafting of meaning that is sketched out in the materiality of the drives, according to an unstable logic of pleasure and displeasure, a logic that precedes the stability of the subject/object distinction, or the distinction between presence and absence, a logic that is as yet unfixed by language. Such a logic is in pursuit of what might later come to be designated survival, need, or self-preservation, but which, prior to the comprehension of I/other, and prior to the delineation of biology from language, or animal need from human desire, figures only as want. From the perspective of the symbolic, the semiotic will always stand in a relation of excess: in whatever ways the semiotic is taken up by the symbolic, this accommodation will remain a partial transcription of a drive economy that can never be fully represented, although our only access to it remains symbolic. Through a return to the semiotic as in excess of the symbolic, Kristeva puts into question any account of system or subject that presents itself as autogenetic or autotelic.[12] Kristeva's sensitivity to this issue is reflected in her construction of the semiotic as a precondition of the symbolic (see 1984, 48), and her simultaneous positing of the symbolic and the semiotic as preconditions of one another (see 1984, 66). Careful to avoid either positing the semiotic as some unthought condition wholly outside the symbolic, as if it were a condition impervious to thought, or positing the symbolic as a system that presents itself in the end as self-generating, Kristeva construes the semiotic as that which can only be approached—but always inadequately—from within the symbolic. Hegel's response to the same problematic was to avoid positing any conditions of absolute knowledge as extrinsic and anterior, as if they were preconditions in their own right. As Terry Eagleton puts it, for a system "to be complete . . . the dominion it exerts over the world must be deployed at the same stroke over its preconditions. A discourse of absolute knowledge would otherwise never be able to get off the ground, since whatever it launches off from is rendered in that act anterior to itself, and so extrinsic to its hegemony. Simply by starting, such a work risks jeopardizing its own transcendental status, undercutting its own claims in the very act of enunciating them. The system, it seems, must somehow always already have begun," (1990a, 126).[13]

For Kristeva, the symbolic is neither completely self-grounding, nor does it contain its own ends entirely within itself. It does not spring out of nowhere, and it is not self-legitimating. Yet neither is it merely the translation of needs or drives for self-preservation, as if society merely amounted to so many ways of structuring, organizing or acquiescing to our essentially animal natures. The deferred effect of abjection makes itself felt as an irruption into the symbolic. The mutilated or amputated bodies that populate the masculine imaginary in the form of abject, castrated, feminized, or raced bodies, figure in narcissistic attempts to control the material origins of birth that would otherwise elude thought and social organization. A fabricated, fetishistic myth of origin holds at bay the apparently uncontrollable materiality of maternity, in much the same way as the mirror stage can be read as an elaboration of a narcissistic myth of omnipotence, which serves to defend against the severed limbs of fragmented bodies. In the words of Susan Buck-Morss, whether it is Benjamin's "'great mirror' of technology . . . where one sees oneself as a physical body divorced from sensory vulnerability" (1992, 33), or Lacan's "mirror stage," (37), in both cases what is at stake is an attempt to protect against physical fragmentation. Lacan's mirror stage extends Freud's reflections on narcissism, developed in 1914, at a time that coincides with the beginning of World War I, while Benjamin is responding not so much to the shell shock of the war machine, as to the "fragmentary impressions" that bombard us in modern life, to the point of "overstimulation and numbness" (Buck-Morss 1992, 16–18). Not only are our senses deadened by the factory system, which causes over-whelming bodily injuries in the form of loss of limbs and life (see 27), so too are our cognitive systems impaired by repetitive, uniform motions required by assembly line production, as if workers were mere automata (see 17). In much the same way, the entertainment system blocks out our capacity to "respond politically even when self-preserva-tion is at stake" (18). Kristeva is also concerned with the way in which our senses are assaulted by the spectacle of media such that little space is left for meaningful political responses.

In *The Intimate Revolt,* Kristeva distinguishes between the "culture of the image" and the "culture of words" (2002, 5). This distinction is symp-tomatic of a polemical divide between the "society of the spectacle"—a phrase often employed by Kristeva, and borrowed from Guy Debord— and the imaginary.[14] Taking up Guy Debord's "society of the spectacle," Kristeva declares that "we are in the society of the image" (2002, 63). For Debord, "the real consumer becomes the consumer of an illusion" (1994, 32). The society of the spectacle is one in which "all community and crit-ical awareness have ceased to be" (1994, 21). Debord calls the spectacle "a permanent opium war waged to make it impossible to distinguish goods from commodities" (1994, 30). Alienation sets in for the spectator: "the more he contemplates, the less he lives" (1994, 23). A dual concern can be discerned in Kristeva's suspicion of the image as spectacle, and her pro-posed solution of a rehabilitation of the imaginary, one that cannot be thought without understanding that Kristeva believes we live in a crisis-ridden era. We live in an age in which we are particularly subject to vari-ous versions of malaise, in which we exhibit symptoms that are produced, in part, by the political and ethical traumas imposed on us by contempo-rary society—Kristeva often cites the Holocaust, and Hiroshima. First, the danger of our being invaded by normalizing images is that they not only offer us false, idealized solutions, detached from the real meaning of our malaise, but they also distract us from pursuing the deep causes of the pervasive crises of our times. Secondly, language becomes emptied of meaning, no longer connecting with the drives or affect that shape our psychic lives. Kristeva is worried about the "extraordinary power" of the image to "suspend" the "meaning" of one's "anxieties and desires" so that the "visual depiction" of desires that we watch on the "television screen" (1995a, 8) amounts to the "psychological poverty" of an "amputated subjectivity" (1995a, 7). "Modern man," says Kristeva, is losing his soul" (1995a, 8), and turning instead to the palliative of mass media to provide an "artificial soul" (1995a, 7). We find ourselves "unable to tell a story," our desires lack "narrative" (1995a, 10)—we have "run out of imagination" (ibid.). According to Kristeva, "both the producer and the consumer of images suffer from lack of imagination" (ibid.). For those turning to analysis, the solution Kristeva points to is the restoration of "drives and language," to our otherwise disembodied "phantasmatic . . . constructions" (1995a, 26), which, rather than representing psychic life in nuanced ways, resort to formulaic, normalizing, stereotypical, empty phrases. Following up her suspicion of the "society of the image" (2002, 63), Kristeva says, "We are inundated with images, some of which resonate with our fantasies, and appease us but which, for lack of interpretative words, do not liberate us. Moreover the stereotype of these images deprives us of the possibility of creating our own imagery, our own imaginary scenarios" (2002, 67). Kristeva's interpretive discussions of works of art, abject or otherwise, can be read then as attempts to reconnect drives and signs.

Kristeva isolates what she calls "an other cinema" from cinema characterized on the one hand as that in which "stereotypical soap opera images reduce the viewer to a passive consumer," and on the other hand as the "so-called auteur cinema" that "pulverizes fantasy and invents a veritable cinematic écriture with ambitions of conceptualizing the specular" (2002, 69). In both of these alternatives, cinema "destroy[s] fantasy," whereas the cinema Kristeva considers to be "great art, from Eisenstein to Godard" is a "realist" cinema that "projects fantasies" (69). There are reasons to be skeptical about the grounds on which Kristeva differentiates what she construes as stereotypical soap opera images from "great art" and the assumptions that she makes about their reduction of the viewer to a passive consumer.

If Kristeva's remarks about stereotypical images give pause for thought, at the same time, one wonders about the criteria according to which Eisenstein, Godard, and Pasolini (see 2002, 73) are celebrated as great artists, while presumably others—designated only by Kristeva's silence—do not qualify as such. How far might Kristeva's own appeal to a cinema in which "fantasy is called on to find or recognize itself" (2002, 74) be couched in terms that remain oblivious to the racial phantasmatics embedded within the Freudian language that Kristeva appropriates uncritically? Fantasies, Kristeva tells us, "are transitional organisms, hybrid constructions between two psychical structures—between the conscious and the unconscious—that play with both repression and the return of the repressed" (2002, 65). She goes on to quote Freud: "We may compare them with individuals of mixed race who, taken all round, resemble white men, but who betray their coloured descent by some striking feature or other, and on that account are excluded from society and enjoy none of the privileges of white people" (66; quoting "The Unconscious" [1953w, 138]). The same passage is cited by Laplanche and Pontalis (1973, 317), whose discussion in *The Language of Psycho-analysis* provides the starting point of her consideration of fantasy and cinema.[15] Neither Kristeva nor Freud pause to raise questions about the legitimacy of such racialized exclusions, or that of the standard of resemblance they are said to "betray," nor do Laplanche and Pontalis.[16] Even in a discussion that concerns itself with thinking fantasy as fantasy, there is no attempt to think through how racial stereotypes inform the psychoanalytic imaginary that grounds Freud's comparison. The question that imposes itself is how to regard Freud's notions of prehistory, of heredity, of "savages" as somehow constituting the ground on which civilization is construed. How do these notions populate the unconscious of psychoanalysis?

Not only is Kristeva's appropriation of it unmarked, but she takes up the analogy of mixed race, seamlessly incorporating it into the first subtitle of the chapter, "Organisms of Mixed Race (Didier, the Collage Man)." Again, the image goes unremarked, so that we are left to wonder whether those who are excluded from the privileges of white society, and thereby aligned with the unconscious aspects of fantasy, are also excluded from the purview of psychoanalytic theory. If so, how might such exclusions be characterized? As abject? No doubt Kristeva would dismiss the question as an "ideological protes[t] of a politically correct sort," which "extol[s] ethnic and sexual difference" (11). Nevertheless, having raised the question of how racial exclusions function to ground social fantasies, I will return to it at length in subsequent chapters. First, however, I want to follow Kristeva's adumbration of fantasy and cinema.

Kristeva focuses on the instability of the object relation, on the staging of objectality prior to its resolution into signs. It comes as no surprise, then, when, in specifying the "different gaze" (2002, 73) that characterizes the "other" cinema—the cinema Kristeva proclaims "great" and to which she wants to direct our attention—she opposes it to "the gaze by which I identify an object, a face: mine, that of another. It offers me an identity that reassures me, for it delivers me from facilitations (*frayages*), unnamable fears (*frayeurs*), sounds prior to the name, to the image: pulsations, somatic waves, waves of colors, rhythms, tones" (2002, 73). In Freud's case study of Little Hans (1953a), his nameless fears—the sounds of the street, and so on—are condensed in his phobia of horses, which thus functions to deliver him from the unnamable nothingness (the rumbling of Levinas's *il y a;* the nothingness of Heidegger's *Angst*). The phobia reassures Hans precisely because it enables him to locate it, to fix it, to name it. If the Heideggerian resonance finds confirmation when Kristeva posits the "image as compensation for anxiety" (2002, 79), the Levinasian echo is confirmed when Kristeva goes on to say, "So-called intellectual speculation derives from this identifying, tenacious gaze" familiar to the hysteric who "unable to find a sufficiently satisfying mirror . . . finds herself in theory," having "delegated to another (to philosophical contemplation) the concern of representing a (my) identity, as reassuring as it is false, because it blacks out fear, facilitation. So-called intellectual speculation socializes 'me' and reassures others of 'my' good intentions as far as sense and ethics go" (2002, 73). Just as Levinas is critical of philosophical contemplation, so intellectual or contemplative speculation presents "a deeroticized surface," says Kristeva; "of my dreamed body it offers only what the doctor's speculum maintains" (2002, 73).[17] Thus her criticism of cinema that conceptualizes the specular—rather than thinking through its connection to the drives—comes into its own.

Prior to Lacan's mirror stage—which has proved so crucial for film theory—prior to castration and to separation, before objects begin to exist, when, like François our bodies are "still experienced as scattered" (70) in the fragmentation that accompanies a lack of motor-coordination. Before language, drives come to be represented metonymically by "the tape recorder," the "'bad object'" (70). Similarly, "when facilitation and fear burst into view," the "different gaze" that Kristeva associates with the "other" cinema "stops being simply reassuring, *trompe-l'oeil,* or the start of speculation and becomes—if you will—the fascinating specular, that is, at once charming and maleficent. Cinema seizes us here, precisely. This is its magic" (73). This "cinematic image makes what is behind identification identifiable (and there is nothing more patently identifiable than the visible): the drive, not symbolized, not caught in the object, neither in the sign nor in language. Or, to put it bluntly, it conveys aggression" (74). Thus the specular can "distance itself from itself" (74). It is the cinematic image that makes what is behind identification identifiable, which can distance itself from itself, that preoccupies Kristeva. The "hollowing out of fantasy" or the "exhibiting" of "its main themes, its skeleton logic" Kristeva designates the "thought specular" (75). This "logic" is "a certain music," "the movement that associates, displaces, condenses" (74), "the lektonic traces, the bones of fantasy that must adjoin a

'rhythmic,' 'plastic' dimension" (76).[18] The thought specular is not intel-
lectualizing or contemplative because it is not a question of abandoning
or evacuating the fantasy in order to reach its true meaning, as if it
could be sublated for a higher level of thought. Cinema, Kristeva tells
us, has "assumed the power of thinking the specular. Thinking it in a
way that is itself specular: using the visible, not evacuating fantasy but
being protected from it while demonstrating it" (75). If the "specular is
fascinating because it bears the trace—in the visible—of . . . aggression
of this nonsymbolized, nonverbalized, and thus nonrepresented drive"
(74), what qualifies the thought specular is that in these images "fantasies are referred to as such; they exercise their power of fascination
while at the same time mocking their fascinating specular" (74). The
"problem of the thought specular" is "how to remain in idolatry (fantasy),
while at the same time exhibiting symbolic truth" (78). The "thought
specular," then, is the term Kristeva reserves for "the visible signs that
designate fantasy and denounce it as such. This information no longer
refers to the referent (or to the object) but to the attitude of the subject
vis-à-vis the object" (74). In such a cinema, of which Godard is representative, for Kristeva, signals are "captured, cut up, and arranged in such a
way that the phantasmatic thought of the writer-director can be made
out" (74). Such a cinema "invites you first to locate your own fantasies
and then to hollow them out" (74). Having found or recognized itself,
fantasy can be put into question.

    For Kristeva, cinema is representationalist, yet it represents not
events, but fantasy. "The most direct cinema, which projects more or less
modified fantasies, seizes us in this place in our psychical lives where
the imagination lets itself be controlled by fantasy, which I call the
specular" (73). By characterizing fantasy itself in terms of "montage,"
Kristeva suggests that the task of cinema is to represent as directly as it
can the movement inherent in fantasy toward meaning: "fantasy, in its
visibility invents an instinctual montage and a drift toward meaning,
language, thought" (73). The drives, organized by primary processes, or
in semiotic rhythm, are what inform fantasy, especially the death drive
(aggressivity, destructive impulse), for Kristeva.

    If the fantasies themselves are "boneless, dislocated" (74), Kristeva
draws attention to the "logic of fantasy" (79), inviting us both to locate
our fantasies within the fantasy with which cinema presents us, and to
hollow them out, to recognize them as fantasies, to distance ourselves
from them. While there are moments in which she pushes up against
their decisiveness, Kristeva does not always interrogate Freud's "primal
fantasies" (66), including that of castration. When she says, for example,
"Cinema constantly offers a vision of th[e] trial of sexual difference, as

well as that of homosexuality, this collision with our impossible identities to the point of psychosis" (73), it is the "untenable" or "discordant,
ironic logic" to which she draws attention, referring us to Hitchcock. I
pursue Kristeva's suggestion that we hollow out our fantasies, that we
recognize them as such, even while remaining fascinated by them—
what Kristeva calls the "fascinating specular"—in a direction that enables
us to ask what happens when film encourages us not so much to switch
our identificatory allegiance from one character to another, but from
one fantasy to another. When film confronts the foundational fantasies
in which its own fantasies participate, it makes them available for
interrogation, and reworking.

In making the spectator self-conscious about the suspense he
induces, Hitchcock, a master of horror, draws attention to the manipula-
tive strategies he employs, even as they successfully engage his audience.
As Kaja Silverman points out, in contrast to classic cinema "Hitchcock's
Psycho . . . deliberately exposes the negations upon which filmic pleni-
tude is predicated. It unabashedly foregrounds the voyeuristic dimensions of the cinematic experience."[19] In *Psycho,* there is a moment at which
the car that contains Marion's body looks as if it might not completely
sink. In Silverman's words, "*Psycho* obliges the viewing subject to make
abrupt shifts in identification . . . thus the viewing subject finds itself
inscribed into the cinematic discourse at one juncture as victim, and at
the next juncture as victimizer" (141). It is as if Hitchcock catches his
spectators in an act of complicity, as, in the moment before the car finally
disappears, we have time to become aware of the fickle nature of our
allegiance to his protagonists. We have just followed Marion on her
emotional journey, as she flees, having stolen money from her boss, and
having arrived at the Bates hotel, only to have second thoughts. Before
she can act on her decision to "come clean" Norman Bates murders
her—and within the space of a few diegetic moments we find ourselves
willing the car in which he has placed her body to sink. All at once, we
are on Norman's side, having deserted our earlier allegiance to his victim with such alacrity that we would be alarmed, if we stopped to think
about it. And Hitchcock gives us the opportunity to reflect upon the
success of his having orchestrated our identificatory regimes. Adhering
to the absolute power of the director as the "absent one," Žižek says,
"when the car stops sinking for a moment, the anxiety that automati-
cally arises in the viewer—a token of his/her solidarity with Norman—
suddenly reminds him or her that his/her desire is identical to Norman's:
that his impartiality was always-already false. At this moment, his/her
gaze is de-idealized, its purity blemished by a pathological stain, and what
comes forth is the desire that maintains it: the viewer is compelled to

assume that the scene he witnesses is staged for his eyes, that his/her gaze was included in it from the very beginning" (2000, 223). It is the distancing of the spectators from their own processes of identification that Kristeva admires in Godard, who capitalizes on Hitchcock's playful reflection about the ease with which he can control his audience's reaction. For Kristeva, Hitchcock has managed to achieve identification between the spectator and the sadomasochistic drive. We find ourselves identifying with the desire of a psychopath to cover up the murder he has just committed, but we do so within the safety of a darkened cinema—or within the security of a living room—in which we pay to watch images produced for our entertainment.

Moments at which we become aware of our own complicity can be all the more significant if they prompt us to question the stability of identificatory regimes by engaging foundational fantasies that operate to stabilize identities by participating in imaginary social scripts that reinforce hegemonic relations. We are not only asked to catch ourselves in the act of being caught in a net of fascination—which can become self-referential.[20] We are also asked to confront how identification is facilitated by social and political prejudices, which are themselves sanctioned by imaginary regimes.[21] Works of art can help us detect imaginary assumptions at play in the symbolic networks that are constituted as the basis for meaningful exchange, and can thereby help us uncover unconscious commitments, including those that participate in racist and heteronormative regimes.[22]

What happens when horror works either to unsettle the sanguine ways in which we typically, systematically, and invisibly abject others due to their gender, sexuality, race, or class? What happens when the fantasy we thought was unfolding transforms itself into another fantasy? What happens when horror is produced because we discover that the person with whom we thought we were identifying is not in fact the person we took them to be, and our discovery has implications for our own self-understanding? Or when we identify with film character resembling those with whom we might be precluded from identifying in "real life"— on account of engrained political prejudice, or unfamiliarity.

The very immediacy that cinema makes available to the spectator can also be undercut, as in *The Crying Game* when Neil Jordan presents Dil as a character capable of being read either as a heterosexual woman, or as a transgender character, thus bringing to the fore the fact that our reading of Dil will depend upon the regimes of sexuality that we bring to that reading. Fergus's response to Dil's transgender identity is to hit her, and to vomit—he cannot assimilate his discovery. To the extent that we identify with the disruption of Fergus's heteronormative desire, we too are presented with a question about our desires. To the extent that we identify with Dil, the normative abjection of transgendered individuals comes to the fore. *The Crying Game* disrupts the viewer's unproblematic identification with the director's gaze, undercutting that gaze in ways that draw attention to its artifice, precisely by exploiting the pleasurable fascination of cinematic narrative realism. At the same time it offers a social commentary on various aspects of class, race, imperialist, colonialist and transgendered relations. It does so by allowing the fractures in symbolic discourse to gape open at certain key moments, in which drive or affect—in the form of a breakdown, or crisis—impose themselves as horrific. Perhaps more importantly, it also brings into question the origins of such horror.

The immediacy with which identifications are effected is in fact a product of a sustained process of our exposure to certain images, rather than others, images that, as Silverman says in her discussion of Jean-Louis Comolli, "we have learned to accept as reality" (1996, 127). So too Tony Kaye seduces his audience in soliciting an identification with Derek in the first part of *American History X*, only to undermine his racist rhetoric in the second part of the film. He thereby elicits identification precisely to disrupt it. Even if we do not agree with Derek's racist rhetoric, we find him sympathetic, charismatic. Derek's conversion from a neo-Nazi to someone who looks out for "the brothers" occurs in part due to his association with a black teacher, Sweeney, in part due to the friendship he develops with Lamont (Guy Torry), and in part due to the disillusionment and violence he suffers at the hands of his neo-Nazi prison friends. The fantasy that fuels Derek's neo-Nazi beliefs collapses, and the structure of that fantasy is laid bare.

There is an interruption of the popular consumption of easily recognizable, stereotypical heroes and heroines that facilitates seamless identification with ideal images, and which reassures me, by providing me with a settled identity. Such identification resembles the practice of critics who theorize about the art of "Matisse, Klee, Rothko, Schoenberg, and Webern" (1986, 237), only to "suppress that dimension in which the subject chooses to trace, for others and hence in the expressible (image or word) his aggressivity and/or his dread [frayeur]" (ibid.). Kristeva's emphasis on dread—anticipating her later emphasis of the horror of abjection—and on lektonic traces, can be read as an effort to prevent an overly idealizing tendency from taking hold in film theory, as a reminder of the materiality of the discharged, rhythmic energy communicated.

The thought specular "is essentially a matter of . . . putting into play what Freud called the 'primary processes' (the 'semiotic' . . .) underlying the symbolic, this primary seizure of drives always in excess in relation to the represented and the signified" (2002, 74). That which is represented, then, in Eisenstein, is "horror." His "organic drama . . . takes the form of represented horror" (2002, 77). Usually repressed, subject to the prohibition of social organization, drives are allowed free reign in the fantasy of cinema. Eisenstein "pursued the project of conveying . . . a network of lektonic traces," that is a distribution of "objects, actors, and lines" of dialogue (2002, 76). His attempt is to "give shape, in the specular" to "a subjacent conflict" (2002, 76), which is "at the borders of the unrepresentable" (2002, 77). In an example of the "primal scene," in which a soldier returns home to find that his wife is pregnant, the conflict concerns "the desire of knowing 'where the child came from' and 'how evil has functioned'" (2002, 76). The dynamic conflict between "two spatial complexes," "a straightforward, frontal tendency and an oblique, diagonal tendency" gives rise to "rhythm" (2002, 76). One can "hear the signifier" not as "deadly symbol" (2002, 77) but as concatenation of "organic" rhythm. In short, what is at stake is "represented horror" (2002, 77). The "[c]atharsis" that the figures of tragedy provided for the Greeks, we find in Hitchcock. When Kristeva identifies Hitchcock as the "filmmaker par excellence" she does so because he "unites Eisensteinian rhythm with the vision of terror" (1986, 238). In horror film, "the image itself signifies aggressivity" (1986, 238), thereby affording a direct representation of the drive. But in restoring terror to the symbolic order, specular fascination has the calming effect of "catharsis" (1986, 238), which shelters us from semiotic drives, and allows representation or language to be "divorced from the body" (Kristeva 1987, 6).

The means by which horror is communicated is the rhythm of montage—yet this rhythm is already characteristic of fantasies, according to Kristeva, who specifies that "great filmmakers have always known to include the facilitation of fear in cinematic seduction, in explicit themes as well as the rhythm of images" (2002, 75). In this sense, horror is at stake both in form and in content. Does montage constitute the syntax or language of film, then? If the spatial arrangement of objects, actors, lines of dialogue amount to a network of lektonic traces—and if the rhythms of montage echo those of the semiotic—montage itself is not quite comparable to the syntactical, logical, symbolic aspect of language. Like Deleuze, Kristeva is at pains to stress the specific visuality of film. The cinema of the thought spectacle is the thinking of fantasy, or the specular, by way of the specular, by means of images themselves (see 2002, 75). Yet, since it is what makes identification identifiable that is crucial for Kristeva, the processes that precede, give rise to, and make possible our recognition and comprehension of images preoccupy her.

Just as a whole range of sensual/tactile/vocalic registers are synthe-sized into abstract linguistic signs, so it is for the visual sign. That sen-suality will not fail to be imprinted by the social/political forces always already at work which render familiar some sensations and unfamiliar others. Tastes, odors, feelings, qualities, colors, sounds and so on, will all be culturally specific, tied to a time and place. For Kristeva "the visible" lends itself "to a primary and fragile synthesis of drives, to a more sup-ple, less controlled, riskier representability of instinctual dramas, the games of Eros and Thanatos" (2002, 69).

The "specular transforms drive into desire, aggression into seduction" (2002, 72). It is already a "diversion of the drive" (2002, 72), one that allows "identificatory allure" (2002, 72). The "specular remains the most advanced medium for the inscription of the drive (in relation to sound or tactile material, for example). The specular is therefore also the ear-liest point of departure of the signs, narcissistic identifications, and phan-tasmatic traces of one identity speaking to another" (2002, 72). Already specular, when identification is explored and unfolded in film, it can be thought at a distance, even while maintaining its allure.

The greatness of film, for Kristeva, is tied to its tendency not just to present, but also to thematize fear. One of the effects of Kristeva's analysis is that horror film takes on a certain privilege. Horror film becomes the specular par excellence. Moving away from the priority Kristeva attributes to horror film—and thereby also questioning the privilege she accords to what she dubs "great film"—I focus rather on cinema that is concerned not only with the representation of horror—not only with abject moments—but also with the fantasies informing the social and political contexts that help to structure and produce abject moments. Such cinema facilitates the exploration of the processes that coalesce in such a way as to produce moments of abjec-tion. It concerns itself with the symbolic and the imaginary that help to constitute the real as inexplicable. It allows the interrogation of the symbolic assumptions and imaginary fantasies that shore up and give meaning to the systematic exclusion, denigration or persecution of certain groups by other groups. It exposes certain moments of abjec-tion when the norms that support the ascendancy of certain groups in relation to others—an ascendancy marked by racial or sexual or class barriers—come tumbling down, or experience fracture and dislocation. In other words, it helps us locate our fantasies as fantasies. It would not be a representation of reality as such but rather an exploration of the forces—and their representation in fantasy—that drive subjects toward abjection, an interrogation of how those forces interact with symbolic requirements.

The films I examine here are narrative, and—to various degrees— what could be loosely designated realist, although most of them are shot through with motifs of hyper-realism, magical realism. As such they include identifiable characters and plot, but they also invoke the fantasies that inform, and make permissible or impermissible, certain identifications. Sometimes these fantasies "take on flesh," in fantastical moments, as in *Ma vie en rose*, when Ludovic escapes to his fantasy world of Pam and Ben, as the stringent and confusing demands of his real world become too difficult to negotiate.[23] This fantasy world, ironically provided by a very heteronormative continental equivalent of Barbie and Ken, does not impose the strictures he finds constraining him in the suburban world of his parents and schoolmates. Ludovic situates his fantasy in relation to the stereotypical fantasy promoted by Pam and Ben. In the real world he is expected to be the boy that his anatomy might suggest he is—but Ludovic has other ideas. Far from perpetuating the banal or the stereotypical, Berliner exposes the stereotypes that inform the social and political mechanisms shaping the parameters of characters' views, beliefs, hopes and expectations. In the process of identifying with these characters we are asked to confront our own desires, the symbolic matrix that informs them, and the imaginary that underlies them. This cinema complicates the identificatory relation between spectator and protagonist, between the viewer and what is presented to us, not only by drawing our attention to how easily we succumb to directorial control, but also by putting us in a position to interrogate our own socially sanctioned norms. In doing so, it declines to offer its audience an uncontested, privileged, or idealized point of view, but neither is it content to merely multiply points of view, as if such a modernist multiplication offered a fundamental challenge to the classic idealization of the spectator/director/bird's eye view. The emphasis is neither on one idealized view nor on multiple views. At issue rather is the need to think through the identificatory mechanism in a way that facilitates an interrogation of the abjection constitutive of the wider social field.

I am put in mind of an aporia at the heart of the debate between realism and the avant-garde practices of Godard et al. Is the key question whether films are realist (as Godard's rejection of realism would have it), or is it rather, as Andrew Higson says, "why they seemed realist (and significant) to a particular group of critics" so that the "socio-historical conditions" in which films are produced become relevant? (1998, 506). Or, as Kaja Silverman puts it, "The look is exhorted from many sides to perceive and affirm only what generally passes for 'reality'" (1996: 3). In the somewhat more pointed language of Fernando Solanas (one of the authors responsible for launching the term third cinema), if Hollywood, or first cinema, "expresses imperialist, capitalist, bourgeois ideas," second cinema "is often nihilistic, mystificatory. It runs in circles. It is cut off from reality."[24] In reaction to both the overt manipulation of Hollywood, and the sometimes reactive, and equally dogmatic response of avant-garde cinema, Third Cinema can be seen as balancing a commitment to the political, with a variety of aesthetic practices that emanate from the specific cultural conditions of the locale in which it is produced.[25] Counter-cinema, or avant-garde film, concerned itself with disrupting the apparently unproblematic identification between spectator and filmic image by making use of an array of strategies intended to render visible the procedures employed by the cinematic apparatus to create the illusion of reality. But in so far as avant-garde practices preoccupy themselves with creating a distance that interrupts the fascinated pleasure of the spectator, they not only risk self-indulgence, but also allow themselves to be little more than thinly veiled reactions to the Hollywood norms of entertainment that they are supposed to put into question. By making the audience self-conscious of their position as spectators, and by interrupting the pleasure gained by audiences losing themselves in the illusory, fictional world of the screen, counter-cinema (influenced by Brecht) drew attention to issues of power and ideology. However, counter-cinema, or avant-garde film also seemed to dictate certain methods and impose certain rules of its own. In its endeavor to displace narrative realism, it tended to require a suspension of pleasure, a celebration of confusion and dislocation, and a distancing of the spectator from the image portrayed on the screen. This suspension of pleasure is what is at stake in Kristeva's concern about conceptualizing the specular.

The international, independent cinema to which I attend does not fall strictly under the rubric of revolutionary Third World national cinemas, although I find the debates provoked around the term third cinema to be informative.[26] I am concerned with films dealing with issues of racism as well with other minority issues such as gender, sexuality, and class. While not conforming to the privilege Kristeva accords horror film, or to avant-garde films, such films can at once fascinate, distance, and question the social norms within which traditional cinematic practices have occurred. If it is true, as Solanas and Gettino claim, that film is the "most valuable tool of communication of our times," and if it is also true, as Kristeva claims, that it represents the spectacular par excellence, then presumably it is able to distill in a dramatic fashion the dominant ideology that it so often uncritically reflects with great precision.

The recent exacerbation of the "disconnection between verbal signs . . . and drive representations," which is accomplished, in part, by the normalizing, stereotypical and idealizing images of consumer culture,

Kristeva also attributes to attempts to purify the paternal signifier (1982, 49).[27] Kristeva takes account of our over exposure to stereotypical images in developing the notion of abjection, which offers a clinical diagnosis of borderline personalities, whom she differentiates from neurotics on the one hand, and psychotics on the other hand. If abjection falls within neither of the classic psychoanalytic clinical designations of neuroses and psychoses, it also issues a challenge to the primacy of the conscious/unconscious distinction, and hence to the central role that repression has assumed in psychoanalytic discourse. Abjection is a defense mechanism not wholly accounted for by the operation of repression.[28] Kristeva says, "The theory of the unconscious . . . presupposes a repression [un refoulement] of contents (affects and presentations) that, thereby, do not have access to consciousness but effect within the subject modifications, either of speech . . . or of the body (symptoms) or both (hallucinations, etc.) As correlative to the notion of *repression*, Freud put forward that of *denial* [dénégation] as a means of figuring out neurosis, that of *rejection (repudiation)* [rejet (forclusion)] as a means of situating psychosis" (1982, 7). If Freud put forward repudiation or foreclosure as a way to approach psychosis, he also restricted the vast majority of this attention to neurotics (and within that designation, paid more attention to hysteria than to obsessional neuroses), since psychosis, in as much as it refuses meaningful discourse altogether, tends to be outside a realm susceptible to meaningful psychoanalytic treatment or intervention, while neurotics show themselves to be more amenable to treatment. A deject (un jeté) then, one who is situated in relation to abjection, occupies a new clinical position with regard to language/reality, a position Kristeva diagnoses as appearing with greater frequency in the twentieth century, in the wake of its traumatic events, but also due to the way in which we are increasingly overwhelmed or seduced by images that are cut off from any meaningful connection with the drives that give rise to them.

The abject is not a response to repression, but to suffering (see 1982, 2). Kristeva distances abjection from neuroses; in abjection it is "as if the fundamental opposition were between I and Other or, in more archaic fashion, between Inside and Outside. As if such an opposition subsumed the one between Conscious and Unconscious, elaborated on the basis of neuroses" (1982, 7). Situating abjection as prior to the mirror stage, Kristeva sketches out a situation that is pre-objectal, prior to naming or language. "The abject is not an ob-ject facing me, which I name or imagine" (1982, 1). The autonomy of the mirror stage cannot be assumed. The "twisted braid of affects and thoughts" has no proper "definable *object*"—this is not Lacan's *objet petit a*, not "an otherness ceaselessly feeling in a systematic quest of desire," nor is it "my correlative, which providing me with someone or something else as support, would allow me to be more or less detached and autonomous" (1982, 1). Abjection is not to be thought then, as akin to the mirror stage—but as prior (albeit in a way that must be qualified, given that any access to abjection is assumed only by a subject who has already negotiated the mirror stage) to the support of the granting of autonomy that is facilitated by the image, which confronts me as independent, anticipating a future independence that is not yet mine (the infant's) but will be. The only thing the abject shares in common with the object is "that of being opposed to *I*" (1982, 1). Rather than meaning, the abject threatens meaninglessness, rather than the homology of intellection, or adequation, or thought—in which my coming to know the object is conceived as a process in which I conform my idea to the object, or the object conforms to my idea of it—in abjection there is radical exclusion.[29] "If the object, however, through its opposition, settles me within the fragile texture of a desire for meaning, which, as a matter of fact, makes me ceaselessly and infinitely homologous to it, what is abject, on the contrary, the jettisoned object, is radically excluded and draws me toward a place where meaning collapses" (1982, 1–2).

Kristeva's analysis of abjection attempts to explore that region in which the subject-object relation is not yet fixed or determined, and yet this attempt is launched from a position that assumes such a relation, within a language that depends upon the coherence of such a distinction, and that operates in terms of the signifier/signified distinction. The conventions of psychoanalysis include not only a correlation between subject and object (see 1982, 1) but also an assumed equivalence between the father and the law—such that paternal authority is the mainstay of the symbolic—and an equivalence between the mother and the first object. Challenging the classic psychoanalytic equation of the father with the law, and the mother with the first object (1982, 32), Kristeva attempts to get at what is behind the object relation. She does not want to take it for granted that the object is already constituted for a subject; rather it is precisely the instability of the relation between object and subject that abjection stages (see 1982, 43).

The true object relation, as understood in classical psychoanalysis, rests upon a triadic relationship, and appeals to the Name of the father. "The paternal agency alone, to the extent that it introduces the symbolic dimension between 'subject' (child) and 'object' (mother), can generate such a strict object relation" (1982, 44). Interrogating the processes by which such equivalences are set up and sanctioned, Kristeva follows the unstable contours by which the relation to the object is initiated, and observes the unsettling of the fixity of its conventional connotations.

At the same time, she conceives of the site of abjection as "the rejection and reconstruction of languages" (1982, 45). Out of the collapse of conventional meaning that occurs in abjection, then, new meanings, new symbolic chains, new ways of signifying can be produced.

If abjection is situated outside the dichotomy between neurosis and psychosis, if it focuses on primal, rather than secondary repression, if it is a defense against suffering that invokes as fundamental the unstable boundary separating inside from outside, rather than the conscious/unconscious opposition, and finally if it stages the instability of the object relation, it also moves beyond the discourse of negativity: "The dynamics of exclusion challenges the theory of the unconscious, seeing that the latter is dependent upon a dialectic of negativity" [dialectique de la négativité] (1982, 6–7). Having already cast doubt on the term negativity in *Revolution in Poetic Language*, as an appropriate term both for the movement by which the symbolic economy comes into being, and for the disruption of symbolic hegemony, Kristeva drives the point home in *Powers of Horror.*[30] With the introduction of the term abjection she reformulates her suggestion in *Revolution in Poetic Language* that rejection might be a more apposite term for the thought she is trying to sustain. An extreme form of rejection, abjection is thought as exclusion.

Kristeva opens the section of *Powers of Horror* entitled "Beyond the Unconscious" in the following way: "there are lives not sustained by desire, as desire is always for objects. Such lives are based on exclusion [l'exclusion]. They are clearly distinguishable from those understood as neurotic or psychotic, articulated by *negation* and its modalities, transgression [transgression], denial [dénégation], and repudiation [forclusion]" (1982, 6). Already preoccupied with the various operations of negativity in *Revolution in Poetic Language*, Kristeva returns to them with a slightly different emphasis in *Powers of Horror.* In *Revolution in Poetic Language* she distinguishes between negation, disavowal, and foreclosure (or repudiation) in the following way: "Negation-as-denial (Verneinung) or disavowal (Verleugnung) in perversion, which may go so far as the foreclosure (Verwerfung) of the thetic phase, represent different modalities capable of obscuring castration and the sexual difference underlying it as well as genital sexuality" (1984, 63–64). In *Powers of Horror*, placing the emphasis on exclusion, Kristeva specifies a modality not subsumable by "negation and its modalities," within which she includes not only denial/negation, and foreclosure/repudiation, but also transgression (previously emphasized as the movement that grants access to the semiotic, and allows for a transformation of the symbolic).[31] In her emphasis of exclusion Kristeva specifies "borderline" personalities, or dejects—those who are jettisoned by abjection.[32] Denial, says Kristeva, bears "on the object whereas repudiation affects desire itself" (1982, 7). She thereby differentiates between hysterical neuroses, in which the object is repressed, but returns in the form of symptoms—the return of the repressed—and psychoses, in which there is an outright refusal of language, understood as the desiring relationship itself. It might be helpful to refer to Table 4.1, where the various modes of negativity are represented—so many ways of negotiating the castration complex, understood as the entry into language. The fetishistic operation of disavowal is included as an example of obsessional neuroses.

Abjection is neither a complete repudiation of language/castration—which would condemn the subject to meaninglessness, to nonsense, to asociality—nor is it merely the adoption of a neurotically perverse relation to language (such as fetishism).[33] Rather, abjection enables a crossing of the thetic border, a reworking of the authority that is set up under the sign of the name of the father. Like fetishism, which deals in the currency of ideas and affect, abjection is "composite": it is both "judgment and affect, condemnation and yearning, signs and drives" (1982, 10). The fetishistic compromise of disavowal posits one idea, not in order to cancel out another, but in order to distance the fetishist from the anxiety with which he would otherwise have to be confronted—the anxiety of castration trauma. The myth of castration, taken up as an idea, is covered over by the fetish, a competing idea, which does not so much negate the reality of the first idea as defuse its affective impact. The operation of disavowal involves precisely the ability to avow castration on the one hand, yet also to maintain on the other hand—and at the same time—a contradictory idea. Despite the contradiction, both positions are maintained. Difference is maintained, without leading to the conclusion that one idea must trump the other. Fetishism is a way of sustaining, without resolving, contradiction.

If fetishism is a response to castration anxiety, abjection registers a more primal fear: separation from the mother. Unlike abjection, in fetishistic perversion one merely "dodges" castration, whereas the

Table 4.1. Modalities of Negativity

Medalities of Negativity:	Exclusion l'exclusion	Repudiation forclusion Verwerfung	Denial/Negation dénégation Verneinung	Disavowal déni Verleugnung
Clinical Diagnosis:	dejection	psychoses	neuroses (hysteric)	fetishism

"borderlander . . . risks his whole life" (1982, 55). Kristeva says "a true abject . . . spares himself the risk of castration. . . . Abjection then takes the place of the other" (1982, 53–54).[34] Abjection is not so much a refusal of the law as it is a resituating of it, a semiotic inscription, a return to the real that is also a writing, an etching out of what will become a new object—a return to the familiar but forgotten object, the insides of the maternal body—which has always, already been prohibited by the paternal law. The "'object'" of abjection is the "body's inside," those "flows from within"—"urine, blood, sperm, excrement," which "show up in order to compensate for the collapse of the border between inside and outside" (1982, 53). "It is as if the skin . . . gave way before the dejection of its contents" (1982, 53). Through "immersion" in the "bad object that inhabits the maternal body" the deject possesses/becomes "jouissance" (1982, 54).

Kristeva observes that the abject makes "those articulations of negativity germane to the unconscious . . . inoperative" (1982, 7). In abjection, "the unconscious contents remain excluded but in a strange fashion: not radically enough to allow for a secure differentiation between subject and object, and yet clearly enough for a defensive *position* to be established—one that implies a refusal but also a sublimating elaboration" (1982, 7). An essentially defensive position, "abjection is directed against a threat" (1982, 1). More specifically, it is a response to maternal hatred. Instead of love, Kristeva says, the deject "has swallowed up . . . emptiness, or rather a maternal hatred" (1982, 6). She goes on: "That is what he tries to cleanse himself of tirelessly" [c'est de ça qu'il essaie de se purger, inlassablement] (1982, 6). Maternal hatred results in part from the lack of motivation on the part of the mother to encourage the child to separate, to realize autonomy. Since society values women by restrictive stereotyping that construes them as good mothers, Kristeva points to the "difficulty a mother has in acknowledging (or being acknowledged by) the symbolic realm—in other words, the problem she has with the phallus that her father or her husband stands for," which "is not such as to help the future subject leave the natural mansion. The child can serve its mother as token of her own authentication; there is, however, hardly any reason for her to serve as go-between for it to become autonomous and authentic in its turn" (1982, 13). The mother thus has an interest in perpetuating the illusion of the phallic mother, a situation that can lead to a suffocating maternal attitude. From this point of view, the father provides welcome and necessary relief.[35]

While not explicitly invoking Freud's imaginary father, which will play a central role in *Tales of Love*, Kristeva nonetheless appeals to the help of the father in *Powers of Horror*: "In such close combat, the symbolic light that a third party, eventually the father, can contribute helps the future subject" (1982, 13). In another, similarly implicit, reference to the imaginary or loving father, Kristeva suggests that perhaps some solace can come from "a father existing but unsettled, loving but unsteady [aimant mais instable] merely an apparition but an apparition that remains" (1982, 6). The loving or imaginary father, then, while not yet thematic, is already gestured towards in *Powers of Horror.* Yet, the emphasis remains on the strict father, internalized as the superego. "To each ego its object, to each superego its abject" (1982, 2) says Kristeva. Unlike the object, which "settles me within the fragile texture of a desire for meaning" (1982, 1–2), "what is *abject,*" "the jettisoned object, is radically excluded and draws me toward the place where meaning collapses" (1982, 2). The superego has "driven it away . . . And yet, from its place of banishment the abject does not cease challenging its master" (1982, 2).

If "meaning collapses," and if it is "driven away" by the superego—an "'ego' that merged with its master" (1982, 2)—abjection occurs for a subject who has developed a superego, and thus internalized paternal authority. If abjection seems not to play by the "rules of the game" (1982, 2), there is a sense in which the deject knows those rules. Although exiled, the abject challenges its master. It is not "repression" but "brutish suffering that 'I' puts up with, sublime and devastated, for 'I' deposits it to the father's account." It is perhaps worth noticing that at the point where Kristeva introduces the notion of the sublime and the uncanny, it is the father for the sake of whom abjection is "endure[d]"—"for I imagine that such is the desire of the other" (2). It is after all, "the working of imagination whose foundations are being laid here" (5) as Kristeva observes. There is a return implied in the "emergence of uncanniness [étrangeté], which, familiar as it might have been in an opaque and forgotten life, now harries me as radically separate, loathsome" (2). The idea of "forgotten time [le temps oublié]" (9) recurs when Kristeva describes the time of abjection as "double: a time of oblivion and thunder [temps de l'oubli et du tonerrre]" (9). The suggestion is that something familiar but forgotten now pursues me. This can perhaps be thought of as the existence that preceded the birth of the subject, which now figures as that from which I must have separated, "a 'something' [un quelque chose]," which "if I acknowledge it, annihilates me" (2). Abjection protects me from this something "on the edge of non-existence and hallucination" and in this sense, the "abject and abjection" are "primers of my culture" (2).

Kristeva approaches abjection through a consideration of phobia.[36] A metaphor of want, phobia "is inscribed . . . in the heterogeneity of the psychic system that is made up of drive presentations *and* thing presentations linked to word presentations" (1982, 35). Commenting on the restrictive ways in which psychoanalysis tends to take account of the "experience of want" by paying attention only to its more or less fetishized occurrence (1982, 5), Kristeva interprets the fear exhibited by little Hans for horses, or by Sandy for dogs, as a hieroglyph that condenses not merely other fears, but the fear of the unnamable, the fear of nothingness (see 1982, 34).

While Freud interprets Hans' hieroglyphic phobia—to be afraid of being bitten by a horse—by substituting it for another fear, namely that of castration, Kristeva worries that to do so is to remain "at the level of the fantasy" (1982, 36). She asks whether Freud's cure "actually revives the phobia," telling Hans "that he is right: you cannot not be afraid of castration, and upon your fear I found the truth of theory. In doing so, he rationalizes that fear" and runs the risk of providing a "*counter-phobic* treatment" (1982, 36). Wary of Freud's "linear, transferential approach," "Kristeva asks, what about "the more subtle workings of the *metaphoric elaboration*" of the phobic object? (1982, 36). Hans's phobia must stem in some way from a "frailty of the signifying system" that Kristeva attributes to "a father" who "does not hold his own" (35). Recall that abjection, as a narcissistic crisis, "can be brought about either by "*Too much strictness on the part of the Other*" or by the "*lapse of the Other*" (15). By focusing on the gaps that appear within secondary repression (see 1982, 12), which punctuate Hans's phobic discourse, Kristeva glimpses behind the fear of horses a more primal fear—that of want itself. Primal repression, Kristeva says, returns "in a phobic, obsessional, psychotic guise, or more generally and in more imaginary fashion in the shape of *abjection*" (1982, 11). Laplanche and Pontalis note that for Freud, primal repression is a "hypothetical process," which is "postulated above all on the basis of its effects" (1973, 333–34). Similarly, Kristeva approaches abjection indirectly, as what must have occurred prior to the subject's inception, and as that which returns, for example, in the guise of Hans' phobia. She thus reads in this phobia not merely a condensation of namable fears, but also of the unnamable. The "phobia of horses becomes a *hieroglyph* that condenses *all fears,* from unnamable to namable. . . . The statement, 'to be afraid of horses' . . . [b]y means of the signifier of the phobic object—the 'horse' . . . calls attention to *a drive economy in want of an object* . . . fear, deprivation, and nameless frustration. . . . It is a metaphor for "*want itself*" (1982, 34–35). The "stupendous verbal skill" exhibited both by Hans and by Sandy is read as an instance of cathecting "*symbolic activity itself*" (1982, 44).

Both Hans and Sandy have a special mastery of language. Sandy speaks a great deal, and has an "extensive vocabulary" (40). Words make up for the missing mother, or "elaborate that want" (41). This verbalizing is an attempt at introjection. Language has "become a counterphobic object" (41). The "phobic hallucination" is "halfway between the recognition of desire and counter-phobic construction: not yet . . . defensive . . . nor [yet] a recognition of the object of want as object of desire" (42). The "phobic object is precisely avoidance of choice" (42) (and in this, limited, sense similar to fetishism). There is a "*condensation* of intense *symbolic* activities" which leads to "phobic hallucination"—a "metaphor" but one with an "added" "*drive* dimension" (42). Something "unknowable" is hallucinated. A hallucination of something stands for the "nothing" (42). This phobic writing is a "confrontation with the abject" (42). Hans puts "into flesh (a horse) those logical constructs that set us up as beings of abjection and/or as symbolic beings" (43).

Hans's fear of being bitten by horses is in fact a form of protection from "some not yet localizable cause" or a projection of fear in general onto horses in particular. The "fantasy of incorporation" is an "attempt to escape fear," like Klein's incorporation of the breast—by which "I hold on to" the mother, which nonetheless threatens me, since I learn at the same time of the paternal prohibition. This second threat, a symbolic one, prompts a second procedure: "I am not the one that devours, I am being devoured by him" (1982, 39). The "aggressivity of drives" is never in its "pure state," but always infused with the "deprivation" (maternal absence) and "prohibition" (paternal law) of the symbolic. Aggressivity might appear to come after primary narcissism, but "what can be *known*" of the connection between aggressivity and want is their coextensive relation, their adaptation to one another (1982, 39).

Since, as speaking beings, separated and autonomous, we are always this side of abjection, we must have gone through some kind of confrontation with castration anxiety, and so can only approach abjection, in which the subject gives birth to itself (see 1982, 4; 15), from this side of language, or within symbolic terms, as subjects who have taken a position in relation to castration. And yet in true abjection the subject spares himself the risk of castration, and, through displacement, abjection takes the place of the other (1982, 3–4). Thus the position of the speaking subject is not determined. One can take a position in relation to castration, but one can also go back and rework that position, in which case meaning collapses—and has to be reconstructed, with the possibility that it might be constructed differently. Conventional meanings are thereby capable of transformation, sometimes in revolutionary ways, but sometimes also in reactionary ways that reconfirm the authority of established laws. Indeed, for Kristeva, Freud's "master stroke" was to have avoided imbuing Oedipus, polymorphous sexuality, or the death drive with a "fundamental determinism" by understanding them in terms of "a completely symbolic causality" (1982, 38). Since the symbolic is normative, as speaking beings we are structured, in some way or other, in relation to symbolic determinations.[37] How far Kristeva endorses the particular normative requirements of classic psychoanalytic scenarios is in question. In abjection, the drive "since it is not sexually-oriented denies [dénie] the question of sexual difference; the subject can produce homosexual symptoms while being strictly speaking indifferent to them: that is not where the subject is" (1982, 45). That is, as prior to castration, in abjection the subject has not yet assumed a position in relation to sexual difference, and has consequently not yet distinguished between mother and father. If it remains the task of the psychoanalyst, according to Kristeva, to adhere to established paths of meaning, there are also times at which the collapse of meaning will divert these paths. The psychoanalyst must "follo[w] or divert the path [of desire], leading the patient towards the 'good' object [not in a moral sense, Kristeva specifies, in a gesture subverted by her normalization of fantasies privileging heteronormative desire]—the object of desire, which is, whatever may be said, fantasized according to the normal criteria of the Oedipus complex: a desire for the other sex" (1982, 48).

Yet Kristeva also points to the possibility of the "collapse of Oedipal triangulation" thereby casting doubt on the "unitary bent" of Lacan's "Name of the father" (1982, 53). When there is an "outburst of abjection" (1982, 48), a collapse of the sign, heterogeneity breaks through. "A language now manifests itself whose *complaint* repudiates the common code, then builds itself into an *idiolect,* and finally resolves itself through the sudden irruption of affect" (1982, 53).[38] Thus Kristeva suggests that new languages can break through the hegemony of that endorsed by the paternal law.[39] Kristeva's own reflections on the scope and meaning of such new languages is restricted by her adherence not so much to the foundational status of castration and fetishism, but to the (white) heteronormative Oedipal fantasy informing psychoanalysis. Within certain limits, one might think these new languages beyond such a register, as akin to Gayatri Spivak's thinking of the subaltern.[40] Certain hegemonic meanings circulate in dominant postcolonial narratives, in ways that preclude the coherence of counter-narratives—making it impossible for the discourse of subaltern subjects to be recognized as significant without a transformation of the very terms in which dominant systems grant subjects recognition. Similarly, in abjection, there is both a collapse and a rebirth, a renewal that gives rise to a reconfiguration of symbolic meaning, a transformation of practice, which is not restricted to the meaning of a particular object within discourse, but which concerns the very possibility of an object becoming meaningful, and thereby addresses the processes in terms of which meaning is granted. Kristeva thus emphasizes that in abjection "revolt is completely within being" and it is "eminently productive of culture. Its symptom is the rejection and reconstruction of languages" (1982, 45). The deject is a "deviser of territories, languages," and never stops demarcating (1982, 8).

Deriving from the Latin, abjectus (rejected), stemming from jacere (to throw), the abject—as Kristeva emphasizes, when she asserts that the corpse is a primary form of abjection—is concerned with a falling away. She draws a connection between the cadaver and the idea of falling [*cadere, tomber*]. Death, waste, is that which falls away from me. Just as "body fluids," "defilement" and "shit" are what "life withstands" (3), so "refuse and corpses *show me* [m'indiquent] what I permanently thrust aside in order to live" (3). Kristeva's emphasis is on decay, on the putrefaction of death, not as that which signifies death, for in the signification of death, I would be able to understand it, accept it. Rather, when I am confronted with a "wound of blood and pus" there is an unmasking of death, such as in "true theater." Kristeva says, "I am at the border [aux limites] of my condition as a living being"; "My body extricates itself, as being alive, from that border. Such wastes drop so that I might live, until, from loss to loss, nothing remains in me" (3). While "dung signifies the other side of the border, the place where I am not" the "corpse, the most sickening of all wastes, is a border that has encroached upon everything. It is no longer I who expel, 'I' is expelled. The border has become an object" (3–4). Sophocles' Antigone, in her burial of Polynices, attempts to keep at bay the degeneration of the body by natural forces. Or recall Lorde, for whom the border also becomes an object. In this case the border of her coat, which separates her from a white woman, disgusted by the color of her skin in such close proximity to her own, turns into a roach.

The elsewhere is here, *jetted, abjected,* into my world; the corpse "is death infecting life" (3–4). "The corpse, seen without God and outside of science is the utmost of abjection" (4). In *Black Sun*, Kristeva will take up Hans Holbein's *The Body of the Dead Christ in the Tomb* in a way that emphasizes the wounds of his body, his suffering. Hegel had already pointed to the importance of abjection and suffering in Christian and Romantic art, which takes "the abject as its privileged object. Specifically, the tortured and crucified Christ, that ugliest of creatures, in whom divine beauty became, through human evil, basest abjection."[41] Hegel cites Count von Rumohr on the Byzantine tradition, who, like Kristeva in her account of abjection, emphasizes suffering: "what they had in view as their subject was physical suffering as such. . . . the succumbing of the body."[42] Holbein's *The Body of the Dead Christ in the Tomb*, with its emphasis on corporeal wounds and suffering, illustrates this perfectly.[43]

By contrast, as Danto puts it, "The tendency in the Renaissance to beautify the crucified Christ was in effect a move to classicize Christianity by returning the tortured body to a kind of athletic grace, denying the basic message of Christian teaching that salvation is attained through abject suffering" (2003, 57). The return to the abject in secular art is an exploration of aggressive forces, in which the suffering of certain groups becomes the site of transcendence for others. When the logic of "it is either us or them" predominates, the violent struggle characteristic of imaginary relations takes over, and becomes institutionalized politically; abjection asserts itself. Thus, for Kristeva, Céline's *Journey to the End of the Night* qualifies as abject because, "far from taking the cathartic path of abjection taken by religions (I support the idea that all religion is a purification of the abject)" it "relentlessly tracked down imaginary abjections that he transformed into political realities. His anti-Semitism and his abject compromises with Nazi ideology were expressed in his sorry pamphlets" (2002, 260). Picasso and De Kooning are among the artists whose work is concerned with that state in which "separation between subject and object is not yet clear but where these two quasi entities are exhausted in fascination and repulsion," where that "archaic relationship of nonseparation with the maternal container: the mother being the primary ab-ject" (260) holds sway.

In a 1995 interview with Charles Penwarden, Kristeva says that abjection is a "soliciting by the other in such a way that I collapse. This solicitation can be the result of fascination, but also suffering: the other disgusts me, I abhor it, it is—we are—waste, excrement, a corpse: it threatens me."[44] If Kristeva points to the corpse as a possible site of abjection in the same moment she underlines the ineliminable ambiguity of abjection. She says, "I abhor it, it is—we are—waste, excrement, a corpse," underlining the way abjection is not easily containable within secure boundaries. The "it is—we are" signals the fluidity and contamination of abjection. I expel, reject or exclude the abject, but I also become it. I am it. "When one is in a state of abjection," says Kristeva, "the borders between the object and the subject cannot be maintained" (22). It is, says Kristeva, "not only murder, excrement, menstrual blood that are dirty, but anything which endangers a structure. When you have a coherent system, an element which escapes from this system is dirty. It begins with something fairly anodyne. Tears, for example, are considered dirty because they escape the limit of the body" (24).

Some art is directed toward eliciting disgust by depicting that which normally passes without comment in such a way that renders it unacceptable. The films with which I am concerned challenge the Kantian dictum, as Danto puts it, that "disgust cannot be disguised."[45] The normative and political force of film can be to suggest what we should find disgusting in life, but often don't. Communities are called into being that are disgusted by that which passes muster as decent. This is what happens when horror is represented in such a way as to elicit in the spectator a horror precisely at our normative identificatory regimes, when the structure of our social fantasies is laid out in its bare bones, when idealization breaks down, meaning collapses, abjection erupts. Film can also elicit identifications with figures that in "real life" might provoke disgust, but within the context of the film, fascinate us, or even seduce us.

When abjection becomes politicized in art, there is a refusal to accept the logic by which a community constitutes itself as cohesive in its mutual disgust, as if that disgust were produced by anything other than (misplaced) convention. It cannot merely be a matter of giving form to the semiotic, but must also be a question of acknowledging the potential revolutionary impact of reintroducing the residual semiotic that is left unthought by dominant symbolic forms of thought. To make good on this suggestion, let me turn first to Lars von Trier's *Breaking the Waves*, then to Thomas Vinterberg's *The Celebration*, and finally let me return to *Ma vie en rose*, three films that exhibit contrary relations to the political logic of abjection. If *Breaking the Waves* corroborates the symbolic status quo, while *The Celebration* upsets and reorganizes it, *Ma vie en rose* engages the organizing fantasy informing a social imaginary driven by the heteronormative order.

Confirming the sacrificial role of women, reiterating the need to exclude or scapegoat certain members of society, even as it explores the religious overtones of such abjection, *Breaking the Waves* celebrates conventional masculine/religious/symbolic forms that relegate women to peripheral roles—just so much matter or content to be worked over, re-formed, in the name of a masculine imaginary, the authority of which remains undisturbed. On the one hand the connection that Kristeva draws between the abject and the superego, as representative of paternal authority, and on the other hand her understanding of abjection as perversely related to the law, renders *Breaking the Waves* amenable to interpretation in terms of abjection. Nor is the overprotective relationship that Bess's mother demonstrates towards her daughter insignificant—a phallic mother? Bess (Emily Watson) puts herself in an antagonistic relation to the law, prostituting herself in the eyes of both the religious and secular orders, but she does so in order to pervert their logics, creating a new order, imposing her own, abject logic. According to Bess, her destiny is to save her husband's life. In a sense, then, she has taken the law into her own hands. In a perversion of the social contract, she sets herself up as executor of God's law, transforming Jan (Stellan Skarsgård) into the

ultimate father—God. At the same time, she sets herself up as the sacrificial object of the law. She mimes the inaugural, founding sacrifice—but
she uses her body, and ultimately her life, to do so.

Abjection, says Kristeva, does not ignore "Religion, Morality, Law,"
but "takes advantage of them, gets round them and makes sport of them"
(1982, 16). Bess transposes her religious faith in God into an unwavering
belief in Jan, carrying out his desire. The transposition is underlined when
she adapts her approach to prayer, in which she verbalizes both her own
thoughts, and those she imagines to be God's, as a technique for talking
to a sleeping Jan, thereby eliciting a declaration of his love for her. Yet, as
Bess's best friend, Dodo (Katrin Cartlidge) puts it, Jan, hospitalized and on
drugs "is not right in the head." Bess's abjection of herself is an attempt
to ward off the greater threat that Jan's impending death presents—his
absence. Bess would rather sacrifice herself to his desire than lose him
altogether. She would rather lose herself than lose him.

Initially, Bess is reluctant to abide by Jan's request that she engage
in sexual relations with other men so that she can tell him stories of
these encounters, and thereby ostensibly keep his love for her alive. After
her first sexual encounter with a stranger, Bess vomits. As Kristeva puts
it, "vomiting . . . protects me. The repugnance, the retching that thrusts
me to the side and turns me away from defilement, sewage, muck.
The shame of compromise, of being in the middle of treachery. The fascinated start that leads me toward and separates me from them" (1982,
2). Bess's vomiting protects her from the repugnance she feels at the
compromise she has made, when, after her husband, Jan, is paralyzed
in an accident on an oil rig, she agrees to act out Jan's fantasies by engaging in sexual relations with other men, so that her "tales of love" will
keep him alive. Having vomited, Bess catches sight of a rabbit, which she
imitates—a gesture at once childlike and defensive, one in which she
distances herself from the world of compromise in which she has just
implicated herself. Bess will reconcile herself to Jan's desire, conforming to his fantasies as she puts herself in increasingly dangerous and
life-threatening situations, convincing herself that she is saving him.
One might say that Bess becomes the bad object. Her corpse will
become the waste product of Jan's desire.

The picture of abjection, Bess collapses outside the church. Barred
from the house by her mother, and cast out of the church in which
women are not allowed to speak, Bess has nowhere else to go. Bess's
prostitution of herself for the sake of Jan provides the grounds on which
she is excluded both from the house of God and from the house of her
mother. A shot of Bess's disheveled, used up, exhausted body lying on
the ground in front of the church, wearing shiny red hotpants, recalls the

provocative poses of Cindy Sherman's photographic series, *Centrefold Photographs*. Sherman's photographs mimic the glossy spreads of *Playboy*, but instead of evoking an alluring or captivating sexuality they depict depression, anxiety, or boredom—abjection.[46]

The minister, who fails miserably to live up to the example of the Good Samaritan, and who has warned her that God "looks with anger on those who fail him," now abandons Bess, walking away, without a second glance. Bess's body has become the site of abjection. An outcast of the church, Bess's identification with Jan's desire, which will eventually kill her, intensifies. Bess becomes the outsider that Jan once was. To the question of whether Bess abjects herself—or at least allows herself to be abjected—whether Jan abjects her, or whether religion abjects her—the film provides no easy answers. Bess's self-sacrifice for Jan is explored in a context that constantly presents her as a Christ-like figure, yet the repercussions of such a transposition remain undeveloped. The film ultimately confirms a familiar paradigm, in which a woman's body becomes the site of sacrificial abjection in order to facilitate a man's desire, when church bells inexplicably, perhaps miraculously, ring out to signify the transcendent meaning that Bess's suffering and death facilitate, namely, Jan's recovery.

Bess in *Breaking the Waves*.
Courtesy of Photofest.

The well worn pop/rock songs (Elton John's *Yellow Brick Road,* Procol Harum's *Whiter Shade of Pale,* Leonard Cohen's *Suzanne*) that accompany the all but frozen scenes—still lifes, or stills?—of the Scottish Highlands in *Breaking the Waves* might be intended to achieve a feel for the 1960s. The story-like chapter headings might evoke a children's tale that formed part of the inspiration for the film.[47] Yet they also serve as a breathing space in which the audience can take stock, exempting themselves from the narrative, even as we wonder why the river is running, or the car is still moving in what appeared to be a still. All is not necessarily as it appears, and if the musical interludes slow us down, they also give us a chance to stop and think, to interject our own reflections. So we reflect on Bess's relation to the religion that governs her life, and disciplines her body, the authority of which is supplanted by a husband who usurps the role formerly allotted to God. We are given free rein to reflect on the patriarchal organization of the community in which Bess finds herself ensconced, on the interdiction of female speech imposed by the church, and on the exclusion of women from funeral services. Commenting on the difference between painting and film, Walter Benjamin observed that "[b]efore the movie frame we can do nothing," and that "[n]o sooner has his eye grasped a scene than it is already changed. It cannot be arrested." Whereas "[p]ainting invites contemplation"—we can abandon ourselves to our own associations, in film we are directed, manipulated.[48] By interspersing the more usual filmic fare with (what appear to be) film stills, Lars von Trier questions the boundaries between painting, photography, and cinema. If *Breaking the Waves* remains entrenched in some of the patriarchal assumptions it permits, at times, the space to explore, it ultimately employs religion—however much its attitude to religion might remain tongue in cheek—to close down the opportunities offered to the audience as moments in which to subject those assumptions to critique. As a meditation on voyeurism, the film remains provocative, especially since in witnessing Bess's sexual encounters the audience is exposed to precisely the scenes that are visually withheld from Jan.

The rough jolts to which the handheld camera subjects the audience in *Breaking the Waves,* as the camera follows Bess to her death, serve to disorient the audience, reflecting Bess's own disorientation. The final scene, however, in which Bess's corpse breaks the waves, a burial in water that is accompanied by the ringing of bells, represents a reassertion of the patriarchal order. Bess has died for the sake of Jan, whose miraculous recovery is attributed to her sacrifice. The fantasy driving this resolution is hardly revolutionary. Abjection might be displaced from its traditional role as consolidating religion, but only to have its meaning taken up in a new form of dogma, that of patriarchal desire. The doctor's ultimate judgment that the appropriate term to describe Bess is "good" does nothing to dispel the sacrificial myth of femininity underlying the fantasy enacted.

In Thomas Vinterberg's *The Celebration,* also a Dogme 95 film, the stumbling camera pursues Christian (Ulrich Thomsen), as he is herded out of the aristocratic family home and into the forest, or the sylvan glen, where, contrary to the insistent song of the patriarch's mother, nothing is calm, still, or tranquil. Christian's ostensible transgression is to have upset the apparent order and decorum of a family that can only sustain its coherence by refusing to acknowledge the incestuous turmoil at its heart, by requiring that its victims suffer the emotional burden of that disorder, and by scape-goating Christian when he tries to publicly acknowledge it. As Christian runs through the woods, pursued by his older brother, the precarious juddering of the handheld camera refuses to let the audience pretend with the rest of the family, who are still celebrating the anniversary of the master of the house, that all is as it should be. By juxtaposing the treatment of Christian with that of Gbatokai (Gbatokai Dakinah), the film underscores the outsider status of both the incestuously sullied other and the racially marked other, indicating that aristocratic society has drawn its boundaries around itself not only by indulging in behavior that it designates taboo but also through establishing racial exclusions. As far as Christian's brother, Michael (Thomas Bo Larsen), is concerned, Gbatokai is permitted access to the aristocratic house so long as he adheres to the stereotypes whites have established for him—he can be a musician but not a guest. That he turns out to be the partner of his sister, Pia (Trine Dyrholm), is all but intolerable to Michael.

Christian can remain in the house so long as he follows the hypocritical rules established by his father, and observed by his family—he can remain part of the family only as an abused and silenced casualty of it. It is with the help of the staff that Christian finally prevails, a circumstance that points up the sympathetic alignment of the lower classes with his plight. Informing Christian's insistent, and eventually successful attempts to give voice to his abuse, to force his family to bear witness to his father's incestuous conduct, is the suicide of his twin sister, whose victimization at his father's hands went unvoiced. By shifting the parameters of abjection, Christian draws attention to its inherent mobility. By making his father an object of public disgust and ridicule, he reorders the phallic scene, refusing to bear the brunt of his father's incest.

If Bess reshapes religious abjection, giving it the form of patriarchal abjection, she does nothing to disturb its underlying logic of exclusion.

By contrast, Christian reshapes the symbolic, and the forms of authority that sanction it. He recasts abjection, protesting the logic that has allowed his father to disown it, resulting in the suicide of his sister. Subjects can be abjected through the abuse of other subjects. They can also use abjection as a way of protecting themselves from abuse, recuperating the dynamic of their suffering. Abjection can occur when a social group unites against particular subjects, consolidating its boundaries by excluding those it designates as other. We can attempt to map the effects of abjection in particular instances and to ask about the political landscape that informs the abject, and how its contours both shape, and are shaped by, abjection. In doing so, we can resist the tendency to restrict, as Hal Foster puts it, "our political imaginary to two camps, the abjectors and the abjected" (1996, 166). Abjection can be thought as a process that is inherently mobile, which has no intrinsic object, but which circulates, and attaches to specific sites, objects, and persons, only to be re-engaged, and re-deployed, through projection. Sometimes those who are abjected, turn abjection back on itself, so that it is thrown back to those who abject. Sometimes abjection is projected somewhere else entirely, on to some foreign object. These processes do not form a closed circuit, since abjection cannot be appropriated without loss, and perhaps it cannot be signified without creating, often unwittingly, new sites of abjection.[49]

Christian in *The Celebration*.
Courtesy of Photofest.

Bataille points to the failure to assume with sufficient force the imperative act of exclusion of abject objects (which constitute the basis of collective existence).[50] If Bataille is correct when he suggests that "the imperative act of exclusion of abject things is the fate of all men but its efficacity and its rigor varies according to social conditions," then the issue is not so much how to avoid abjection, as how to figure it differently.[51] The poles of abjector and abjected will inevitably reassert themselves, but they will not do so in a fixed or determinate way. It is, then, not a matter of hoping to eliminate abjection altogether, but rather a matter of critically tracing its effects, taking seriously its affect, and thinking about how it might be refigured or reshaped. Bataille says that "it is impossible to give a positive definition, at once general and explicit, of the nature of abject things" (1970, 220). He thereby reminds us that abjection is not about designating anything as inherently abject, but concerns the act of ordering or structuring, an act that defines the abject as excluded or rejected only in producing lawful identities as lawful.[52]

In an essay included in the volume *Visions capitals*, whose title replicates that of her 1980 book, *Powers of Horror*,[53] Kristeva revisits the theme of abjection and art, with specific reference to works by Warhol, Picasso, Delacroix, Bacon, Klee and Artaud, among others (see 1998, 132). Kristeva says that without the horror of the feminine the power of horror would be insignificant (see 127). Depicting demented, fearful, and idiotic heads, decapitated, grimacing, and tearful heads, heads of the damned, heads of the dead, ravaged heads, Kristeva ends her essay with Picasso's *Bust of the Woman*, with its hair "confounded with a gigantic nose" (133), in which she sees the "sublime horror of the archaic feminine" (137). Although the abject denotes a stage prior to the Oedipal confrontation, it already borrows from it sexual connotations, which, although they might not yet be set in stone, prefigure the normative associations of paternity with law, and the maternal-feminine with abjection. The abject mother is already that from which the child must separate itself in order to become a subject capable of formulating its desires in accordance with paternal laws—foremost among them the taboo against incest. I want to insist on the necessity of analyzing the power of the abject, in all its disruptive capacity, not just from the point of view of a discourse that assumes the ultimate teleological authority of an Oedipal subject, but also from a point of view that garners the disruptive force of the abject in a direction that allows for an interrogation of the social parameters that it usually tends to produce.

Following up her suspicion of the "society of the image" (2002, 63), Kristeva says, "We are inundated with images, some of which resonate with our fantasies, and appease us but which, for lack of interpretative words, do not liberate us. Moreover the stereotype of these images deprives us of the possibility of creating our own imagery, our own imaginary scenarios" (2002, 67). Kristeva emphasizes the importance of renewal, describing her attempt to think the "work of revolt" as that which "opens psychical life to infinite re-creation" (2002, 6).

What does Kristeva propose in order to protect against the invasion of the spectacle, or the inundation of images? In order to prevent fantasies becoming merely mesmerizing, reductive, and repetitive, one must retain the role of interpretation that the symbolic can contribute. "The role of language is essential to the formulation of fantasies" (2002, 68) says Kristeva, or "when the imaginary implies creative work and fiction it involves linguistic signification" (1995a, 104). She neither wants to jettison images, nor to focus exclusively on symbolic representation, but rather to find the meaningful connections between them. "I seek the specular in the imaginary, that is, the trace of fantasy," says Kristeva (2002, 75). Aggression inscribes itself in the symbolic; the semiotic is rendered in the spectacle. The "specular," according to Kristeva, is "the final and very efficient depository of aggressions and anxieties," a "brilliant purveyor-seducer" (2002, 72).

Drawing on Freud's notion of primal fantasies, Kristeva says, "A presubjective structure, the primal fantasy, like the fantasy of the primal scene, the fantasy of castration, and the fantasy of seduction, does not necessarily constitute a sedimentation of individual experiences but hereditary schemas. The child invents these scenarios, which he represses, but the invention is only an eternal return of hereditary schemas that have actually taken place in preceding generations and are mysteriously encrypted in the psyche. . . . If it is true that all fantasies have analogous structures and reflect unconscious fantasy, the subject's entire life would appear to be shaped by the phantasmatic. Literature and art are the favored places for the formulation of fantasies, not their realization" (2002, 66). Kristeva goes on to say that the privileged place, "not for the realisation, but for the formulation of fantasies, is literature and art" (ibid.). "In this regard," she adds, "art and literature are allies of psychoanalysis; they open the way verbally to the construction of fantasies and prepare the terrain for psychoanalytic interpretation" (2002, 68). Since our drives and "originary fantasies" cannot "find psychical representation, they search for a way to act or for somatization" (ibid.). When our representations fail to connect up with the drives and pulsions that both underlie and give rise to them, when the symbolic becomes completely abstracted from the semiotic, crises ensue. While they stop short of identifying the Oedipus complex with original fantasy, Laplance and Pontalis show how Freud eventually has recourse to a phylogenetic account of fantasy.[54] Given her reliance on Freud's Oedipal formulation of fantasy, how far does Kristeva's celebration of narrative end up being akin to the ability to formulate our relationship to oedipal fantasies? And how far does the apparent open-endedness of the work of revolt that Kristeva endorses turn out to be seriously compromised by the confining normative appeal to an Oedipalized version of fantasy? If the crises that become recognizable are resolvable by such an appeal, imaginaries that run counter to this version, or that are abjected in order to shore it up, will be taken for granted and at the same time rendered unthinkable. As such they will constitute legitimating fantasies, but will not be capable of being thought as fantasy.

In capturing the imagination in unorthodox ways, by shaping desire in non-conventional modes, by fascinating the spectator in ways that she or he did not expect—perhaps did not want, had no (conscious) desire to become complicit in—Berliner manages to expose his audiences to the force of the socio-symbolic matrix that facilitates and constitutes the identificatory regimes that legitimate abjection. When Ludovic (Georges du Fresne) climbs into a freezer in *Ma vie en rose* (1997), tiring from his

Ludovic in *Ma vie en rose*.
Courtesy of Photofest

attempt to simply be who he is, we do not see a monstrous individual who challenges the fundamental lines of gender demarcation we might have supposed were in place. Ludo, an innocent child who finds himself caught in the maelstrom of societal boundaries and expectations, does not appear abject, but rather the society that tries to force him to identify as a boy. By making us see Ludo's world not only through the eyes of his parents but also through Ludo's own eyes, Berliner succeeds in rendering Ludo as a thoroughly sympathetic figure. Drawing us into his world, he exposes the rigidity of those who expect Ludo to simply conform to his body-type. Berliner asks us to confront our own preconceptions about who is allowed to be a girl, and who is not, by fusing social commentary with humor, whimsy, and fantasy. He doesn't preach; he shows how difficult life is not only for Ludo, but also for his parents, he explores how well they cope, but also how they, in turn, reach their breaking points. He thereby poses the question: how quickly would we reach ours? He challenges us to ask ourselves what it is like to be designated an aberrant other: how would we cope if we were Ludo, or Ludo's parents, or how might our being who we are rendered more comfortable by the fact that there are Ludos who we are not? How might our lives made more livable by the fact that we so easily relegate others to the domain of the unlivable, constructing our world according to definitions that reflect our own experience, and not allowing others to inhabit those worlds, requiring their abjection?

When Ludovic dresses in his sister's dress because he wants to look pretty, the reaction of his parents and neighbors is to make a joke of it. Their laughter deflects attention from the question Ludovic keeps asking throughout the film: am I a boy or a girl? "Laughing is a way of placing or misplacing abjection" (1982, 8), says Kristeva. Despite the laughter, Ludo persists in trying to be the girl he feels himself to be, refusing to go along with the deflection. The parents of the children in his class sign a petition to get Ludovic removed from the school, and the headmaster concedes their point, citing as his reason Ludovic's eccentricity. Ludovic moves to another school, where he is beaten up for being too much like a girl. His father is laid off from work shortly afterward and the family is forced to move to a lower class neighborhood. But before they go, there is an episode in which Ludo's mother takes up and turns around the abjection that this respectable neighborhood has visited upon Ludovic and his family by refusing to tolerate his behavior, by putting it out of bounds, by excluding his desire from the public arena. As a parting shot not only to Albert, the man who has just fired her husband because of Ludovic's inability to stop raising the question of his sexual identity, but also to the community that has just expelled them, she kisses Albert. She is an attractive woman. She kisses Albert on the mouth, a full, sexual, and passionate kiss, in front of his wife, on the front lawn of their house, and in full view of the neighbors. In doing so she upsets the boundaries of decorum. She thereby takes up the abjection that Ludo and his family have suffered, and redirects it to the people who have excluded, banished, and refused Ludo. A maverick kiss, a kiss that flies in the face of social boundaries and expectations, a kiss that takes on and throws back at the community the label of misfits with which it has designated them. A kiss that flirts with the boundaries of the acceptable and tolerable and the inadmissable and outrageous. I will be what you are asking me to be, I will accept what you have forced me to accept, I will incorporate your attempt to exclude me, I will become the perverted mother that you take me to be for my failure to force my son to be the boy that you want him to be, and I will cross the sexual boundaries with you that you think I have overstepped with him. I will put my tongue in your mouth, and leave you and your wife, your family, your symbol of respectability, to deal with the mess it puts you in.

The dynamic according to which marginalized subjects in turn abject others, often in an attempt to repudiate their own abjection, must be thought through. These others, in turn, often produce "other others." When those of us who maintain relatively privileged positions find ourselves rendered vulnerable, our reaction is often to re-inscribe still further the lines of demarcation separating those who inhabit zones that are livable, and those who are relegated to the unlivable marginal domains. Often this happens by appealing to dominant narratives that are secured by foundational fantasies, which Hollywood typically recycles and perpetuates. Yet film can also help us learn new ways of seeing—new ways of seeing ourselves and new ways of seeing others. Deepa Mehta explores this theme by means of a series of short, idyllic dream/flashback scenes, including the opening and closing images of *Fire*. We see a meadow of yellow flowers, in which a young Radha, frustrated in her attempt to follow the advice of her parents to "see without looking" but who finally announces "I can see the ocean." Sometimes we try too hard to see things differently, and often it is difficult to isolate the forces that converge and render possible a sudden shift of vision. In *Fire*, Sita acts as a catalyst to help the adult Radha see things differently—to see her duty toward her husband in a different light, and most of all to see the repression of her desire in a new light. Film can contribute to shifts in our ways of seeing things by eliciting affective investment in ways that challenge routine political identifications, organized according to legitimated fantasies. The symbolic effects of orchestrating such temporary interventions in social imaginaries demand to be articulated.

In her 1995 introductory essay to the catalog for the "Rites of Passage," an exhibit at the Tate Gallery, Kristeva identifies the artists as responding to the "banalisation" of the image. Pictorial signs, she suggests, "have lost their sensorial and instinctual force, as if they were no longer able to speak of corporeal experience and remained neutral. The artists seem to be trying to react to this banalisation or extenuation of the image."[55] Commenting on the Tate Gallery exhibit in an interview, Kristeva expresses concern about the tendency of the abject to become a "fetish."[56] She says, "Modern art was supposed to replace the absence of rites of passage, and to exhibit the abominable from which, by giving it form, the human being purifies himself" (ibid.). Kristeva indicates that verbal art carries with it less danger of fetishization than the image: "I find that, in a way, verbal art, insofar as it eludes fetishization, and constantly raises doubt and questioning, lends itself better perhaps to exploring these states that I call states of abjection. From the moment that you establish it in a sort of image or something representable, salable, exposable, capitalizable, you lose it."[57] The thought specular is Kristeva's attempt to answer to this problematic, since it resists on the one hand abstract speculation devoid of drives, and on the other hand mindless fascination devoid of critical reflection.[58]

In order not to suffer from a de-eroticization, in order to hold on to the images of our dream—"that private cinema of the public" (1986, 240)—we must acknowledge, with Kristeva, both that "Specular fascination captures terror and restores it to the symbolic order" (1986, 241), and that without the "demystification" that "hold[s] the spectator, still inside a phantasm, but at a distance from his own fascination" (1986, 242), and without symbolic, critical, discourse, "the cinema would be nothing but another Church" (1986, 242).

5

The *Exotica*-ization and Universalization of the Fetish, and the Naturalization of the Phallus: Abject Objections

> Abjection . . . is immoral, sinister, scheming, and shady: a terror that dissembles, a hatred that smiles, a passion that uses the body for barter instead of inflaming it, a debtor who sells you up, a friend who stabs you.
> —Kristeva, *Powers of Horror*

FILM HAS LENT itself peculiarly well to fetishistic analysis, from the heteronormative fascination with the fetishization of female body parts to the demystification of the magical transposition by which the increasingly technologically complex, labored, collective, and mediated enterprise of filmmaking enables immediate identification between the spectator/consumer and the characters on the silver screen. Does this marriage of fetishistic theory and the impact of film image conceal another identificatory process that is covered over by the excessive capital film theorists have invested in theories of fetishism? I suggest that there are moments of abjection, which both facilitate and are upheld by fetishistic structures, but which are also capable of undermining and refiguring those very structures. Such moments can constitute the most compelling and disturbing filmic experiences, and at the same time often the most politically salient dislocations. Moments of dissolution in which the identification that has been narratively built up breaks down or transforms itself into the distanciation of horror or revolt can illuminate for us assumptions hitherto inhabited relatively unthinkingly, offering up those assumptions for reflection and possibly for reworking.

The trajectory of this chapter will move from Jacques Lacan to Julia Kristeva, via Karl Marx, Claude Lévi-Strauss, and Sigmund Freud, and finally to a reading of Atom Egoyan's *Exotica*. By returning to Marx, and using the moment at which he calls for a new symbolic to supplant the form of commodity fetishism, I suggest that phallic logic should be cast against the background it disavows, against abjection. The logic of abjection exhibits an opportunistic exploitation: exploiting weak links, its divisive strategies territorialize along fissures of racial and class differences, as well as sexual difference—which does not privilege sexual difference over racial and class differences, as does the Oedipal, Western narrative. My use of psychoanalysis is motivated by the belief that we cannot do without a theory of the unconscious in order to confront dynamics such as that of white privilege, although neither can we use the traditional psychoanalytic formulations of the unconscious, which are themselves complicit with racist and sexist histories. Yet abjection reveals that repression is not the only operation at stake. As a radical form of exclusion, abjection is characterized not just by exclusion, but also by usurpation and expropriation. Symbolic systems benefit from what they exclude, without allowing the excluded proper representation.

My return to Marx is motivated by a belief that he offers us a way of thinking the difference between the symbolic formations of capitalism, and the possibility of forging new symbolics. If Marx's own analysis failed to analyze the surplus value arising from labor performed by women in housework, childcare, and the psychic work of mourning, it also needs to be supplemented in order to take account of the racial dynamic of labor patterns. While neither Marx nor Lacan shed light on women's subordination, Kristeva's notion of abjection helps to move in this direction, and can be applied beyond this reference to facilitate a thinking of the racialized other that feminist theory itself has help to reify.

Like social contract theory, which also posits a kind of prehistory—a state of nature—psychoanalysis appeals to a mythic time that might, must, or could have existed, the characteristics of which are read, negatively, off current socio-symbolic forms, and then projected into a lost and inaccessible past, which is nonetheless incorporated into the symbolic, in a way that marks it off as differentiated from the symbolic. Psychoanalytic theory repeats the gesture of social contract theory by appealing to a mythical past, which is thereby marked as primitive, uncivilized, and outside culture, at the same time as being incorporated by culture in a way that either inscribes it as deviant, or requires it to conform to its own logic, as preparatory.

Through an economy that is stipulated in terms of a series of oppositions that he associates with the mother-child dyad and the paternal metaphor, Lacan develops an account of the imaginary versus the symbolic. The alignment of the mother-child dyad with the imaginary and of the paternal metaphor with the symbolic is dependent upon the oppositions of presence to absence, immediacy to mediation, and mythical coherence or completion to division or splitting. The mother-child dyad thereby comes to represent a relation of immediacy, and comes to be posited as prior to symbolization or representation, while the phallus comes to represent splitting and division, and comes to be associated with the capacity for language. Lacan's account is also dependent upon a retroactive logic that consigns the imaginary to a prehistory, which is designated after the fact, and within the terms of the symbolic, as preoedipal.

The way in which psychoanalysis establishes itself as a myth of origin that guarantees its claim to symbolic authority by enshrining the phallus as an uncontestable law has been remarked by feminist theory.[1] Feminist responses to Lacan have also focused on the problematic of the phallus as transcendental signifier and its dependence upon constituting women's bodies as lacking or castrated, such that a masculine morphology is presupposed in a way that makes its normativity unavailable for interrogation. They have pointed to the slippage in Lévi-Strauss and Lacan between *a* symbolic and *the* symbolic.[2] But these insights have not been followed through to their logical conclusion by a rigorous questioning of the work that the trope of fetishism continues to accomplish, as it is exported from psychoanalytic theory to race theory and film theory and the field of cultural studies more generally. The extent to which psychoanalytic theory remains dependent on the logic of fetishism, and the consequences and ramifications of this for cultural theories that continue to draw on it as a resource, is in need of exploration.

To say that the logic of fetishism has been exported from psychoanalytic to race theory is to describe only the most recent history of a complex and multilayered series of fetish discourses that can be traced from the late Middle Ages to the twentieth century.[3] While my focus here is restricted to Marx's commodity fetishism and Freudian fetishism, I am interested in the ways in which discourses on the primitive that peripherally inhabit the texts of Marx and Freud have been suppressed by Marxist and psychoanalytic theorists, only to reemerge in new forms in race theory. This reemergence has in turn occurred in a way that tends to marginalize or repudiate the insights into class and sexuality that Marxist critics and feminist theorists had unearthed. It is as if the logic of disavowal at work in fetishism reinvents itself strategically, perpetuating a univocal meaning, suspending the multiplicity of its historical referents. Religion, race, imperialism, colonialism, sex, gender, class—all these terms surface as signifiers that articulate the discourse of fetishism at various historical epochs and locations, and each of them do so in such a way as to elide the significance of the others.[4]

Lacan's reliance on Lévi-Strauss has long been problematic for feminist theorists because the idea of exchange at the heart of Lévi-Strauss's

account appeals to women as the supreme object of exchange. By the end
of his study of kinship, the exceptional status of women seems to have
attained a logical necessity. "The emergence of symbolic thought must
have required that women, like words, should be things that were
exchanged. . . . In the matrimonial dialogue of men, woman is never
purely what is spoken about; for if women in general represent a certain
category of signs, destined to a certain kind of communication, each
woman preserves a particular value arising from her talent, before and
after marriage, for taking her part in a duet. In contrast to words, which
have wholly become signs, woman has remained at once a sign and a
value."[5] The moment at which women began to serve as things that were
exchanged is consigned to a prehistory, a kind of Rousseauan state of
nature, which can only be posited as what "must have" occurred. Lévi-
Strauss acknowledges that while women "in general represent a certain
category of signs," women also have a "particular value," but it is unclear
whether such particular values remain capable of representation. In
effect, the material or sensuous aspect of female sexuality has been cast
out of the symbolic system, taking on the status of the real, leaving only
women's status as signs that can be exchanged capable of signification.
Like Marx's commodities, women's function in exchange usurps their status as particular, disguising their particularity and rendering it inaccessible
to interrogation. The use value represented by women tends to fall out of
Lacan's account of women as signs, since the materiality/corporeality/sex-
uality of women as objects of desire and sites of reproduction is abstracted
in their representation as tokens of exchange. As Chase says, Lacan
"understands 'value' as exchange value or the condition of signification. . . . In this context, to identify with the phallus is to invest in a system of meaning ruled by language as a system of abstract values, signs
with a determinate difference between signifier and signified guaranteeing the presence of meaning. Language so conceived is a system of preex-
istent positions in which gendered subjects find their assigned place"
(1989, 71–77). Not only are these positions prearranged according to the
oedipal myth but also the contingency of that myth is not admitted into
the determinacy of the system of language or meaning. The symbolic
order now appears to be dependent on a particular social configuration—
the signification of women as gifts to be exchanged in marriage. If the
prohibition of incest is "the link between" the biological and the social,
doesn't the particular form it takes when it endows women with the status of "supreme gift" suffer a transposition into the realm of the natural by
virtue of the necessity Lévi-Strauss confers on the exchange of women?
     The equivocation embedded in Lévi-Strauss's account is one that gets
carried over to Lacan, and transported into the function of women as

facilitating the exchange of signs that constitutes communication, so that women come to be understood in terms of their function as sign, representation, or phallus.[6] This equivocation is one that allows Lévi-Strauss and Lacan to relegate women to their natural status as second-class citizens, whose role is to bear children, cement communities, and serve as conduits through which lines of inheritance can establish communal identities—all without noticing, or at least without acknowledging, that the move they employ is a naturalizing one.[7] So long as there is no confrontation with women's equivocal function as both the "natural" ground or constitutive outside of society, and as the cement that glues society together, facilitating the flow of signification, and constituting meaning, it hardly matters whether the symbolic is construed as either ideal or contingent. Whether one defends the symbolic by insisting on its ideal status, thereby attempting to divorce it from any normative or social definition, or insists that the symbolic is precisely normative rather than natural, one ignores the double valence of the category of woman. The point is that woman as a concept that facilitates communication functions both as a guarantor of meaning within society, and is expelled outside the system, as if it could function unproblematically as a ground—conventional or essential. To insist that the symbolic system is the only system of intelligibility that we have is a truism that avoids the salient question of how, in what ways, with what effects, and with what casualties, that system remains capable of challenge or transformation. Lacan says, "It is the world of words that creates the world of things—the things originally confused in the *hic et nunc* of the all in the process of coming-into-being. . . . Man speaks, then, but it is because the symbol has made him man. . . . the life of the natural groups that constitute the community is subjected to the rules of matrimonial alliance governing the exchange of women, and to the exchange of gifts determined by the marriage."[8] The question as to why it is women who serve as tokens of exchange, or how the status of women is conflated with the term "natural" in Lacan's discourse, and how women therefore operate as placeholders for the presocial, is one that is never raised. The equivocal status of women as both prehistorical, preoedipal bearers of material meaning, and symbolic members of a society, is therefore consigned to an unthinkable, imaginary past—the amorphous here and now of becoming. The value of women's bodies as reproductive vessels is presupposed in an untheorized way, so that they perform the function of use-values in a way that immediately appears in a disguised form, namely in terms of their exchange value not just of *a* mode of production, but as *the* mode of production, as meaning itself.[9] Since the system of exchange that women facilitate constitutes the very means by which signification is instituted, since their function as signs is what allows women to pass from one group to another in a move that is then identified as the founding moment of society, since there is an assimilation of meaning *per se* to the exchange or, in Gayle Rubin's words, "traffic in women," it becomes very difficult—if not impossible—to posit an alternative system of meaning.[10] The patriarchal system appears to be the only one, but that is because it presents itself as naturalized. If this appearance is left unchallenged, an array of questions that are crucial for confronting issues of social oppression are simply left aside. As Castoriadis puts it, "Why *this* system of symbols and not another? What are the meanings conveyed by the symbols, the system of signifieds to which the system of signifiers refers? Why and how do the symbolic networks become autonomous?"[11] Just as Marx argued with regard to the categories of bourgeois economy, which came to appear implacable and fixed within the mode of commodity production, so the symbolic economy of psychoanalysis appears to be unassailable within a patriarchal organization of society.

Jacqueline Rose suggests that Lacan's later conception of language does not fall prey to the same objection as Lévi-Strauss, but her differentiation between the early and later work only succeeds in shifting the problematic to another level, not in dissipating it. In her discussion of Lacan, Rose does not address the extent to which the Lacanian phallus is thoroughly implicated in a fetishistic discourse.[12] Neither does she acknowledge that the imaginary, masculine morphology that is assumed by Freud prevents him from developing a theory of maternal identification.[13]

While feminist theory has firmly established that the Freudian subject is modeled on male experience, and that this privilege is conflated with the universality of language, the implications of this insight have been applied inconsistently to one of the most dramatic examples of such an investment, namely, Freud's account of fetishism.[14] Freud's masculinist morphology is coupled with the failure of the male imagination to acknowledge sexual difference, a failure that nonetheless has done little to dislodge the transcendent status taken on by the myth of castration, a myth that is intimately tied to the logic of fetishism.[15] The value of the phallic economy sustains itself by imposing its measure of what constitutes pleasure on any body that does not immediately conform to masculine sexuality. Hence, the fact that women's bodies lack a penis does not deter Freud from providing them with one, in one way or another, in a logic that conforms to the apparatus of fetishism. Freud thus manufactures for women the missing penis that nature is constructed as having failed to provide for women. It is not merely that nature is found wanting according to the masculinist imaginary that Freud refrains from questioning, but rather that even nature is made to confirm the expectation that women should have a penis. Freud finds that the "science of biology . . . justifies" the prejudice that "all human beings have the same (male) form of genital" in that it "has been obliged to recognize the female clitoris as the true substitute for the penis."[16] Science is thus constructed by Freud to conform to the expectations of the fetishist, and biology is understood to provide women with a substitute penis, a copy that provides a prototype for the phallic mother.

It becomes clear that psychoanalysis has not effected a return to the body as such, but has merely elevated and idealized the experience of the masculine subject, abstracting from the bodily pleasures afforded by masturbation, and universalizing the value of these very specific, corporeal experiences into an economy of satisfaction that can be represented according to the measure of the phallus. Meanwhile, the specific bodily pleasures of female sexuality are neglected, and female anatomy appears either as a site of difference that would threaten the universal value of the phallic economy, or as a gap or hole in an economy that sustains the myth of the same, which imposes its measure of what constitutes pleasure on any body that does not immediately conform to masculine sexuality. The missing part, the lack of the penis, must be compensated. Woman must be made whole, made to conform to the always already phallic male model. The clitoris is designated a penis-equivalent, which prevents Freud from having to bring into question his one-sex model, or from having to confront female sexuality as differing from male sexuality. The mother is represented as phallic, which keeps at bay the horror of the female genitals, or the fetishist invents for females the missing penis that they lack. Perhaps it will not have escaped notice that the various maneuvers that Freud employs to prevent women from interfering with the myth of the same replicate kettle logic (I didn't borrow the kettle; it had a hole in it before I borrowed it; I gave it back without a hole).[17] Women already have a penis, albeit an inferior copy or an inadequate version in comparison to men. Women don't have a penis: they are always already castrated. Women always already have a penis: the phallic mother. The hidden agenda is the myth of the same. Instead of a lack, the phallic economy produces penis substitutes: clitoris-penis, phallic mother, fetish. The inability of boys to imagine that girls lack a penis, despite the evidence of their senses, and the proclivity to provide them with the missing penis that would otherwise figure as a lack, testify to the powerful assumption of the myth of sameness. The myth of the same fuels the masculine imaginary, which is grounded in an unthematized privileging of male anatomy.

Not only does the myth of sameness infect psychoanalysis, in a way that makes unavailable for interrogation its masculine, white biases.

The metaphysical prejudice of presence also informs castration theory. Girls are assumed to be wanting, given the evidence of the absence of a penis—a lack, however, that is based on the disparity between what is seen and the *expectation* that they should have a penis. The normative force of such an expectation resides in an attachment to the following unstated assumption: the basic similarity of all humans, where humanity is defined by default according to male traits (phallic activity, for example). Once that similarity is found to be wanting, its lack is met only with the insistence on such similarity, and its production, even in the face of evidence to the contrary. Taken together, the assumption of sameness and the fetishistic reaction to its empirical lack reveal a more fundamental ideological commitment to an account of experience that is in fact based on pleasure derived from white, male anatomy, but which takes on an idealized and independent existence, precisely as imaginary. This imaginary achieves creative potential and becomes capable of grounding new ideas about subjectivity, ideas that proceed in ignorance and oblivion of their repudiation of their feminine and racialized others. In this way the discourse of disavowal has taken hold in both race theory and neo-Marxist theory, which are able to proceed without paying any attention to the abject status of the feminine and racialized others that fetishism both produces and disavows.

In its celebration of the phallus as a transcendental signifier, as a signifier in relation to which the only possibility of meaning is relative to its privileged status, theory reenacts the denial that is at the heart of commodity fetishism. The substitution of use-value by exchange-value is now reproduced with a slightly different twist, one that is somewhat reminiscent of Adorno and Horkheimer's critique of enlightenment thinking for endorsing the currency of abstraction, in which all meaning comes to the same thing, and only one meaning is recognized, an abstract uniformity divorced from objects in themselves.[18] Unfortunately, Adorno reproduced some of the problems that his critique of enlightenment thinking was intended to expose when he not only allowed his critique of the fetishism of consumer culture to succumb to a somewhat arbitrary division between high and low culture but also unthinkingly drew on racialized language that needs to be problematized. Adorno compares the ecstasy that "takes possession" of "jitterbugs" who "differentiate themselves by pseudoactivity" from "the mass of the retarded" to "the ecstasies savages go into in beating the war drums" (1982, 292). He thereby manages at one stroke both to enact an unthinking racism and to denigrate the musical taste of the "retarded" masses by implying that their cultural and intellectual debasement puts them on a level with those who are assumed to occupy an even lower level of humanity, namely "savages."

Adorno thus repeats the racializing gestures that inhabit Freud's texts, gestures that I am suggesting should be read as abject moments.[19] Here the abject is inhabited not by the feminine, but by the racialized other, as if the abject is—despite Lacanian protests—capable of resignification.[20] Its inherently mobile momentum or charge gets passed on from feminine sexuality to race, so that it circulates from one discourse to another, in a resignification that presupposes a colonialist imaginary.[21] The redemptive move that saves women by associating them with their white, male counterparts is one that puts the racialized other completely beyond the pale.

By focusing attention on the maternal relation as the locus of a primal mapping that is not yet symbolic or syntactic, but is on the cusp of the semiotic and symbolic, Kristeva's notion of abjection offers a way of reworking the dominant psychoanalytic model.[22] Maternal authority involves an ordering of the world in terms of the proper and the improper, or the inner and the outer, which in turn presents the infant with a means of organizing the world into self and other. This ordering, which is not yet fully symbolic (but borders on the symbolic), and does not presuppose the development of a superego, does not require the installation of paternal authority in the form of the law, although it is referred to a third—a loving, imaginary father, which Kristeva models on Freud's father of preindividual history.[23] The infant must, by means of rejection, distance itself from its source of sustenance and protection. It must abject the mother. Yet, since abjection is prior to the onset of sexual difference, it is not quite accurate to speak of the mother, insofar as to do so assumes that the mother is gendered, and as such differentiated from the father. In other words, to designate the first object as maternal, is already to assume the acquisition of language and acculturation from the standpoint of an oedipalized and castrated subject. The abjection of the mother is bound up with the need to establish autonomy, which is figured in terms of becoming a speaking subject (and perhaps what needs to be added to the psychoanalytic account is a subject that can be heard, since not all subjects are positioned in a relationship of authority to speech). To abject the mother is to move away from the immediacy of need and toward the mediation of desire. Abjection is the initial and unstable site of differentiation for the infant, not yet of sexual differentiation, but in terms of separation from what comes to be designated, retrospectively, as the maternal body. Since that which is constituted as abject is already shaped by the masculine imaginary, the value of which is secured by a phallic economy that assures its predominance by reproducing fetishes, it becomes clear that the privilege attached to the maternal proceeds from the phallic psychoanalytic privileging of sexual difference. Perhaps, then, the paternal metaphor cedes its role as the organizing principle of discourse, in certain instances, to the economy of race. So long as the myth of castration continues to posit as ideal (even if unrealized for masculine subjects) the completed masculine corpus, a completion that is disavowed, the fragmentation of the female body continues to serve as the abjected feminine. Its status as incomplete, as a body in parts, lacks the organizing phallic principle, unless provided with one through the manufacture of fetishes. If the logic of castration is transferred to race, the trope of fetishism is recycled in a way that privileges whiteness as an alternate principle of completion, making the racialized other play the role of abjected other. The constitutive outside of a system that produces its contrary is displaced onto race, but the logic of the system remains unchallenged. Now the raced other is spat out of an unmarked economy of whiteness, but such a displacement merely transfers the cultural capital of fetishism to race, rather than altering the logic of displacement. The abjection of the feminine remains in place, but its place is no longer marked as such. The sexuality of women, and the racialization of bodies, become unthinkable and impossible from the point of view of a white, patriarchal symbolic. Ejected from the system of equivalent and exchangeable signs, they come to occupy the site of the real.

Since, for Kristeva, the mother must be abjected in order for the infant to become a subject, it might seem that the discourse of abjection can only achieve a more detailed account of the differentiation of the mother-child dyad than either Freud or Lacan provide, and indeed, at least in some of its registers, this rather limited role is confirmed in Kristeva's discourse. Abjection merely plays the role of precursor to castration theory, consolidating the mother as expendable, as outside the symbolic system, containing her in the imaginary, preoedpial realm, and representing her as that which must be rejected, thereby carving out her role as signifying the castrating, fearful other. If Kristeva herself affirms such a reading on the whole, a more dramatic reorientation of psychoanalysis can be opened out by following through her insights into abjection in a way that points beyond the confining oedipal narrative into which Kristeva's own account falls back. Far from abandoning the phallus, Kristeva reaffirms it.[24] She also recognizes that it does not have the same affect on the girl as it does for the boy. "The phallic phase is structural, therefore for both sexes, but it is so in a different way for the girl and for the boy. Each confronts (phallic) power and (paternal) meaning (removed from the sensible connection to the mother) . . . but the boy tries out that confrontation with the conviction of 'belonging to it,' and the girl with the impression of a *strangeness*" (59). So, "the girl will be part of the phallic order. But since she will remain a stranger there, she will preserve a sense of inferiority, of exclusion, or, at best, of irony" (59).

Thus, strangeness can confer "on certain women the appearance of a dis-abused and benevolent maturity, a serene detachment that . . . is the true sense of what Hegel so enigmatically calls the 'eternal irony of the com-munity'" (60). Thus *"detachment"* is the "very mark of femininity" (ibid.). Kristeva relates this "distance" or "irony" to the maternal (ibid.).[25] Antigone is thus read as an abject figure, as constitutive of a system that both excludes and incorporates her, as the unassimilable part object that is only included in the dialectic in terms that have already decided in favor of its teleology. The terms that contest that teleology are marked out pre-cisely not only by her exclusion from that system but also by her refusal of its logic, a refusal that amounts to a transgression of that logic and thereby opens up the possibility of new logics, new symbolic meanings.

At the same time as affirming the phallus, Kristeva introduces a map-ping, or ordering of the world, a "first cartography of identity" that admits of an authority that precedes the phallic order of castration, that subtends the symbolic, linguistic meaning it introduces.[26] This "maternal authority" is "warded off" by "sacred rites" (95), which designate certain substances as "dirty or contagious or dangers 'in themselves' only because they fall under the prohibition" (92) ordained by a *"system of classification"* (92). The "rules of separation or exclusion" (91) operate, according to Kristeva, in line with "two prototypes of filth (excrement and menses)" (95).[27] Filth is "always related to the orifices or boundaries of the body, as so many land-marks constituting the corporeal territory" and it is either "excremental" or "menstrual" (94). "Excrement (and its equivalents: rot, infection, ill-ness, cadaver, hair, and so on) represents the danger stemming from what is external to the 'proper' or to the '(logical) order'; conversely, menstrual blood threatens the relation between the two sexes and represents the danger stemming from within sexual and social identity" (95). The abject then is the always improperly excluded other, that which is expelled in an attempt to maintain the sanctity and integrity of the subject.

In effect, Kristeva reworks the logic of Freud's *Totem and Taboo,* by offering an interpretation of ritual, of the forging of distinctions between what is clean and proper on the one hand and unclean and improper on the other hand.[28] Religious and sacred rituals perform divisions between the sacred and the profane, between the pure and the impure, by mapping the world into territories. This mapping is linked to the cor-poreal mapping that divides excrement from the body, the infant from the breast, the I from the not-I, and, ultimately, society from its outcasts. The abjection of the mother is a necessary and primordial process that divides the child from the mother, defining the boundaries of the self, and in doing so designates what was previously conflated with the I as that which is to be rejected. Prior to the prohibition of the incest law, an originary process of discrimination takes place, a semiotic ordering, which is not yet the symbolization of language, but which gives rise to and shapes the symbolic. As social practices, rituals of division and separation already partake of the social structure, but they do so at a mythical, rather than a symbolically articulated level. Kristeva associates the semiotic with the Platonic chora for good reason: it is what gives rise to spatial differentiation, making possible the ordering of bodies that language will, retroactively, organize into codes. While I think the notion of abjection provides a useful interpretive device, unlike Kristeva I do not think its scope should be restricted to a description of the infant's rejection of the mother. On the contrary, I see abjection as inherently mobile, and as descriptive of a mechanism by which various others are stipulated as excluded, in particular, raced, classed, and sexually deviant others. I also think that rather than seeing processes of constitutive differentiation as coterminous with socio-symbolic myths as Kristeva does, there is a need to reflect on their divergence from symbolic legitimations.

To untangle the theoretical complexity of the excluded other, marked by the maternal-feminine, is to confront the history by which psychoanalytic categories have converged around castration theory and the logic of fetishism. The mother comes to represent lack within an order of representation that operates retroactively to situate the mother's body as a sign that is constitutive of a lost past. The closure of the system of signs that the maternal body effects erases its specificity at the same time as consigning it to a prehistory that is unintelligible strictly in terms of the system it facilitates. Materiality, lack, and the maternal thus become inscribed in a complex web that is both constitutive of the system of representation, and excluded as its unthought outside, its prehistorical other. Three strands of this problematic can be analytically isolated from one another. First, there is the temporal problematic of how the unconscious is constructed through a process of selective memory and repression. Second, there is the problem of abstraction from materiality, a process that invokes universality, idealization, and homogenization, and that finds its ultimate expression in the birth or acquisition of language. Third, there is the historical circumstance by which the maternal body comes to be a privileged site of constitutive loss as a corollary of privileging the phallus. Each of these strands has been confounded with one another in a series of historical configurations that have produced various polemics at the intersection of film theory, psychoanalytic theory, and feminist theory.

Might it not be possible to use the lesson inscribed in Marx's account of commodity fetishism not only to confront Lacanian assumptions about women's status as representative of the phallus but also the racist economy that is typically left intact even by feminist revisions of psychoanalysis?

In commodity fetishism, commodities take on, as Marx famously puts it, "a life of their own," becoming the master of men (instead of vice versa).[29] The social/personal relations between men become obscured, as they are transposed into the commodity form. This process of mystification constitutes the riddle of commodity fetishism. Once the products of labor no longer serve as strict use-values, once they leave the level of pure need, and enter into a cycle of production where they are produced not only to satisfy needs but also for the purpose of exchange, something decisive has changed. Similarly, a displacement of the value of women's bodies takes place, such that female bodies cannot be figured as valuable, except in symbolic terms, which are already marked as masculine/universal. Commodities are now produced for the express purpose of being exchanged, such that their nature as commodities is now figured into the production process. The abstraction that capital represents renders quantitatively equivalent the duration or magnitude of labor time that it takes for two different objects to be produced. In this process of abstraction, which already liquidates the specificity of workers by appealing to a notion of the average worker (thereby rendering irrelevant sex, race, and sexuality), the particularity of the labor power, its qualitative features, and the materiality of the object are all rendered irrelevant. All that counts is that the amount of time it takes a worker to produce a loaf of bread can be calculated in units equivalent to the amount of time it takes another worker to produce a certain garment. Taken to its logical conclusion, this entails the replaceability, or substitutability, of one worker with another (along with all the aspects of alienation that goes along with the worker's estrangement from his own creative process, which is exacerbated by the factory system).

Marx says, "If I state that coats or boots stand in a relation to linen because the latter is the universal incarnation of abstract human labour, the absurdity of the statement is self-evident" (169). Yet, the same kind of absurdity is at work when producers use "gold or silver" as a "universal equivalent" by which to render the value of coats and boots. The "relation between their own private labour and the collective labor of society" appears as if it were fixed and implacable, when in fact the proportions dictating exchange are merely a result of "customary stability" and not at all the result of "the nature of the products" (167). Having established the absurdity of assuming that such stability resides in any natural facet of the product itself, Marx argues that, "The categories of bourgeois economics . . . are forms of thought which are socially valid, and therefore objective, for the relations of production belonging to this historically determined mode of social production, i.e. commodity production. The whole mystery of commodities, all the magic and necromancy that surrounds the

products of labour on the basis of commodity production, vanishes therefore as soon as we come to other forms of production" (169). Could it
be that Freud has made the mistake of naturalizing the phallus by taking
it to provide the gold standard by which all pleasure is to be measured,
such that he even finds confirmation in biology and science?[30]

Much as bourgeois categories of thought are taken by the economists
to be fixed, when in fact they only apply to the capitalist class, so the phallus is taken to be naturalized by Lacanians. The failure to situate the categories of psychoanalysis within a cultural context amounts to a refusal to
admit that the very way in which the unconscious is figured might entail
masculinist, racist, and classist assumptions. Irigaray says, addressing
Lacanians, "You refuse to admit that the unconscious—your concept of the
unconscious—did not spring fully armed from Freud's head, that it was
not produced *ex nihilo* at the end of the nineteenth century, emerging suddenly to reimpose its truth on the whole of history—world history, at
that—past, present and future. The unconscious is revealed as such, heard
as such, spoken as such and interpreted as such within a tradition. It has a
place within, by and through a culture" (1991, 80). The purported universality of the symbolic order, Irigaray suggests, is in fact based on an
imaginary configuration that prioritizes masculine morphology. "The symbolic, which you impose as a universal innocent of any empirical or historical contingency, is *your* imaginary transformed into an order, into the
social" (1991, 94). What needs to be added is that the morphology that is
prioritized is not only masculine, but also, by default, white. And that the
discourse of fetishism elaborated by psychoanalytic theory not only owes a
debt to Marx's commodity fetishism, but also to a racialized interpretation
of religion—with which Marx famously compares fetishism. The trope of
race is erased by both Marx and Freud (and, by extension, by neo-Marxists
and Lacan), appearing only in isolated pockets, in passages that line up
"savages" with the primitive state of the feminine, such that women and
raced others function at the level of an originary, mythical, excluded other,
outside civilization, banished to the unconscious of psychoanalytic theory.

Both Marx and Freud appeal to a notion of substitution in their theories of fetishism. In the case of Marx, what gets replaced is the sensuous,
material, physical aspect of that which is produced as a use-value, including the variety of qualitatively different forms of labor that result in the
production of manifold use-values through a division of labor. Considered
as a commodity, as having value conferred upon it through exchange,
this physical, sensuous dimension is abstracted from, such that a uniform equality now represents the total amount of labor expenditure
that goes into the production of each product. The substitution of the
sensuous dimension for the supra-sensuous dimension is at the same

time a transferal of the social dynamic between human beings to the abstract realm of quantitative determination, where all that counts is the duration or magnitude of labor, and not the quality of individual skills, talent, or originality. Thus the product itself seems to be endowed with a power that in fact derives from a personal relationship, but which now stands over against the worker, and confronts it as alien. Marx can there-fore refer to value as a "social hieroglyphic" that is in need of deciphering (167), and of the "determination of the magnitude of value by labour-time" as "a secret hidden under the apparent movements in the relative values of commodities" (168). In the case of Freud the meaning of the fetish is likewise obscured, but this time it is hidden not from the fetishist but only from other people.[31]

For Freud, it would seem at first glance that the nature of the sub-stitution is similar to that of Marx's commodity fetishism, insofar as the penis (sensuous, material, physical) is replaced by the fetish (which, in its capacity as representational, is suprasensuous, symbolic, abstract). Yet, there are two vital complications, not only because it turns out that the penis that is substituted by the fetish never existed in the first place, but also because it also turns out that the status of the fetish is not so easy to determine. A closer examination of fetishism is called for. What, if not an actual penis, does the fetish replace, and what, if not merely symbolic, is the exact nature of the fetish?

It emerges from Freud's earliest (1905) discussion of fetishism, sup-plemented by additions in 1910, 1915, and 1920, that fetishism substi-tutes a body part (a foot or hair) or an inanimate object (a piece of clothing, fur, or underlinen), and that the choice of the fetish is often bound up with the childhood expectation or imagination that the female genitals are in fact male.[32] As such, the fetish is a material object, but it also carries with it from the beginning a symbolic weight of an earlier memory. It is the (perhaps unconscious) residue of the childhood belief that women have penises. In his 1927 essay "Fetishism," Freud puts the matter "more plainly: the fetish is a substitute for the woman's (the mother's) penis that the little boy once believed in and—for reasons familiar to us—does not want to give up" (1953f, 152). The fetish then, is not a replacement for the penis as such, but a replacement for the boy's *belief* that the mother has a penis.

At the most general level the fetish replaces the "sexual object" (1953r, 153), but what becomes clear in the essay on fetishism is the sym-bolic function of the fetish as a "memorial" to the "horror of castration" and the fact that "an aversion . . . to the real female genitals" is "never absent in any fetishist" (1953f, 154).[33] Freud compares the repression that occurs in the setting up of the fetish to that of "traumatic amnesia": "it is as though the last impression before the uncanny and traumatic one is retained as a fetish . . . pieces of underclothing, which are so often chosen as a fetish, crystallize the moment of undressing, the last moment in which the woman could still be regarded as phallic" (1953f, 155). By the time Freud writes "An Outline of Psycho-analysis," the castration complex is not just compared to trauma, but is regarded *as* the "greatest trauma" of life (1953p, 155). What the fetish stands in for is the "horror," "aversion," and "fright of castration at the sight of a female genital" (1953f, 154). The fetish functions as a "token of triumph" (1953f, 154) in that it affirms that "the woman has got a penis, in spite of everything; but this penis is no longer the same as it was before" (1953f, 154). The fetish also functions as a "protection" (1953f, 154) against castration, since for the fetishist "if a woman had been castrated, then his own penis was in danger" (1953f, 153). Perhaps even more importantly for Freud, the fetish "saves the fetishist from becoming homosexual, by endowing women with the characteristic which makes them tolerable as sexual objects" (1953f, 154). The logic of fetishism, then, is to make women seem like men in order to (i) save men from the threat of castration, and (ii) save them from becoming homosexual. By endowing women with fetishes, men can tolerate us, that is, they can accept that we are not men only by conferring upon women the appearance of men, by using fetishes to disguise women as men, and to distract them from the horror of the reality: women are not men! Women, in fact, do not have penises. The only way in which the fetishist is able to retain a woman as a sexual object, it would seem, is by effectively denying her sexuality. Recall that for Freud "a certain degree of fetishism is habitually present in normal love" (1953r, 154) and it becomes clear that a certain degree of denial is habitually present in all men—or at least in those men that love in ways that Freud would deem "normal," that is, heterosexual.

To the question of why the child expects the woman to have a penis in the first place, where this belief derives from, Freud can only appeal to self-evidence. "It is self-evident to a male child that a genital like his own is to be attributed to everyone he knows and he cannot make its absence tally with his picture of these other people" (1953r, 195).[34] Or, as he puts it in "On the Sexual Theories of Children," the boy attributes *"to everyone, including females, the possession of a penis,* such as the boy knows from his own body . . . the boy's estimate of its value is logically reflected in his inability to imagine a person like himself who is without this essential constituent" (1953t, 215). It is clear then that the law of sameness derives from the assumption that everyone's body must be like the little boy's own body. It is also clear that the value attributed to the penis is responsible for the boy's *failure to imagine* a person *like himself* without such a valuable organ. Freud says that the "effect of th[e] 'threat of castration' is proportionate to the value set upon that organ and is quite extraordinarily deep and persistent" (1953t, 217). There is, then, a logic of equivalence set in motion between the threat of the absence of the penis and the immense value of the penis, a value based on the pleasure it gives. Just as for Marx, twenty yards of linen is equivalent to one coat, or ten pounds of tea, and these proportions are represented by a third measure provided by the money form, and represented by two ounces of gold (see 1977, 162), so, for Freud, the effect of the threat of castration is proportionate to the value placed on the penis, both of which are measured by the assumption of likeness. The more pleasurable the sensations of the penis, the more concerned the boy will be about its loss, and the more he will be impelled to compensate for its absence in girls, as a means of assurance against his own castration.

In the "Splitting of the Ego in the Process of Defence," Freud picks up again both on the failure of imagination, and the language of value: the boy "cannot easily imagine the possibility of losing such a highly prized part of his body" (1953u, 276).[35] Rather than giving up "the satisfaction of the instinct" the fetishist "created a substitute for the penis which he missed in females—that is to say, a fetish. In so doing, it is true that he had disavowed reality, but he had saved his own penis. So long as he was not obliged to acknowledge that females have lost their penis, there was no need for him to believe the threat that had been made against him: he need have no fears for his own penis, so he could proceed with his masturbation undisturbed . . . he effected no more than a displacement of value" (1953u, 277).[36] An economy of pleasure, circulating around the penis, is in operation. The pleasure of satisfaction gained from the penis is what confers value on it. A certain equivalence is therefore assumed by the boy, along the lines that any human being must be like himself. To put this in the language of Marx's commodity fetishism (read via Adorno) for a moment, it is as if the boy is saying that any other human being must of necessity be the same as himself, and if this turns out not to be the case, he will simply make it the case. The language of abstraction that is in play here deals in the currency of a masculine imaginary that protects itself from confronting any threat to its uniformity by providing alibis, which also protect against any confrontation with the truth that would otherwise emerge: were it not for the universalization of fetishism, Freud would have to confront the reality of his claims, which consist in construing all men as basically homosexual in their desires. This is the hidden message of fetishism, its secret, one from which Freud himself is at pains to distance himself, one that must remain veiled and covered up.

For Freud, in one sense the answer to the question "what is it that the fetish replaces?" is the female sexual organs. The material, physical, sensuous reality for which the fetish becomes a substitute is women's genitals, and the symbolic status of fetishistic discourse universalizes sexuality, by abstracting from the unique sexuality of each woman and putting in its place fabricated fetishes that come to represent the productivity of the masculine imagination, and the strength of his prejudice. Freud says of the penis "the boy's estimate of its value is logically reflected in his inability to imagine a person like himself who is without this essential constituent. When a small boy sees his little sister's genitals, what he says shows that his prejudice is already strong enough to falsify his perception. He does not comment on the absence of a penis but invariably says, as though by way of consolation and to put things right: 'Her ——————'s still quite small. But when she gets bigger it'll grow all right.' "[37]

If in one sense what the fetish substitutes itself for is the female sex organs, in another, what it substitutes is the pleasure the boy derives from his own penis. The failure of imagination, and the boy's refusal to see the reality of the situation except in terms that mystify it, due to his assumption of likeness between the sexes, combine to attribute to the girl a penis that she does not in fact have. The boy only supposed its existence, and in his reluctance to give up the idea that the girl must have a penis—since he cannot imagine her not having one—he finds a substitute for it. It must be emphasized that, since the penis that the fetish replaces never existed, except as imaginary, in Freud's account of fetishism, rather than the sensuous being replaced by the supra-sensuous—as in Marx's commodity fetishism—the movement is the reverse. Here we have an imaginary penis being replaced by a stand-in that does in fact have a real sensuous existence. Yet the value of the fetish lies not in its sensuous aspect, but precisely in the symbolic value that accrues to it by virtue of its substitution as equivalent to male morphology. The labor of the masculine imaginary that has produced the fetish by modeling it on the male penis was rendered invisible by its conversion into the symbolic economy of the phallus.[38] Freud says, "The meaning of the fetish is not known to other people, so the fetish is not withheld from him: it is easily accessible and he can readily obtain the sexual satisfaction attached to it. What other men have to woo and make exertions for can be had by the fetishist with no trouble at all."[39] Two points are of particular interest. First, the fetish hereby takes on an exceptional status with regard to the circuit of meaning, such that its meaning is veiled from others and thus it seems to signify outside the symbolic, signifying in a way to which only the fetishist has private and privileged access. Secondly, access to the fetish appears to dispense with the necessity of effort. The fetishist expends no labor: he makes no "exertions" but obtains satisfaction without any "trouble at all."[40] While others have to work for satisfaction, the fetishist has an easy way of achieving it, one moreover that remains opaque to others. It is as if the fetish retains its hieroglyphic status for society in general, while the fetishist alone can decipher its secret. There is no need for social change, no need to unravel the mysterious nature of the fetish by confronting the form of its production with another mode. At one stroke, Freud seems to have safeguarded the fetish, exempting it from possible critique by privatizing its meaning. The fetish is both a universal strategy—Freud says that due to the "overvaluation of the sexual object, which inevitably extends to everything that is associated with it [a] certain degree of fetishism is . . . habitually present in normal love"—and yet retains its particular meaning for the individual because its significance is disguised from others.[41] Critiques of such phallic economies need to recall that the imaginary production that has fashioned fetishism has done so on the basis of an unarticulated abjection of the feminine and the racialized other. Atom Egoyan's *Exotica* (Canada, 1994), to which I now turn, performs such a critique, by exploring the dynamic of fetishism in a context that restores the context of racialized, commodified, exploitative relationships within which it is enacted, but from which it is so often abstracted. I want to show both how *Exotica* follows the logic of fetishism, and how it undermines or interrogates that logic, at least as it functions within the narrowly defined sphere of psychoanalytic theory.

Through his identification of Christina (Mia Kirshner) with his murdered daughter Lisa, Francis (Bruce Greenwood) sets up Christina as a fetishized memorial to his lost object.[42] In doing so he preserves a melancholic attachment to his dead daughter, while at the same time reenacting the trauma of castration, confronting his failure to protect her, thereby trying to regain a sense of his identity as a father-figure. His need to protect Christina, his desire to fetishize her, is also a failure to confront the death of Lisa. By displacing his paternal desire for Lisa onto Christina, he can continue to deny the loss of his daughter, and to enact the fantasy of completion and omnipotence that his fetishistic relationship to Christina facilitates. His melancholic and fetishistic denial of his lost object also finds expression in his relationship with another young girl, Tracey (Sarah Polley). The daughter of Harold (Victor Garber), Francis's brother, who was in the car accident that killed Francis's wife, "babysits" for Francis while he visits Christina at Club Exotica. The fact that there is no baby to sit, that Lisa is dead, is one that Francis conveniently circumvents by maintaining the façade that Tracey is house-sitting, while at the same time having her practice the piano, thereby once again substituting for his daughter, who played the piano so well. As fetish, the piano covers over the actual loss of his daughter, and elides the difference between Tracey and Lisa, just as Christina's schoolgirl uniform masks her castration and her identification with Lisa. That said, the fetishistic resemblances among Tracey, Christina, and Lisa will only take us so far—unless, of course, we take up the trope of fetishism (replete with its imaginary castration), and apply it not only to gender but also to race—as has indeed been done by film and race theorists. For Francis's daughter and wife were black, as we see from a photograph of Lisa, which depicts her in school uniform, with her mother. Unless we read over this racial differentiation, or assimilate it to fetishism, we must ask what it means for two white females to come to stand in for Francis's loss of his daughter and wife. Both Tracey and Christina play the role of babysitters for Lisa, which also places them in the position of mother substitutes, stand-ins for Francis's wife. As a stand-in for Francis's wife, Tracey covers over her loss in more than one way. Francis's brother and Tracey's father, Harold, not only survived the crash, but allegedly had an affair with Francis's wife. How, then, is Francis's symbolic replacement of his daughter and wife with the white-skinned Tracey and Christina to be read? Is Francis compensating for his transgression of racial taboos? Is he masking the racial signifiers that mark his loss? Is he rewriting history as a concession to the fact that white middle-class society might not have been ready to tolerate racial diversity to the point of miscegenation? By installing Christina and Tracey in place of his daughter and wife, is Francis conforming to the racial boundaries that he had disrupted by marrying a black woman and giving birth to her child? Or has he himself come to identify with the racialized other, having been accused of murdering his daughter, and finding himself on the wrong side of the law that, as a tax inspector, he is used to upholding in his role as overseer, ensuring that others comply with the law? Why was Lisa murdered, and why was Francis a suspect? Was he a suspect even before the murder was committed, due to his transgression of the racial law, was he a suspect waiting for a crime to happen, of which he could be accused? Had his racial transgression already put him on the wrong side of the law?

Before the death of his daughter and wife Francis seemed to have the perfect, middle-class, heterosexual life. The fact that his marriage was interracial has been read as a product of Egoyan's progressive, normalizing agenda.[43] Even if Egoyan could be said to employ normalizing racial strategies, it still remains to ask: how are we to read Francis's fetishistic and melancholic identification of his black wife and daughter with two white girls? What does it mean to position a black woman as the object of desire of two white men?

If Christina's schoolgirl attire serves as a fetish for Francis, the transference of Francis's paternal attention into a fetishizing sexuality serves to feed Christina's need for the attention she so desired but was denied as a child. How does Lisa's black skin play into this? Does Francis's substitution of Christina for his racialized daughter provide Christina with added affirmation? Has Christina appropriated the exotic role of Lisa, by assuming the role of fetish? Does her exotic dancing reappropriate the fetish for white sexuality? The extent or nature of the abuse or neglect Christina suffered as a child is not clarified, but her deprivation is made evident in a flashback sequence, in which Francis drives home a young and awkward Christina, after babysitting. Christina, whose family life clearly falls short of Lisa's, is envious of the pride Francis exhibits for his daughter. Unappreciated as a child, Christina dresses as a schoolgirl in adulthood, commanding the attention she was unable to attract as an actual schoolgirl, and allowing Francis to become a substitute paternal figure. In Club Exotica, Christina is everybody's object of desire. Zoe (Arsinée Khanjian), Eric (Elias Koteas), and Francis are all entranced by her schoolgirl attire. Her dance is one that embodies untouchable childlike innocence and at the same time figures the forbidden fruit of Eden. As we, the audience, watch Eric observing Francis, who in turn looks at Christina—and by doubling the voyeuristic relationship Egoyan also draws our attention to its structure—it becomes clear that if Christina's relationship to Francis is circumscribed by the fetishistic structure that her appearance seems to endorse, it also provides her with something that is vital for her, a type of female agency that the Freudian/Lacanian account of fetishism neglects. Her schoolgirl uniform wins her the attention she craved but was deprived of as a schoolgirl. In this sense she is by no means a mere victim of the gaze. On the contrary, she solicits it, and is empowered by it, as it wins her the approval she missed as a child. At the same time she participates in a perhaps unconscious redirection of the gaze, away from the black skin of Lisa, restoring its proper path. Christina and Francis find in one another resources that help them survive their past, resources that at the same time implicate them in a legacy not only of women's sexual objectification but also in the hegemony of the white gaze. For Francis, Christina's schoolgirl uniform operates as a fetish that allows him to deny the past, to mask his failure to protect Lisa, to erase his racial transgression, and to enact a fantasy of power, control, and completion. For Christina, Francis's fetishization of her combines the paternal attention she lacked as a child with the sexual approval her phallic substitution wins for her. She is thereby compensated for her neglect as a child, through her adoption of a stereotypical, fetishistic relation to the voyeuristic gaze of the club, and affirmed in her whiteness as the proper object of the white male gaze.

Adopting the role of the fetish serves Christina's need for attention, but does nothing to contest either the phallic organization of the gaze or

Christina in *Exotica*.
Courtesy of Photofest.

its racial signification. It maintains Christina as a sexualized object of the white male gaze, while facilitating Francis's fetishistic disavowal of the past, which is also an abjection of his mixed-race marriage. It is Tracey who facilitates a break with the past, when she expresses her wish to discontinue "babysitting" for Francis. Unlike Christina, Tracey is not dependent upon, or invested in, the fetishistic relationship Francis has with her, nor on the whiteness of his gaze. Coupled with Francis's ejection from the club, which Eric orchestrates, and Zoe's refusal to allow him back, Tracey's refusal to adopt the role of the fetish allows Francis to move on.

In order to successfully commodify sexuality, its presentation must be divorced from the context of life, personal histories, particular desires. What bothers Eric about Christina's relationship with both Francis and Thomas is not its commodified sexuality, but precisely the fact that her connection with them is "real," or rather that she seems to have a "thing" for Francis. Eric doesn't use words like "real" or "authentic," but rather the language of commodification, reification, as if he wants to hold on to what is liable to "slip away." Christina's connection to Francis might be articulated within a fetishistic structure but it also escapes the economic and artificial boundaries imposed by the club, in a way that Eric wants to rein in. His manipulation of Francis's ejection from the club is accomplished by encouraging Francis to violate the rules, to touch

Christina. In Eric's mind, Francis has already violated the rules of the club, by establishing a meaningful connection with Christina that transgresses the commodified relations that alienates workers from their feelings.

Thrown out of the club, Francis lies on the ground, in the rain, his face bloodied. The picture of abjection, Francis, who has already lost everything—his wife, his daughter, his trust in his brother, his white prerogative—now loses his fetish, Christina in her schoolgirl uniform. And Christina, who never had very much to lose in the first place, loses her paternal figure of authority, whose gaze she realigns with whiteness. The breakdown of the symbolic system that coalesces around fetishism, in both Marx's and Freud's sense, allows both Christina and Francis to start anew, to create new meanings, to fashion a new symbolic. Eric's forcible separation of Francis from Christina expresses his failure to tolerate the passionate connection between Francis and Christina, which exceeds the bounds of commodification, yet at the same time as it provides them with an opportunity to abandon the structure of fetishism.

There is, of course, a danger in abruptly breaking off the coping mechanisms—fetishistic or otherwise—that individuals have developed. Christina and Francis facilitate one another's denial of the past, while providing one another with a lifeline that enables their psychic survival, providing a fantasmatic completion for one another, compensating for loss. Christina is made whole by Francis's gaze, which sexualizes her as an object by reading over her castration with the means of a fetishistic strategy, while at the same time it provides her with the paternal attention she missed as a child, and reassuring him that he has not lost his daughter, that he is a capable father, that he is in control, that he is white, that he has phallic power. Christina's schoolgirl uniform fulfils the condition of the fetish. Francis is made whole by fetishizing Christina, thereby obviating the threat that she would otherwise represent as a castrated female, a threat that also represents the desertion of his wife, the murder of his daughter, and his implication in the crime. He recovers his sense of completion by abjecting the racial contamination of this past. Deprived of their coping strategies, which take place within the fetishistic structure, whereby Christina offers Francis the opportunity of disavowal, both Christina and Francis encounter psychic crisis. The form that Francis's psychic eruption takes is phallic and violent, predictably so, given the confirmation of his paternal role with which Christina provided him. He wants to murder Eric with a gun he finds in Thomas's shop, he wants to eliminate the person who has severed his psychic lifeline. Equally predictable is the childlike character of Christina's response to Francis's ejection from the club. She exchanges the inaccessibility of her onstage persona, the captivating image that predominates throughout the film, for a childlike, abject, animal loss of control. All sense of boundaries or decorum desert her at she hits out at Eric, the man who has manipulatively deprived her of her connection with Francis, in which she found validation. Abject, she reverts to animality, to the child that she is dressed as in her schoolgirl outfit, exhibiting behavior that sharply contrasts with how she will appear the following night, having regained her composure, doing her job as always, reverting to her sexual, fetishistic persona, in control of the gaze she elicits.

The fragility of the solutions adopted by Francis and Christina consists in part in the fact that they attempt to extract a meaningful relationship with one another from a context that is designed for the production of profit, based on the controlled circulation of desire in the form of women's commodified sexuality. Within this circuit of meaning, Christina adopts the position of the sexual object, by regressing to a childhood position. She plays out her Oedipal complex in relation to Francis by soliciting and sexualizing his attention as a father figure. Francis has lost everything, the daughter of whom he was so proud, his wife, whose relationship with Francis's brother is never clarified, his confidence in his ability as a father. Yet he is able to deny his loss of power, his castration, by adopting the position of father-figure in relation to Christina.

The commodification of women's sexuality in which Club Exotica trades is informed by a series of assumptions that specify the scopophilic desires of its male clientele. Far from being a space for the free expression of sexual desire, Club Exotica enforces stringent codes of conduct that reflect the requirements of a capitalist, heteronormative economy, and appeal to the strict separation of pleasure from work. You can look, but you cannot touch. The gaze is authorized, but the material and emotional connection to sexuality is not. In order to successfully commercialize sexuality, its presentation must be divorced from the context of life. In order to take their place in the economy of exchange, to circulate as saleable goods, women's bodies must be constructed according to desires that have already abstracted a certain interpretation of sexuality and race from their complex and differentiated existence.

Emphasizing the extent to which the scopophilic practices of voyeurism and fetishism are governed by a series of culturally specific constraints, Egoyan draws attention not merely to the fact that desire is always already structured by the law, but also to the imaginary constructions that feed into the erection of the law. By framing it against the background of an alternative economy, Egoyan exposes the white, heteronormative assumptions of power and desire within the confines of which the fetishistic solution typically operates. From the opening scene, in which a black, gay customs officer is taught how to position himself in relation to the gaze by subjecting Thomas (Don McKellar), who will later become his lover, to scrutiny, the policing of borders is at issue. If international boundaries are at stake in Thomas's smuggling operations, the boundaries between therapeutic institutions as opposed to the entertainment industry are at stake in Club Exotica. When Eric tells Zoe that he finds it "therapeutic" to introduce Christina, Zoe's response is to remind him of his contractual obligations: "that's not what you are getting paid for," just as she tells Francis that Club Exotica is there for his "entertainment" and "amusement," not for "healing." "There are other places for that," Zoe admonishes him, offering to "give him a list" of addresses he can go to get treatment, designating the proper domain of legitimate medicalized discourse as outside the business of entertainment that the exotic dancers of strip clubs provide.

The question of whether one is performing the job one is being paid for, or whether one is consuming the product one is paying for, is thematized throughout the film. Thomas shares a taxi with a passenger who gives him opera tickets in exchange for paying his part of the fare, an exchange that that turns into something neither Thomas nor his taxi companion anticipates. It becomes an opportunity for Thomas to meet a man with whom he will have an erotic encounter, but one who will also disappear with the valuable Hyacinth Macaw eggs that Thomas has illegally imported. The question of whether or not payment is appropriate, and what is being paid for, recurs in Francis's payment of Tracey for "babysitting," and in Thomas's payment of Christina for her exotic dancing. Christina is reluctant to accept money from the gay Thomas, whose true intentions are to elicit information from her on behalf of Francis, and not to voyeuristically gain pleasure from her sexuality. As Thomas says over the phone to the person who is working on his apartment, "you did the job, but it's not the one I asked you to do." Or, in a symbolic exchange that deals in legal abstraction and currency rather than monetary transactions, as Eric says to Zoe, who is pregnant with his child, he has to be careful about his feelings—that's why they have a contract.

Leonard Cohen's lyrics reflect the fact that everybody knows about Francis's trauma. "And everybody knows that you're in trouble. Everybody knows what you've been through . . . Everybody knows it's coming apart." Francis's fascination with Christina reenacts the fascination of the murderer who abducted and killed his daughter, for whom Francis himself was mistaken when the police arrested him on suspicion of her murder, only to release him after the real murderer is found. Francis falls under suspicion because police suggest a motive of revenge, after revealing an affair between his wife and brother, which they imply Francis believes might have resulted in the birth of his daughter.

Appealing to a boundary that is established according to the commodification of bodies, sexuality and pleasure are separated by the procedures of capitalism, which in turn depends upon disciplinary practices that codify some forms of sexuality as acceptable and commercially viable, while other forms are classified as deviant or certifiable. Zoe's pregnant body, for example, must be kept under wraps, since it is liable to make the clients uncomfortable. So long as desire at least appears to conform to the commodified and packaged form of sexuality to which the club caters, everything runs smoothly, but as soon as the conventions of commercial viability are openly flouted, and their contingency challenged, desire can no longer be appropriately channeled along the path of white, heteronormative, fetishistic desire. Like Eric's, Francis's attachment to Christina is too personal. It does not adhere to the convention that Zoe wants to maintain that the club is a place of entertainment, a place of voyeurism, a place in which the dancers are there to be looked at for the pleasure of the clientele, who are there to enjoy a temporary respite from their hardworking lives. Francis and Christina have mixed up the categories of business and personal history, of pleasure and the psychic work of dealing with trauma, confusing the boundary that Zoe tries to re-erect in the interests of maintaining the success of the business she inherited from her mother.

The club is where the entrepreneurial business executive comes to relax after a long, hard day's work, having earned the right to be entertained, the right to look but not to touch, the right to the anonymity of voyeurism. Eric exhorts the clientele to observe the boundaries between work and play as he entices them to treat themselves to what they deserve "for just five dollars." Their just desserts are the reward of female spectacle, so long as they obey the rules, keeping intimacy, touch, physicality, bodies at bay, even while they allow themselves to be seduced by the visual display of sexuality that they have paid for. It is the job of the employees of the club to entertain the clientele. As employees, their personal histories and desires should not enter into the realm of their work.

Subverting the expectations of voyeurism and surveillance, where the power of the gaze is not usually associated with black males nor with gay sexuality, Egoyan sets up a context in which the rules of voyeurism that structure Club Exotica are brought into question.[44] This interrogation of the white, male, heterosexual gaze is continued as we follow Thomas through a series of gay encounters, and finally witness his discomfort in Club Exotica, as Christina dances for him. Thomas has no sexual desire for Christina, and under his embarrassed gaze her commodified sexuality becomes superfluous, faintly ridiculous. For her part, Christina's ability to communicate to Thomas is perhaps premised on the fact that he has no

Christina and Thomas in *Exotica*.
Courtesy of Photofest.

interest in her sexual commodification. As a substitute father figure, standing in for Francis, Thomas represents the possibility of Christina moving beyond the need to solicit sexual attention in the guise of a schoolgirl. His ability to nurture exotic birds, and to cross sexual boundaries, has been established through his smuggling operation of rare eggs. Throughout the film, a parallel is suggested between the exotic birds in Thomas's pet shop and the dancers in Club Exotica.

The boundaries that sanction and are sanctioned by the power of the gaze, the pleasures of looking, and the mechanisms of surveillance are under interrogation in Atom Egoyan's *Exotica*. Penalties are exacted for transgressing boundaries without respecting the law. The crossing of boundaries requires the observance of certain rules, the violation of which is liable to warrant investigation and punishment. Financial transactions are subject to international law, and the commodification of women's bodies is structured by codes of sexuality, desire, and competition. Egoyan problematizes the mirror image that has been such a dominant trope for film theory, alluding to the regimes of power that structure the image of the subject in ways that escape the subject's control (if not their knowledge).[45] As Thomas gazes into what appears to be a mirror, he is in fact subjected to the gaze of customs officers, and as Christina dances in front of what appears to be a mirror, she is in fact observed by Zoe, whose mother built the one-way window at the behest of a customer, telling the dancers that it was for their protection. When Francis opens the door to a young Christina, who has arrived to babysit Lisa, he holds a video camera, having been filming his wife and daughter at the piano.[46] The scene that he has videotaped is one that haunts him, one that excludes Christina from the family embrace, and also one that asks the audience to explicitly confront the relation between Francis, the character, and Egoyan, the director, as the look of the male protagonist and that of the camera/director are made to coalesce.[47]

The fetishization of exotic birds, which appear everywhere in "Exotica"—the club, Thomas's pet shop, the apartment that Tracey shares with her father—alludes to an illegitimate borrowing of, and disavowal, of cultures marked as exotic. Thomas's smuggling of Hyacinth Macaw eggs stands as a metaphor for the systematic cultural pillaging of "faraway" places accomplished by Western capitalism, and reproduced in the décor of Club Exotica. Egoyan thus draws attention to the colonial history of fetishism that Freud and Lacan suppress, but that has been well documented by William Pietz and others. The following exchange between Francis and Thomas, ostensibly about the temperatures that can be endured by exotic birds, pertains both to the exotic dancers, and to exotic, racialized others. "They're a lot hardier than you'd think," says Thomas, to which Francis replies, "I wouldn't think they are not hardy. Just because they are exotic, doesn't mean they can't endure extremes."

What imaginary ideals continue to inform both the privileging of fetishism, and the erasure of its racial history from the psychoanalytic corpus and from Marxist analyses?[48] I suggest that the continued need to marginalize others, in order to keep in place the fictional supremacy of the phallus, and the particular social order it legitimizes, rests on a dynamic of abjection that requires the abject to circulate among various dejects. The abjection of Francis and Christina, when they are deprived of their fetishistic coping mechanisms, is also an abjection by Egoyan of the capitalist system that cannot tolerate the expression of genuine emotion or affection in the commodified world of contracts. After all, "It is a jungle out there." The club represents a refuge by inviting customers to come in from the cold, pay to have women conform to the ideal of sexual objects, pay to have the illusion of control over them. But this refuge is itself illusory, circumscribed by the rules of profit. Once the boundary is crossed, once Francis touches Christina, Eric—who incited the desire to touch—enforces the law, and the limitations that commodified desire imposes come to the fore. These limitations are constructed by the objectification, commercialization, and racialization of women's sexuality along rigid lines of demarcation. The exotic atmosphere that Egoyan creates in

Club Exotica is a highly contrived one, and no less a jungle than the outside, borrowing the lush vegetation of tropical climates, just as it soothes its customers with the strains of Middle Eastern music. Egoyan is critically presenting the norms of capitalism, at the same time as commenting on the illegitimate borrowing from cultures that softens the hard edges of commodity culture, while maintaining the balance of power in its favor.

For Marx, one only has to compare the form of commodity production to other social forms of labor organization, and the mystical quality whereby values appear to be fixed, and whereby men appear to be governed by commodities that seem to be endowed with transcendent powers, vanishes. Similarly, until and unless new forms of symbolic production—those created by feminist imaginaries for example—not only circulate but gain a certain legitimacy, the mystery of the phallus, and the natural status it confers on its particular version of the symbolic, will not be exposed in its particularity. The problem is that the process of gaining legitimacy tends to proceed by way of spawning new abjects, so that the very practices through which new symbolics are generated and sustained as meaningful are liable to operate to the detriment and invisibility of those not specifically articulated as subjects in need of legitimation.

If the successful introduction of new symbolics is taken to mean the legitimation of situations in which the terms of a feminist or race theory discourse are recognized as worthy of engaging, situations in which the terms comprising such discourses can be mobilized as common currency in cultural and intellectual exchanges, the success of any new symbolic is inherently problematic. Establishing feminist or race theory as legitimate discourses involves at the same time their necessary reification, fetishization, or the celebration of these discourses as hegemonic. In particular, there is a tendency for apparently radical or progressive agendas to reinvent with solipsistic and unreflective gestures the isolation of their own terms of analyses in ways that exploit socially available forms of oppression. Rather than thinking through its own status as a discourse implicated in racist structures, feminism has typically exempted itself from this responsibility, thereby blindly repeating or even exacerbating existing racist tendencies. Hence, the production of feminist symbolics, unless they proceed with the specific intent of correcting racial biases, will tend to reproduce them, in much the same way that Freud's theory of fetishism rests upon an abjection of homosexuality.

6

Prohibiting Miscegenation and Homosexuality: *The Birth of a Nation, Casablanca,* and *American History X*

A FOUNDING AMERICAN MYTH of innocence is reenacted in *Casablanca*. The propagandist subtext of *Casablanca* is well known. Critics point to the message it sends to Americans to join the allied forces against Adolf Hitler's Aryan motives of purification.[1] It was used to support America's involvement in World War II, and it thus played a role in the decision of the United States to help the allied forces prevent Hitler's attempt to exterminate Jews and ostensibly purify the world. *Casablanca* offers fertile ground for a consideration of how nations imagine themselves on the basis of legitimating myths of racialized, gendered, and sexualized identities. A complex network of myths concerning sexuality, class, and race function as the subtext of *Casablanca,* facilitating America's representation of itself as the savior of Europe. This mythical self-representation of America rests upon a repression of its own racialized history, and the perpetuation of a myth of purity around which it seeks to consolidate its national identity, a myth that appeals to the purity of Ilsa (Ingrid Bergman) as a white, heterosexual, feminine woman. American imperialism establishes itself in *Casablanca* as originary by putting in place boundaries that constitute America as a safe place for white women to continue a legacy of purity that never existed.[2] Through the marginalization and appropriation of Sam's desire, a symbolic and imaginary value accrues to white, heterosexual, male heroic action in a way that allows America to perform a denial of its own racial history, while representing itself as a savior to Europe.

Discourses surrounding the prohibition of miscegenation, homosexuality, and unproductive sexuality subtend America's nationalist representation of itself in *Casablanca*. More recently, in justifications for the war against Iraq, the values that the United States stood for were invoked in terms of a history that recycles enduring racial and sexual mythologies by giving them a new twist. Once again America articulated its role on the world stage by appealing to ideologies that stipulated its identity with reference to a mythology that required an implicitly white, middle-class, heterosexual, Western idealized version of women to be representative of the alleged purity of its intentions. A racist subtext underlies the invidious comparisons that were drawn between Hitler and Saddam Hussein, as the United States set itself above the authority of the United Nations, portraying itself as the protector of the true interests of Iraqis and appealing to the need to liberate Iraqi women from their oppression. The implicit message was that Iraqis should become more like the ideal of a liberated, middle-class, white woman of which America imagines itself to be representative, conveniently forgetting all those "other" women, whose economic, racial, or sexual status precludes them from enjoying the ideal of freedom America represents itself as exporting—while systematically undercutting that ostensible freedom.[3]

Robert Ray has suggested that *Casablanca* "reworks many of the motifs of Twain's" *Adventures of Huckleberry Finn,* but the mapping of the world that establishes an affinity between Twain's archetypal tale and *Casablanca* is suggestive of unconscious white American desires that escape Ray's analysis.[4] The infantilization of Sam (Dooley Wilson) that girds the narrative has not been fully thought through, even by critics such as Robert Gooding-Williams, who fills in some of the lacunae created by Ray's partial reading, and in doing so helps to make visible others, without pursuing them.[5] By situating the fetishistic role that has been attributed to Sam against the background of abjection, my contention is that his subordinate but necessary role in the narrative plot can be explored more fully. Not only is Sam the motivator of Rick and Ilsa's memory of the past, but he also situates Ilsa, as a white, heterosexual, and ultimately passive woman in relation to Rick as the active, and ultimately decisive, white heterosexual male, capable of thinking and acting for the "good" of America. By thinking Sam's subordination through the motif of abjection we can see that he is construed as not yet fully human, and that his lack of humanity preserves a mythical white symbolic America from which blacks, women, and homosexuals are either carefully excluded or in which they know their very precisely circumscribed places. In what sense, then, does the representation of Sam in *Casablanca* represent an advance over the overtly racist depiction of Gus as a black rapist in *The Birth of a Nation*—whose director, Griffith, seemed to be saying, in Donald Bogle's words, "that things were in order only when whites were in control and when the American Negro was kept in his place"?[6]

In the wake of the blatant racism of early films like *The Birth of a Nation*, some critics, such as Cripps and Harmetz, welcome the racial depiction in *Casablanca* as more positive than previous, demeaning images.[7] Cripps says that in *Casablanca* "a strong black role not only survived but gave dramatic underscoring to important themes and incidents" (1977: 371). Gooding-Williams contests these readings, suggesting that Casablanca "recodes racial difference not by creating a new kind of racial stereotype, but by depriving its only black character of a distinctive personal identity. . . . Playing the deferential role of white desire's devoted minstrel, [Sam] epitomizes the subordination of black bodies to white ends" (1995, 151).

The invisibility of whiteness in the critical reception of *The Birth of a Nation* depends upon the occlusion or bracketing of its racism as a pertinent concern in the relentless attempt to champion its unparalleled aesthetic achievements. The fact that, rather than employ black actors, white actors wore blackface in the film represents a more overt instance of the invisibility of whiteness, while illustrating its highly convoluted logic: blacks could not be relied upon to represent themselves accurately, so whites had to do it for them. In *Casablanca* the portrayal of race, which at first sight might seem more benign, in fact constitutes, as Gooding-Williams shows, one more twist in the history of racism that has gone hand in hand with the development of Hollywood. Sam might not be might be a "black simpleton," or a "sexual black male," but he is deprived of "a distinctive personal identity" (151). He plays the "deferential role" of "devoted minstrel" and remains marginal to the white protagonists, adding "allure" (148) to Rick, but not enacting his own desires (ibid). Here, the invisibility of whiteness consists precisely in whites being lulled into a false sense of security, borne of the civility that apparently characterizes the relations between Rick and Sam, but which masks—unless we look closely, as Gooding-Williams asks us to do—a marginality so familiar that it is in danger of being overlooked. If Gooding-Williams is right—and I think he is—to insist that far from representing a departure from the pernicious and stereotypical representation of African Americans, *Casablanca* recodes racism in damaging ways, how does such a reading play out in terms of miscegenation? If *Casablanca* reinscribes racism, albeit departing from the overt racism of earlier films—and that racism is nowhere more glaring than in *The Birth of a Nation*—what impact does its implicit reinscription of racism have on race-mixing? How does it subtly redraw the boundaries between black and white, and how does it remain in thrall to the idea that America must preserve for itself a myth of whiteness, purity, and innocence, which must not be contaminated with the blackness it pretends to have integrated in its postslavery era, but in fact continues to abhor, diminish, and fear? How does the homo-sexual subtext that Gooding-Williams points to exacerbate and elabo-rate Sam's marginality, and how does it expand his effeminization, as a passive, ineffectual entertainer, whose purpose in the world is to amuse, and enliven the collective memory not of his own race or people, but of a couple of white heterosexual stars who steal the limelight, and insist on taking center-stage? The message of *Casablanca* is that Sam must remain marginal to America's understanding of itself. In ultimately sell-ing him to Ferrari, Rick does not merely treat him as a saleable com-modity, but dispenses with him in a way that renders palpable his status as deject. It is not just that he no longer has any use for Sam in his capac-ity as glorifying or romanticizing Rick's aura, that he no longer needs him to mop up the romantic mess that Rick finds himself in. It also that his very presence is a threat to the myth upholding the symbolic America to which Rick's resolution of his relationship with Ilsa is in service.

Sam metaphorically holds Rick's hand, and dries his tears, when Ilsa deserts him. He plays a maternal figure as he puts an arm around his shoulders as it becomes clear that Ilsa is not going to meet him at the station as she had promised. Once Ilsa is dispatched back to America with Victor Laszlo (Paul Henreid), Rick no longer needs Sam, who would only serve as a reminder of his vulnerability to her. As Rick saunters off in the night toward some new adventure, Rick remains true to his outlaw-hero, authentically American self, replaying the mythological Western hero, going off to new frontiers, conquering new horizons, and never set-tling down in a permanent homestead. The American tours the world, spreading his own peculiar brand of swaggering bravado, and speaking in the name of rugged, heroic individualism. Rick is himself, and, in the end, all the other characters are dispensable. He has finally managed to put his romance with Ilsa to rights: she deserted him in Paris, and he must revenge himself by tricking her into leaving for America with Laszlo.

If the gangster motif is reinvented by *Casablanca,* so too is that of sublimated homosexuality, which subtends the relationships between men in so many gangster films. Even friendship is redefined—according to what is useful and expedient at the time. American isolationism is reconfirmed in the figure Rick cuts, brandishing—instead of Ilsa's gun—righteousness, as the moral of the tale undoubtedly celebrates America as the savior of Europe's Nazi problem. Meanwhile, America can con-tinue to fail to confront its own race "problem," the one right on its own doorstep, the one it will not have been able to contain, and which will ramify in the upheaval of the civil rights era, the repercussions of which remain to be fully measured. Its reverberations continue to ricochet around America, and continue to inform America's relationship to the rest of the world. One might even say that those of us engaging in post-colonial and/or feminist critique, and who operate in an American context, assume the right to set the race agenda in the Western world. To that extent, I offer this discussion less in an attempt to continue to dictate the terms of the agenda, and more as a contribution to thinking through American hegemony, as represented in one of America's most enduring, canonical mythic films, in which sexuality, race, and imperialism play themselves out on a world stage. More than ever, this is a time in which those of us living in America have a responsibility to be self-conscious about the image of America projected by Hollywood, and the material suffering and foreign casualties on which this image is grounded.

Gooding-Williams has argued that Rick's allure for Ilsa in *Casablanca* can be illuminated by interpreting Sam's role in terms of commodity fetishism. On this reading, Ilsa remains an object of exchange, an object of white, heterosexual desire, for which Rick Blaine (Humphrey Bogart) and Laszlo compete, while Sam, an African American, carries the erotic baggage of the relationship between Rick and Ilsa. As the minstrel figure, Sam's role is confined to that of a worker who produces entertainment for the customers at Rick's café, but at the same time his singing conjures up the mythic past of the Parisian romance between Rick and Ilsa. The apparently Edenic, innocent past, represented by the idyllic relationship of Rick and Ilsa's Parisian encounter, operates as a prehistorical myth, whose mythical status is unearthed when Ilsa reveals to Rick that all the time—even if she believed her husband to be dead—she was in fact married to Laszlo. Gooding-Williams suggests that there is a homoerotic subtext to Rick and Sam's relationship, one that is only allowed to come to the fore in the scene where Sam tries to protect Rick from an encounter with Ilsa. Afraid that Ilsa will hurt Rick, Sam suggests that they take the car, drive into the night, go fishing, and get drunk. Rick, reinscribing the heterosexual and racial boundaries of their relationship, refuses him, thereby putting Sam back in his place as subordinate employee.

Ray has explored the ways in which *Casablanca* takes up and reworks Western gangster themes, particularly in respect to the frontier status Casablanca occupies, and Rick's "outlaw hero" status, which contrasts with Laszlo as the official hero. Yet if French Morocco is still a safe zone, and if Casablanca is still a neutral location, a fact on which Laszlo's arrival there depends, its status as a boundary town on the edge of North Africa has not been parsed out in terms of Euro-American racial history. Keeping Sam in Africa is a way of making America a safer place, a way of preserving it from the potential conflict that was to rise to the surface when civil rights became a contentious, divisive issue. In *Casablanca*,

America is kept safe from the playful, licentious, slightly seedy character of Rick, who breaks the rules, and whose romantic allure derives in part from his association with Sam. Sam must be kept where he belongs, in Morocco, on the edge of the civilized world, in its marginal, colonial relation to France, the imperialist, cultured center of Europe. America can thereby protect itself from a threat that is never articulated, but which informs Sam's smiling repudiation of his history: the black savage, the quintessential primitive. If Rick returns to America with Ilsa, the construction of America's image of itself as pristine, pure, uncontaminated—as white—will be destabilized. The mythical origin of America as a country discovered by Columbus fails to acknowledge the humanity of its Native American residents, just as Laszlo's credentials as a leader of the resistance movement establish him as the appropriate man to return with Ilsa to the homeland, without confronting the relevance of his unassailable whiteness. He assures America's mythical future as non-racist, as white, as heterosexual—and as innocent.

Building on the contrast between Rick as the outlaw hero and Laszlo as the official hero that Robert Ray (1985) had drawn, Gooding-Williams suggests that Sam's racial identity lends Rick a sexual attractiveness that he would not otherwise have. Yet in circumscribing Sam's role within the trope of fetishism, he does not give himself scope to explore the ramifications of this as fully as he might. If it is true that Rick's association with Sam lends him a sexual allure that Laszlo lacks, this reading serves to confirm Sam as the fetish, the condition that allows Rick and Ilsa's heterosexual, white desire for one another to flourish. Yet to read Sam's desire for Rick merely from this point of view is to accept the rules of the game as white and heterosexual. It is to confirm Ilsa as the white castrating female, and Sam as the black fetish that Rick employs in order to ward off the threat of castration that Ilsa represents. Sam's homo-erotic desire for Rick is disavowed, and he is reduced to his black body, which constitutes a fetish with which Rick protects himself against Ilsa, the castrating female. Such an interpretation fits well with Freud's observation that the fetish "saves the fetishist from becoming a homosexual, by endowing women with the characteristic which makes them tolerable as sexual objects" (1953f, 154).

In order to conform to Marx's commodity fetishism, the value of Sam's singing would have to be reducible to the capital it produces. At first glance it might seem that commodity fetishism adequately describes the relations that bind Sam to Rick. Marx says, "A singer who sings like a bird is an unproductive worker. If she sells her song for money, she is to that extent a wage-labourer or merchant. But if the same singer is engaged by an entrepreneur who makes her sing to make money, then she becomes a productive worker, since she *produces* capital directly" (Marx 1977, 1044). Yet Sam's singing is not reducible to the capital it produces, since Rick's exploitation of Sam is not limited to that of an indifferent capitalist. The nostalgic value of Sam's rendition of "As Time Goes By" sustains the romance between Rick and Ilsa. The song "As Time Goes By" is inseparable from Sam's persona, and from his racial history, as subordinate. This dynamic is not adequately explained by fetishism, in which Sam creates the surplus value that accrues to his white masters, while at the same time rendering himself superfluous—only his labor is valued, and not himself, since he is replaceable as a laborer (there are other black singers). Such a reading ignores both the specificity of Sam's contribution to Rick and Ilsa's relationship—it is not just any song by any singer that serves to promote the idyllic memory of Paris—it is "As Time Goes By" sung by Sam. It is this song played by Sam in the way that he plays it that conjures up memories of the past for Ilsa and Rick. His "productive labour" is not "like any other," and his singing is not "simply a means of reproducing the means of subsistence" (Marx 1997, 1046). The product of Sam's art is not "distinct from the artistic achievement of the practising artist" (1048). His "product is not separable from the act of producing" (1048). For Rick and Ilsa the "character of the actual concrete labour employed" in Sam is far from being a matter of "complete indifference" (1046). The difficulty of applying Marx's theory of commodity fetishism to Sam's role as musician stems in part from the nature of his labor, but also in part from the inability of commodity fetishism to account for the racial and sexual economies that inform his role. Sam's singing falls under the rubric of those "types of work that are consumed as services and not in products separable from the worker" (1044). Hence it is "not capable of existing as commodities independently of him" (1044). Marx designated such service work as "of microscopic significance when compared with the mass of capitalist production" (1044–45). While he acknowledges the existence of such work, where the "product is not separable from the act of producing," when he says "I want *the doctor* and not his errand boy" (1048), he nonetheless thinks it can "be entirely neglected" (1045). "Such peripheral phenomena can be ignored when considering capitalist production as a whole" (1048). Marx thereby preempts the possibility of analyzing in detail Sam's singing both as a significant contribution, as part of the entertainment economy, and as a labor of love that anchors and stabilizes the heterosexist and racist values that it allows to flourish. There is a sexual and racial economy in operation that cannot be accounted for within the terms of Marx's commodity fetishism. The phantasmatic production of bodies by fetishism continues to produce the integrity of some bodies by the abjection of

Sam, Ilsa, and Rick in *Casablanca*.
Courtesy of Photofest.

others, without confronting the specific dynamics of racialization or
sexualization that maintain that integrity. Abject, fragmented bodies thus
continue to be produced as the waste products of systems of representation that do not own the processes by which they abject their necessary but unrepresented others.

Sam's desires are barely recognized, and consequently, in psychoanalytic terms, he is barely a subject. He is, precisely, abjected. Sam is
not yet allowed to be a subject, let alone take responsibility for his
desires, be they his or someone else's, someone to whom he still, perhaps,
belongs. The vessel that Sam's musical body is pours the romance into
the white relationship between Rick and Ilsa. His song "As Time Goes
By" utters the truth that neither of them want to see: that the past is
over, and never was what it seemed to be. Their idyll is a myth. Ilsa was
never free to be Rick's lover. She was always, unbeknownst to her, still
married. According to convention, she was not allowed to be occupied
elsewhere, she was owned by another man. The only way that she can be
a diegetically sympathetic love interest for Rick is by not knowing that
Laszlo is still alive, although one must wonder what her assumption
that he is dead can mean at an unconscious level. Is her attachment to

Rick melancholic, is it a desire for the lost husband that she never had, even when she thought he was alive? If she thinks he is dead, her attachment to Rick operates as a melancholic attachment to him. Judith Butler has suggested that any strong libidinal attachments occur after the loss of an object, and has invested this suggestion with the valence of homosexuality (1997). Perhaps it could equally be invested with Ilsa's sublimated attachment to Sam's blackness, an attraction that is only available to her in the acceptable form of her desire for Rick—whose romantic allure is nonetheless assured by Sam. Sam's minstrel existence allows Rick to be invested with the eroticism of blackness that attracts Ilsa. Sam contaminates the whiteness that the collective unconscious of the studio-produced *Casablanca* works to achieve, and which the world of Hollywood serves to protect, even as he facilitates its desire and subjectivity. The quasi-object that Sam's eviscerated, emasculated body becomes as it lends its phallic status to Rick, producing the music that flows and, in flowing, stimulates the desire that cements Ilsa and Rick, while feminizing Sam, invests Sam with a maternal, nurturing, compliant role. As their muse, he eroticizes Rick and Ilsa's relationship, while marginalizing his own desire, a desire that is only allowed to subsist so long as it is sublimated in the white, heterosexual, legitimated desire of the co-stars. Sam's desire is only allowed to exist as subordinated to, yet supportive of, a white narrative of heterosexual desire. The narrative hypocritically holds out the promise to Sam that his desire can also be legitimated, but only at the cost of mirroring the desire it helps to produce and sustain, or rather to recapture and establish retrospectively as legitimate. Sam's song is what breathes life into the relationship that has foundered on Ilsa's desertion of Rick, and her rediscovery of her legitimate husband. That he agrees to indulge her, albeit reluctantly, to sing it for Ilsa, despite Rick's longstanding prohibition, amounts to an instance of insurrection. Sam's transgression opens up the floodgates of the past, with results that both he and Ilsa find impossible to contain. Rick must reassert his control by banishing them both, reasserting his patriarchal, white authority over them.

One can see the attraction of applying the trope of fetishism to Sam. He serves as a substitute for the mythical relationship that never was, and his song preserves its memory. To read Sam as fetishistic does not capture the sense in which he is disenfranchised by the role he plays— it only captures his value from a white point of view. The promise to Sam is that you too can become like us, but you can never be us, because we are what we are partly because of you. You are not one of us, and if we create you in our image, you will still always only be becoming us—even as you helped us become us, since we profited from your labor. We'll make you no more than one of us, no different from us, since to acknowledge your difference might also be to acknowledge our guilt and your productivity. You can only exist in comparison to us, as subordinate to us, as lesser than us, as created by us, as allowed to exist by us, but how you helped us be us cannot be acknowledged. As soon as any attempt is made to take seriously the ways in which Sam makes Rick who he his, lends him romance, adds to his allure, the trope of fetishism is shown to be wanting as explanatory not only of how Rick functions for Sam and Ilsa, but of how they are who they are, they become what they are, in part through excluding Sam from full humanity.

While Rick absorbs the primitive, magical, bestial sexuality Sam has on offer, Sam is also replete with uncontrollable, insupportable myths of negroes (see Fanon 1967a). Sam's body communicates, channels, directs, lends itself as a vessel, containing raw unformulated desires, to Rick, his master, who shapes those desires into something new, or some new version of the same—white, heterosexual desire born of the sublimation of homosexuality (see Irigaray 1985a). Sam's desires have no value in this system, and as such are not desires. Their delegitimation occurs before they can be recognized, so that even their expression is only ever indirect. Sam can be the cupid, the gelling agent, the go-between, the feminized glue, the simple, uncomplicated innocent, whose raw, untrained, natural, unformed musical talent is harnessed in the service of white desire, cultivated by white law, regulated by heterosexual, paternal authority.[8] He is not a man with legitimated, well-formulated desires of his own. In short, he is not a subject, but neither is he an object, commodified or fetishized. He is precisely abject. Sam is constitutive of Rick and Ilsa's relationship in a way that goes unacknowledged.

Not only is there a need to gain access to the imaginary, phantasmatic structures that uphold unconscious symbolic structures that are sexist, racist, heterosexist, and classist, but there is also a tendency of these abjecting discourses to reify or congeal into new forms of discrimination that abject one another. Hence the difficulty of articulating forms of oppression and domination without succumbing to the tendency to homogenize or universalize discourses that privilege one opposition over another. The trope of fetishism, which is itself subtended by masculinist claims masquerading as universal, collapses race and class. It fails to see the intricacy of relationships in all their constitutive complexity. In *Casablanca* Ilsa's construction as a heterosexual white woman is constituted by Sam's abjection in a way that assures America of a myth that it has constructed for itself, a myth of innocence and racial purity, driven by a fear of miscegenation and fuelled by a denial of slavery. Ilsa must go to America with the white, heterosexual Laszlo, who is uncontaminated by the black and homoerotic allure of Rick, with which Sam contaminates the outlaw hero. She can thereby reproduce white babies, preferably male, who can grow up and perpetuate a logic of com-modification that continues to exploit racialized others. This logic assures for America its purity as unassailable, its goodness as unimpeachable, and its mythical origins as white. Colonialism and slavery are consigned to a prehistory that cannot be thought, and white, heterosexual America can be safeguarded by a white, European, heterosexual woman, Ilsa, who becomes the ground on which nationalism is supported and protected by white, heterosexual, capitalist patriarchy. This can only be sustained against a background in which Arabs are represented as thieves and cheats, living in a country to which Sam is consigned, keeping his black-ness and homosexuality well away from America, on the periphery of Africa, in a border zone, that free town, Casablanca. The point is not to outlaw the discourse of fetishism, which remains useful and illumina-ting within certain contexts, but rather to point out that it has taken on the role of a currency that is often ignorant of its legacy, and thereby inadvertently perpetuates that legacy.

Sam has not escaped oppression, but only found an (arguably) less intense version of it, one that moreover allows the American conscience to salve itself by pretending that oppression no longer exists. To trans-port Sam first to Europe, then back to Africa, is to send him back where he came from, and thereby pretend to have solved the problem of slav-ery. Rewriting history, or wanting to forget slavery, or insisting that we move on, because all that is in the past, is not a way of confronting it, but a way of continuing to evade history. It is a way of continuing to deny slavery's lasting impact not only on the collective white psyche, but also on the material distribution of wealth and the economic and psychic opportunities available to African Americans. This strategy of denial is all too obviously in play in conservative arguments that frame ostensible answers to racism by wanting a colorblind society, and then assuming that a colorblind society already exists. Such obfuscation leads to the denial for the continued need for affirmative action, a denial of the realities of discrimination, which at some level surely does remain invisible to those who do not suffer it and do not want to see it. Collapsing an imaginary possible future into an existing present, the refusal to see discrimination becomes the refusal to see the salience of race, a refusal that relies upon a disingenuous appeal to a colorblind principle—an ideal future which proponents of affirmative action invoke. To pretend that this future is here is to perpetuate a blindness that can only be explained on the basis of a relentless and unexamined white privilege.

Sam is not allowed to be quite human. He is barred from becoming a subject capable of articulating his desire, which is not recognized by others, especially if those others are white men and white women. He is not represented as a desiring subject in control of his own destiny. He is not permitted to enact his desire, or to constitute himself as an I. He is too full of the desires of others, a repository of myths that prohibit him from becoming fully human. He remains a black body that makes music for others, and he is only allowed to desire by proxy. His desire to protect Rick can be justified, some critics might argue, as a desire that anyone would have to protect a friend from a potentially damaging relationship. Ilsa has let Rick down in the past, and since she is a married woman, the chances of her letting him down again are good. Yet, if Sam is merely a friend to Rick, the desire to protect a friend is not reciprocated by Rick, who dispenses with Sam's services as soon as he dispatches Ilsa to America with Victor Laszlo. This confirms Robert Gooding-Williams' suggestion that Sam's raison d'être is to carry the erotic baggage of Rick and Ilsa's desire. Despite his earlier claim that Sam is not for sale, Rick has no trouble transferring him to Ferrari once he has decided to send Ilsa away with her lawful husband. Sam's reluctance to play "As Time Goes By" cannot be read simply as a protective gesture toward Rick, expressive of a mutually respectful friendship, for Sam, after all, is not Rick's friend and equal. He is an employee, a sidekick, and Rick is his employer, and master of the plot.

Yet there is something to the idea that, even if it would be incorrect to see Sam as an equal to Rick in *Casablanca,* the distance between the benign, if misguided, representation of Sam and the caricatured, hyperbolic, representation of Gus as a rapist in *The Birth of a Nation* needs remarking. What does it mean to see, and to capture that difference? In what way does the racism informing and recreated not only by *The Birth of a Nation* itself, but also by its critical reception, differ from the less blatant but perhaps for that very reason more insidious racism of *Casablanca*? Perhaps the difference can be remarked by pointing to the way in which the racial history of America is effectively repressed in *Casablanca,* which presents us with a smiling minstrel figuration of African Americans, in which the ugliness of slavery is conveniently forgotten. Slavery is never mentioned in the film. It is merely a past that was never present. It is a past that was not what it has become since its demise, and yet, in reconstructing its significance, cultural theorists find themselves creating a history that is still in the process of being told, a contested history that still has to be legitimated. The history that is still in the process of being written is the history that has been written out of schoolbooks written by white historians, who present Native Americans as wily, cunning people, in tune with nature, and ready to teach the white European invaders how to catch fish in the rushing brooks, while African slaves are depicted as a happy, compliant, if essentially lazy people, in need of the firm hand wielded by their white masters. This portrait reemerges in a new guise in the figure of Sam, who smiles, sings, and entertains, while remaining in the background of the relationship that is conducted in the foreground between Ilsa and Rick. Sam the muse also performs the role of spiritual advisor and caretaker of Rick, whose well-being seems to be his ultimate concern—as it might well be, since Rick remains his employer and source of income.

The danger confronting Europe in World War II was one that was also played out on the grounds of race, in an irony that Hollywood could all too easily sublimate. Remaining, at least on the surface, oblivious to the racial tension *Casablanca* embodies, critics heralded the film as a departure from the negative stereotypical depictions of race, epitomized in *The Birth of a Nation*. Since stereotypes are capable of withstanding contradiction, indeed their capacity to be infinitely malleable is what makes them so hard to undermine, the recoding of race in stereotypical ways in *Casablanca* represents less a departure from stereotype than its reaffirmation, in a new guise. Homi Bhabha's "concept of stereotype-as-suture is a recognition of the *ambivalence* of . . . authority . . . and orders of identification" (1994, 80). Yet, the concept of the fetish that drives Bhabha's analysis, as it does the analyses of Fanon (1967a), Krips (1999), Mulvey (1990), Taylor (1996), and Gooding-Williams (1995), needs to be questioned. Bhabha goes on, "The role of fetishistic identification, in the construction of discriminatory knowledges that depend on the 'presence of difference' is to provide a process of splitting and multiple/contradictory belief at the point of enunciation and subjectification" (1994, 80). By turning to the abject, as the excluded ground of the fetish, in order to account for the multiple and contradictory beliefs that infuse film narrative with its racist, colonialist, classist, sexist, and heterosexist inflections, we avoid re-inscribing and privileging another stereotype that has proved itself ingeniously adaptable to myriad patriarchal structures, colonial and otherwise. The discourse of abjection allows us to bring into question the phallic monism that ultimately underlies even Bhabha's apparently versatile reworking of the fetish for the purposes of elaborating the previously neglected postcolonial positioning of subjects. Not only does abjection offer the advantage of not yet assuming the solidity and coherence of sexual differentiation, it also operates at a semiotic level that is capable of restructuring the self-affirming discourses that solidify into the competing narratives of race, sex, class, and heterosexism, whose relationships we spend so much energy trying to articulate. To displace the fetish from sexuality to race is to act as if these narratives were not always already connected in labyrinthine and mutually supportive ways.

As caretaker of Rick's emotions, and regulator of his desires, Sam plays the role not so much of coon, or buck, or sambo, but rather of mammy. His effeminization, both as potential erotic carouser with Rick (à la Gooding-Williams), and as servant-Sam, who carries Rick's and Ilsa's erotic baggage, speaks to the maternalization of his role, and yet is read against the background of servitude that slavery has assured for African American stereotypes.[9] The narrative of Western imperialism spun out by *Casablanca* requires the sacrifice of Sam's desire for the reinstallation of Ilsa's passivity as a good white woman. If Ilsa temporarily disrupts this passivity when she pulls a gun with which she threatens Rick, her resolve quickly melts, only to confirm all the more rigorously her subordinate role. When she famously asks Rick to do the thinking for both of them—for all of them (thereby including her husband in her own reinstatement of her passive feminization), Rick complies. Ilsa thereby fits herself neatly back into the heterosexist norms that require women not to think for themselves, but rather to safeguard the alleged purity of an illegitimate national identity. By allowing herself to be manipulated by Rick, Ilsa conserves America both from the threat of miscegenation and from that of homosexuality that Sam's relationship with Rick represents. The legendary, phallic power of black men is thus borrowed by the world-weary and cynical Rick, who must act decisively to save the world. Sam, as both maternal figure, and yet (always ambiguously) phallic figure, can't be read straightforwardly along the lines of sexual differentiation. Yet, his maleness eviscerated by his blackness, he is ultimately reduced to a powerless maternal figure. His metaphorical children, Rick and Ilsa, grow up, separate, and leave him, putting him firmly back in his place: Africa. Although Rick finally dispenses with Ilsa—the outcome advised by Sam—in the process, Sam's reason for existing (as protector of Rick) evaporates. Sam becomes the casualty of his own good will and selflessness. Not only is fetishism an inadequate explanation for this dynamic; it also ignores the mythic phallic powers associated with blacks, of which Fanon reminds us.

A reworking of the disavowal of castration is called for. Sam (we assume) has a penis, but Rick acts as if he does not have it, in the sense that he appropriates it for himself, and thus castrates Sam; as castrated, Sam is feminized, maternalized. He can look after Rick, but the care he provides is repudiated. What is significant here is that if Ilsa is the castrating, threatening female, of whom Rick is wary, Sam is ultimately the castrated figure. It is Sam's romantic allure as a black singer that adds to

Rick's cachet, and it is Ilsa's attachment to Laszlo that makes her threat-ening.[10] Part of Rick's attraction for Ilsa lies precisely in the rogue element that Rick's association with Sam lends to him. Ultimately Rick transfers his identificatory allegiance, his homosexual attachment, to Renault, thereby making Ilsa his new transitional object, on the way to a homoso-cial pact. In doing so, Rick substitutes a white European for his black "friend" Sam.

Once we take seriously Gooding-Williams's suggestion of a homo-erotic bond linking Rick to Sam, the homoerotic subtext emerges else-where in the dialogue of *Casablanca*. Gooding-Williams does not do an extensive analysis of this motif, largely restricting his treatment of it to the only scene in which, he claims, Sam's desire comes to the surface, only to be abruptly repressed by Rick, the outlaw hero. Yet when Renault meets Laszlo, the scene reveals Renault's jealousy of Rick for the atten-tions of Ilsa, although Renault's statement is ambiguous. He says to Rick, "I can't get over you two. She was asking about you earlier, Rick, in a way that made me extremely jealous." He clearly holds Rick in high esteem, and is a close observer of his character and actions, comment-ing on the number of precedents broken when Rick not only sits down and drinks with Ilsa and Laszlo, in contrast to his usual refusal to drink with customers, but even pays for the drinks. As Laszlo and Ilsa depart, Ilsa asks Rick, "Will you say goodnight to Sam for me?" to which Rick replies "I will." Ilsa follows up by observing, "There's still nobody in the world who can play 'As Time Goes By' like Sam," thus rendering her request that Rick "say goodnight to Sam" perfectly innocent of homo-erotic undertones. Sam's reason for being, we are reminded, is solely to conjure up the lost past with his musical talents, and thereby conserve the memory of that lost past for the white protagonists. To think through Sam's own role in this romance is perhaps to perform what Toni Morrison refers to in *Beloved* as "re-memory." To recollect the past from Sam's point of view, or at least from a potential point of view he might have on his situation—were he granted full subjectivity within the narrative of *Casablanca*—would be to construct his role within the film in a way that does not pretend to be innocent of America's history of slavery. As it is, the relationship implied by the dialogue is not allowed to surface in the film. In perhaps the most explicit recognition of the homosexual bond that remains largely below the surface between Rick and Renault, Renault describes Rick to Ilsa as "the kind of man that, well, if I were a woman, and I were not around, I should be in love with." The position-ing of the I in this confession first imagines being a "woman," then reverts to being a man, but absents this man—if "I" as a man "were not around" then "I should be in love with" Rick.[11] If Renault's womanly/homosexual side were to emerge, and if he were to leave his masculine/heterosexual façade behind, he seems to be saying, then he too would be in love with Rick. Clearly, he identifies with Ilsa in her capacity to love Rick, and wishes he could too. Later, on he says to Rick that he didn't think he was interested in women, and at the end of the film more than a hint of their close friendship is resasserted, as Rick and Renault "walk off into 'the equivalent of the lovers' sunset'" (Ray 1985, 112).

If classical Marxist theories of commodity fetishism fail to explain the specificity of Sam's musical contribution to the dynamic between Ilsa and Rick, classical Freudian fetishistic theory doesn't work for the figure of Sam either. Rick's own romantic allure is assumed only on the basis of his usurpation of the supposed legendary phallic powers of black men—in this case of Sam—powers that invest Rick with the prowess he has as an outlaw hero. Sam thus has, and does not have, the phallus. He is ambiguously phallused. He has the phallus in the sense that as black he is invested as oversexed—black men ostensibly, according to white, racist mythology, have large penises. But if this phallus turns out to be a white fetish—a compensatory substitute put in place by a white imaginary that invests blacks with a hypersexuality all the better to align them with animality, and dismiss their humanity, while accessorizing their own sexuality with his—its condition is Sam's dejection. Sam is therefore nothing but sex, compared to the white man, and at the same time he lacks the phallus in the sense that as black, his maleness is compromised. He is an effeminized subordinate.

In asking Rick to think, to make her decision for her, Ilsa capitulates to her fate, which Rick will determine. At the same time she appears to give up her castrating, threatening demeanor, but she does so only to revert to a traditional feminine role. The moment at which she softens, requiring Rick to make the important decision, confirming, true to Freud, the inability of women to be trusted with morality, is precisely the moment at which the issue of miscegenation surfaces. Her fate is to safeguard America, by returning to her proper, wifely role as homemaker. Evading responsibility for her actions, she confirms Freud's belief that women's sense of morality is not very well developed, that our superegos are weak, a belief that echoes a long legacy, and mimics Aristotle's belief that women's deliberative capacity is weaker than men's. Yet Ilsa's passivity also draws on and re-inscribes the boundaries separating black from white, homosexual from heterosexual, and America from Europe. Sam will stay on the edge of North Africa, where he belongs; Rick will wander off, thus continuing his vagabond, outlaw existence, abandoning Sam, while playfully indulging in the possibility of a new homoerotic but still sublimated bond.[12] Meanwhile, white, heterosexual Ilsa will go to America, embodying all that is good and pure and right. She can therefore represent the mythical essence of white purity that America has produced for itself, and sets out to preserve in the context of a messy world, of which it can wash its hands, having set itself up to heroically intervene to solve Europe's problems and win the war. At the same time as presenting its heroic ideals to the world, America can forget its own genocide of Native Americans, its own history of slavery, and restore itself, with Ilsa's help, to its illusory, fictional, powerfully imaginary origins of white innocence. The Edenic paradise, the mother-child bond, is reasserted, but this time its whiteness is guaranteed. When Rick sends Ilsa to Europe with her white, heterosexual, official, anti-Nazi, moral husband, the unlawful contamination of his liaison with Sam is contained in Morocco, on the periphery of Europe, far from America, on the edge of Africa.[13]

Essentially unproductive, Rick cannot go back to the United States because he is contaminated by Sam, who must also remain outside of Europe and America. Now for the first time Sam does become a subordinated commodity who can be sold to the highest bidder once his function as the indispensable go-between who facilitates the romantic liaison between Rick and Ilsa ceases to be necessary. The United States must remain the province of white manly men and womanly women—the kind of woman Rick has insisted Ilsa be—compliant and married to a man who can reproduce white, straight children. Hence the children that America produces will be purified of the unproductive (black/homo) sexuality that Sam represents, and of the lawlessness that is fostered by Rick's association with him.

It is not to that overdetermined origin that we call Oedipus, a Greek who casts out his eyes in refusal to look upon what he had done, to whom we must appeal in order to shed light on *Casablanca*—or rather in order to allow *Casablanca* to shed light on our world.[14] Oedipus, who so relentlessly insisted on discovering who he was, and whose knowledge was also a self-discovery, constitutes the element in which the myth of mastering the world continues to thrive. In a raced rewriting of Eden, it is not a blinding, castrating, self-evisceration that is enacted, as Oedipus cuts out his own eyes, symbolically inscribing on his own body the cut, splitting himself in two, before and after, past and present, inscribing history on his body, in order to confront the future, disfiguring himself as he dissociates himself from the horror of the past, defacing himself, gouging out his eyes, castrating himself, marking himself as monstrous, as he signals the unnatural acts he has committed. Literalizing the blindness that plagued Oedipus and his city, Oedipus takes on his own punishment, recognizes himself as the guilty one: the sinner effectively removes himself from the city of which he was once savior, putting himself outside its bounds in order to secure it. He acts, he speaks as a subject who takes responsibility for his desires, even though those desires were unknown to him in their true nature.

By challenging the hegemony of the psychoanalytic narrative, which always returns to Oedipus in order to tell its story, by complicating the story that Western European philosophy and its psychoanalytic spinoffs incessantly replay, in a narcissistic repetition of its ancient Greek origins, perhaps we can also locate the logic of fetishism as part of this recurrent narrative. With the rise of nationalism and capitalism, with the birth of colonialism and expansionist territorialist ambitions, first of Europe, and then of America, perhaps a new myth of origin needs to be thought through. Perhaps psychoanalysis invested so much time investigating the psychic archaeology of ancient Greek tragedy in an effort to distract itself from the issues of colonialism and slavery that were much nearer at hand. In this more recent history, certain subjects have played the role of constitutive others within representation—including social, economic, cultural, and political representation—that both relegates them to an unmarked zone outside of legitimating discourses, and includes them peripherally, siphoning off what it can from them.

Gooding-Williams provides a provocative and productive reading of *Casablanca,* which succeeds in showing how Sam's blackness not only lends Rick a "romantic allure" that is lacking in Victor Laszlo, Rick's competitor for Ilsa's attention. He also suggests that the heterosexist relationship between the two white protagonists is sustained by Sam's denial of his own homoerotic desire for Rick. Rick's mastery—albeit the kindly paternalism of the antebellum era—of the situation, as the white hero, prevents him from acknowledging that Sam might be a love-object, or any avowal of his homosexuality. In this reading, Sam's marginality is constituted both by his race and by his sexuality, while Rick's success as the rogue hero is dependent upon his repression of the homosexual subtext that is only allowed to state itself indirectly. Like Taylor's interpretation of *The Birth of a Nation,* Gooding-Williams's interpretation of *Casablanca* appeals to the interpretive device of fetishism. For Taylor, this strategy involves a bracketing of gender, a concern that is allowed to intrude into his text, only to be subordinated to the main narrative of race. Unlike Taylor, Gooding-Williams does not restrict his reading to only one dimension. Not only does he acknowledge Ilsa's passive, womanly, and stereotypical subordination to Rick, who complies with Ilsa's request to do the thinking for both of them. He also understands the value that accrues to Rick through Sam's musical labor in terms of Marx's commodity fetishism, thereby alerting us to the homoerotic undertones of the relationship between Sam and Rick. I have suggested that despite Gooding-Williams's nuanced and multidimensional reading of the film in terms of race, gender, and sexuality, he is ultimately limited by his adherence to the trope of fetishism. I think that Gooding-Williams closes down the possibilities his reading opens up by appealing to fetish as the motif by which to understand Sam's marginality. While such a reading remains illuminating and persuasive at the level of racial politics within the United States, in order to follow through the racial motif it is necessary to think about how the image of the United States is constructed against the background of Europe. The discourse of abjection helps to elaborate the sense in which the marginalization of Sam's desires supports a vision of racial purity in America, one that is eerily mirrored by the threat of Nazism that *Casablanca* pits itself against. Released in 1942, intended to motivate U.S. troops to join the allied forces against Hitler, *Casablanca* can also be seen as assuring the American populace that it is secure from the threat of racial contamination. By drawing on the concept of abjection, the implicit discourse against miscegenation that *Casablanca* embraces can be elucidated. By taking up the homoerotic tendencies uncovered by Gooding-Williams in Sam's relationship to Rick, and reworking them in the context of a reading of Sam as abject, Sam's homoeroticism is set against the broader context implied, but not developed, by Gooding-Williams's designation of him as "servant" Sam. Using the notion of the abject as a reference point for the homoerotic bond between Sam and Rick, we see that Rick's repudiation of Sam's advances can be read as a final attempt to overcome the reliance that he has indulged upon Sam as a maternal figure. Reading the attachment between Rick and Sam through the lens of the maternal, we are able to see that Rick breaks free of his dependence on Sam, in a gesture that prepares the way for his eventual sale of Sam to Ferrari.

The reading that Gooding-Williams provides has the merit of bringing to light the way in which Sam is doubly marginalized, and doubly exploited: he lends both his musicality and his sexuality to Rick. If Sam is a fetish, an accessory to the white, heterosexual narrative, his usefulness comes to an end once Ilsa returns to America. If he serves to link Rick to his past with Ilsa, his dismissal serves as a definitive break with that past. Sam's function as fetish must be read against a history in which his abject, racialized status allows him to perform this fetishized role. Rick's success as an attractive hero rests on his ability to exploit and sublimate the power of black sexuality and to tame the wild abandon of homoerotic undertones. At the same time, the ambiguity that Rick both embodies and represses makes him ultimately an unacceptable American hero. By sending Ilsa, the white heroine, off to America with Laszlo, Rick secures his homeland from the nascent threat of miscegenation, and contains any homosexual subtext that the film might endorse within the borders of Morocco. Thus the film restores the authority of a white, patriarchal, heterosexual order by allowing the disruptive forces of Ilsa's independence, and Sam's emergent homosexuality, to briefly appear, only to reestablish their marginality. Ilsa does not merely submit to Rick's will. She does so only after threatening Rick with a gun (a phallic embodiment of the threat of castration Laszlo's symbolic position as her husband represents), and accusing him of cowardice. She thereby calls him to action, reminding him of his heroic and national duty, and at the same time reinforcing the boundaries of law and the heterosexist order. She displaces Sam as the fetish, taking matters into her own hands. It is only after recalling Rick to his duty as an American that Ilsa retreats back into the predictable feminine role that after all defines her. That role is circumscribed not only by gender, not only by heteronormativity, but, crucially, also by whiteness. Laszlo must be the one to stay with Ilsa, so that America is protected from the possible contamination that would ensue from her potential union with Rick. Sam must be eliminated from the equation. Rick must be the strong, dominant, courageous male, and she must collapse back into the feminine role, under his protection.

As Gooding-Williams points out so effectively, Rick's sexual attractiveness is inextricably bound up with the cachet he accumulates from Sam. I have extended (and to some extent challenged his reading) in suggesting that Casablanca effectively contains the threat of homosexuality that Sam and Rick's relationship portends within the geographical limits of a foreign place that is far enough away from America that it does not represent a threat. It thereby reestablishes the boundaries between whites and blacks in a way that safeguards the homeland from the threat of miscegenation. It suggests that as long as black folks are kept in their place, and white women are kept with their white husbands, everything will be as it should be. Sam is allowed to be a companion to Rick, so long as he plays the piano and preserves for Rick and Ilsa the idyllic memory of Paris, so long as he observes the rules of heterosexuality and subordination. At the same time, the superiority of the United States over Europe is established. The message that this resolution sends is that race is dealt with in a much more civilized way in the United States than it is under Nazism. Borders are policed with a great deal more subtlety. Everyone knows her or his place, and everyone keeps to it. That way, no ethnic cleansing has to take place. Of course, the fact that Sam is safely ensconced in Casablanca effectively distances the United States from its own history of slavery, so that it can present itself as the benevolent savior of Europe, coming to resolve its racial problems, while in fact it exports them to other places.

Just as Gooding-Williams uses the notion of fetishism in his discussion of *Casablanca*, arguing that "whites fetishize black sexuality as a black magic that white civilization lacks" (1995, 157), and referring to Mulvey's analysis (158, n. 20), so in illuminating the racial dynamic in *The Birth of a Nation*, Clyde Taylor and Manthia Diawara both rely on concepts that are central to Mulvey, fetishism and voyeurism.[15] While Diawara explicitly acknowledges his debt to Mulvey (214–15), Taylor appeals to the Freudian notion of fetishism and the Oedipal scenario at key points. Taylor shows how the aesthetic achievement of the film can blind itself to its racism, thereby protecting the transcendental value of whiteness (see 1996, 27 and 35).[16]

The concepts of fetishism and voyeurism continue to play a key role in analyses of racial tropes, even in their attempt to go beyond psychoanalytic gaze theory. It is striking that even attempts to theorize the representation of race that are explicitly motivated by the need to correct "discussions . . . that foreground gender and sexuality but not race," as is Robert-Gooding Williams's consideration of the Rick/Sam/Ilsa love triangle in *Casablanca*, still rely on the explanatory value of fetishism.[17] Just as Fanon showed that in order to be applicable to a wider constituency than the white authors who established its outlines, phenomenological analysis needed to abandon its claims for universality, and reap the implications of taking seriously the lived experience of the racial epidermal schema, so it is necessary to ask whether the continued privileging of fetishism, both in feminist and race theory, inadvertently reproduces white, male privilege.[18] A discourse of abjection can help move us beyond the implicit universalism endorsed by theories of fetishism, theories embraced by many race theorists, which reinstall the phallocentric assumptions that are part of the fabric of Freud's work.

D. W. Griffith's *The Birth of a Nation* (1915) was heralded for its innovative film technique, but also heavily criticized for what Thomas Cripps calls its "racial propaganda" (1996, 38), and what Clyde Taylor identifies as its "blatant racist portrayal of Blacks" (1996, 22). Since Griffith's "epic," Hollywood has served up a steady diet of films that could be said to repeat such racist gestures, differing only in how explicitly they do so. Manthia Diawara refers to *The Birth of a Nation* as "the grammar book for Hollywood representation of Black manhood and womanhood" (1993, 3). The most important elements of this grammar, for Diawara, are, first, Hollywood's "obsession with miscegenation," secondly, "its fixing of Black people within certain spaces, such as kitchens, and into certain supporting roles, such as criminals," and third, the mandate that "white people occupy the center," which results in black people being left with "only one choice—to exist in relation to Whiteness" (1993, 3).

In his discussion of *The Birth of a Nation* Taylor observes: "For obscure reasons, narrative works considered landmarks in American culture for technical innovation and/or popular success have often importantly involved the portrayal of African Americans" (1996, 15). The obscurity of these reasons, their enigmatic quality, remains intact in much of the critical literature on the film. Although Taylor does not point to *Casablanca* as exemplary of this phenomenon, a case could certainly be made for it. In *The Birth of a Nation* lynching, according to Taylor, produces "fantastic gratification" in the white witnesses, who "transfer . . . their inadmissible desires to the immolated Black victim" (27). Taylor echoes, here, the words of Fanon, who says, "Projecting his own desires onto the Negro, the white man behaves 'as if' the Negro really held them" (1967a 165; 153–54). A variation of the same trope is at play in *Casablanca*, according to Gooding-Williams, who observes that while Sam himself is not sexually expressive, his "allegorical" role as "mythical Cupid," who "facilitates and sustains the erotic relationshi[p]" between Ilsa and Rick, is crucial (1995, 144).

Taylor's focus is on D. W. Griffith's *The Birth of a Nation*, which "represents two historical landmarks: an incomparable racial assault and a major breakthrough for subsequent filmmaking technique" (1996, 15). Rather than reading the film's legendary racism as inherently separable from the mythical status the film has assumed for its technical sophistication and aesthetic achievements, Taylor's strategy is to argue that, far from constituting separable aspects of the film, "virtually all of the film's formal achievements—its editing, close-ups, iris shots, manipulation of crowds, camera movements, scenic set-ups, literary titles, etc.—are deployed in the cause of aestheticizing and sentimentalizing the principal characters as White people" (22). The evasive strategies of critics who dismiss, excuse, minimize, or justify the film's racism in order to better celebrate the strengths of *The Birth of a Nation* are adopted not merely to preserve its integrity as a great film, but to enshrine it so that it serves an "Edenic" role (see 20–21). It thus comes to serve "almost" as "a myth of origin" (Taylor 1996, 16).[19] The tendency, if not to uncritically accept the film's racism, then at least to look for mechanisms that explain it away, has its basis both in the desire for cinema to establish its aesthetic legitimacy, and in the systematic blindness exhibited by critics who take for granted the privilege of whiteness. In order to sustain this privilege, and to preserve the blindness, complex maneuvers must be undertaken so that the distorted and inequitable social relations that support it do not come to light. Film critics are therefore doubly invested in failing or refusing to see that the film that they take to be originary in so many ways might also be implicated in the racism that

March 13, 1915.   MOTION PICTURE NEWS

Advertisement for *The Birth of a Nation*.
Courtesy of Photofest.

it depicts and at the same time legitimates. To establish film as art, one might say, is to resist any suggestion that as art it might reflect, legitimate, and reinvent the racism of the very institutions from which it is seeking approval. To see that film might be racist is to see that art might be white. If film wants to be art, then it must be white too—but it must be so invisibly. Taylor says that "the passive racism of film studies has led it to neglect the meaning of Griffith's national allegory and the role of racism in it, in striking contrast to the subtle social analysis given other national allegories like the Western or the gangster movie" (17).[20]

Despite the fact that Taylor argues that "the central theme" of *The Birth of a Nation* "is the unification of national sentiment around the theme of miscegenation as a threat to 'civilization'" (22), and that the "issue of Black-White sexual relations, in fact, forms the spine of the text" (21), he admits that he has "been slow to recognize that the largely unconscious cultural symbolism of *The Birth of a Nation* is equally expressive on the level of gender as of race" (30). That this admission is inserted into the text in a paragraph that is bracketed produces an irony that is apparently lost on Taylor. His bracketing of the salient question of gender uncannily mirrors the bracketing of Griffith's racism that he so skillfully exposes in the critical reception of *The Birth of a Nation*. His blindness to gender unconsciously reproduces exactly the same kind of gesture he exposes in his criticism of Gerald Mast. As Taylor says, Mast's "approach to the issues of racism and aesthetics is to condemn the film's bigotry, but in a way that mitigates its severity, then turn from that subject as a troublesome intrusion to examine the film's artistic achievements as landmarks in 'human' expression" (18). Just as "Mast's exploration of the movie's cinematic qualities" can proceed by celebrating the "human" in a way that—now that the "intrusive issue of race" is "out of the way" (18)—inadvertently understands humanity as equivalent to whiteness, so Taylor's own insights about race can proceed unencumbered by the neatly bracketed question of gender. Having made his bracketed confession that he has failed to apply the same kind of focused attention to the gendered dimension of the rape scene as he has on its raced dimension, having got this intrusive issue of gender out of the way, Taylor picks up the thread of race again: "Let me return once more to the common assertion that Griffith's racism was largely unconscious. What does that mean? The assertion is made as if to bracket Griffith's racist attitudes from further analyses ... the notion that *The Birth of a Nation* merely reflected contemporary racial prejudice is another way of bracketing the phenomenon of the film from wider significance in our understanding of American culture and media" (30). Can we say of Taylor's concession to gender what he says of the attitude other critics adopt toward Griffith's racism, that he "elaborates this bracketed perception without, finally dissolving the brackets" (30–31)?

Sam's marginality in *Casablanca* resides in the fact that his character expresses sexuality, yet his sexual expressivity yields a return not for himself, but for the white protagonists. He is there to entertain, to supply the romance in the relation that will take center stage, but his own desires are denied. As Gooding-Williams argues, "Sam's tie to sexuality is, primarily, a tie to a sexuality belonging to others . . . Servant Sam, one might say, produces and carries the baggage of Rick's and Ilsa's desire, but displays no desire of his own" (146–47). Yet the implications of this usurpation extend beyond national boundaries in a way that requires Sam's abjection to secure the myth of America as the pristine savior of Europe. If Sam carries the baggage of Rick and Ilsa's desire, does Lamont (Guy Torry) carry the moral baggage for Derek in *American History X*? Do they both constitute the ground on which the conflicts of the white characters are worked out? Moreover, does Lamont revert to the more stereotypical embodiment of sexuality that Sam's character had shifted to an allegorical level? The scene in which he bonds with Derek is one that represents him not only as highly sexualized but also highly comedic. He also ends up saving Derek, acting as his protector. But, unlike Sam in *Casablanca*, he is not the only major black character. Sweeney, in contrast to stereotypical representations of blacks, is urbane, highly educated—he has two Ph.D.s—and represents the modulated voice of wisdom. Whereas *Casablanca* can be read for its unconscious replication of racist gestures, good intentions notwithstanding, *American History X* can be read as a study in the invisible privilege of whiteness, and a meditation about what it might take to undo that privilege.

   American History X exposes whiteness as the norm by confronting us not only with the violence of white racism but also with its logic. The film both dissects the dynamic of racism from a white point of view, and challenges us to come up with the arguments it doesn't present very forcefully—at least not at the symbolic level—arguments against racism. Film critic Scott Renshaw makes the following comment: "For all its flaws, *American History X* grabs you because it throws you inside the racist mind more effectively than any film I can remember. . . . Derek is chilling because he's not merely spewing bile and epithets—he's making racism make sense—like a master rhetorician. . . . We get that racism is bad. *American History X* works because it risks showing us why some people believe it's good."[21] One of the strengths of the film is that it not only risks showing why some people believe racism is good, but it exposes the dynamic of class oppression that makes such a belief plausible. At the same time, it displays little regard for gender equity. None of the female characters are well developed, and none of them are shown a great deal of respect, nor are there any women of color depicted as major characters in the film. How far screenwriter David McKenna and director Tony Kaye were consciously trying to accurately reproduce the sexist attitudes that they thought would be displayed by a group of white, working-class, neo-Nazi skinheads, and how far they unconsciously reproduced the standard marginalization of women that society displays, is an open question. The depiction of women in the film might not be particularly positive, but it is believable. The film succeeds in representing in a convincing way the marginality of women. The problem this presents is whether or not the film can be seen to perpetuate the marginal status of women by neglecting to portray any strong women. While I am reluctant to demand that films only engage in positive portrayals of women, because I think there must be room for the realist depiction of the ways in which women continue to be peripheral figures whose voices and ideas are dismissed as unimportant, the particular problem that *American History X* confronts us with is more complex than this. While the antiracist points that Davina (Jennifer Lien) and her mother make are trivialized by Derek at the time of their expression, they are validated by the conversion process that Derek undergoes. This can be read as an instance of the power of the semiotic erupting into the symbolic, yet we are still left with a problem. It is all too often still the case that those who understand the marginalization of others, partly because of their own marginalization, remain inarticulate and marginalized. In this case we see two women, Davina and Derek's mother, and a Jew, Murray, express—albeit in a halting way—the forces that ultimately come to shape Derek's thinking. Derek's sister suffers violence at Derek's hands for daring to contradict him, his mother is silenced, and her love-interest is peremptorily dismissed by Derek for putting forward a liberal view. The fact that Murray (Elliot Gould) is Jewish aligns him with the women in Derek's family—as effeminized. By the end of the film not much has changed in this respect. Derek paternalistically insists that Davina finish college, rather than getting a job in order to help with the family's finances, while his sickly mother languishes, her Jewish lover nowhere to be seen, having been successfully run off by Derek.

James Berardinelli offers the following view of *American History X:* "Despite a tendency to become preachy, this film, the directorial debut of Tony Kaye, is no mere piece of propaganda . . . *American History X* does not easily dismiss the rhetoric of pro-white groups. Decoupled from their actions, some of their less-volatile arguments, borne of insecurity and frustration, sound plausible."[22] The film points to the death of Derek's racist father as a major source of the insecurity of Derek (Edward Norton), the white neo-Nazi protagonist, whose charismatic but historically flawed speech incites a mob attack on a local, Korean-owned store. Without naming it as such, the success of the speech rests in large part on its appeal to class.

This is about your life and mine. It's about decent, hard-working Americans falling through the cracks and getting the shaft because their government cares more about the constitutional rights of a bunch of people who aren't even citizens of this country. On the Statue of Liberty it says "Give me your tired, your hungry, your poor." Well it's Americans who are tired and hungry and poor. And I say, until you take care of that, close the fucking book. Cos we're losing. We're losing our right to pursue our destiny. We're losing our freedom, so that a bunch of fucking foreigners can come in here and exploit our country. And this isn't something that's going on far away. This isn't something that's happening in places we can't do anything about. It's happening right in our neighborhood, right in that building behind you. Archie Miller ran that store since we were kids here. Dave worked there. He went under. And now some fucking Korean owns it, who fired these guys and he's making a killing because he hired forty fucking border jumpers.

The frustration Derek is able to tap into has its origins in the fact that Derek and his friends feel like they are at the bottom of the pile, on the lowest social rung—and in terms of white America, they are. Their reaction is to hit out at those who are seen as taking away the jobs that they assume to be theirs, to remind them that they are less than nothing, that they should go back where they came from. This reaction is blind to the fact that illegal immigrants are willing to work for wages that allow the new Korean owner to make "a killing" because they are escaping a poverty unknown to most Americans. The economic threshold of expectation for the Mexican workers is such that to work as illegal immigrants, no doubt earning less than minimum wage, represents an improvement that is worth risking the illegal status of being "border jumpers." An irony that is not confronted by Derek's easy assumption that he and his friends are "losing" their "freedom" is that the European explorers on whom he bases his inheritance could equally well be regarded as a "bunch of fucking foreigners"—a designation Derek reserves for Mexican immigrants—who exploited the Native Americans already living on the land Derek claims as "ours." There is, then, not only a blindness to the economic poverty endemic to those who risk their lives to enter America illegally, but also a blindness to American history, and, most pervasively, a blindness to the qualification of "whiteness" that is assumed to constitute being American. If this whiteness escapes verbal conceptualization, we are confronted with its graphic depiction when, upon entering the store, Derek's friends relentlessly humiliate one of the female workers, physically assaulting her in a scene that culminates in what could be seen as a ritualistic repudiation of the threat that she poses, as they pour milk over her brown skin. Putting a new spin on Kristeva's observations about milk, the refusal of which "separates me from the mother and father who proffer it" (1982, 3), this image condenses within it not only a reference to the sustenance of the maternal body, but also a reference to the mother-nation. The message is clear enough: become like us. Be white. The moment is one of abjection. You are not one of us. You can never be one of us. The only way we could accept you is if you were one of us. The message is that she and her kin should return to her country of origin, to her motherland, and stop taking the jobs that her attackers see as theirs.

As a number of critics have observed, the film contains other scenes whose shock value might be more potent, but the violence of this particular scene resides in its condensation of the themes of miscegenation with sexual control into a single image of relentless humiliation, and its graphic erasure of a skin color that dares to deviate from the white norm, eerily underlined by the decision to shoot the scene not only as a close-up but also in slow motion. That the liquid used to erase the color of the skin is milk reminds us that women must be kept in their place, and that place is circumscribed by traditional, domestic activities such as breast-feeding. At the same time there is a symbolic appropriation of the maternal act of a liquid usually associated with nurturing, a perversion of its sustaining function, that enacts a refusal of the idea that women be allowed to deviate from the white norm. Immigrant workers, especially women, accept low wages, transgress the boundaries of acceptable white femininity, and encroach on territory that is not their own. If they stayed at home, like good white women should, there would be more jobs for the white boys.[23] The pouring of milk over the worker's face is a way of infantilizing her and punishing her: here, you drink the milk that you should be feeding your children with, the job that you should be staying at home to do, and which should not have allowed you to leave your home. We will teach you a lesson that will nearly choke you, even as it paints your face the right color. Go back to where you came from, and give us back our jobs.[24]

As an act of violence that discolors the skin of this woman whose only speech consists in cries for mercy, cries of terror, it etches on her face the symbolic imperative that America purify itself of immigrants in order to survive. It reinstates the boundaries between Mexico and America, between black and white, a border that has become too porous and uncontrollable, a border that the police, undermined by a government that is represented as caring more about the welfare of illegal immigrants than its "own" people, seem to be incapable or unwilling to effectively patrol. As I edit this Republicans are introducing a bill that fuels the fear of illegal immigrants among white citizens by requiring citizens to inform on them, while also effectively distracting attention from the war in Iraq.

In *American History X* the myth of the purity of nation is evoked with the pouring of milk over a Mexican woman's face. The myth that America was born white, and should stay white, is one that needs to be enacted over and over again, in order for America to be able to efficiently bury its "forced inclusion" of Native Americans, and its reliance on immigrant workers and slave laborers, who, often at the cost of their lives, built its infrastructure. In order not to remember that whereas civil rights have largely functioned in a liberatory way, and have even become the ground of white feminist advances, for some women, enforced American citizenship operated in a way that was far from liberatory for America's racially marked underclass. While the procurement of civil rights has been cast as a major victory for mainstream feminists, Guerrero shows that, far from contributing to the liberation of women across the board, this supposedly feminist victory has in fact constituted an oppressive colonialist agenda for native women.[25]

The critical reception of *American History X* is peppered with observations that fail to take up the challenge that this film represents. Critics such as Roger Ebert see the film as one-sided, because it does not do justice to antiracist arguments. In his review in the *Chicago Sun-Times*, Ebert writes, "The movie's right-wing ideas are clearly articulated by Derek in forceful rhetoric, but are never answered except in weak liberal mumbles (by a Jewish teacher played by Elliot Gould, among others)."[26] Alexander Walker agrees: "Kaye allows their [fascist's] rabid bigotry to set the predominant tone by being aired more regularly and forcefully than the wishy-washy counter arguments of their liberal-minded opponents."[27] While the film might not showcase cogent arguments against racism, its outcome is in fact driven by the very arguments that are only weakly stated. The dramatic events that unfold, and the images onscreen, are what add substance and force to the arguments that are only briefly introduced in the dialogue. We are shown what racism does, not told about it. What speaks against the chain reaction of racism and revenge is not only the murders—including finally that of Derek's brother Danny (Edward Furlong), who narrates Derek's story through the vehicle of a school essay Sweeney has him write as a substitute for one on Hitler—that are so graphically depicted. More importantly, one by one, for all the forcefulness of their rhetoric, every racist argument Derek presents is directly addressed, not merely by the arguments put forward—and quickly dismissed—by Davina and her mother Doris (Beverly D'Angelo), figures marginalized by their gender, and by Murray (marginalized by his Jewish identity)—but also by the events that happen to Derek and the relationships that transform him. These include his encounter with Lamont, the African American prison inmate with whom Derek finds himself working in the laundry, his relationship with Sweeney, who asks him whether anything he has done so far has made his life better, and Derek's disillusionment with the unprincipled behavior of the neo-Nazis he meets in prison. It is through the affective or semiotic impact of these events and encounters on Derek that their significance is revealed, and not through any obviously symbolic or well-articulated argumentative dimension. The fact that the film not only focuses on racist arguments but also puts them in the mouth of a charismatic figure, while it also resists the idea that there are any easy answers to racism, leaves the audience with the task of doing the hard work of countering Derek's rhetoric. It is up to us to put into words what the film shows us, but what it does not argue for effectively at an overtly syntactic level. It is up to us to translate the affective content of the film into meaningful symbolic change.

When Murray suggests that rather than indicating a "racial commitment to crime" the number of black males in prison might have more to do with "prejudice in the correctional system," Derek remains unimpressed. When Derek's sister, Davina, backs up Murray by adding, "Yeah, if you want to talk about statistics, you might want to take a look at the social inequalities that produce them," her argument is not granted any weight by Derek, at the time. Yet it is precisely the "prejudice" and "social inequalities," to which Murray (the Jewish "kike") and Davina (the silenced sister) appeal, that come into their own, when Derek processes his incredulity at his black coworkers' prison sentences. One of the turning points in Derek's conversion process is his realization that only racism institutionalized in the legal system can explain the fact that someone is in prison for six years for stealing a television (which he accidentally dropped on a policeman's foot in his attempt to escape), while Derek's own sentence for killing two black men is a mere three years.

Lamont does more than befriend and protect Derek. He helps to change his racist frame of mind. If Sweeney helps him see things differently, and if the rape he suffers at the hands of those he took to be friends forces him to rethink his priorities, above all it is out of loyalty to "the brothers" for whom Lamont exhorts him to look out as Derek leaves prison all in one piece that Derek tries to turn his life around. Lamont uses humor to get through to Derek, turning the bed sheets it is their job to fold in the library into a KKK costume, and parodying Derek's racist beliefs. A second comedic scene, in which Lamont performs the role of an imaginary girlfriend engaged in what he calls "make-up" sex, has Derek in fits of laughter. From then on, the stony silence on Derek's part is relinquished for friendship. If Sweeney's influence on Derek largely takes shape on an intellectual plane, Lamont's operates on the affective level, and the confluence of the two has a powerful impact on Derek, both of them in different ways, displacing Cameron as Derek's father-figure.

Before prison, Derek announces that "One in every three black males is in some phase of the correctional system" and asks, "Is that a coincidence, or do these people have, you know, like a racial commitment to crime?" His loyal girlfriend, Stacey (Fairuza Balk), chimes in, "Not only that, they're proud of it." Although critics have drawn attention to the triumphant expression on Derek's face when he turns toward his brother Danny, having just brutally murdered a black man for attempting to steal his car, they have not made the connection between Stacey's words and Derek's own jubilant pride. The gleam in Derek's eyes reflects his supremacist belief that he has just rid the world of unwanted vermin. Clearly he does not think of those he has just murdered in human terms. His expression is one of pure joy. This is a defining moment for Derek: he is master of his world. By obliterating those he has made to stand for everything threatening in his world, he has made his mark on it. Referring, in a footnote, to Lacan's mirror stage, Fanon writes, "When one has grasped the mechanism described by Lacan, one can have no further doubt that the real Other for the white man is and will continue to be the black man. And conversely. Only for the white man The Other is perceived on the level of the body image, absolutely as the not-self— that is, the unidentifiable, the unassimilable" (1967a, 161, n. 25; 151, n. 25). While Fanon does not have the benefit of having available to him Kristeva's notion of abjection, he does appeal to Sartre's concept of nausea (112; 110), a concept that Kristeva connects to abjection.[28] One could read the critique of phenomenology that Fanon's racial elaboration of the corporeal image accomplishes as a nascent theory of abjection. In his own narrative, this nascent theory is subordinated to the discourse of fetishism, although his appropriation of Lacan has a tendency to substitute one foundational discourse for another, so that the reference point is no longer (white) male sexuality, but becomes black male sexuality. Nonetheless, Fanon's rewriting of the Lacanian mirror stage foreshadows Kristeva's concept of abjection, while at the same time suggesting that the body image operates in racialized ways, and is not confined to the register of sexual difference.

By showing that Derek's redemption is not enough to stop the cycle of violence that racism has set in motion, by leaving the audience with Danny's murder to contemplate, the film does not allow us to rest assured that the conversion of one neo-Nazi is enough to stop the insidious cycle of racism. It suggests that to be implicated by racism does not allow the drawing of neat boundaries that impact only the targets of racism. It requires its audience to formulate more adequately the arguments that the liberal Jewish mumblings of Murray only begin to deliver. It prompts us to remark on the irony that Derek's condemnation of the Rodney King "riots" follows a logic that is reproduced exactly in his own incitement to loot the Korean store in his neighborhood. When Murray points out that "most of the stores that were destroyed during the riots were owned by black people," Derek's younger brother, Danny responds with the words, "That's stupid, though! I mean, why trash your own neighborhood?" Murray responds with the observation that "It's an irrational act. It's like an expression of rage by people who feel neglected and turned away by the system," and Derek passes a judgment that also repudiates the idea that the looting of the Korean-owned store might have anything to do with his own rage, while also inadvertently condemning his own actions as opportunistic: "Calling a riot an irrational expression of rage—that's such a cop out. It's opportunism at its worst. It's a bunch of people grabbing any excuse they can find to go and loot a store."

Far from being isolated and ineffective, almost every "weak, liberal" mumble comes back to haunt Derek. Perhaps if Ebert had seen this, he would have been more convinced than he is by the motivating forces behind Derek's conversion process. The film asks us to think about the insufficiency of the logic in Derek's father's arguments against affirmative action and multicultural curricula. It asks us to comment critically

Derek in *American History X.*
Courtesy of Photofest.

on the fact that when Derek's father balks because Derek's teacher, Dr. Sweeney, is having him read Richard Wright's *Native Son,* he equates "great books" with "white books."[29] "Look, now you've got this book, *Native Son.* What happened to the other books? They're not any good any more, because Mr 2 Ph.D. says they aren't? You've got to trade in great books for black books? Does that make sense, huh?" That some school curricula are still plagued with the legacy of the "great books" or "Western civilization" syndrome, which has made the precise equation that Derek's father commits, points to the institutionalization of racism by the education system to which Derek's father was no doubt exposed.

When Derek's father tells Derek why affirmative "blaktion" isn't American, there might not be an immediate, cogent response from Derek, but the film as a whole asks us to question the occlusion of American history that is at work in his rejection of it. "There are two black guys on my squad now, who got their jobs over white guys, who actually scored higher on the test. Does that make sense, huh? Yeah, sure, it's equal now, but I got two guys, watching my back, responsible for my life, who aren't as good as two other guys, who only got the job because they were black, not because they were the best . . . is that what America is about? No, America is about the best man for the job. You do your best, you get the job." Affirmative action is a policy intended to redress the past history of racism, and to foster conditions that will, in the future, allow everyone to compete on genuinely equal grounds. As long as racism dictates that racialized minorities are imprisoned for disproportionate terms, because of a white imaginary that has not yet come to terms with the history of slavery Derek is so keen to leave behind and forget about, such equality will not be possible.[30]

The death of his father is taken up by Derek in the form of a melancholic attachment to his father's racist ideals. Derek blames his father's death on blacks, and installs Cameron as a father-substitute, whose neo-Nazi views Derek acts upon, as if in revenge for his father's death. The hyperbole of Derek's racist views express in the form of aggression the affection in which he held his father, in the absence of the object of that affection. Derek turns his identification with his father into a hostility against African Americans. In prison, having been raped by those who ostensibly espouse the very neo-Nazi ideals to which Derek himself has become committed, Derek's emotional breakdown signifies not only his physical and sexual violation, but also the moment at which he lets go of his attachment to Cameron, and begins to mourn his father. Rather than holding on to the symbolic, racist views of his father as a way of refusing to acknowledge his loss, Derek's defenses, allegiances, and attachments all desert him. Bereft, disillusioned, humiliated, and vulnerable, he listens to Sweeney, the African American teacher who had such a powerful affect on him, and whose authority the racism of his father had succeeded in supplanting.

Throughout the film, there is a breaking down of the symbolic and imaginary domains that Derek has constructed for himself by drawing on an unconscious construction of whiteness as racially privileged over blackness. The arguments that Derek presents are interrupted by a series of crises that fragment his racist discourse, creating fissures that allow the illegitimacy of his arguments to show through. These crises erupt until the coherence of his racist rhetoric no longer holds. The trauma of rape reduces him to a victim, so that his position in the world is radically altered, and for the first time, he is able to see the world through the eyes of those whose belief in themselves is shattered. He no longer knows what he thinks. His feminization at the hands of those with whom he thought he had something in common is an act of violence that helps him put into perspective not only their inhumanity, but his own. With Sweeney's help, he pieces himself back together, forging a new imaginary, drawing anew his boundaries. Through Derek's own abjection, he reshapes his understanding of the world, and once out of prison he begins to reeducate Danny by telling him his own story. The events that happen to Derek, and the experiences he undergoes, give substance and weight to the liberal arguments that, at the level of the symbolic, carry little authority. It is the brute, material fact of rape, its violently uncompromising, harsh, and inassimilable reality that challenges the simplistic division of the world into white and black, as if the world could easily be divided into those represented by purity and goodness versus the impurity and evil of others. The fact that the flashback sequences of the past are filmed in black and white, in contrast to the use of color in the rest of the film, highlights the oversimplified vision of race that Derek used to hold. The psychic reordering that takes place is fragile and underpinned by the traumatic experiences he undergoes in prison. There is no telling what impact the death of his younger brother, Danny, will have on the shift that has taken place in Derek's imaginary reordering of the world. Whatever its effects, what remains in place is the impact trauma has in shaping how we see the world. By implication, the history of slavery that Derek is so quick to dismiss is granted a decisive role in shaping the collective memory of African Americans. Perhaps more importantly, as Fanon shows, this history also shapes the white imaginary.

American History X focuses on the forces that shape the racism of a white, working-class youth from Venice Beach, and those that combat it. It suggests that it is the responsibility of white people to be reflective about the white privilege we have been able to assume. If *The Birth of a Nation* and *Casablanca* represent two stages of the playing out of race relations in American film, *American History X* represents a third. Both *The Birth of a Nation* and *Casablanca* have overtly propagandist agendas, and both of them write out of the historical narratives they tell any point of view but that of white America, but in the former the racist projection of blacks as evil, violent, disruptive, unruly, and threatening is overt. In *Casablanca,* race is still depicted in accordance with a pejorative myth, but the myth is one that appears more benign, even as it relegates Sam to the periphery of a narrative, driven by two white, heterosexual protagonists. As a marginal figure, one moreover who lends desirability to Rick, Sam's legendary talents are usurped, appropriated, consumed, and reshaped in the form of Rick's prowess, while Sam himself is cast aside, once he outlasts his function, a deject, a waste product, sent back to where he belongs. Blacks and homosexuals, we are reminded, were among the targets of Nazism, not only Jews.

In *American History X,* the spotlight is focused on white racists, on the social and familial causes of racism among the working class, and on what it takes to overcome racism. Derek looks up to his father, and listens to what he is told—and what he is told is racist. What it takes for Derek to question his father, and to overcome his bitterness over his father's death, is abjection, humiliation, and shame, but also great literature written by African Americans such as Wright, and friendship, protection, and support from members of one of the very races he hates so vehemently. The achievement of *American History X* is that it shows us the effects of racism, and imposes on us the responsibility of articulating the logic of its subtext—its history, injustices, and blind spots.

One can point to what has been referred to as "the toxic humiliation of shame" in order to explain if not exonerate the systematic blindness that afflicts one oppressed group when it comes to seeing the oppression of another group.[31] Such a gesture acknowledges the extent to which the specific violence suffered by subjects who find themselves amputated from humanity is liable to impair the vision of those subjects such that recognition of another's humanity is rendered impossible. Or one can invoke a utopian future that appeals to the similarity between the dynamic of racism, sexism, homophobia, and classism. Neither gesture captures the complexity of a situation in which the specific dynamic of one form of oppression has been sustained by the existence of other forms of oppression. What demands more reflection is that the affliction that typically blinds us to oppression of others does not emerge because in principle one cannot make the imaginative leap from one's own suffering to that of another. Rather, it is because the resources to which I turn in my incessant attempt to shore up my own humanity in the face of the ideological war that is waged on it continue to have recourse to myths and legends that partake of racism, sexism, homophobia, and classism. Thus not only is any assurance I might acquire of my own humanity unremittingly fragile, but it is also liable to distortions that I must work hard and vigilantly to keep at bay, by supplementing them with new imaginaries. Given that these mythical distortions have been built up over a long period of time, it will take time to break them down. It will also take imagination and critical reflection: the production of new images, and a willingness to reflect on what these images mean.

To assert an easy and uncomplicated commonality between different forms of oppression is tempting because it yields a harmonious vision of how society could be, but it overlooks the fact that disenfranchisement is crippling to the spirit, and often results in a desperate attempt to consolidate a workable, defeasible ego, and a willingness to blindly throw up all kinds of protective barriers that reinstall precisely the kind of violence they were intended to forestall.[32] When psychic survival is at stake, people take what they can get—and the most readily available defenses often involve the putting down of others in ways that are socially sanctioned. The weak and disenfranchised are easy targets. This does not of course mean that they are the only targets, only that the frequency with which they become so, and the difficulty of addressing such dejection, is compounded by historically sedimented ways of seeing. Just as Klein's notion of projective identification has explanatory purchase in accounting for how the child sets up the bad, threatening breast as dangerous—it is not me that is dangerous, it is the other who is biting me—so white, heterosexual men set up immigrants as the threatening other. It is not me that is always already privileged, it is you who are threatening my privilege, threatening to undermine my stability.

The overenergetic or premature effort to get rid of race as a meaningful category is worrisome precisely to the extent that it is allowed to obfuscate the profound and multiple ways in which race continues to structure material and intellectual privileges, and continues to facilitate the invisibility of whiteness.[33] The rhetorical force of invisibility coalesces with that of the melting pot, hand in hand with the ideology of the American dream, and aligns itself with the spirit of competitive individualism, which is alive and well. As Derek's father would have us believe: "America is about the best man for the job. You do your best, you get the job." It's as simple as that.[34]

7

Abject Identifications in *The Crying Game:* The Mutual Implication of Transgender/Race/Nationalism/Class

W<small>HEN</small> F<small>ERGUS</small> (S<small>TEPHEN</small> R<small>EA</small>), in *The Crying Game,* arrives in London, the first shot we see of his face has him covered with dust from the construction site at which he has found work. Fergus has just arrived from Northern Ireland, and he is in hiding. His gaze is directed toward a quintessentially English scene—a cricket pitch, which nonetheless recalls the sport that Fergus's former hostage, Jody (Forest Whitaker), played in the former British colony of Antigua, a sport that is resolutely ensconced in middle-class privilege in England. While in captivity, Jody had complained to Fergus that he had been sent to "the one place in the world where they call you nigger to your face." We are reminded, when we see Fergus in a modified version of blackface, that in London, Fergus is the "nigger," and that there is a world of difference between his lowly class status and the leisurely cricket game in progress on the pitch. Feminized by a face mask that also marks out his working-class status as construction worker—typical employment for Irish immigrants to England—the image of Fergus's dirt-covered face indicates his marginality, anticipates the sexual relationship about to unfold, and signals at the same time the political anonymity that Fergus is trying to achieve in London, after having fled from the scene of his crime, which does not fail to catch up with him.[1] The discoloration of his skin resonates with the way in which Jody's skin racializes him, and conveys the need to disguise one's identity, a theme that is explored at a variety of levels in the film—not only do we hide from others, but more importantly we hide from ourselves. Fergus is about to become embroiled in a relationship with Dil (Jaye Davidson) that will challenge his sexual identification, and follow through on the homoerotic transference that took place between himself and Jody, the black prisoner he held hostage for the IRA.[2] That Dil is also racially marked as other, but that her skin is lighter than Jody's, renders her less taboo as an object of white desire than Jody's dark skin marks him. That her skin renders her more accessible as an erotic interest for Fergus obscures from him another socially prescribed taboo, that of Dil's transgendered identity.[3] Gender ambiguity is thus veiled by racial ambiguity in a way that allows Dil to pass as a woman. The issues of race, gender, nationalism, sexuality, and class—all of which are at play in *The Crying Game*—are condensed into the image of Fergus's masked appearance.

In order to deal with the identity crisis that Dil's passing provokes, once it is unmasked for him, Fergus serves prison time for a murder he did not commit. Serving a prison sentence in isolation is not so much a punishment, or a means of protecting the world from Fergus's violence— on which he ideologically reneged when he failed to kill Jody—as it is a respite that protects him from his gender confusion. It is easier for Fergus to serve a term of life imprisonment for a murder that he did not commit, thereby aligning himself again with the IRA, whose violence he repudiated when he let Jody run, than it is for him to deviate from the norm of heterosexuality to which he believed he was so firmly attached. He would rather serve time for something he did not do, than do something that his idea of himself cannot serve.[4] Paradoxically, prison allows him to regain control of a situation that has been spiraling out of his control for most of the narrative, and it allows him to adopt the protective stance toward Dil that he has vowed to himself, and to her, to deliver. He thus redefines the boundaries of masculinity and femininity that Dil—precisely by adhering momentarily to the masculine violence that society usually condones for those who possess penises—had shot to pieces, disrupting, albeit at Fergus's request, the consistency with which she passes. Yet prison also allows Dil to care for Fergus—albeit only at a distance.

In prison, by assuming the identity of a killer, Fergus takes up the masculine guise that he never quite managed to live up to, but he does so by retreating back into the symbolic safety of the IRA persona that he tried so hard to escape. He thus fabricates a masculine (active, aggressive) persona by adopting a passive (feminine) relationship to the traumatic discovery that he was not who he took himself to be. He thereby mimics the ambiguity that he cannot process or thematize. He does so because it is easier for him to foreclose the meaning of his affection for Dil than it is to come to terms with what his love for Dil might do to the ideal of masculinity that Jody had already revealed to him as mythical, by seducing Fergus into deviating from the stereotype of the violent IRA killer whose nature is not to let their victims go.

Fergus's incarceration functions both as moral compensation for the death of Jody—for which he was indirectly responsible—and as a strategy that prevents him from having to resolve the uncertainty that his relationship with Dil has created for him. He would rather return to inhabit his role as a member of the IRA—the very thing that he was fleeing from—than confront the difficulty of negotiating what his romantic attachment to Dil might mean for his sexual identification. Fergus is a good deal more comfortable behind the safety of the bulletproof glass of his maximum security prison cell, which places tangible limits on any exchange he has with Dil, than he was on the outside, where he dressed Dil in Jody's clothes in his attempt not only to save her from the IRA, but also to save himself from the predicament he found himself in. Having brought to fruition the fantasy of Jody in cricket whites that has haunted and informed his sexual relationship with Dil, Fergus seeks to remove his relationship with Dil to the same relatively safe plane of friendship that he developed with Jody, in which sexuality remained sublimated, circumscribed by the political definitions that categorize Jody as a British soldier, and a powerless hostage, and Fergus as an IRA volunteer soldier and his captor. In the maximum security prison cell where Fergus serves his sentence for the sake of Dil—thereby proving that he would do "anything" for her—he is separated from Dil by a glass panel, which recalls the glass greenhouse in which Fergus kept Jody hostage at the beginning of the film. The greenhouse or glasshouse in which Fergus held Jody captive is exchanged for another glasshouse, one in which Fergus consents to incarcerate himself.[5] Now it is Fergus who is captive, and Dil who brings him not cups of tea but vitamin pills. She too seems quite at ease with the glass pane through which she can see but not touch him, and behind which he is doing time for her.

Is Jordan's message that the borders differentiating male from female, and heterosexuality from homosexuality, are policed more intransigently than those differentiating British, imperial, Protestant pretensions from the nationalist, Catholic opposition of the IRA? Are we meant to believe that the decision as to whether Fergus should remain a member of the IRA, or betray his ideological commitment to the independence of Northern Ireland, is grounded on a political instability that is more pliable than the borders by which gender identity and sexuality are policed? Or is the point rather that national identities and loyalties are played out on the grounds of race and sexuality, and

policed by racial and sexual taboos? Is it that sexist and racist mythologies dictate the terms in which national collectivities tend to represent
themselves, and find themselves represented in relation to the colonial
histories that determine their identities? In these mutually supporting
scenarios, myths of nationalism, race, class, and sex feed off one another
in a way that makes all of them appear to be implacable, despite the
multiple refiguring the film enacts. The colonial relationship that
England exercises over Ireland is often represented in feminized terms.
Ireland is seen as the passive, feminine other, as a fertile land to be harnessed, cultivated, and conquered under the masculine dominion of
England.[6] *The Crying Game* exposes the multiple mechanisms by which
identities are created and borders are policed, while it raises the question
of who polices these borders, and whose authority ensures their integrity.
The various aspects of identity the film explores—nationality, race, gender, sexuality, and class—are shown to constitute one another.[7]

With some notable exceptions, critical responses to Neil Jordan's
The Crying Game (Ireland, 1992) tend to be organized around three
approaches.[8] There are those who herald the film as radical, basing their
arguments on the claim that the film transgresses sexual norms, forcing
us to confront the instability of gender identity.[9] Such readings tend to
emanate from gender theorists, who focus on the ways in which Dil's
gender instability is echoed by Jody, Fergus, and Jude (Miranda
Richardson). Then there are those, for example, hooks (1994) and Edge
(1995), who argue that the film's exploration of shifting sexual identity
is only superficial, and at a deeper level the appearance of radicality
gives way to pernicious stereotypes that are reinforced in terms of both
gender and race.[10] Finally, there are those who approach the film
within the terms set by the study of Irish cinema and particularly in
terms of its Anglo-Irish political context, for example, Rockett and
Rockett (2003) and Lloyd (1999). Situating the film with reference to its
relationship to Frank O'Connor's "Guests of the Nation" (1931),[11] a
short story in which two British soldiers are taken hostage in an attempt
to forestall the execution of two IRA men, and Brendan Behan's play
The Hostage, which was inspired by O'Connor's story, establishes the literary precedents for *The Crying Game.*[12] Informed by the presuppositions
of the theoretical discourses out of which these readings emerge, each
of them tends to repudiate any sustained consideration of other aspects
that are central to the film. Hence, those who approach the film from
the perspective of gender theory typically do so at the expense of a serious interrogation of its racial motifs and its nationalist concerns, while
those who approach it from the point of view of race often do so at the
expense of taking seriously its gender and nationalist implications.[13]

Critics who approach the film from the perspective of national cinema theory tend to highlight the history and politics of the Anglo-Irish conflict effectively but for the most part fail to critically engage its racial and gendered aspects.[14] Very few theorists have thought in any sustained way about the class politics that also structure the film.[15]

As should be clear by now, I think that the notion of abjection can be mobilized as a theoretical device that can contribute productively to feminist and progressive analyses of film, just as I think certain films can shed light on the abject. *The Crying Game*, and its critical reception, both implicate, and are implicated in, various forms of social discrimination that can be usefully read in the light of abjection.[16] Reading *The Crying Game* as a critical intervention in debates not only about gender and race but also about class and nationalism, I grant that the film subverts gender assumptions in a productive way, while at the same time acknowledging that it also reinscribes some racially coded, discriminatory, and misogynist gestures, even as it disrupts others. Abjection can serve as an interpretive device that can illuminate the film at a number of levels. First, the break or rupture of the narrative plot, around which the sexual identities of Dil, Fergus, Jody, and Jude are organized, can be analyzed in terms of abjection. Secondly, the impact that this rupture has on the spectator, either by encouraging the viewer to become self-reflective about her/his identification with Fergus's heterosexually privileged desire, or by revealing how the heterosexual narrative proceeds only by a consistent reference to homosexual desire, lends itself to an interpretation that takes abjection as its cue. Finally, certain patterns emerge in the critical responses to the film that conform to the dynamic of abjection. I am particularly interested in the apparent necessity that surfaces in the critical literature either to repudiate the suggestion that *The Crying Game* has any racial significance at all, or, in the process of establishing that it replicates certain racist gestures, to insist that Dil is "really" a man, thereby repudiating—or abjecting— whatever sexual radicality is contained in the film's exploration of transgendered identity.[17] A similar tendency surfaces in approaches that treat the film as part of the corpus of Irish cinema. Thus Rockett and Rockett allude to "Dil's true gender" (2003, 138), as if the penis as a bodily referent unproblematically identifies Dil as really a man, thereby lapsing into the kind of biological essentialism that transgender studies makes a concerted effort to disrupt. By the same token, critics who claim that the second part of the film abandons its focus on politics are assuming that sexuality is not shaped by politics, and that the concerns of nationalism showcased in the first part of the film are not played out with insistent reference to sexuality. The effect is to naturalize one part of the film at the expense of abjecting another.

The unassimilable is what Fergus comes face to face with in *The Crying Game*, in an encounter that renders unstable the heterosexual matrix that structures his self-understanding. Critics such as Sarah Edge and bell hooks have argued that *The Crying Game* is not as radical as many film critics hailed it. Edge (1995) suggests that Jude is demonized, a monster, an abject figure, and hooks (1994) suggests that stereotypical notions of race prevail—in the end, the interracial relationship cannot work.[18] While informative and interesting on a number of levels, these readings also seem problematic to me, since they recuperate some of the most radical aspects of the film in attempting to draw it back into a conservative narrative about gender and race, one that supports, rather than disrupts, the status quo.[19] These readings undercut the radicality of the challenge that the film's exploration of transgender offers, recuperating this theme within a rather traditional insistence that there are no good real women in the film, and refusing to acknowledge the implications of the shock that Fergus feels at the realization that the person he has fallen in love with is anatomically a man. While hooks is right to point out that Dil's function could be read as conforming to the stereotypical, exotic other as a tragic mulatta, she allows this objection to neutralize not only another pervasive disruption that Dil effects on Fergus's discovery that Dil is not anatomically the female he has assumed she is, that of Fergus's heterosexual gender identification, but also the specific imperialist history that informs the events depicted in the film.

Despite the fact that race plays a prominent role in *The Crying Game*, some critics have been able to completely ignore its significance, while others have either downplayed or reduced the gender ambiguity introduced by Dil's transgender identity, in order to argue that the film replays some very traditional racial stereotypes. Bruzzi provides a highly nuanced discussion of the film with regard to the "complexities of sex and gender" (1997, 186), in which she reads *The Crying Game* as "an extended interplay of inconsistent, fluid identities" (187), but in which she fails to even mention race. bell hooks provides a much needed corrective to the neglect of race by many critical reviews of *The Crying Game*, but in doing so, she erases the radical effects of both Dil's transgender identity, and the less-than-radical effects of her status as mixed race, in a reading that insists that "Dil is really a black man" (1994, 61).[20] One could argue rather that it is not only Dil's apparent sexuality, but also her lighter skin, which makes her, rather than Jody, a possible object of Fergus's sexual attraction.[21]

Many critics have commented on the homoerotic overtones of the relation between the IRA man, Fergus, and Jody, his prisoner, who is tied up, prefiguring the scene in which Dil ties Fergus to the bed, thus preventing him from carrying out the suicide mission that Peter and Jude have arranged for him. By tying Fergus to the bed, Dil is unknowingly doing to him what Fergus has done to Jody—and, as David Lugowski says, "In both cases, male bondage is caused by or juxtaposed with the IRA's activities."[22] Fergus's discomfort with Dil's sexuality is compounded with the history of his oppressive relationship to Jody, so that any signifier of intimacy between them is mixed with the violence of the IRA having taken Jody hostage. As Leighton Grist argues, while readings of *The Crying Game* that privilege homosexuality have a certain validity, they are also "partial and delimiting" in that they "foreclose" other "significant matters regarding gender and sexual identity. . . . In discussing how *The Crying Game* problematizes the masculine-feminine binary, analyses of the film seem all too eager to replace one binary with another, that of hetero-homosexuality" (Grist 2003, 5). This eagerness is not confined to sexual binaries, but is replicated at a number of levels in the critical literature.

The insufficiency of a logic of reversal for a radical politics has been amply remarked. The politics of gender, class, or nationalism is inevitably shaped by an oppositional politics that it nonetheless seeks to go beyond, and which it must put in question, or else condemn itself to repeating the same logic.[23] The difficulty in avoiding such repetition resides both in the extent to which nationalist (or class or gender) claims are formulated in reaction to colonial (or capitalist or patriarchal) oppression, and in the danger that such claims, which are produced precisely in the attempt to throw off oppressive ideologies, will collapse into naturalistic claims.[24] In the case of Ireland, the dangers of a nationalist rhetoric that casts itself as inherent takes up the various ways in which the Irish have been constructed by the British as in need of cultivation, and in turn constructs the Irish as wild, untamable, and anarchic.

The artificial reversal of roles, by which the IRA temporarily turns the tables on the British, gaining the upper hand, at least within the limited terms of Jody's capture, cannot be sustained as a viable political strategy. The sheer might and force of the attack on the IRA safe house so obviously outweighs any military strength that could be mustered against it by the IRA, that it prompts the question of why Jordan represents the scene in this way. As David Lloyd points out, such high-profile violence runs counter to the policy of low-intensity campaigns adopted by the British in Ireland.[25] Assuming that the scene is played neither for the sake of gratuitous violence, nor for any concerns of realism, what is its function? The show of military prowess by the British army in its rescue mission functions not merely at the level of sensational, Hollywood-style violence, but allegorically, demonstrating graphically the power differential between the IRA and the British army. The scene can be read as underlining the extent to which any maneuver by the IRA is politically overdetermined by the presence of British troops in Northern Ireland, and the continuation of British rule. The IRA's arbitrary use of an individual as symbolic of national interests might successfully mimic the ideological violence experienced by the Irish at the hands of the British Empire, but the relative powerlessness of this gesture inscribes it in a dynamic that can only perpetuate the logic of colonial style–rule over individuals in the name of protecting their interests.

The stability of political categories in *The Crying Game* is in question from the start, not least because the representative of the British army that the IRA has chosen to take hostage is hardly the obvious choice. Given the racist regimes that underlie the racial epithets to which Jody takes exception (even as he himself engages in similar practices by calling Fergus "paddy"), it is hardly plausible that the IRA would target Jody as a hostage.[26] As Lloyd comments, such narrative implausibilities—which he establishes as rife—engage in a parodic impersonation of narrative probability by which *The Crying Game* distances itself "from the ethic of realism, which insists on bringing individuals into conformity with what is given as the facts of life."[27] Jordan allows Jody to stand as representative of the British army in order to complicate the moral absolutism that tends to construe nationalist discourses as if they were a function of metaphysical, racial essences, rather than of politics and history.[28] For the same reason he allows Dil to police the boundaries of femininity more effectively than any of the characters that identify as male. Jude moves through a succession of roles, becoming progressively more masculine-identified as the narrative develops, and as one masquerade replaces another. Her role as sexual temptress (dressed in a short denim skirt and high heels) is replaced in quick succession by that of a subordinate who makes the tea (dressed in an Aran sweater and jeans), a ruthless terrorist whose violence against Jody finds its counterweight in Fergus's increasing sympathy with Jody, and finally, in London, the spurned lover (dressed as a femme fatale), whose terrorist credentials are now apparently so well established that even Peter accepts orders from her.[29] If in Ireland the communication between Jude and Peter (Adrian Dunbar) ranged from Peter's dismissive "Shut up Jude" to "Shut the fuck up, Jude," in London the tables are turned, and the balance of power now operates in Jude's favor.

Dil becomes the vehicle through which Jude's transgression of traditional tropes of femininity is punished, thereby resurrecting and re-creating the boundaries of what is permissible for femininity and what is not. She does so from the position of someone who identifies as a woman and who has a penis. Yet, at the moment of Jude's murder, Dil is dressed not as a woman, but as Jody. Is Dil's punishment of Jude, the femme fatale who must die, to be read as a reversion to her real, true, underlying masculinity—after all she has the body that is normatively associated with that of a man, and is dressed in conformity with that body for the first time in the film?[30] Or is it rather to be read as consistent with her hysterical femininity, a hyperbolic mimicking of the ideal of femininity to which her body does not conform, but which her behavior takes to its extreme? If it is to be read as consistent with the ideal of femininity to which she aspires, though, according to deeply embedded cultural norms, she will always fall short of this ideal, does Dil merely confirm what Freud thought he knew, namely, women's incapacity for morality, their inconsistency, dependency, proclivity for jealousy, and excessive narcissism? Does she add substance to the Lacanian view that there can only be one woman? Or in killing Jude, does Dil rather confirm the myth that, as a woman of color, she cannot be relied upon to make sound judgments, because of an alleged irrational, untrustworthy, and emotive nature? I want to make some preliminary observations about the scene in which Dil murders Jude, to which I will return toward the end of this chapter.

When Dil switches her excessively feminine persona for that of violent murderer, she is motivated not only out of revenge for Jody's death, and not merely by her jealousy of Fergus's commitment to Jude, but also by her jealousy of what Dil refers to as Jude's "tits and that cute little ass." According to social dictates, in order to be accepted as the woman Dil identifies herself as, she is required to have the bodily anatomy that is presumed to accompany femininity. That she lacks this anatomical social prerequisite provides the ground on which she mercilessly unloads bullets into Jude's dying body—as she "overkill[s]" her (James 1995, 39). In Dil's eyes, Jude's crime consists more than anything in having so effectively mastered the art of performing femininity in its various guises. The urgency with which she demands of Fergus (who cannot remember—for him, clothes are just extraneous "details"): "Tell me what she wore" reveals the importance of clothing to Dil's own success at passing.[31] The external signifiers of clothing and hairstyle are all she has to rely on, so that the strength of her initial resistance to Fergus's proposal that he cut her hair comes as no surprise. What Jude wears is all we have to go on with regard to how to read her gender, since, unlike Dil, there is no unmasking of her sex—as if such an unveiling could tell us anything definitive anyway. Whether Jude has a penis or not we do not "know," but most of us probably make conventional assumptions about the presence or absence thereof.[32]

For Lloyd "it is Jude who most effectively performs femininity" and as such "threatens both Dil's 'femininity' and her possession of Fergus *and* Jody" (1999, 71).[33] If it is true that Jude is the one who performs femininity most effectively, it is also true that she does so with an ease that is underwritten by the fact that she (we presume) has the body type that society prescribes for femininity, that is, she conforms to the gender hierarchies and stereotypes that the film asks us to disrupt. To ignore this is to elide the challenge with which Jordan presents his audience in providing the space in which an all-too-predictable abjection of Dil's transgendered identity occurs. Dil's inadmissible sexual ambiguity becomes the ground on which more conventional stereotypes of femininity and masculinity are allowed to masquerade as radical.[34] Thus, Jude's adoption of masculine norms, as she totes a gun, toughs it out, and remains loyal to the cause that Fergus abandons, might desert the norms of femininity, but only in order to perform a complete reversal, by inhabiting the norms of masculinity. As such its radicality is severely limited, if not entirely compromised, by the fact that she merely enacts a reversal, inhabiting masculine gender norms, but doing nothing to challenge the content of traditional feminine or masculine tropes. While the range of feminine roles adopted by Jude proves to be elastic, there is no reason for anyone to question the stability of her gender at the level of generic correspondence between anatomy and social mores. Jude's heavily coded styles might vary, but the audience has no trouble in understanding that she remains a woman—according to traditional conceptions of womanhood—despite the masculine roles she performs. In this sense she does not so much participate in gender instability, as reinforce the traditional, received meanings of what it means to be a woman (and therefore what it also means to be a man). We understand her to be deviating from the norm, but this deviation causes no disruption in what we take to be the norm. By contrast, Dil's success at passing as a woman—for Fergus, and perhaps for us—proves to be debilitating once it is revealed for what it is. Yet, this revelation does not have the effect that one might have expected. Far from clarifying Dil's gender identity, the revelation maintains, rather, its instability. As Helen Hanson says, "although Fergus and the film audience see Dil's body, her/his gender identity remains in question. . . . Dil cannot be recuperated to figure 'masculine' even when s/he is seen naked."[35]

Like Ilsa in *Casablanca*, Dil tries momentarily to adopt the pose of phallic woman when she threatens the man she loves with a gun, but she cannot sustain the role any more than Ilsa could.[36] Both Ilsa and Dil revert to type (although of course Dil severely complicates what constitutes type), taking up the role of passive females who need a man to assure them of their continuing affection, or to take up and resolve the moral questions that defeat them. In *The Crying Game* it is left up to Jude to inhabit the role of the phallic, castrating woman, who must be punished. In one more twist, in the end it is Dil who murders Jude, taking on as she does so the callous persona that Jude has portrayed up until this point. In a reversal that the critical literature on *The Crying Game* so consistently repudiates when it refuses Dil the status of a real woman, the film asks us to read Dil as the woman she identifies herself as—until, one might think, the moment at which she adopts Jody's masculine persona, having allowed Fergus to perfect the identification between Jody and herself that he has imagined in his dreams. In fact, however, apart from when she kills Jude, Dil is at her weakest and most vulnerable when dressed as Jody. She sheds the pathologically feminine and masochistic persona that she exhibits until she realizes that Jude is not only her rival for Fergus's love and loyalty but also that she used her sexuality to trap Jody, thereby leading him to his death, and so Dil turns the gun on Jude. Dressed in Jody's cricket whites— replete with the white, upper-class, heterosexual connotations of this quintessentially British sport—Dil's newly empowered self has no trouble performing the masculine-coded violence that is also encoded in racial signifiers. Taking revenge on Jude as Jody's bereaved lover, she also revenges herself on the white, heterosexual mores that intrude upon Fergus's ability to accept her for what she is. That she does so in the guise of cricket whites signals her usurpation of power, usually reserved for more conventionally privileged figures, at the same time as it aligns her with Jody, the other racially and sexually marginalized figure in the film, whose capacity to act has been foreclosed both by his captors and by the British army, who are thereby shown to be united in their common antiblack racism—albeit a legacy of the British Empire from whose grip the IRA is trying to loosen itself. Just as Jody claims to be a "shit hot" bowler, so Dil, inspired and focused by the memory of her dead lover, and her desire for retribution, turns out to be a remarkably good shot. At another level, Dil becomes the vehicle for the symbolic supremacy Britain maintains over Ireland, as her murder of Jude, following quickly on the heels of Peter's murder of "some judge," can be read as swift British retaliation. Dil's position as a (presumably) British subject—despite the evidence of her depoliticized sensibilities—positions the meaning she herself attributes to her actions differently, functioning as a reminder that not only her subjectivity but also that of Fergus and Jody is produced by the symbolic, imperialist forces that do not fail to govern the narrative even now. As Althusser puts it, *"There are no subjects except by and for their subjection."*[37]

If Dil adopts a masculine, phallic, and empowered relation to Jude as she mercilessly unloads bullets into her body, she only arrives at this moment after having traversed a stereotypically feminine-coded psychic collapse, even as she is dressed as Jody. Without her man, she is a mess. Assuming that Fergus has abandoned her, or will do so, she staggers across the cricket field, bottle in hand, emerging out of the darkness as Jody has done so often in Fergus's fantasies/dreams, drunk, in need of medication, suffering from an unnamed blood-disorder (AIDS?), she is hardly the man that Jody was. But she takes her cue from him in the matter of killing or letting be.[38] After her unceremonious murder of Jude, Dil once again finds herself unable to dispatch Fergus: the memory of Jody won't let her. Apparently still watching over Dil and Fergus, Jody's ghostly moral authority thereby informs Dil's displaced love for him, and Fergus's act of contrition, also an act of loyalty to Jody. If Fergus takes responsibility for Dil's murder of Jude, this maneuver allows him to figuratively pay for both the death of Jody and his deceit of Dil, but, as already noted, it also facilitates his retreat from the confusion of his sexuality that Jody represents for him, and Dil provokes in him.[39]

True to the continuity between Ilsa as *Casablanca*'s leading woman, and Dil as *The Crying Game*'s, Joy James points out that "The mulatta, as hybrid, supplanted both the African and European woman in her representation of the female sexual fetish" (1995, 35). Yet to read Dil as fetishized is also to eclipse precisely the racial identification that James intends to point out, reinscribing the emphasis on the heterosexual, white, male gaze of the director. By reading Dil's transgendered identity as abject I suggest that the critical literature spawned by *The Crying Game* mirrors the abjection that Dil suffers diegetically, as Fergus accomplishes his moral redemption by bracketing the need to resolve the identity crisis his romantic involvement with Dil constitutes.[40] I think that Dil's abjection can be seen most clearly at the moment at which Fergus, on discovering her penis, hits out at her, drawing blood from her mouth (as Jude had earlier drawn blood from Jody's) and then vomits. It is a moment in which the sexual identity Fergus thought he had established for himself is thrown into question, a moment at which those in the audience who had identified with what they (and he) took to be Fergus's heterosexual desire for Dil are abjected. While I agree with James that Dil serves "as food for thought for white moralizing" (39), as the "vehicl[e] for [Fergus's] redemption" (1995, 41), and that Jordan recycles "stereotypes of black *femmes fatales*" who are "prone to sexual abuse," I think that the stereotypes he trades in are also put into question, and that abjection does more explanatory work for Dil's role in *The*

Fergus and Dil in *The Crying Game.*
Courtesy of Photofest.

Crying Game than either the trope of fetishism or that of voyeurism.[41] I also think that a good deal of the critical literature on *The Crying Game* proceeds by abjecting transgendered identity. Fergus abjects Dil in his sickened response, which is not only a rejection of her but also a repulsion of himself for having fallen for someone who has a penis—something that does not fit in with the norms by which he had previously understood himself. Jordan thus abjects his heterosexually identified audience in and through Fergus's abjection of Dil.

If first Jody and then Dil function as vehicles for Fergus's confrontation with his identity on multiple levels, the film does not abandon the political for the personal, as some critics suggest.[42] To claim that it cannot deal at a serious level with the Anglo-Irish conflict because it degenerates into a narrative about sexuality is to refuse to think through the sense in which assumptions about miscegenation, sexuality, and class thoroughly infuse the construction of national identity. It is also to relegate sexuality, class, gender, and race to the realm of the private, as if these aspects of identity were not constructed in relationship to highly visible, public myths. Which subjects are allowed to take on the legitimate representation of nationality, and which are not, has everything to do with their class, gender, and sex. To relegate sexuality—or gender, or race, or class—to the private realm, is to evacuate it of political significance, and to misconstrue the ways in which national identity asserts itself. It is to do so not in a way that might attempt to isolate itself from, and set itself above, other socio-political mechanisms, but in a way that makes constant reference to them. Finally, to minimize the film's thematization of the political ignores the sustained parodic discourse that is maintained in *The Crying Game* about the pathology of terrorism, to which Lloyd has drawn attention (1999). To assume that Jordan falls prey to a depoliticization of the Anglo-Irish conflict by subordinating this aspect of the narrative to a more personalized narrative about gender confusion is to underestimate both the film and the complex relationships that pertain between national, gender, race, sexuality, and class identity.[43] Jody challenges Fergus at multiple levels, becoming the catalyst that provokes Fergus to question his moral commitments as an IRA member, and thus his nationalist identification, at the same time as throwing him into confusion over his sexuality. What sexual relationships are socially sanctioned, who is publicly deemed to be allowed to have sex with whom? These are the nuts and bolts of kinship boundaries.

The inseparability of class from other aspects of identity, for example, resides in the frequency with which conventional codes of racialization, sexuality, and gender inform and construct one another. Fergus's fellow construction workers participate in the conventional sexism of catcalls when Dil visits Fergus at the construction site. Fergus's distraction causes him to drop a pane of glass, and his boss, Mr. Deveroux, wields his class authority over Fergus not only by telling him the cost will be deducted from his wages but also by having recourse to a gesture that can be read as both racist and sexist. He refers to Dil as a tart, prompting Fergus to gallantly and intuitively defend her honor with a threat of violence that marks Fergus as physical, visceral, and corporeal, thereby reinstating the boundaries along which Irishness is stereotypically delineated from its ostensibly urbane English other. The joke, of course, is that in coming to Dil's metaphorical rescue, Fergus aligns her with the gender that he can apparently only accept when others call into question its respectability—even as he acknowledges (in accord with definitions of gender bound by anatomical convention) that while she is not a tart, neither is she a "lady."

After Fergus playfully picks up a cricket bat (a gesture that identifies him with Jody), Mr. Deveroux reminds him in a middle-class English accent of his class position, as he calls Fergus by a string of indiscriminately Irish-coded names. "I don't actually give a fuck whether it's Jim, Pat, or Mick, as long as you remember you're not at Lord's, alright." He thus constitutes Fergus as a generalized Irish other—whose individuality doesn't matter, as long as he knows his place. That place is not on the cricket ground below, a space of leisure, reserved for white, middle-class England, but is determined by the physical work Fergus has been employed to do, which requires that he tow the line, keep his head down, and not get into any trouble—in particular he should observe the boundaries separating the privileged from the working class.[44] The equation of the Irish in London with physical labor aligns them with the corporeal—thus feminizing them—as opposed to the English, whose masculinized capacity resides in their overseeing of the bodies whose physical strength is needed to erect buildings in which corporations can continue to pedal the values of capitalism.

As Fergus's class position is clearly marked in England, Jody's class is firmly established in Ireland. His working-class identity is signaled when he responds to Fergus's question "why did you sign up [for the army]?" with disarming simplicity: "It was a job." We get an insight into both his ethnic and his class background when he explains that cricket might be a game "for toffs" in Tottenham, but not in Antigua, where he comes from.[45] While Fergus's class aligns him with Jody, his naiveté sets them apart. In contrast to Jody, Fergus's provincialism is heavily enmeshed in a heterosexual matrix of desire that prevents him from picking up the cues that Dil wants to assume are too obvious for him to miss. When Jody asks Fergus to hold his penis while he "pisses," because his own hands are tied behind his back, Fergus's discomfort with the task presented him is palpable.[46] If the symbolism of having his hands tied signifies Jody's having got himself into this situation by signing up for the army, the scene's reference to male bondage also anticipates the homosexual bond that Fergus will have so much trouble assuming with Dil. Displaying prophetic qualities about the difficulty Fergus will encounter when he discovers Dil's biological sex, Jody says, "It's amazing how these small details take on such importance," and then, when Fergus is reluctant to touch his penis, "It's only a piece of meat." Back in the safety of distance, in the glass outhouse where Jody is being held hostage, their laughter dissipates the tension, and signals to Peter, who appears on the scene to reprimand Fergus, the inappropriate bond that has sprung up between Fergus and Jody.[47]

Initiating another of the repetitions that structure the plot of the film, when Fergus leaves for London, he finds the hairdressing salon where Dil works, and he has her give him a trim—a gesture that will be reciprocated when Fergus, overcoming Dil's feminine protests, cuts her hair in order to disguise and protect her, but also in order to make her identity conform to Jody's.[48] Dil assumes from Fergus's accent that he is Scottish and he allows her assumption to stand, since he is hiding from the IRA, and hiding his implication in Jody's death from her.[49] The film thus continues its pursuit of the question of identities, and the need to hide the truth about who you are. Adopting the name of Jimmy, Fergus conceals his true identity and nationality from Dil, and fails to recognize her biological—what the world considers to be "true"—sex.[50] Much of their relationship is staged in the presence of a third party, a constant reminder of the socially mediated nature of gender configuration. Dil seems to have less trouble choreographing other people's lines than she does in speaking in the first person. At dinner Dil tells Fergus that "now is the time you are meant to do something isn't it . . . make a pass or something. Isn't that the way it goes?"—as if she is writing a script.[51] She is, after all, a performer, a nightclub singer, as we discover when we are treated to a rendition of *The Crying Game*.[52] Dil feeds to him the dialogue she wants to hear from Fergus, just as she instructs him to tell her he loves her and will never leave her, that he would do anything for her (which, as it happens, turns out to be true, at least if we except the possibility of continuing a sexual relationship with her). Like Jody, she uses the third person to refer to herself.[53] The performance is often mediated by Col (Jim Broadbent), the bartender, who dispenses not only margaritas but also advice to Fergus about how to treat Dil.[54] On another occasion, as we've seen, the third party is Fergus's boss and coworkers, when Dil comes to see him at work one day. Their first kiss is orchestrated, ostensibly to get ex-boyfriend Dave's "goat," as is their first date. Thus, in a variety of ways, a social context is woven from conventional, heterosexual expectations. At the same time, those expectations are undercut by multiple cues that establish Dil and the club in which she performs as transgender. Col speaks for Dil's expectations, at one point almost telling Fergus what he suspects he does not know, while the onlookers in the restaurant, Dave (Ralph Brown) and the construction workers, provide the heterosexual substance of Fergus's expectations.[55] The series of triangular relationships (Fergus/Jody/Dil, Fergus/Jude/Jody, Fergus/Jude/Dil, Fergus/Dil/Dave, Fergus/Dil/Col, and even Fergus/Mr. Deveroux/Dil), whether consciously or not, replicate the triangular relationships that characterize *Casablanca*, in which Sam is the go-between linking Rick and Ilsa, while Laszlo forms another triangle with Rick and Ilsa.

At first sight, to the extent that Dil has successfully passed as a woman, both for Fergus and for those who have identified with his desire as heterosexual, the moment of revelation might be said to have the effect of castration. This reverses Freud's insight that the sight of female genitalia is a moment of castration because the absence of the penis is threatening.[56] Here it is the presence of the penis that is castrating—or

Jude, Fergus, and Dil in *The Crying Game.*
Courtesy of Photofest.

rather, as I suggest, abjecting—because Fergus has taken Dil to be a woman, and his desire for her to be heterosexual.[57] This brings to the fore the often-unstated presumption of castration theory that it is not the penis per se that has phallic implications, but the penis when it is read as embodying masculinity in an uncomplicated way.[58] In other words, by embodying what might seem to be the logical outcome of Freud's fantasy of disavowal, Dil exposes it as impossible and unthinkable within the binary and heteronormative assumptions that are the basis of Freud's theory. By presenting us with the logical result of what fetishism wishes to keep at bay, *The Crying Game* exposes the illogicality of the theory of fetishism within its own terms, at the same time as it makes clear the extent to which the theory of fetishism relies on the differentiation between the phallus and the penis. That is, it brings into focus the necessity of allowing the phallus to remain at the symbolic, metaphorical, signifying level, the necessity of preserving a substitutive relation between the penis and the phallus. The moment the maternal phallus is collapsed into a maternal penis, the power of the phallus *as maternal* is destroyed. Confronted with Dil's penis, the audience for whom Dil has passed, through their identification with Fergus, as a woman, does not experience Dil as threatening, or castrating, as phallic, but precisely as abject. Fergus's horror refracts the audience's horror. What is horrific in this instance is not—as Freud would have it—female genitalia, but the penis in place of the female genitalia that Fergus (and those who identified with him) expected. What Dil makes painfully clear is that for Fergus femininity only operates as femininity if it is backed up by what can be read as a body consistent with femininity, a body that thereby functions as a stable, anatomical ground of gender. If it is not, it becomes uncategorizable, horrific.[59] The horror consists not so much in the fact that Dil has passed as a woman as it does in the unmasking of Dil's passing. Hanson acknowledges this when she says "it is only in the exposure of an act of passing that its subversion of identity categories is made plain" (1999, 50). What is subverted then is our attachment to the stability of gender categories, and our assumption that such categories function in reliable, predictable, self-transparent ways. For Fergus, the subversion that takes effect at the sight of Dil's penis is not limited to Dil; it implicates him, and the world he lives in, destabilizing not only his own sexual identity but also the heteronormative order he assumed to legitimate him.

The figure of Dil clarifies not only the sense in which femininity and masculinity depend upon a heteronormative understanding of gender, in which a body that is read as female grounds femininity, but also the imaginary status of fetishism. It is essential to fetishism that it deals in substitutes, that it function as a series of signs, that it replace the "missing penis" with objects that stand in for the penis, but which do not approximate to it or resemble it in any straightforward way. Part of the allure of fetishism lies in its obscurantism, in its suggestiveness, in its necessary failure to present directly what it nevertheless hints at through innuendo. Once the indirect, circuitous, veiled nature of the fetish is short-circuited, once the necessity for signs, stand-ins, substitutes is dispelled, the fetish not only loses its alluring power as fetish, but becomes repulsive. Masquerade is crucial to the fetish. When it becomes clear that the fetishistic mechanism operates at the level of fantasy, and this fantasy has been debunked, the phallic mother is no longer what she was. Far from being powerful, castrating, or threatening because of any quality inhering in maternity or femininity, the operation of the maternal phallus is exposed according to a logic of replication that retains the father as the model to be copied. The phallic mother is only threatening if she *seems* to echo paternal authority, but as soon as that appearance—with all the ambiguity and veiling it allows—is dislodged, as soon as the logic of fetishism is demystified, its magical power dissolves. The viability of fetishism relies upon disavowal. An actual penis on a woman is not powerful or castrating—it is sickening, abject, at least for the heterosexual order that maintains the myth of fetishism as its necessary other. That is, it is sickening for Fergus, and for those who identify with him sexually, but it is not sickening for Jody. Jody's desire for Dil thus puts in question the binary, heteronormative boundaries by which those who are sickened by Dil are determined, at the same time as showing how those boundaries inform the Freudian discourse of fetishism.[60]

Rather than reading the scene as a reversal of the classic castration scenario, abjection provides us with a more adequate theoretical device. It allows us to account both for Fergus's bodily registering of his revulsion, as he violently pushes/hits Dil out of the way, bloodying her mouth, and vomits, expelling a truth that his mind cannot process, and for Dil's feeling of humiliation, betrayal, and abandonment, as what was meant to be a moment of sexual intimacy turns into a moment of abjection—she is not what he has taken her to be, and he cannot accept her for what she is.[61] The moment is abject precisely because, in the classic oedipal view, Dil is meant to substitute morphologically for Fergus's mother, and her penis makes her an inadequate stand-in. For Freud, the sexual maturity of men, in other words, their ability to surmount with some degree of success their oedipal complex, depends upon their substitution of another woman for the mother. This other woman must not be phallic, but must rather be capable of giving birth. The realization that women give birth is the corollary of overcoming the idea of the mother as phallic. How can Fergus have successfully separated from his mother, if the substitute woman he finds to replace maternal desire turns out not to be a real woman? His failure can only mean one thing: that he is not a real man. His identity as a hardheaded IRA man is already in question. Now he is asked by Dil to confront the fragility of his heterosexual identification, and all the privilege and stability that it entails. The impact that Dil's penis has is disruptive precisely because it shows that the maternal phallus cannot be embodied by a "real" penis without a profound disruption of the heteronormative, fetishistic order.

Jordan refuses to allow identification to be a matter that is settled. By utilizing and then disrupting received ideas about race, gender, and class, Jordan both addresses the viewer as a desiring, embodied, socially situated being—as raced, gendered, classed, nationalized—and requires his audience to put into question socially prescribed mechanisms of identification. In doing so, he refrains from substituting one set of norms for another—say, homosexuality for heterosexuality or transgendered identity for sexual dimorphism. Rather, he first exploits the prevalence of a white heterosexism that exoticizes the raced other, by seducing his audience into fetishizing Dil, and then he exposes the mechanism of the fetishistic trope. He plays into audience expectations, granting them access to an ideal point of view, while at the same time carefully staging an alternative view via a series of cues that are available to those who are socially predisposed to pick them up. Jordan trades in a kind of visual literacy that leaves some of his audience floundering in a sea of heteronormativity, while others will be tuned into the lip-synching performances of the singers at the Metro, and the transgendered identity of its clients. Jordan thus holds open the question not so much of which characters we identify with, or with whom we should identify, but rather why we identify in the particular ways that we do. He thus draws attention to the fabricated nature of both the socially privileged heteronormativity and that of homosexuality and transgendered identity.

Employing what seems to be a classic Hollywood approach, at the beginning of the film, Jordan solicits our sympathy for Jody, the innocent IRA captive, but then turns the tables on us. Jordan deprives us of our "hero" halfway through the film by killing Jody off, encouraging us to shift our allegiance to his former captor. Like Hitchcock, he thus intervenes in the classic Hollywood convention of hero presentation. Thus far, Jordan's strategy is similar to Hitchcock's strategic manipulation of the viewer in *Psycho,* where we catch ourselves in the act of switching our identificatory allegiance from Marion to Norman Bates, but Jordan goes further. Not content to demonstrate to the viewer the staging of the idealizing identificatory compulsion, upon which Žižek comments, as if this problem were confined to the orbit of the consumption of film, Jordan also compels the viewer to confront the idealization of the heteronormative order, which film reproduces and utilizes. Jordan cuts the ground from under his viewer in more than one way. The alignment of Dil's femininity with the body type typically assumed to support or underlie femininity is rudely interrupted by the appearance of a penis, suggesting not only the instability of filmic identification, nor merely that of sexual identity, but that of the identificatory mechanism itself—filmic or otherwise.

If we have identified with Fergus's heteronormative desire for Dil, the stability of our own sexuality is called into question at the moment that Fergus's reaction of vomiting calls into question his desire for Dil. Yet Fergus's reaction is not the only one made available to us. A history of Jody's unquestioning desire for Dil has been established, and it is with reference to this background that Fergus constantly reads his own interaction with Dil, wanting to know what Jody would think, whether he would have approved, what he would have done. If Fergus fetishizes Dil, and idealizes Jody, by staging Fergus's negotiation of his fetishization and idealization, Jordan insists on the complexity and construction of the identificatory mechanism itself, and its tendency to stabilize that which is inherently unstable. Fergus's idealization of Jody complicates the audience's identificatory adoption of Fergus. At the same time, Fergus's relationship to Jody, as a substitute for Jody whose emulation of him is shown to be wanting, mimics, as we will see further, the structure of fetishism.

Jordan allows dialogue to stage the instability of identificatory processes, exposing the mechanism by which apparently universal claims are constructed, and confronting them with their false universality. The apparent complicity of the heteronormative male camaraderie in an exchange between Fergus and Jody illustrates both the false ideality of heteronormativity, and the way in which such heteronormativity sustains its stability by processes of abjection that render untenable and unstable other positions. When Jody presents Fergus with a photograph of Dil in a scene that is charged with homoeroticism, Fergus responds to Jody's attestation, "Now *she's* my type," with the words, "She'd be anybody's type." At one level, this loaded phrase expresses the unreflective prerogative that Fergus assumes as a white, male heterosexual, where "anybody" appears to mean "everyone," but in fact means anybody like Fergus. At another level, it expresses a much more radical claim—no matter what race, sex, or class, anybody would find Dil attractive. We see, first, a reference to a very specific male, heterosexual desire that masks itself as (second) a statement about all desire, the unmasking of which reveals (third) not only a radically different meaning that transforms rather than supports heteronormativity, but that also reveals the abject operation of false universal claims. This triple inflection is at stake throughout the dialogue of *The Crying Game*.[62] The audience is seduced into the conformity and hypocrisy of the first interpretation, where a statement that appears to have universal application in fact designates an unspoken privilege that silently abjects women and homosexuals (who are not recognized as "anybody"). The impossibility, for Fergus, of taking the statement "she'd be anybody's type" literally, rather than conventionally, is exposed when Dil's penis is revealed. In the same stroke, those abject others who do not count as "anybody" are exposed as casualties of convention. Their desire has no place in convention, but their exclusion facilitates, is constitutive of, the inclusion of those who count as somebody.

If men require women to occupy abject positions in order to assure themselves of their masculinity, both men and women require those who challenge the boundaries separating male and female to occupy abject positions. To be neither male nor female but both at once (according to conventional interpretations) is impermissible. Yet at the same time this impermissibility serves to police the boundaries of what is permissible. Transgender identity is outlawed as unlivable, consigned to a zone that is unthinkable, in order to render stable, feasible, and uncontestable the differentiation between male and female. The mobility of abjection is discernible here. If men abject women, and heterosexuals abject homosexuals, women also participate in the abjection of transgendered individuals.

The hypocritical abjection of unspoken heteronormative privilege becomes available for interrogation, and Jordan also deprives us of assuming the familiar trope of fetishism as a stable interpretive framework by presenting Dil's body as the site of its impossibility. Disrupting the abject status of the phallic/fetishistic interpretation of women as "castrated," Jordan stages the necessity of the veiled or masked status of the fetish as a stand-in penis. Once that which the fetish represents is presented as transparent, unmediated, precisely unrepresented, one might say, far from being reassuring, it becomes horrific. The staging of the scene in which Dil's penis is revealed is replete with drapes, curtains, and veils. The décor of Dil's abode reflects the permanent veiling that is part of the structure of fetishism, and the fabric of her life.

Fetishism itself operates on the basis of the abject status of women, who are not acknowledged as anything other than horrific or terrifying unless they are made to resemble men. Yet that women only resemble men is crucial. The veiled nature of the fetish, its opacity, is indispensable. As soon as women no longer merely resemble men, as soon as they transcend their strictly fetishistic status, as soon as they vacate their role as signifying mimetically men's superior phallic position, or exhibiting an inferior, stand-in phallus, the ploy of fetishism is exposed for what it is. For Fergus, but not for Jody, Dil's penis elicits disgust, not titillation. Fetishism rests upon the heteronormative abjection of the female as female, requiring women to imitate masculinity and in doing so to retain their imitative status, as inferior. What is precluded is that this imitation be completely successful. Dissimulation is essential to the structure of fetishism. The fetish must present itself not simply as a substitute but as a failed substitute—it must present itself precisely only ever as a copy. Its representative function must not be completely obscured. The fetish must appear as a fetish.

The revelation of Dil's penis makes clear that the fetish fails insofar as it covers over its status as a substitute. To imitate the penis successfully is to evacuate the phallic status of the fetish. It is essential that the fetish maintain its difference from that which it imitates, even as it imitates it. To imitate the penis without also exhibiting its status as imitative, to represent the penis in such a way that there is no distinguishing between the fetish and the penis, is to fail to carry out successfully the function of the fetish. It is no longer to be a fetish. The function of the fetish is to stand in for, to substitute for, to seem to be the penis while at the same time maintaining its difference from the penis. The fetish must therefore not be the penis but must precisely represent it. Its not being the penis must be visible at one and the same time that it signifies that penis. Opacity is essential to its representative function.

What happens if we assume Dil's transgendered identity from the start? There are plenty of cues, visual and otherwise, which Jordan plants in the film for us to read if we are so disposed. Fergus's crisis operates metaphorically as representative of the crisis that society would experience were the normativity of heterosexuality challenged. How far we take Fergus's crisis to be indicative of society's normative condemnation of homosexuality, and how far we take it to be a function of his own inability to come to terms with the transformation in his identity that his affection for Dil signals, is perhaps a moot question. Fergus's reaction to the situation is inextricably bound up with his own normative conditioning—or perhaps it is nothing else but that.

Unlike Edge, I do not think that Jude is the central site of abjection; rather, the scene in which Dil reveals her penis is the scene of abjection. One could argue that the moment that Jody is hit and killed by a British army Saracen (the irony of which, particularly in the light of Jody's own relationship to British colonialism, cannot be overlooked) also prefigures the abject. Jody is reduced to a corpse by the British army, of whom he is taken by the IRA to be a representative, and he thus prefigures the reduction of Dil to her body by Fergus, who takes her to be a representative of the heterosexual norm. Dil then reduces Jude to nothing more than a body, a corpse—which, by extension, becomes abject. In his shock of discovering Dil's penis one could say that Fergus vomits the mother (see Kristeva 1982, 47). Derailed from the heterosexual path that his identification as a man, and his attempt to separate from the mother, has prepared for him, he is confronted, in his love for Dil, with the unacceptable other. The boundaries he has created for himself collapse, as he reverts to the fear and aggression that Kristeva suggests are inseparable from one another. He hits out at Dil for not being the woman he took her to be. Just as his failure to murder Jody represents a collapse of the political and normative principles to which he has adhered as an IRA member, so his violent, threatened, and sickened outburst at Dil represents the collapse of the uncomplicated heterosexual norms he had assumed were his own until this moment. Dil's words, "Even when you were throwing up I could tell you cared," are heavily ironic, but they

Fergus and Dil in *The Crying Game.*
Courtesy of Photofest.

also speak the truth. Fergus does not stop loving Dil, despite her disruption of the conventional matrix of desire. When Fergus vomits, what he finds intolerable is his unwitting transgression of the gender boundaries he was assuming were fixed in place according to the societal boundaries to which he adheres. The moment of abjection is a moment when all his prior assumptions come tumbling down, and he is faced with an abyss. He must renegotiate his identity, come to terms with who he is, what he has done—or left undone, who he loves, and what he will become. The film does not resolve the issue of how successfully he will ever be able to do so.

The tale of the scorpion and the frog is told twice in *The Crying Game,* first by Jody, and then by Fergus.[63] The first time, Jody relates it to Fergus as part of his ongoing plan to seduce Fergus into letting him go, to turn him away from his "nature" as a member of the IRA, a pathological, "deluded motherfucker," who doesn't give up. If Jody can establish that Fergus is not in fact like the scorpion, that he will not sting Jody and go down with him, that it is his nature to give, rather than to take, then he can save himself. He can, and he does. Unfortunately the world is more complex than Jody's fable makes it appear. As Jody runs into the path of a British army Saracen, which is traveling at speed, he has no chance of surviving. The irony that the military whose job it is to find him accidentally ploughs over him reminds us not only that

death can occur at any moment for any reason but also that soldiers are
likely to die: Jody's death could have been predicted. That Jody joined
the army because "it was a job" might provide Fergus with a reason to
scoff at him, but it also constitutes the rationale for the overwhelming
number of army recruits in many countries, and certainly both in
America and in Britain. That he dies in the service of duty is representative of occupational hazards that members of the working class take
on disproportionately, whether in the army or working in a mine or
factory.

That Jody appeals to the scorpion and the frog as part of his seduc-
tive campaign to persuade Fergus that it is "not in his nature" to kill
him complicates the content of the fable. Rather than allowing the
fable to stand on its own, as if it could be allowed to declare that goodness or badness, generosity or meanness, the ability to give or the tendency to take, inhere in nature, Jordan has Jody persuade Fergus that
his IRA persona and the moral accoutrements he has acquired under
its guise can be shed. Jody's appeal works not simply because identity
is inherently unstable or even because he appeals to Fergus's better
"nature," but because Jody, who hails from Antigua, is no more viable
as a representative of the British Empire than is Fergus—and Fergus
knows this. The complexity of their relationship is signaled by the fact
that Jody hails from a former West Indian British colony, which complicates Fergus's relationship to him, since Jody is himself subject to
Britain's colonial imperialism. As a hostage of the IRA, Jody is therefore far from being a representative of the British army's imperial relationship to Northern Ireland in any straightforward way.[64]

Fergus tells the same tale to Dil when she visits him in prison
where he is serving time for her murder of Jude. Juxtaposed with
Fergus's quotation from Paul's first letter to the Corinthians, "When I
was a child, I thought like a child . . . but when I became a man, I put
childish things away," the fable not only divides the world into good
and bad but also into male and female, white and black, heterosexual
and homosexual, British and Irish.[65] Yet Jody subverts these clean divisions precisely because he succeeds in muddying the waters by turning
the fable into an appeal for Fergus's help. In this sense Rockett and
Rockett are right to say that "Jordan's message is that appearances are
precisely that—appearances" (2003, 139), yet such a message should
not be understood to imply that race, gender, national identity, sexuality, or class do not matter.

The second time the fable is told, Fergus has established himself as
"good," by serving time for Dil. In doing so he has entered into the
symbolic identification with the IRA that he sought to flee, at least in

part, in order to avoid what to him is a greater harm. He has fled another confrontation, his encounter with his homophobic constitution, and he has found protection in a jail cell. In order to preserve intact his heterosexual identification, he has effectively bracketed the question of his sexual attraction to Dil, camouflaging his denial as moral guilt for Jody's death. His goodness is predicated on the repudiation of homosexuality, which figures prison as the lesser of two evils. He would rather abase himself as a criminal, accepting responsibility for a crime that he did not, in fact, commit, and at the same time purify himself of his intention to kill Jody, than engage in "unnatural" acts. If Oedipus accepted the punishment for the crimes that he unwittingly committed, Fergus avoids confronting the meaning of his intimacy with Dil, which thereby becomes an act of sexual transgression that cannot be incorporated into his account of himself.[66] Fergus cannot go there. He prefers to incarcerate himself, which also conveniently serves the purpose of looking after Dil, as he has promised to do. His fear of asking fundamental questions about his own homophobia, sexuality, and identity is conveniently masked by the appearance of goodness. The question of who he is can be cloaked with a veneer of morality. He seems to be a man who is protecting Dil, rather than a man who is too cowed by the meaning of his love for Dil to be able to accept her endearments, too afraid to engage in an ongoing, physical relationship with her. Prison allows him to procrastinate: so long as he is in prison he does not have to confront the question of physical intimacy. Notwithstanding his apparent isolation, as a result of having been convicted of murder as an IRA member, the fact that he is in an all-male prison suggests the symbolic likelihood that he will encounter male homosexual activity—an irony that is surely not lost on Jordan. Will prison thus serve to prepare him for a relationship with Dil?

When the fable is retold by Fergus in the last scene of the film, its meaning has changed. Now it signifies Jody's lasting influence upon both Dil and Fergus, and therefore the possibility of people influencing one another across the boundaries of race, gender, nationality, and sexuality. At the same time it enshrines Jody's ghostlike presence, which haunts Fergus throughout his sexual relationship with Dil, with a goodness that belies the stereotypical representation of blacks in film.[67] In this sense, Jody has the last laugh, as he is depicted in one of Fergus's fantasies of him. Most importantly, by ending the film in a way that demonstrates Jody's lasting influence upon Fergus, Jordan asks us to reread Fergus's abjection of Dil. When Jody successfully pleads with Fergus to take off his hood, he uses a fable to reread racist myths in which IRA terrorists are all "deluded motherfuckers," whose pathological violence puts them in a category that equates their violence with their natures. Similarly, Jordan asks us to reread the narrative in a way that privileges Jody's love for Dil, untrammeled as it is by the binary ordering of sex and gender, over Fergus's abjection of her on his discovery of her anatomy. This gesture is not enough to perform permanent closure—instability has been so consistently exploited throughout the film in so many registers that this rereading is just one more twist of a narrative that ultimately refuses to come down on either side of the multiple binary oppositions it explores.

To read *The Crying Game* as a testimony to Jody's moral authority is not to deny that this authority is exercised only in the wake of his death, or that Dil's comparatively light skin might well have played a role, however unconscious, in Jordan's decision to allow the homosexual bond between Jody and Fergus to remain implicit. Nor is it to deny that Jody's blackness condemns him to death, just as Jude—as the femme fatale who has transgressed the acceptable boundaries of traditional femininity—is condemned to death.[68] As Frann Michel says, while the "interracial relationships" in *The Crying Game* challenge "racist assumptions . . . the fact that the film's two black or biracial characters are also sexual outlaws leaves unquestioned a conventional equation between racial and sexual otherness" (1994, 32). Jordan does not entirely back off from confronting the racist attitudes of his own country, an example of which we see when Jude responds to the prisoner she has helped to capture by calling him a "fucking animal."[69] If Jody is content to stereotype Fergus as "a Paddy," he is not so happy to be called a "nigger." The friendship that develops between Fergus and Jody will not remain confined by the initially strained relations that are both embedded in their structural roles as captor and hostage, and signaled by these racial tensions. Like the IRA men who guard Belcher and Hawkins in O'Connor's "Guest of the Nation," a genuine affection comes to bind Fergus and Jody.[70] The friendly exchange between Fergus and Jody about the relative merits of the British game cricket and the Irish game hurling serves to solidify the connection of each to their own ethnic backgrounds, but it also serves as a ritual of male bonding—the universal language of sport.

The racial and gender stereotypes that Jordan undoubtedly puts in place, often self-consciously, sometimes perhaps unconsciously, can be read in the light of the moral authority Jody exerts over them. Unlike Fergus, Jody, who, in Dil's words knew "absolutely" what Fergus has such trouble assimilating, is attracted to Dil not despite her anatomy but in full, conscious knowledge of it. If we read the film from Jody's and Dil's points of view, they are not sexual outlaws, or marginal figures, just two people who love one another. If we read the film from

Fergus's point of view, when Fergus starts to re-tell the fable of the scorpion and the frog, we are asked to reread his point of view again from the vantage point of Jody's. This demand gathers up the impetus of the intermittent appearance Jody makes to Fergus in the dream/fantasy sequences.[71] Such a rereading profoundly reorients our relationship to Fergus and, perhaps, to ourselves.[72]

If, like Fergus, we did not know what, as the film progresses, it becomes increasingly clear that, in Fergus's words, we "should have known," the question remains: What precisely should we have known? What does Fergus know? What does his knowledge amount to? How does his knowledge change him? Does he discover retroactively, through Dil, his erotic interest for Jody? Does he come to a new understanding of his own sexuality? Does his love for Dil indicate rather—or perhaps at the same time—his identification with Jody? None of these questions are answered by the film, except insofar as they remain unresolved. The enigma of what it means for Fergus—and for us—to know, remains. The fact that his discovery of Dil's penis does not change his affection for her, but does change his ability to express his feelings toward her sexually, points out both how affect runs contrary to knowledge and how its expression is caught up in symbolic codes that have always already constituted the subject. An anti-Oedipus, once he reveals to Dil his failure to commit the murder of Jody, once his crime—a moral one rather than an actual one—is revealed to Jody's lover, Fergus does all he can to hide from himself, bracketing the question of what his knowledge might mean for his identity. Rather than coming to a deeper understanding of who he is, he shies further away from any resolution of the question. Unlike Oedipus's discovery of himself as having unwittingly committed murder and incest, Fergus did not in fact commit the crime he ends up paying for. Unlike Oedipus, his failure to commit Jody's murder is followed by a failure to fully consummate his relationship with Dil. Notwithstanding the gap between his intentions and his actions, he holds himself morally responsible for a murder he did not in fact commit, and in knowingly taking responsibility for a crime he did not commit, he exempts himself from making any decision about how to live out his relationship with Dil. Fergus's refusal to resolve the meaning of his identity leaves the question in our hands.

Audience expectations are confounded, as we, along with Fergus, experience the "shock of gender"—to adapt Seamus Heaney's words in a way that he would probably not approve.[73] Whether or not we have figured out Dil's anatomical identity does not override the fact that to the extent that as viewers we have followed the narrative and invested in the attraction she holds for Fergus—insofar as we have identified with Fergus's desire—we experience a disruption. While our "discovery" of Dil's anatomical identity will have various effects on us as viewers, depending on whether or not, or with what degree of certainty, we have either colluded with Fergus's view of things or seen his delusion for what it is, the suturing effect by which we collaborate with the director is severed, at the same time as being reinforced.[74] We realize that we have been taken for a ride. Perhaps more importantly, as we witness Fergus vomiting in the face of Dil's penis, the expectations that fabricate and inform his/our desire are abruptly thrown up for interrogation. The glaring inadequacy of the castration motif employed not only by classic Lacanian theory, but also by feminist film theory revisions of it, shows up. Fergus's reaction to Dil—and any identification with his abject response, his abjection of her—cannot be explained as if she were the castrating other. It is Dil's penis that makes Fergus literally sick—he is not disconcerted by its absence. Jordan is asking us to examine the heterosexual subtext of castration theory—a lynchpin of film theory—as much as he asking us to examine the subtext of our desire. He is playing with our identificatory regimes at more than one level. We are asked to confront gender ambiguity, whether it is merely in terms of Fergus's expectations, or whether it is also a matter of a more radical challenge to the heterosexual parameters we might have assumed were in place.

By displacing the priority of castration, abjection provides us with a way of theorizing sexual, and, I argue, racial difference, but not through being circumscribed by a simplistic dichotomy that equates heterosexual men with the gaze, and heterosexual women with objects, leaving no room for any other positions. What it means to be a subject or object, a man or woman, white or black, English or Irish, working class or middle class, is up for question in abjection. How far is Fergus's attraction for Dil dependent not only on her identification as a woman but also on the lightness of her skin relative to Jody—whose dark skin haunts Fergus's erotic fantasies as he substitutes Dil for the homoerotic bond that could not be sustained between the white captor and his black captive?

Powerful as it is, the trope of homosexuality is not, ultimately, the decisive one in *The Crying Game*. Rather, it is Dil's transgendered identity that destabilizes most radically our assumptions about gender and nature. Critics who argue that Dil is "really" a black man (hooks 1994 and Edge 1995), or that Jude in fact presents us with the most powerful site of gender instability (Lloyd 1999), fail to take on the challenge that Jordan offers us in the figure of Dil.[75] If Dil lives out the revenge motif of ancient tragedy, quite dispassionately unloading bullets into Jude's writhing body, she also lets her have it for luring Jody into an act of unfaithfulness to her. As we have seen, underlying Dil's anger at Jude is the ineluctable fact that Jude has what Dil lacks: the "tits" and the "cute little ass" that would make Dil approximate more efficiently to the ideal of femininity she performs. Dil's body is an obstacle to her desire to be an adequate love-object for Fergus. The anger with which she dispenses bullets into the body of Jude, having asked Fergus what Jude wore as she seduced Jody, represents not only an avenging of Jody's death but also an avenging of the world that looks at her askance because she does not have the "right" body to be the woman she identifies as. As we have seen, Fergus, typically masculine in this respect—and in contrast to members of the audience who have been alerted to Jordan's highly self-conscious portrayal of Jude as a figure of masquerade, a master of disguise—claims not to remember the short denim skirt that marks out Jude's first incarnation as a working-class lass, apparently out for a good time but in fact plotting to kidnap Jody. His claim to have forgotten, although it can be read at one level as typical of the generic straight man's obliviousness to fashion, also functions as a protective measure toward Dil, saving her from having to compete with Jude. If Fergus cannot remember what Jude wore, Jude cannot be that important to him, and Dil has no need to be jealous of her because of her claim on Fergus's affections. Clothes are such an important part of Dil's identity that the question of what Jude wore is not insignificant. We have already heard a highly charged exchange between Dil and Jude on the appropriate amount of makeup, and the need for "a girl to . . . have a bit of glam-our." The fact that Fergus cannot remember what Jude wore also oper-ates in a more radical way, establishing that he might be coming around to the studied casualness of Dil's dismissal of Fergus's earlier remark that Dil is "not a girl" with her words, "Details, baby, details." If clothes don't matter, if they are merely the superficial accoutrements of gender, then, maybe, eventually, body parts too could become insignificant, and Fergus could accept Dil for who she is.

The challenge that Dil's transgendered identity presents is this. Fergus's horror results not from the "castration" of a woman but pre-cisely from the presence of a penis on a woman. She has thus been read as the phallic mother. But to read her in these terms is to accept the terms of fetishism, which is itself a product of Freud's patriarchal imaginary. The phallic mother is a figure who has been fetishistically produced by a system that cannot tolerate the idea of genuine differ-ence, unless that difference is read as inferior. Women's sexuality is quite literally unthinkable for a male imaginary obsessed with produc-ing mirror images of itself, in accordance with which, it must produce a substitute penis, which it then attaches to the mother, all the while trying to replace the mother with a wife, according to a logic that remains governed by the exclusive value of the phallus.

But if Dil is "not a girl" in the traditional, anatomical sense of the word, neither is she a phallic mother. She is, rather, someone who has a body that would conventionally mark her as a man. She takes herself for a woman, has been taken as a woman, continues to be taken for a woman, wants to be a woman, and in this sense, she is indeed a woman—unless we invoke highly problematic metaphysical assumptions about what it means to be a woman, which involve positing a causal relationship between some untheorized body as the ground and cause of gender.[76] Good anti-essentialists that most of us are in this day and age, we need to be very cautious about agreeing that Dil is "really a man," since this ensconces us in a vision of gender that places bodies in a naturalized context, as if the meaning of bodies were not always already produced by our sexist, racist, and heterosexist contemporary assumptions about what it means to be a woman or a man, black or white, homosexual or heterosexual, working class or upper class.

Acts, states, and beings coded as abject can take up transgressive or revolutionary positions, and these very positions can take on opposite effects. When critics refuse the radical implications of Fergus's confrontation with Dil's transgender identity, in order to criticize its stereotypical race tropes, there is a sense in which they could be said to use race to abject Dil's transgender identity, and when critics ignore the dynamics of race and nationalism with which the film concerns itself, they could be said to abject these aspects of identity in favor of sexuality. The point, of course, is not that we can afford to ignore the ways in which the film continues to trade in racial stereotypes—I have argued that there are some ways in which the film does indeed replicate such stereotypes, although I also think that the discourse on race is more complex than some critics acknowledge, and that it contains some radical moments. By engaging abjection as a mode of analysis I want to resist polarizing society into representative agents of good and bad, oppressor and oppressed, holy and evil, and in doing so to resist the ways in which various accounts of gender, race, class, and nationalism are marshaled as apparent representatives of these polar opposites. I also want to resist the impulse to repudiate whatever radicality the film might exhibit in questioning gender norms in order to argue that it embraces a conservative discourse about race. Equally, I do not think it is necessary to claim that the film is consistently radical around the themes of gender or race.

Fergus's revulsion at the revelation of Dil's penis can be read as consonant with his heterosexual commitment, but it can also be read as signaling the inadequacy both of Freud's account of the need for men to separate from the mother by replacing her with another woman and as a refusal of the normative weight acquired by heterosexuality, and even as a refusal of the ways in which homosexual identity is subjected to policing in a way that often mirrors the strictures imposed by heterosexual presumption. Abjection is a crisis that assumes a subject already structured by language, but one who reverts to its incomplete separation from the mother. The moment of abjection is an irruption of affect into the ordered, stable, and discriminating world of symbolic discourse. Fergus's encounter with Jody leads him to a crisis of confidence in the symbolic world of the IRA that he has taken on, a world whose authority is underwritten in the film by Peter, the father figure. Temporarily shedding his political identity as an IRA man in London, the moral crisis Fergus undergoes with Jody not only prompts him to shed his political identity as a member of the IRA, but also draws him into an encounter with Dil, and to a shattering of his sexual identity. Unable to face its implications, he returns to his former, fractured, political identity as a refuge, a womb of security. He refashions that split identity, reconsolidates it as a mask behind which he can hide. The mask he presents to the outer world, to Dil, the front of moral rectitude, serves a dual function. He pays for a murder he did not commit in order to compensate for one he did "in a manner of speaking," but in adopting this moral stance, he avoids interrogating his sexuality, putting it on hold. He enters into prison, under the watchful eyes of the law, as a haven, which preserves his love for Dil, and hers for him, in an idealized, but physically unrealizable form.[77]

In prison it is Dil who keeps watch over Fergus, in a reversal of roles that turns Fergus into the performer, as he gives his rendition of Jody's fable. The issue of who is watching, who is performing, and who is mimicked, highlights for the audience their own participation in constructing the plot. Both Fergus and Dil share a level of comfort with the distance of the glass between them, and the performance it allows them, which leaves the question of sexuality ambiguous. Fergus still objects to her calling him "honey," but at least the difficulty of how to negotiate sexual contact between them without him throwing up is resolved. Dil seems free to express a conventional femininity that Fergus denied her on the outside, a freedom that is endorsed by the appropriately ironic, dulcet tones of Lyle Lovett's rendition of "Stand by Your Man." Subject to the law, which punishes him for what she has done, he enjoys a respite from the crisis his love for Dil has thrown him into. The law reasserts itself, and plays the role of the loving father, rescuing Fergus from having to definitively alter his symbolic universe.[78]

By using narrative, realist conventions of mainstream Hollywood cinema to draw the spectator into a fantastical plot, only to expose the extent to which heteronormative, binary conventions of spectators help to construct that narrative reality, Jordan draws attention not only to the conventions of cinematographic illusion but also to the social and political codes that inform the assumptions of his audience.[79] In disrupting the seamlessness of identification, and the ease of gender recognition, he asks the audience to question the stability of their own gender identification and to confront the opacity of their own desire. He does not achieve this by suspending identification, fascination, or sexual pleasure, nor does he abandon the use of stereotypes, but he does draw attention to their constructed and thoroughly politicized nature. In doing so he also asks us to heed the unstable and constructed nature not only of sexuality but of race, gender, nationality, and class, all of which prove to be ultimately inseparable from sexual norms.

8

The Fetishistic Temporality of Hegemonic Postcolonial Nationalist Narratives and the Traumatic Real of Abjection

IT IS INADEQUATE to envisage discourses of sexism, racism, heterosexism, and classism as structurally replicating one another in all important respects, since this not only elides important historical and political differences between these discourses, but also makes it impossible to make visible the ways in which each discourse is able to make use of others in order to advance its own agenda. Similarly, it would be a mistake to construe nationalism as if it were a monolithic concept, whose traits are universal no matter what political or historical context is under consideration. British imperialism might be replicated from one colony to another, even to the point of directly transferring practices of colonial rule from one site to another, yet an analysis of nationalism must remain differential, and not merely comparative. While there are both substantive and structural similarities between British rule in India and Ireland that attest to, in Lloyd's words, "the ubiquity and replication of forms of colonial rule," we must also recognize "the remarkably diverse ways its rationalizing drive is deflected by the particularities of each colonized culture."[1] Lloyd points to the inadequacies of models of nationalism that fail to accommodate profound differences that exist between different forms of nationalism, arguing that "accounts of nationalism which are currently hegemonic in the West are locked into a singular narrative of modernity," which is unable "to do historical justice to the complex articulation of nationalist struggles with other social movements" (1999, 20). For Lloyd, "nationalism is formed in articulation or conjuncture with other social movements" whether these movements are "termed 'proto-nationalist,' like peasant movements" or "counter-nationalist, like feminism or Marxism" (1999, 23). I suggest that while nationalist discourses can and do proceed in "articulation or conjuncture" with other social movements, they are equally (if not more) likely to proceed by abjecting them.[2]

In order to develop this suggestion, I raise some questions about Bhabha's influential interventions in the discourse of postcolonialism, in particular his account of Fanon and his reliance on a fetishistic model. While postcolonial theorists have been quick to question linear, progressive notions of temporality, they have been less inclined to question redemptive, Messianic narratives of temporality, and still less disposed to think through the temporality of disavowal, a gesture that they endlessly invoke without challenging its phallic and masculinist underpinnings. One does not have to commit the error of naturalizing the history of nations, as if they unfolded according to some inherent, racialized traits ascribed to their people, in order to fall prey to a linear conception of temporality that implicitly appeals to a cosmopolitan order in which each nation would find its natural place. The future becomes a repository for history's realization of what Kant regarded as the "hidden plan of nature" or guiding thread of nature's design (1983, 6). As Derrida puts it, this guiding thread is not so much driven by nature as it is by a certain conception of Greek history, one with a cosmopolitan purpose that is "too naturalistic and too teleological-European" (2002, 341). Accounts of nationalism that adhere to a vision of history that aspires to be universal and progressive, as if the world were a staging of national conflicts for the perfecting of human faculties, can only do so by ignoring the fact that the ostensibly civilized and rational values attributed to Western nations were achieved at the cost of capitalist exploitation and colonial appropriation. In Fanon's words, "The settler owes the fact of his very existence, that is to say, his property, to the colonial system" (1968, 36). Because the decks are stacked unevenly, "The natives' challenge to the colonial world is not a rational confrontation of points of view. It is not a treatise on the universal, but the untidy affirmation of an original idea propounded as an absolute" (1968, 41). The histories that are written, including the histories of nationalism, are written by and large from colonial perspectives, so that it is hardly surprising if the concept of nationalism that becomes established is a concept that reflects the colonial experience: "the history which he writes is not the history of the country which he plunders but the history of his own nation in regard to all that she skims off, all that she violates and starves" (1968, 51). This history condemns the native to "immobility" that "can only be called in question if the native decides to put an end to the history of colonization—the history of pillage—and to bring into existence the history of the nation—the history of decolonization" (1968, 51).

Neither this history nor the writing of it will be immune from a logic of mimicry since "nationalist parties copy their methods from those of

Western political parties" (1968, 111), and the native intellectual assimilates himself to the colonial world (see 1968, 60). Just as the national bourgeoisie assimilates itself to the colonizing powers, taking over their capitalist values, so the intellectual who takes on the task of writing nationalist histories from an anticolonialist point of view "has assimilated the culture of the occupying power" (1968, 222).[3] As Robert Young points out, Third World theorists such as Fanon and Said tend to reproduce this problem at another level. Both the "Third World" and the "West" are represented as if they were homogenous. "Categories such as 'the West,' or 'colonialism' or 'neocolonialism'—even 'colonial discourse'—are themselves in their current usage often the creation of Third World theorists . . . who needed to invent such categories precisely as general categories in order to constitute an object both for analysis and resistance" (Young 1995, 165). Young defends the necessity for such general categories "in order to counter the divide-and-rule policies of colonial administration" and warns that even the emphasis of "historical and geographical" specificity might amount to an uncritical repetition of "colonialism's own partitioning strategies" (165). It is no doubt true, as Lloyd recognizes, that we need both to construct general categories—even as we remain wary of such categories, while at the same time reflective about their continued symbolic power—and to be alert to the particularities that they obscure.

Even Bhabha tends to perpetuate a Eurocentric idea of the nation precisely in his attempt to distance himself from the universalism of Said's colonial discourse. If Fanon invokes the "whole people" (1968, 240) in a rhetoric of liberation that, for all its emphasis on class difference, continues to envisage the nation as unitary, albeit an internally fractured unity that is articulated through an ongoing and contested address, Bhabha reproduces this logic in his appeal to the performative. The claim of a nation to represent itself is said to take shape as a struggle in which competing versions of nationality are played off against one another. The unstable nation emerges in the form of an ongoing contest that plays itself out between various interests whose successful representation of themselves as capable of defining nationality depends upon the degree of legitimacy accruing to their claim to be representative. The nation thus comes to be represented as an internally fractured, or self-differentiating people, which, in its capacity to become more or less inclusive, is not only able to withstand conflict, but consists in an elaboration of its differences.[4]

By failing to admit that even in the process of articulating for itself a new identity, old identifications will assert themselves, drawing the myth of the nation into old forms of discriminatory logic, Bhabha imagines that there is a space immune from claims that take themselves to be universal and self-authorizing. "The liminal figure of the nation-space would ensure that no political ideologies could claim transcendent or metaphysical authority for themselves" (Bhabha 1990, 299). I am not so sure that anything—let alone a language of liminality, which precisely reinscribes the trope of figure and margin—can ensure that no new hegemonic discourses will be formulated, or that they will not camouflage the partiality of their claims to authority. To narrate the histories of nations and nationalism requires an understanding of both the plurality of nations and the temporality of narration. It also requires an understanding of how a nation comes to represent itself. In order to confront these issues Bhabha has suggested that we need to envisage an idea of the nation subject as split, and to develop a double notion of temporality, that of the pedagogical and the performative. What biases haunt Bhabha's invocation of the double time of the uncanny (295), or the language of disavowal (311)? Underlying this appeal is the logic of castration. As Daniel Boyarin puts it, "no matter how many uses and stagings of the uncanny he describes, Freud always returns it to castration" (1998, 211). In relying on this logic I suggest that Bhabha produces a new version of hegemonic discourse, one that trades in the language of fetishism and disavowal, and thereby partakes of the universalizing gestures that he seeks to put in question. Fetishism—the currency or language in which ideas are exchanged in the name of cultural critique—has extended its purview from psychoanalytic theory to film theory, and postcolonial theory in a way that continues to mask the abject status of women and minorities. Ranajit Guha, Gayatri Chakravorty Spivak, and others have pointed to the limitations of anticolonial nationalist theories, even in the attempt to give voice to the colonized, in their failure to acknowledge subaltern groups marked by class and gender.[5] Yet one of the principal mechanisms of this failure, namely the discourse of disavowal, remains intact. Since this discourse is the product of a patriarchal and colonial mindset, we would do well to be vigilant about the exclusionary logic that is built into it, particularly when it is mobilized as an analogical relation that purports to shed light on an implied structural parallel between the white, colonial, male subject of castration, and the racialized, anticolonial, or postcolonial subject of nationalism. What historical legacies are being written out of postcolonial theory when it translates the implicitly male, white, colonial subject of castration to serve as the model for the racialized subject of postcolonial theory? How does the practice of postcolonial theory consent to hegemonic strategies that operate by foreclosing the possibility of alternative theoretical languages, becoming complicit with those exclusions? Can the history of postcolonial theory be narrated in a way that renders visible the lapses that it repeats and reinvents by passing over in silence the experiences of those subjects that do not conform to theories that are told in the language of disavowal, those whose imaginary bodies figure rather as the site of trauma, as inciting unspeakable horror? What if those traumatic sites that figure only as impossible, excluded, and yet constitutive of the psychoanalytic discourse of disavowal have their femininity conferred upon them by a logic that trades in metaphors that already evoke a still more unspeakable abyss, the abyss of the "dark continent" of femininity?

Recall the dynamic of fetishism, which Bhabha appropriates in his reading of Fanon, and then extrapolates from to provide the foundation of a more general theory of postcolonialism that emphasizes ambivalence. We have seen that the psychoanalytic account is fueled by the myth of sameness, based on an unquestioned priority of masculine pleasure and its value. Thus, according to a masculinist imaginary, all humans are assumed to have penises. The confrontation with evidence to the contrary comes in the empirical shape of the little girl who lacks a penis. Rather than an acknowledgment of difference, the reaction is not so much a denial of the evidence of difference, as a refusal to take on board what is seen, and a stubborn adherence to the assumption of sameness even in the face of this evidence. The duality of this position, or the splitting of subject, comes to be the model of the psychoanalytic subject, and this splitting is taken up by Bhabha in his emphasis on ambivalence. If in childhood there is an attribution of a penis to the girl either in the past (she had one but she lost it) or in the future (she might lack a proper one now but she will have one—it is small now, but it will grow bigger), the divided attitude of the fetishist formalizes the splitting of the subject. With the production of a fetish that can stand in for the missing penis, the fetishist circumvents the anxiety that women's lack of a penis would otherwise provoke, without dissolving the trauma of castration. The logic of fetishism gives rise to a time of representation that makes of the past and the future—and even the present—modified versions of the present. The temporality of fetishistic representation forms a seamless, uninterrupted whole, guided by an appeal to full presence, in the continuity of a belief that stems from a masculine imaginary. This now time is presented as an idealized succession of uniform, identical presents parading along a timeline, as if the future and the past replicated the present, but it is undercut by the trauma that precisely elicits such a narrative of continuity. In its linear representation time becomes an infinitely malleable space of sameness in which each moment is rendered equivalent to other moments in an effort to sustain the myth of the same, and to cover over the horror of trauma. Walter Benjamin's "homogenous, empty time" to which Benedict Anderson appeals in establishing the importance of print capitalism, in particular the significance of the newspaper and the novel for the emergence of the nation-state, is both interrupted and inaugurated by a trauma.[6] The linear narrative time of representation, in which time is taken to be a succession of now-points, equidistant from one another and equivalent to one another, is the time of everydayness, clock-time. The representation of the quotidian life, the humdrum, day to day existence that is the stuff of the realist novel, in which an imagined community is invoked, or the ritualistic reading of the newspaper, in which the synchrony of national consciousness is celebrated, is in fact predicated on the forgotten trace of the violent founding of the nation. As Geoffrey Bennington puts it, "national differentiation does not come along to trouble the state *after* its perfect constitution, but precedes the fiction of such a constitution as its condition of possibility. . . . Nation is, then, always opened to its others: or rather, it is constituted only in that opening, which is, in principle, violent" (1990, 130–31). The imagined community of a nation is possible only on the basis of its self-differentiation from the plurality of nations.

Like the trauma of castration that incites the production of a fetishistic logic, the traumatic past of invasion and conquering, the wounds of war, and the scandal of slavery are forgotten in colonial nationalist narratives that cover over their inaugural founding moments. The trauma of castration is a crisis in the belief of one's omnipotence and power, a rupturing of one's ability to know the world on the basis of one's own bodily, pleasurable experience. The reaction to the irruption of difference is to produce a version of the world that is still consonant with one's former belief and the desire modeled on it. The fetish comes to take the place of the "missing" penis, to cover over the trauma as a way of keeping anxiety at bay. The anxiety of castration is an anxiety based upon one's inability to control the world, to predict its behavior on the basis of one's own experience, an inability to circumscribe the pleasures of others. It is an anxiety generated by one's inability to be master of one's own satisfaction, or the production of one's own desire. When Bhabha says "All men have penises . . . Some do not have penises" (1994, 74), and transcribes this problematic onto that of colonialism, he sidesteps the issue of the masculinist imaginary that fuels the psychoanalytic staging of fetishism, and imports the sedimented representation of masculine desire into a postcolonial framework that all but demands the challenge that Spivak has issued.

To transpose the psychoanalytic problematic of fetishism to colonialism, as if there were an analog between the excluded, abjected feminine and the excluded, abjected, colonized nation, is to foreclose the possibility of asking about how women might be abjected within masculinist counter-narratives of anticolonial nationalist discourse. To retain this analogy is to keep silent about the history of the idea of women that fetishistic discourses generate by excluding that history replete with its colonial and patriarchal legacy, by failing to ask about the racialized and sexist assumptions upon which those discourses are premised. Perhaps that is why Spivak begins *A Critique of Postcolonial Reason* by invoking not disavowal but repudiation and foreclosure (1999). If we were to elaborate the analogical relation to which Bhabha appeals, we might say, in place of Freud's dictum that all humans must have penises: "All men are like us (for us read white, Christian, capitalist, European men)." This would be akin to Bhabha's formulation, "All men have the same skin/race/culture" (1994, 74). Confrontation of evidence to the contrary—discovery of natives who live entirely differently (whose pleasures, beliefs, values, and prejudices do not conform to the capitalist, industrialist economy) is met only with an attempt to make them like us, in our image. By taking their land; exploiting their labor; and imposing Western values, laws, religion, conceptions of property, ways of life, and capitalist work ethics on them, while at the same time holding their visible differences as signs of their inferiority, the colonial expansion of the West sets out to make non-Europeans like Europeans. The threat that the colonized represent is not the open wound of femininity that women's bodies evidence in place of a penis, but the open wound of war. It is the threat that they will not acquiesce to be conquered, they will cling to their culture, to what they know and who they are—in short, that they will insist on their difference. That difference, as we will see further, is transposed by the white colonizer into the phantasmatic "myth of the negro" as Fanon calls it, and mythologized as a threat to European values and culture, so that Europeans adopt the stance of protecting their way of life—including their practices of domination and subjugation. Just as a girl's lack of a penis signifies the possibility that the man too might lose his penis, so the colonizer is afraid that the difference of the colonized threatens the loss of his own familiar culture. As Fanon points out, in colonial confrontations domination is established by nations with superior technical abilities.[7] It is easy to see how such superiority can be used to justify colonial exploitation in the name of progress, and how the need to progress becomes part of the ideological package with which the consent of the colonized is solicited.

The present of colonialism (capitalist, European, age of discovery, reason, science) is upheld by an appeal to the past (mythic origin, we gave birth to ourselves, there has only ever been us, we deserve to rule, it was ever thus), and it is fueled by a desire to progress, to fulfill our destiny, to realize a glorious future that will actualize the potential of the present, which contains the germ of what is to come. An implicit cosmopolitanism informs the commitment to progress—it is part of the destiny of mankind to realize its true potential. Colonial exploitation can therefore be wrapped up in what is effectively a moral imperative: it is the duty of Europe to bring its non-European others out of the past and into the future, which is in the best interests of humanity. I can persist in the childish belief that everyone is like me, while clothing it in the language of progress. If it is not so, I will make it so, since it should be so. In Freud's account of fetishism, castration anxiety sets in not merely due to the sight of a girl's lack of a penis, which is a necessary but not a sufficient condition, as certain philosophers are fond of saying. It is also instigated by the threat, backed up by paternal authority, that the boy will lose his penis if he does not obey the prohibition against masturbation. The threats embedded in the racist mythology that Fanon describes so vividly function similarly. "The negro is an animal, the Negro is bad, the Negro is mean, the Negro is ugly . . . the nigger's going to eat me up" (1967a 38).

In Bhabha's account of fetishism there is an elision of the significance of the fetish object "as the substitute for the mother's penis" (1994, 74), which, let us remember, never existed except in the boy's imagination. Sexual difference is said to be "disavowed by the fixation on an object that masks that difference and restores an original presence"—this "original" presence, though Bhabha doesn't specify it, is the already imaginary penis, produced by a masculine imaginary. Yet, since Bhabha takes for granted that sexual difference is "the precondition for the circulation of the chain of absence and presence in the realm of the Symbolic" (1994, 74), he cannot specify castration anxiety as generated by a masculine imaginary, since it would belie the originary presence that the fetish is supposed to evoke. What does it mean to say that sexual difference is such a precondition, except to endorse the masculine imaginary and embrace its symbolic as the only way of making sense?

Not only does Bhabha's account put off-limits any questioning of the symbolic as predicated on Lévi-Strauss's exchange of women as objects, it also collapses the colonial point of view with that of the colonized. The "colonial subject, both as colonizer and colonized" is denied "that form of negation which gives access to the recognition of difference" (1994, 75). Bhabha reads Fanon's well-known description of the crumbling of the corporeal schema under the gaze of the child who says "Look, a negro" as one of two "primal moments" (1994, 76). Fanon's "amputation" is the equivalent of the reactivation of the anxiety of castration.[8] The second primal moment is the encounter with racial stereotypes. But both these "primal" moments are in fact fabrications by a colonial power. Their primacy resides in the fact that they are already part of sedimented myths of meaning, already embedded in a history of representation whose horizon is indelibly colonial. Fanon discovers himself as represented by the imaginary of the white other, and not as he is. The disavowal of his race by a black child is described by Bhabha in terms of "the positivity of whiteness"—the colonial subject denies his race in order to flee the stereotype and is "returned to the narcissism of the Imaginary and its identification of an ideal ego that is white and whole" (1994, 76). This disavowal already happens, to use Terry Eagleton's phrase, "under the sign of irony" (1990b, 26), it already betrays the radical uncertainty of a colonized subject to know its desires and needs, or to be able to meaningfully represent subjectivity in terms that depart from the values that colonialism holds out for it.

Fanon affirms that the colonial native takes on the perspective of the colonizing power, but this is only one moment, the first of three phases that Fanon describes. It is the moment of imitation, deracialization, "assimilation," and it is qualified in *The Wretched of the Earth* as an identification undertaken not by the mass, but by the intellectual.[9] As becomes clear in Fanon's account of the second moment, it is also predicated on a forgetting of oneself. First there is assimilation, then there is a return to the past in which the native "decides to remember what he is" (1967b, 41–43; 1968, 222), both moments that are characterized by Fanon as phases in which the intellectual in his anxiety to "create a cultural work . . . fails to realize that he is utilizing techniques and language which are borrowed from the stranger in his country" (1968, 223). The first phase of assimilation Fanon describes as "unqualified," a phase in which the intellectual's "writings correspond point by point with those of his opposite numbers in the mother country." In the second phase the colonized intellectual immerses himself by recalling the life of a people that has become "exterior" to him, as the "past happenings of the bygone days." It is only in a third phase that "the native, after having tried to lose himself in the people and with the people, will on the contrary shake the people" (1968, 222). The literature of this phase is a "literature of combat" (1968, 240). "While at the beginning the native intellectual used to produce his work to be read exclusively by the oppressor . . . now the native writer progressively takes on the habit of addressing his own people" (1968, 240). Bhabha implicitly takes up this notion of address in his appeal to the performative.

Were we to map out the dynamic of fetishism as it might be applied to the colonized, subaltern position, without collapsing the colonizer and the colonized into one "colonial subject" as Bhabha does, we might say that the moment of imitation or assimilation, coupled with a "pejorative judgement" (1967b, 38) or the rejection of one's own culture, is followed by a return to the past. Yet it is a return to a lost past, a past that has been "abandoned" but which now becomes "an object of passionate attachment," such that the native accords this past "a very marked kind of overevaluation" (1967b, 41), while the intellectual behaves "like a foreigner" (1968, 223), exoticizing the past (1968, 221). As Rai puts it, the "lost object" is the wretched native of an always prior age (1990, 101). And yet there is still some spontaneity (1967b, 41) to be found, even if the "ecsta[s]y" and "ardor" are deformed by the fact that this culture that the native tries to rediscover is "dying" (1967b, 41). This valorization of the archaic is in fact an attempt to return to an idealized purity, to the "pure and simple" way of life (1967b, 42) that the colonial capitalist invader has displaced by the technical ability he has introduced. This, then, is the moment of harking back to an Edenic, mythical past, as if it were whole, pure, and ideal, it is a return to a past that the colonial power has forced the colonized to abandon, a past that has become reified, fixed, lifeless. The promise of full presence is disappointed. Not only has the past lost its life, its vibrancy, but so too this "cultural mummification leads to a mummification of individual thinking" (1967b, 34). The past is "archaic, inert . . . a caricature" (1967b, 34). To cling to this lost past in an effort to resist the "progress" of colonialism is to adhere to a melancholic logic of compensation governed by one's loss, by installing a static version of the past to stand in for what has become irretrievable. It is therefore to cover over one's loss as irreparable. It is to refuse the narrative of progress offered by colonialism, by returning to a past that is no longer, trying to hold on to what has already slipped away, clinging to the vestiges of history as if one could breathe new life into them. Looking to a past that has already been demolished, the colonized subject retrieves or fabricates an image that is incapable of providing the recognition sought, since this image is produced by a logic of compensation that is governed by the attempt to seek out whatever figures as the opposite of Western narratives of progress. Picking through the shards of history, one discovers oneself only in fragments that lack coherence, which one pieces together in a failed attempt to produce a mythical whole.

Let me briefly return to Lloyd's analysis, which is useful because it elegantly elucidates the problematic of fetishism in relation to questions of representation and irrationality. While I am suggesting that the discourse of fetishism has become part of the machinery of the dominant, hegemonic articulation of cultural theory, and as such it needs to be unsettled, I also recognize not only that it has played a formative role in race theory (Fanon, Bhabha) but also that Lloyd is probably right to regard fetishism as "an inevitable moment of emergent nationalism" (1999, 23), even if it still adheres to a reactive model that allows itself to be governed by the colonial claims it opposes. Its inevitability resides not in any inherent necessity but in the prevalence of colonial and patriarchal tropes, and their apparently interminable flexibility. I agree with Lloyd that the fetishistic atavism that characterizes myths of nationalism needs displacing, but I also think that the adoption of a logic of the fetish as an analytic tool does not fail to spawn its own abjects as it is recycled. The discourse of fetishism constitutes a practice of cultural criticism, a loose assemblage of critical theories around the topics of nation, race, and sexuality, which has come to characterize a cultural imaginary.

According to Anderson's influential book *Imagined Communities,* one of the defining paradoxes of nationalism is "The objective modernity of nations to the historian's eye vs. their subjective antiquity in the eyes of nationalists" (1990, 5).[10] Lloyd restates this paradox when he identifies a contradictory impulse that pervades discourses on nationalism. On the one hand nationalism is seen as a "product of modernity" (1999, 19) and on the other hand it is held to involve "a resurgence of atavistic forces which civilization, in the form of the centralized state, has struggled to expunge or contain" (20). In his attempt to move beyond the failure of discourses on nationalism to historicize the binary of "atavism versus modernity" (20), Lloyd suggests that the role of the state is directed not so much toward eliminating atavism but rather to producing it. Explaining the dynamic of fetishism with reference to Fanon, Lloyd says that for Fanon the " 'plunge into the past' " is "the beginning of nationalism in the emerging intellectual's turn back to 'his' own culture to find another reflection, another human image" (22). Lloyd goes on to emphasize that this turn to the past is fetishistic not only due to the subject's desire but also, more importantly, because of the arrested development of the colonized culture, a reification produced by colonial power.

> If that turn to the cultural past is in a strict sense fetishistic because it involves the desire for an image of wholeness to set against the mutilating experience of deracination and alienation, it is so not merely on account of the subjective sources of the desire. It is in the first place necessarily fetishistic because of what Fanon terms the "sclerotization" of the colonized culture, the paralysis of a society whose previous, relatively autonomous paths of transformation have been blocked by colonialism. What the dispossessed intellectual turns to is fixed, archival and available for fetishistic recovery only in part, because of the intellectual's own relation to it; in large part, it is because that culture no longer exists except as an object of archaeological recovery. It is, indeed, strictly speaking "fetishistic" in involving the disavowal of the intellectual's cultural mutilation by way of fixation on an apparent prior wholeness. (22–23)

In this account fetishism is cast as a joint project in which the colonizer and the colonized are engaged, as if in a dialogical relation, but what this suggests is that a practice and a logic of fetishism unites the colonizer and the colonized in a discourse that remains thoroughly masculinist. Such an account resists collapsing the point of view of the colonized with the colonizer, at the same time as it confirms the homosocial pact that unites the two points of view in their common exclusion of any attempt to represent the female subject, whose imaginary castration is presupposed by the logic of fetishism without becoming available for interrogation, not to mention the fact that this imaginary castration is itself formulated in racialized terms.

While the logic of fetishism has certainly been applied to the reification suffered by the arrested culture, there is nothing inherent in the particular masculine imaginary informing the discourse of fetishism that renders it necessary. So long as the mythical past, idealized as one in which the subject is autonomous and fully present to itself, and contrasted to an actual present in which the subject is mutilated, is envisaged in terms of the myth of castration, there is an assumption of masculinist logic. The phantasmatic completion in terms of which the past is constructed serves as a solace for the mutilating threat of the present. The fact that both Fanon and Lloyd fail to put into question the masculinist imaginary underlying the model of fetishism complicates the argument that Lloyd goes on to make. Lloyd distinguishes between, on the one hand, the "'bourgeois' forms" of nationalism that "most Western accounts" take "at their word," which he associates with "[r]omantic fetishism," and with what Fanon calls the "'sterile formalism' of bourgeois nationalism" and on the other hand the "inventiveness of popular democratic movements." The "contemporary space" of the latter is a "hybrid, 'unevenly developed' culture that is neither traditional nor modern" but in its "contemporaneity" it provides the resources for "means of resistance" (1999, 23). Again, I will merely note here—and I will return to this observation in my discussion of Uma Narayan—that the bourgeois forms of nationalism also remain masculinist. If it is true that the "self-representation" of nationalism remains bourgeois, in a way that goes unmarked by the Western narratives under critique by Fanon and Lloyd, it is also true that it remains masculinist in a way that goes unmarked by Fanon and Lloyd.[11]

The problem of the self-representation of the nation-state is one that Lloyd analyzes in terms of its function as both "form and end" (24). Insofar as the nation-state takes itself as the end toward which nationalism strives, it assimilates any other social movements to its own ends so far as it can. At the same time it relegates any aspect of movements that remain antagonist to it to "the residual space of historical contingency" (24), and "writes such popular movements out of history and into [the] mythopoetic space . . . [to which] national culture is held to recur in its atavistic moments" (24). The movement of feminism, for example, comes to inhabit a space that does not conform to the logic of nationalism, and as such it is dismissed as "non-sense," as irrational, or illegible according to that logic. Yet—and this is an aspect that Lloyd does not develop as much as he might—it is crucial to note that the very forms of nationalism that write such movements out of history also, on Lloyd's own account, appeal to them, and draw on them, only to cast off whatever cannot be absorbed in a fetishistic, atavistic moment. As such, these movements that are written out of the history of nationalism also provide its sustenance, constitute its resources, keeping it afloat even as they are repudiated by nationalism. Feminism becomes an abject casualty of nationalism.

Not only does the drive for nationalism to represent the nation as an uncomplicated unity, as "one people"—a representation that cannot tolerate any fracturing or diversity or self-differentiation in general— reproduce the logic dictated by the project of universal history and its vision of cosmopolitanism (23); it also fails to mark itself as specifically masculinist. By continuing to exploit both the resources of women and of the feminist movement, appropriating for itself what it finds useful at both the material and ideological levels, making those resources conform to its logic, and discarding the rest, the unifying drive toward nationalism relegates feminist and other social movements to the mythic past. The apparent universal project of history into which the identity of nations is slotted for the end of cosmopolitanism is in fact a masculinist project through and through. Not only are the very forms of self-representation that constitute the nation dictated by a particular form of subject—masculinist—whose particularity represents itself as universal, but the path of ascendancy achieved by this form is obscured, as it must be in order for masculinist particularity to mask itself as universal.

Lloyd emphasizes the need to go beyond nationalist appeals to tradition as merely reactive, regressive, fetishistic throwbacks, in the face of colonial aggression, and shows how such accounts are themselves caught up in bourgeois forms of self-representation. At the same time he elucidates the dynamic by which movements such as feminism are constructed as irrational, nonsensical residues that are unthinkable in terms of the nationalist logic that conforms to the idea of cosmopolitanism enshrined in the ideal of universal history. By recasting this argument in terms of abjection, as that which fetishism has always already assumed even in its foreclosure, I suggest that we can provide an account of how the bourgeois and patriarchal biases of representation can be made to account for themselves, and open a space for the recognition of movements such as feminism. Rather than merely contenting ourselves with the account that bourgeois forms of nationalism dictate, in which feminist movements are relegated to some mytho-poetic past, unthinkable under the terms of representation that nationalism has legitimated for itself, the possibility of how women and feminist discourses can contribute to, constitute, and reconfigure viable forms of anticolonial nationalism is opened up. In a discussion that advances reflection on the relationship between nationalism and social movements such as feminism, and on the tendency of different strains of imperialism and nationalism to get caught up in reactionary appeals, and to represent themselves as naturalizing forces, Narayan asks us to think about the need to reimagine communities, whether those communities are colonial or anticolonial. In doing so, while she herself does not use the language of abjection, she helps to make visible the ways in which both imperialism and anticolonial nationalism proceed by way of abjecting some subjects in order to preserve as rational and intelligible the claims of others.

Both Indian nationalists and Western colonizers have oversimplified their competing visions of nation and culture. One of Narayan's concerns is to avoid overplaying the differences between the imaginary constructions of East and West that have been produced due to colonization. As Partha Chatterjee says, "European criticism of Indian 'tradition' as barbaric had focused to a large extent on religious beliefs and practices, especially those relating to the treatment of women" (1993, 9). In response to criticism that their practices are barbaric or primitive, anticolonialists have revalorized traditional practices in a way that positions women as the guardians of what is then construed as a national essence, thereby reducing women to passive, static alibis of history. When these practices involve the symbolic reduction of women to guardians of tradition, coupled with the actual sacrifice of women, we are confronted with the logic of abjection on the basis of which nationalist values are constructed. Narayan's analysis demonstrates the extent to which nationalist values, when constructed according to masculinist, bourgeois assumptions, and in reaction to colonial oppression, not only depend upon the subjection of women but also include the attribution of any resistance to that subjection to the pernicious influence of the West. Thus, it is not just that patriarchal nationalism usurps feminist energies for its own cause, while consigning women to history, as Lloyd suggests. For Narayan it is a question of projecting that which cannot be assimilated by anticolonial nationalism onto its colonial oppressor, so that the myth of nationalism can be preserved, as if it were pure and uncontaminated by feminism. By maintaining that colonialism corrupts the myth of national identity, disrupting the unity the colonized nation tries to formulate for itself, anticolonial nationalism outlaws feminism. Anticolonial nationalism thus benefits from whatever feminist resistance it can recoup for itself but fails to acknowledge this, either by denying feminism and consigning women to their traditional roles, or by attributing feminism to the colonizing West. Local feminism is repressed, only to be projected onto the West. This split legacy of anti-colonial nationalisms testifies to the ways in which they mimic Western narratives of nationalism, even as they set themselves in opposition to them. Western narratives of nationalism thereby sustain themselves through establishing continuities between themselves and the new narratives of nationalism they provoke. There is a refusal to see women who develop feminist narratives as anticolonial national subjects, and a positing of them instead as a corruption of anticolonial nationalist myths, as continuous with Western hegemony.

Like Fanon, Narayan suggests that we need to understand that the very values that purport to stand for what is "traditional" nationalism, are in fact constructed in reaction to colonial forces. According to Narayan, allegedly traditional Third World values, far from being "natural givens," are in fact "constructed" (1997, 402, 405) in response to colonial and postcolonial values.[12] What is at play here is a mere inversion of colonialist ideology. While the West characterizes the Third World in terms of their allegedly backward and barbaric ways, and as therefore in need of liberation and enlightenment by a reputedly benign and progressive benefactor, the Third World masculine elite reacts against this would-be liberator by constructing an idea of itself that appeals to tradition, purity, and spiritual values—of which women come to be representative. Thus while the West and the Third World agree on their divergence—on their differential status, or on their "otherness"—they disagree on their valuations of one another. Reacting against the claims of superiority made by the West, anticolonial nationalist movements "inver[t] the colonialist contempt for indigenous cultures into a contempt for the culture of their colonizers" (402).

For their part, Western governments have represented themselves as standing for a superior way of life, standing for equality and liberty when in fact they practiced slavery and colonialism. Not only do appeals to tradition on the part of anticolonialist nationalist movements remain beholden to, and determined by, Western ideologies insofar as they content themselves with being merely reactive, but both "Western culture" and "anticolonial and nationalist visions of 'national culture' " suffer from "'idealized' constructions" or are " 'totalizations' " (402). So, for example, Western culture takes itself to be concerned with "liberty and equality," while in fact engaging in "slavery and colonization," while "'Indian culture' is often problematically equated with aspects of upper-caste Hindu culture, ignoring the actual cultural and religious diversity of the population" (402).

Narayan points out how women get caught in the middle of the competing narratives provided by colonial powers and the colonized parties, so that any feminist criticism is seen as a betrayal of their national culture, as if feminists are selling out to Western colonial visions. Narayan shows that, far from being imported to India as an ostensibly enlightened Western idea, in fact her feminist practice is indebted to the struggles that she confronted within her own family. She watched her mother struggle with her mother-in-law, in a joint family, which was still patriarchal in many ways. Her feminist consciousness was forged precisely because of the fact that she witnessed the silencing of her mother, who was critical of Narayan's feminism, as if it were due to the corrupting influence of the West. Fusing the autobiographical with the theoretical in revealing ways, Narayan draws out the contradictory messages to which she was exposed. On the one hand, her mother wanted to do her duty in bringing up her daughter well, but on the other hand she encouraged her daughter to get an education—yet the very ideas to which this education exposed Narayan were suspect in her mother's eyes. Asked to uphold traditional nationalist values, Narayan shows how her mother was invested with the expectation that she safeguard the culture that Narayan witnessed as oppressing her mother.

The contradictory messages to which Narayan was exposed in her relationship with her mother in the context of a joint family function as a metaphor for the idealization and totalization at work in the ways that both the East and the West represent themselves. Thus, for example, traditional Indian nationalists constructed sati, the practice of widow immolation, as if it were emblematic of "Indian culture." The religiously and ethnically variegated cultures of India are represented as a homogeneous and monolithic other of an equally imaginary and oversimplified conception of the West. Narayan observes that Indian nationalists evoke a picture of the pristine, spiritual tradition, in which women knew their place, by constructing sati as a much more widespread practice than in fact it is. There is an oversimplification both of what is constructed as Indian tradition, and in what is taken to be Western culture. As Narayan says, "in Third World contexts" "there is an *extremely selective* rejection of 'modernization' and 'Westernization'" (407). Drawing attention to the complexity of hegemony, Raymond Williams also points to what he calls "*selective tradition*"—"that which, within the terms of an effective dominant culture, is always passed off as '*the* tradition,' '*the* significant past'. . . . from a whole possible area of past and present, certain meanings and practices are chosen for emphasis, certain other meanings and practices are neglected and excluded. Even more crucially, some of these meanings and practices are reinterpreted, diluted, or put into forms which support or at least do not contradict other elements within the effective dominant culture. . . . [There is] a continual making and remaking of an effective dominant culture" (1997, 39). Hindu fundamentalists see no contradiction in castigating Western values, on the one hand, and "skillfully us[ing] contemporary media such as television to propagate their ideological messages" (Narayan 1997, 407), on the other hand.

If Narayan points to the partial and contradictory representations of Indian culture, she is also concerned with the fact that the colonial Western world persisted in representing itself in similarly problematic ways, as enshrining the values of liberty and equality, in order to oppose what were consequently perceived as barbaric Eastern practices, while in fact themselves perpetrating the barbarism of slavery and colonialism. The Western world continues to cast itself in the role of liberator of the free world, to claim the high moral ground of innocence and justice, while in fact operating according to the demands of capitalism, and committing itself to continued abuses of freedom, whether in the form of slavery, colonialism, preemptive and unjustified war, or torture.

Narayan conveys a sense of her mother's subordination to the "domestic tyrannies available to Indian mothers-in-law" (398) due to "cultural traditions" that "did not deem it appropriate for a son to reprimand his parents," and which provided a "convenient cultural excuse" for her father to refuse to "interfere" (ibid.). She also points out that "motherlands are spaces where fathers still have most of the privileges and power, and the mothers and mother-cultures relate differently to their daughters than to their sons, imposing different demands and expecting different forms of conformity" (400).

Narayan calls on us to imagine new nationalist communities, to reimagine the postcolonial nation as one in which women are not required to sacrifice themselves for the sake of maintaining what are in any case ossified imaginary visions of a lost past, deriving from a rejection of what is taken to be "the West"—a representation that is itself a mythical and oversimplified characterization. Postcolonial narrators of nation must become more self-reflective about their tendency to reiterate abjection in ways that cannot be wholly accounted for even by the conceptual infiltration of the unity of nationhood by notions of splitting and fracturing, which themselves are susceptible to being related as newly hegemonic.

Third World feminism emerges, Narayan argues, not due to some misplaced allegiance to Western ideas, but out of the particular histories endemic to the local situation, in her case, out of the political struggles of women around issues of "dowry-deaths and dowry related harassment of women, police rape of women in custody, issues relating to women's poverty, work and health, and issues of ecology and communalism that affect women's lives" (400). To attribute the emergence of such feminism to the hegemony of the West is both to insist that all feminisms are the same, and to ignore the fact that patriarchal organization of society is not restricted to the West. Even if patriarchy reinvents itself in postcolonial theory in part by mimicking Western theory, taking over the discourse of fetishism, feminist resistance to it cannot be entirely circumscribed by such processes of mimicry. To contest the hegemony of fetishistic discourse is to take on its language and thereby confirm and reproduce its power, in the very act of putting in question that power. Yet it is not only to do that.

Hegemony, in Williams's words, is "not singular" but rather "its own internal structures are highly complex, and have continually to be renewed, recreated and defended" (1997, 38). It is "a set of meanings and values which as they are experienced as practices appear as reciprocally confirming" (38). The continual renewal of hegemony involves what Williams calls "emergent" and "residual" culture (41). In order to remain dominant, the dominant culture must absorb emergent meanings and transform itself through their reinterpretation (45). At the same time it consists of mutually confirming—at least noncontradictory (39)—elements. If it is true, as T. J. Jackson Lears suggests, that "Subordinate groups may participate in maintaining a symbolic universe, even if it seems to legitimate their domination," it is also true that "the line between dominant and subordinate cultures is a permeable membrane, not an impenetrable barrier."[13] Counterhegemonic discourses will therefore be incorporated, in just the way that the fetishistic logic of disavowal has extended itself to include the postcolonial subject, and in doing so has participated in the exclusion of the female subject. This complicity can be read as the legitimation of postcolonial theory, yet it can also be read as colluding in the abjection of women as legitimate postcolonial subjects. In order to be recognized as counterhegemonic, feminist discourses must use the language of hegemony, even as they point out the ways in which current hegemonic cultures delegitimate feminist concerns. Lears comments that "values rooted in the workers' everyday experience lack legitimacy . . . hegemonic culture depends . . . on the tendency of public discourse to make some forms of experience readily available to consciousness while ignoring or suppressing others (1985, 577). The effort by Indian nationalists to suppress Deepa Mehta's film *Fire* can be read as an attempt to enforce "the boundaries of permissible discourse, [to] discourag[e] the clarification of social alternatives, and mak[e] it difficult for the dispossessed to locate the source of their unease, let alone remedy it" (570). Read as part of the symbolic and

Sita and Radha in *Fire*.
Courtesy of Photofest.

cultural discourses of postcolonialism, whether and in what ways Narayan's and Mehta's interventions have the power to redefine the terms of that discourse remains to be seen, just as it remains to be seen how the terms of feminism will be reinvented so that it does not retain as part of its myth of origins an indelible attachment to the West.

I suggest that through the invocation of fetishistic discourse, the language of postcolonial theory has partaken in a confirmation of patriarchal discourse. Through a common process of othering, through their mutual expulsion of postcolonial women from the scene of representation, postcolonial and patriarchal discourses confirm one another, and they do so by either articulating or endorsing for one another the silences that inhabit each discourse. If male-dominated postcolonial theory reenacts the patriarchal thrust of psychoanalytic theory in taking up the language of disavowal and fetishism, it also opens up a potential space for challenging the repressed colonial other of that patriarchal discourse. Yet by adhering to the language of fetishism, postcolonial theory enacts a certain complicity with the white, patriarchal biases of psychoanalytic theory that is not necessarily raised to the level of theorization. To the extent that the mimetic adoption of the language of fetishism and disavowal remains a practice that is left untheorized, and to the extent that feminist theorists reproduce it, it becomes a universal practice, the universality of which lends it an air of transparency. The discourse of fetishism achieves a cultural hegemony for itself, legitimating itself through its malleability. In Williams's terms the emergent practices and theories of feminism will become articulated in the developing hegemonic discourses of postcolonial nationalism, yet even as this happens "certain other meanings and practices are neglected and excluded" (1997, 39), because they are not yet "defined" (1997, 41) in terms of dominant culture. The question remains as to how hegemony proceeds to include its former others, and what new exclusions are perpetrated in the process. While the development of hegemony consists in a constant attempt to revise the processes that present themselves as inconsistent with dominant culture, to contradict what contradicts it, its dissolution of contradictions is itself the production of new hegemonic discourses. The constant deviation of hegemonic thinking from itself encourages the formulation of contradictions so that it can negate those contradictions.[14] In this ongoing articulation of hegemony, new forms of abjection will arise, and it remains for those sites of abjection to be marked. In marking them, a redefinition of what Lears calls the "boundaries of common-sense" (1985, 572) might take place. Ironically, the very identification of abject sites as abject will tend toward their discursive incorporation and thus to the transcendence of the abject, to its transformation into theory—but not without engaging in the production of new significations that enact new abjects. Already effective at the level of practice, the abject is constituted as outside discourse. In this sense it constitutes something like the "embryonic" working-class conception of the world that is "implicit" in the "activity" of the working class (Lears 1985, 569).[15]

Since hegemony does not, in Williams's words, "exhaus[t] the full range of human practice" (1997, 43), the emergence of new practices will continue to be incorporated at the same time as other practices will not yet be recognized as significant. This failure of recognition involves the production of a series of unintelligible sites, irrational or nonsensical practices that can be read as emergent sites of meaning that enable what counts as significant to dominant culture to shift, since they threaten current dominant meanings. As illegible in the terms of this symbolic, the real is ejected from its embrace. In this sense, as Cole says, "The real of slavery, of ethnocidal terror and subjugation, functions as Southern slave society's symptom—as the enabling condition threatening to undermine this society" (1998, 268). The real of colonialism, the wounds of war and exploitation, would be Europe's symptom. Colonial subjects facilitate capitalism by providing the economic base of capitalism, in the form of labor resources, while at the same time threatening to rebel, to refuse the ideology of capitalism. Deepa Mehta's *Fire* furnishes one instance of what might be called the real abject of postcolonial discourse in the context of

India, namely, the marginality of female desire, the denial of female agency, and the taboo on lesbian sexuality. One might think that to depict lesbian sexuality only as a response to husbands who, in different ways, neglect their matrimonial symbolic roles, is to affirm, rather than contest, the psychoanalytic construction of lesbian desire as pathological. Rather than understanding the lesbian desire of Radha and Sita as adhering to its pathological construction of homosexuality—as Western, feminist theoretical paradigms might encourage us to do—by taking seriously the contradictions that situate Third World women that Narayan examines, *Fire* can be read as contesting reactive, masculinist, postcolonial nationalist narratives.[16] In this context, lesbian sexuality does not constitute a last resort that is only embraced as an alternative to dominant economies of desire, but rather a creative reworking of the privilege that heterosexist imaginaries assume in postcolonial nationalist myths. If in order for the claims of postcolonial nationalism to be upheld by the practices of everyday life, women must adhere to heterosexual and traditional roles—to obey their husbands, to cook, to clean, to reproduce, to preserve the values of "their" culture—what does this say about anticolonial nationalist discourse, whether intellectual or not? What does it say when theoretical discourses relegate the emergence of a counter-narrative of desire and agency to the pernicious influence of the hegemonic grip of the West, by constructing a myth of origin that writes women back into an archaic culture? In doing so, postcolonial discourse continues to draw on the resources of women, while refusing to recognize as legitimate their claims to have moved—and to have been moved—beyond the confines of tradition. The fetishistic temporality of atavistic narratives, whether in the name of colonial or anticolonial nationalisms, produces sites of abjection, sites that elicit both fascination and disgust. An example of such desire/disgust is Ashok's memory/fantasy of Sita and Radha's sexual intimacy in *Fire*. Ashamed because the desire he had spent so many years ago not only reemerges, but that it does so at the vision of his wife making love to Sita, Ashok experiences arousal as giving into temptation. A second abject moment in this film, which bears a close affinity to the issues Narayan raises, is that in which Biji spits at Radha in an expression of her disgust at Radha's relation with Sita. After a stroke that has left her mute and unable to walk, Biji is unable to use words to describe her disdain for Radha's relationship to Sita and for her desertion of her son, Ashok. Instead she resorts to the response previously reserved for Mundu, the servant who masturbates to pornographic videos in the presence of the helpless Biji, whose ill health symbolizes the fading power of matriarchy over the joint household. As Biji spits at Radha, she rejects the person who has devoted herself over the years to caring for Biji's bodily needs.

The trauma of colonialism reiterates itself through history, by spawning new forms of the real. Figured as impossible by the hegemonic terms of the symbolic, the abject does not fail to contaminate the discourses that outlaw it, and in outlawing it the symbolic is invested in abjection, even as that investment is unthinkable or unsignifiable within its terms. That it is unsymbolized by this symbolic does not mean that it is non-symbolizable by a new symbolic. In our attempts to formulate this new symbolic, what as yet untold imaginary will we have repressed or repudiated in our presupposing of it, and how will we come to disavow it? How will the new communities that constitute themselves around this new imaginary come to be hegemonic? What forms of negation will be harnessed to our foreclosure of abjection?

Abjection happens when individuals, peoples, nations, states, or political, religious, or ethnic groups attempt to set themselves up as pure and good by requiring others to occupy a place of impurity, a place of evil. It is not always—perhaps only rarely—that people consciously try to make others represent all that is bad in order to prove themselves as good, righteous, holy, morally rigorous, unimpeachable. As often as not, it happens outside the circuit of conscious, deliberate intentions, or voluntary, well-conceived, well-controlled actions. As often as not, it happens out of feelings of insecurity or anxiety, defensiveness or inadequacy, weakness and fear of contamination. In order to rid myself of my guilt, my feelings of unworthiness, I deny my fear or cowardice, and project it onto others, who then come to represent it for me. I cannot be dirty and disgusting, so another must be it for me. I must purify myself. It is a dynamic that is set into motion despite our best intentions. When a nation sets itself up as benevolent and powerful, and in order to sustain its mythical narcissism, requires that other nations occupy the symbolic place of an axis of evil, it appeals to an imaginary that fosters an image of itself as only good and pure. The often-unstated rhetoric that underlies this abjection of the other as evil and impure appeals to a mythical, Edenic prehistory, a time of absolute innocence.

The abjection of subjects, based on their race, religion, ethnicity, gender, sexuality or class, seems to have become a commonplace. I try in this book to articulate a logic of abjection, as supplementary to dominant fetishistic theories which seem to replicate themselves so prolifically. A logic of abjection is at work in an imperialistic politics that sets itself up as if it were well intentioned, but consists of demanding that other countries conform to its own image. In particular, I am concerned with the ways in which even those who take themselves to be practitioners of and supporters of progressive politics are liable to reinvent logics of abjection in their attempts to shore up their own claims to validity. Insofar as such logics target other minority and disenfranchised groups, they need to be rigorously challenged. If a politics of abjection is to be practiced at all it should be directed at those who take it upon themselves to invade, and abject whoever presents themselves as a convenient, profitable, target. The power of representation remains both a formidable foe, and an ally for those of us who remain committed to thinking through how it is that we are abjected, and how we in turn abject others. If abjection marks the birth of thought, if the affective moment in which a separation between I and another occurs is also the moment at which representation becomes possible, it is necessary to return to such formative moments in order to reshape representation, in order to redraw, infinitely, boundaries.

9

Concluding Reflections on the Necrophilia of Fetishism

In the close-up of Ludovic applying lipstick and looking at his image in a mirror, Berliner withholds from his audience any visual cues that would render determinate the character's gender, thereby putting into question the normative assumptions typically in play as identifiers of gender, assumptions that will be interrogated systematically throughout *Ma vie en rose*. Cowie says:

> Identification . . . arises not with the visual view of a character but with a close-up of the character looking. The use of a full-face close-up can invoke a transitivist identification not merely because we can then see the face clearly, but more importantly because in filling the screen it also obscures the space and time of the narrative. . . . The transitivist identification with the image of the face is but a moment, and just like the mirror stage itself, it is no sooner constituted as identification than it is flipped over into identification in a chain of desire, and the figure of the Other intervenes. In the cinema it is the moment when movement, narrative, the shift to medium-shot from close-up, or to the object of the glance, breaks up the absorption in the image of the other and forces it to give way to the chain of signification, to the movement of desire which is figured. (1997, 105)

If identification arises with a close-up of the character looking, when that character is Ludovic, looking into a mirror and seeing the girl he wants to be, how does identification play out? The reflection in the mirror that Ludovic sees is his ideal ego, not the ego ideal or superego that admonishes him to identify as a boy. As the narrative unfolds, how viewers position themselves in relation to Ludovic's identification will depend in part on how critically they reflect on the heteronormative, binary fantasies that fuel the social order, defensive fantasies that abject the Ludovics of this world. In *Ma vie en rose* the assumption that male bodies entail masculine genders while female bodies entail feminine genders also proves to be constitutive of middle-class cohesion. Ludovic identifies as a girl, and cannot understand why his family and society frown upon his desire to wear his sister's clothes and red lipstick. Identificatory regimes can be made available for reconstitution when we discover ourselves as having identified with such a desire. *Ma vie en rose* encourages critical reflection on the necessity of such constitutive relationships. A transsexual who views the film will be likely to entertain a different relationship to gender assumptions than another viewer, just as those who gasp in surprise or horror when they see Dil's penis in *The Crying Game* will not see it in the same way as those who are, as it were, in the know. Yet Jordan works to undermine the certainty not only of those who did not "know," but also of those who claimed to "know." What exactly did they know, and how does such knowledge perpetuate sexual and racial binaries that continue to dictate the imaginary possibilities of those that are lovable and those that are not? The spectators who view *The Birth of a Nation* as aesthetically groundbreaking, while minimizing its racism, stand in a very different relation to its images than that of viewers who refuse to divorce its aesthetic achievements from its use of racial stereotypes. Those who read Sam in *Casablanca* as Rick's equal fail to see as significant—that is they fail to see at all—the fact that his character remains largely undeveloped and that he remains Rick's sidekick and subordinate. The invisible regimes of whiteness and heteronormative desire that orchestrate his subordinate status fail to signify.

The ways in which spectators identify themselves in relation to racial, sexual, class, and nationalist regimes are not coincidental to what we will see and what we will not see. This suggests that the continued adherence to Christian Metz's contention that the spectator is "all-perceiving" (1982, 48) needs to be revisited. Commenting on Metz, Cowie says, "What is specific to the cinema as visual performance is that all the spectators see from the same position—everyone sees Garbo's face as a profile—but this point-of-view will be continually changing: now close-up, now long-shot, now from this character's position now from another's. In other words, the spectator's look is aligned with and made identical to another look, the camera's which has gone before it, and already 'organised' the scene" (Cowie 1997, 100). To say that "all the spectators see from the same position" is to obliterate the significance of the difference between someone who reads Dil as transgendered from the start, and someone who doesn't, a difference that depends on the position one takes in relation to prevailing foundational social fantasies of desire. The director who has organized the framing of the film is not in control of the meaning it takes on for its viewers, even if that director provides for ambiguous readings. There is more than one spectator, and some spectators will see what others fail to see. Metz posits an ideal spectator, while espousing a theory of cinema that adheres to the trope of disavowal, a trope that Rose identifies as an "exclusively male construction" (1986, 202). The terms in which Metz posits the spectator as ideal also covertly privilege whiteness, heterosexuality, and middle-class identity, at the same time as they tend to underline the passivity of the spectator. Even as he acknowledges that the spectator "constitutes the cinema signifier (it is I who make the film)," Metz construes the spectator as a "great eye and ear," in which "material is deposited," as the "place" in which a "really perceived imaginary accedes to the symbolic" (1982, 48–49). This reflects a more general tension in Metz's analysis between his attestation on the one hand that the "ego is already formed" (47) and his refusal of the idea on the other hand that "the psychical apparatus" is already "fully constituted" (47). Feminist theorists are among those to have emphasized that for Freud, not only must the ego be constituted, rather than assumed from the start, but that it continually elaborates itself in response to loss, through shifting identifications.[1] Yet these identifications are often explored either within the restrictive framework of castration theory and fetishism, or from a feminist framework that questions the trope of masculinist disavowal, but continues to privilege sexual difference over other differences. The attention Kristeva pays to the infant's abjection of and separation from the mother, which occurs prior to the infant's developing a capacity to signify its desire symbolically—prior to the subject's situating itself in relation to castration—opens up the possibility of attending to class, racial, and heteronormative power regimes not as secondary to sexual difference, but as mutually constitutive of one another. To say that such regimes are mutually constitutive of one another is not to say that all differences will signify equally for all subjects at all times, but to acknowledge that they will signify differentially and unequally for subjects, not in ways that necessarily reflect the social identity of spectators, but according to how spectators situate themselves in relation to dominant social norms. This differential operation of symbolic forms of cohesive identity has been consolidated precisely by the insistence of psychoanalytic theory that sexual difference is constitutive of taking up a meaningful position as a subject, and that it is therefore foundational to any meaning. When race theory takes over the trope of fetishism without critically addressing the psychoanalytic assumption that sexual difference is foundational to meaning, its insights continue to operate differentially around the question of sexual difference, even while making available for interrogation the elision of race by psychoanalytic theory.

If the trope of fetishism reemerges in the discourses of race theory and film theory, it does not do so without a significant recasting of its meaning. Thus, if Fanon retains fetishistic discourse, he radically recasts its meaning so that the racial connotations that appear in Freud, but tend to be repressed in standard, white, psychoanalytic theory, signify a history of colonialism. The racialized mapping and fragmentation of the corporeal schema that Fanon describes in terms of the historico-racial schema and the racial-epidermal schema has been rendered invisible by the dominant regimes of whiteness upheld by colonialism.[2] The corporeal mapping that Kristeva describes in relation to the mother's body has been repressed by the phallic, symbolic order of representation, which thereby subsumes it under the discourse of fetishism. When this repression and invisibility are interpreted by means of the fetishistic trope of disavowal, new forms of repression and invisibility are set in motion, this time in the name of feminist and race theory, which fail to mark themselves as masculinist and white.

If the abjection of subjects has been fetishized, sometimes precisely by theorists who attempt to address forms of social discrimination, it stands in need of demystification. Like the retaliatory maneuvers of Klein's projective identification, characteristic of the paranoid-schizoid position, and the reparative, creative responses characteristic of the depressive position, the play of abjection and transference/identification provides an interpretive tool that acknowledges the existence of multiple, sometimes conflicting, ways of splitting up the world. The defenses put in play in abjection are intended to safeguard subjects from greater threats (annihilation, nonexistence, nothingness). It should not surprise us that such defenses are liable to recuperation by fetishistic discourses, which in addition to their classic feature of disavowal—I know (that women are castrated/that blacks are inferior) but all the same (my fetish will cover over this deficiency)—consolidate difference according to a master discourse (patriarchy/whiteness). If abjection is a defensive response to the horror of disintegration or nonexistence—the threat is not limited to castration, rather my very being is threatened—it can follow the logic of projective identification, in which retaliation is projected outside, onto some other. Such logics operate by way of a refusal intended to cleanse the subject: I cannot be the bad object (disgusting, or impure), so you must be it. Works of art can perpetuate such logics, by acquiescing to available forms of marginalization, sustained by racist, homophobic, sexist, or classist fantasies. Or they can intervene in ways that disrupt and reorganize the social fantasies that fuel identifications legitimated by the symbolic order. As such, they can facilitate the work of reparation, by eliciting identifications against socially sanctioned norms.

While Metz wants to affirm the "permanent play of identification" (1982, 46) and sees the play of identification as definitive of "the cinematic situation in its generality, i.e. *the* code" (54), he also insists that "the spectator can do no other than identify with the camera (49). Yet the spectator critical of the racism of *The Birth of a Nation* does not identify with the camera.[3] Metz is careful to say that it is the "film" that confers its "gift of 'ubiquity'" on the "all-powerful" subject (48) and the "camera" (49) with which the spectator identifies (49), but this privileging of technology, which he understands with reference to the trope of fetishism, must itself be treated with suspicion. It merely mystifies the choices made by the director not only in privileging certain shots over others or editing them in certain ways, but also in using them to build up a narrative that conforms to, or undercuts, foundational fantasies. Metz conflates an implied universal spectator with the subject of fetishism, whose knowledge that he is watching a film that he takes for reality is theorized in a way that, in Rose's words, makes sexual difference the "vanishing point" of the theory.[4] When the trope of disavowal is transferred to the discourse of race theory in a way that disavows sexual difference, racial difference, we might say, becomes the vanishing point of theory.

Film theory has tended to emphasize either the ways in which film facilitates identification, how it covers over any dissonance, to produce a harmonious narrative flow in keeping with the fantasy of the director, or how it disrupts that identification. When such disruptions have been the focus, as in Brechtian-inspired readings of film, whatever distanciation is explored tends to dislocate the pleasure of fantasy.[5] What matters, however, is how disruptions of affective identifications translate into disjunctive relationships that symbolically appropriate social and political norms, or how affective identifications are effected that harbor the possibility of rearranging more permanently our ways of seeing. Film can play a part either in perpetuating normative identifications or in educating viewers to see differently through becoming invested in scenes, characters, and desires that move us beyond the normatively restrictive identifications of our daily lives. Their semiotic address can operate in tension with prevailing symbolic forms, alluding to an alternative symbolic. If film can elicit temporary, imaginary identifications that are dissonant with symbolically normative identifications, such identifications might have a lasting impact in rearranging the symbolic order. Yet even such interventions are susceptible to reification, will be liable to conform to rigid, doctrinaire beliefs, and must be ready to called, in their turn, to account.

No matter how metaphorically it functions, the name of the father remains the governing trope of psychoanalysis for Lacan—and the phallus remains its referent. The impetus behind this invocation of the phallus is concomitant with the priority accorded to symbolic meaning. Yet to assume such priority covers over the question of what legitimates symbolic meaning, who governs what is sanctioned as meaningful, and who is disqualified in advance as arbiters of meaning by a symbolic system that systematically evades the questioning of its own historically and socially established privilege.

To say, as Rose does, that the symbolic is inaugurated by the sense that "something is missing," and that words must be spoken only when the "first object is lost" (1986, 54), covers over a number of problems. What, precisely, is missing, and how does it come to be an object? How does a subject come to be a subject capable of representing an object as missing? How does an infant separate from the mother, and come to conceptualize itself as a subject? And how does the psychoanalytic account of language acquisition come to represent this necessary separation from the mother as only making sense as a function of the father? By explaining language as a function of the third, and by installing the paternal metaphor in the place of the third, Lacanian psychoanalytic theory consigns the mother to the status of the excluded other, who initiates the subject into the order of representation, but who is consigned to a past history that can never be adequately represented or spoken—except insofar as she is situated in relation to castration theory.

Rose's argument hinges on a shift in Lacan such that the fantasy of completion is no longer located in the imaginary but is now assigned to the symbolic: "there is no longer imaginary 'unity' and then symbolic difference or exchange, but rather an indictment of the symbolic for the imaginary unity which its most persistent myths continue to promote" (1986, 71). For Rose, if Lacan's early work is open to the same charge as Lévi-Strauss, namely that to define women as objects of exchange is to presuppose "the subordination which it is intended to explain," (69), Lacan moves away from the idea of women as objects of exchange in his later work. Woman is now "a category within language" (71), "constructed as an absolute category (excluded and elevated at one and the same time)" (71), but this status "as an absolute category and guarantor of fantasy . . . is false" (72). Yet to constitute woman as a category within language—even if the phantasmatic closure that she produces is illusory—is not to transform women's status as objects of exchange, as the guarantor of the possibility of meaning, but only to inoculate it from interrogation. To enclose women's generative capacity for representation within representation effectively closes off the possibility of questioning the legitimacy of this system of representation, while retaining the phantasmatic assurance of completion that women's imaginary castration accomplishes. The universalization of the language of disavowal, for which Freud can already be credited, has established a cultural monopoly.[6]

In Lacan's return to Freud, the game that is played by Ernst, Freud's eighteen-month-old grandson, is given peculiar importance as the staging of the acquisition of language. As such, it constitutes one of the primary sources of Lacan's elaboration of the symbolic. This essay, "Beyond the Pleasure Principle," is also one of the essays, along with Freud's "Negation," to have had a special importance for the Kleinians. The different emphases developed by Lacan on the one hand and Kristeva, following Klein and Isaacs, on the other hand, in their readings of Ernst's game, are therefore instructive for delineating their divergence, particularly around the question of the emergence of symbolic meaning. Lacan privileges the signifier, the object, the symbolic, or the phallic order, while Kristeva is more attentive to the pre-linguistic ordering of the world.[7] For the Kleinians, fantasies, and therefore also the splitting, schizoid mechanisms by means of which the infant attempts to control pleasure and pain, are operative from the beginning, prior to language.[8]

According to Lacan "man thinks with his object . . . the signifier is the first mark of the subject" (1977b, 62). Lacan's emphasis is on "the world of words that creates the world of things" (Lacan 1977a, 65), or on the symbolic order (1991, 172, 179). He reads the significance of Freud's well-known account of the game Freud's grandson played, throwing and retrieving the spool, bobbin, or reel, accordingly (1953b). Whereas Freud had emphasized Ernst's pleasure in mastering his mother's absence, Lacan will understand Ernst's repetitive game as having revealed to us that "the moment in which desire becomes human is also that in which the child is born into language" (1977a, 103). In Freud's account, says Lacan, Ernst substitutes for "the painful tension engendered by the inevitable fact of the presence and absence of the loved object . . . a game, in which he himself manipulated the absence and presence in themselves and took pleasure in controlling them. He achieved it by means of a little reel at the end of a thread, which he threw away and pulled back" (1991, 172). For Freud, "the child makes up for the effect of his mother's disappearance by making himself the agent of it," but for Lacan, "this phenomenon is of secondary importance" (Lacan 1977b, 62). As we will see shortly, for Isaacs, on the contrary, this compensatory mastery remains of primary importance.

Drawing out what is "implicit" in Freud, Lacan focuses attention on language, on the symbolic, on the fact that this "game with the cotton-reel is accompanied by a vocalization" (1991, 172). "What is important" Lacan tells us "is not that the child said the words *Fort/Da*, which, in his mother tongue, amounts to *far/here*—besides, he pronounced them in an approximate fashion. It is rather that here, right from the beginning, we have a first manifestation of language. In this phonematic opposition, the child transcends, brings on to the symbolic plane, the phenomenon of presence and absence" (1991, 173). The absence of the mother is explained as a function of the father. "*Fort! Da!* It is precisely in his solitude that the desire of the little child has already become the desire of another, of an alter ego who dominates him and whose object of desire is henceforth his own affliction" (1977a, 104). Referring to Henri Wallon, Lacan specifies that the child's "vigilance" is aroused not when he sees his mother, the loved object, exit the room but "earlier, at the very point she left him, at the point she moved away from him" (1977b, 62). It is in the attempt to negotiate this "ever-open gap, introduced by . . . absence" (1977b, 62) that the child's back-and-forth game with the cotton-reel, accompanied by the sounds "oooh" and "aaah," expresses "self-mutilation" (1977b, 62). For "that which falls is" the "cotton-reel linked to itself by the thread . . . in which is expressed that which, of itself, detaches itself in this trial, self-mutilation on the basis of which the order of significance will be put in perspective. For the game of the cotton-reel is the subject's answer to what the mother's absence has created" (1977b, 62). The object, the cotton-reel, is understood as a mutilated part of the subject, an object that is linked to the child by the thread he holds. Lacan will give to this object the name "*petit a*" (1977b, 62). It is not the mother who is represented—or rather jettisoned—in the *objet petit a*, but a part of the self. The game of little Ernst is thereby understood as the overcoming of a split caused in the subject by the mother's departure (see 1977b, 63).

This splitting of the subject in turn is, according to Lacan, orchestrated by the castration complex, which retroactively "orientates the relations that are anterior to its actual appearance—weaning, toilet training, etc. It crystallizes each of these moments in a dialectic that has at its center a bad encounter" (1977b, 64).[9] Accordingly, we can see that Lacan's *petit a* comes to perform the work that is accomplished under the heading of castration. Kristeva's notion of abjection delineates the separation from the mother without recuperating it immediately in the name of the phallic, paternal signifier, and in doing so provides a space in which the imaginary of psychoanalysis can be rewritten in a way that opens up other avenues of interpretation, which do not necessarily follow the language of fetishistic disavowal. Just as for Lacan the object only comes to exist through its absence, so for Kristeva the mother only comes to be abjected through separation, through moving away. In contrast to Lacan's and Kristeva's derivation of an emerging sense of subjectivity from Hegelian particularity or "thisness," through differentiation, Isaacs understands what she calls "me-ness" on the basis of "sensations (and images)," which "give the phantasy a concrete bodily quality" (1989, 105). For

Isaacs, the "earliest phantasies are built mainly upon oral impulses, bound
up with taste, smell, touch" and so on (1989, 104). As Kristeva puts it,
"The Kleinians' focus was on the experience of the drives underlying
vision," preceding the "scopic hold" and prefiguring "the *Bejahung* [affir-
mation] of judgment that takes place before the gaze and immediately
through taste" (2001, 172).

Where Lacan reads Ernst's game in terms of the "birth of the symbol" (1977a, 103), Isaacs reads it in terms of fantasy, emphasizing the
child's "phantasied satisfaction of controlling his mother's comings and
goings" (1989, 73). For Isaacs, as for Freud, "phantasies . . . are the 'mental expression' of an instinct'" or "the psychic representatives of a bodily aim" (1989, 104). If for Lacan the compensatory pleasure Ernst takes
in substituting for his mother's absence is of secondary importance, for
Isaacs it is central. As she says, "forgoing . . . the satisfaction of an instinct,"
Ernst "compensated" for his mother's absence "by himself enacting the
same disappearance and return with the objects within his reach" (1989,
73). For Isaacs, on discovering a mirror Ernst "delight[s] in making his
own image appear and disappear in the mirror," confirming "his triumph
in controlling feelings of loss, by his play, as consolation for his mother's
absence" (Isaacs 1989, 73). In Kristeva's words,

> Isaacs concludes that the emergence of language is preceded, though not
> in a linear way, by a generic continuity in which the mastery of the pres-
> ence or absence of the object, which culminates in the mastery of the
> appearance of the baby's own image, is a sine qua non for understanding
> language—which itself develops well before the active use of language.
> Her conclusion serves as a good introduction to what will become Lacan's
> "mirror stage," but here it is portrayed as a process of a heterogeneous
> negativity consisting of movements, fantasized acts, and verbalization,
> and only then of scopic images. (2001, 170)

For Lacan it is "the symbol" that "cancels the existing thing" and "opens
up the world of negativity, which constitutes both the discourse of the
human subject and the reality of his world in so far as it is human"
(1991, 174). Recall that language, for Lacan, is manifested right from the
start, whereas for Isaacs, words "are a late development in our means of
expressing the inner world of our phantasy" (1989, 91), yet "[p]hantasy
and reality-testing are both in fact present from the earliest days" (1989,
107). Fantasy, for Klein, in Kristeva's words, is "anchored in the drive"
(2001, 172), while "the judgment of existence focused on reality" (172).
Kristeva, who highlights Klein's proximity to Hyppolite, emphasizes the
"asymmetry" (2001, 173) of these two stages, the first of which constitutes a kind of "*primary* symbolization" (2001, 172), neglected by Lacan.

This is already "thinking" but "it does not appear . . . as such" (Kristeva 2001, 173). As Isaacs puts it, "some measure of 'synthetic function' is exercised upon instinctual urges from the beginning . . . play creates and fosters the first forms of 'as if' thinking" (1989, 110–11).

For Klein and Kristeva, fantasy, a kind of primary symbolization, and negativity precede language; they are akin to what Freud calls "judgment[s] of attribution ('this *is* good or bad')" as opposed to judgments "of existence ('this *exists* in reality outside the scope of my representation')" (Kristeva 2001, 173). The birth of the subject proper emerges with the "judgment of existence," which

> presumes that "I" rediscover in "my" memory (and thus that "I" attribute myself to "me"—who thus becomes a "subject") a representation that *belongs* to an object and that *de-sign-ates* an absent object for the subject that "I" have become. Put another way, the judging subject cannot exist without a lost object: by relying on memory, "I" can signify the object only as it is—lost for the "ego" who, as a result of losing the object, is held out as a "subject." The interaction between the judgment of existence and the judgment of attribution forms the basis of intelligence, in the sense of a symbolic thought that is distinct from the imaginary or from fantasy. (2001, 173)

When foundational fantasies, of race for example, inform collectivities in such a way as to have become all but indistinguishable from symbolic forms of thought, the work of identifying the various ways in which such fantasies are enacted becomes crucial. Not only do such fantasies help to shape our social realities, such that the availability of services can be based on racial myths of exclusion; they also help to shape our theories. To develop this thought, let me turn to Mike Leigh's *Secrets and Lies,* a film that Kalpana Seshadri-Crooks has discussed from a Lacanian perspective. My own reading of it, inspired by Kristeva, attends not only to the role of the absent father, but to the exclusionary racial fantasies that are rendered visible in the eruption of a crisis, precipitated by the redrawing of familial boundaries that Hortense's black skin represents.

When Mike Leigh in *Secrets and Lies* presents his audience with a series of photographic portraits, the fruit of Maurice's labor, he asks us to think about the difference between photography and film, and between commerce and art, as the inexorable unfolding of the narrative is interrupted by a sequence of photographic stills.[10] Presented as works in which Maurice, a commercial photographer, has revealed the inner truth of the clients who pay him to take their pictures, the stills prompt Leigh's audience to ask themselves what his film reveals about us. Tongue in cheek, Leigh plays with the idea that people resemble their dogs, presents us with a bickering couple, or with obsessive behavior. In the background of Leigh's exploration of the relationship between photography and film, one cannot help but detect a reflection on the status of "art" films in relation to their commercial success or their critical acclaim. *Secrets and Lies* garnered more awards and more recognition than Leigh's previous films, and it is thus ironic but fitting that he uses this film to reflect on the role of the business of commercial art, and whether or not its success is to be judged by how well it pleases its consumers. At the same time, despite the insistence of many reviewers that the film has nothing to do with race, the film raises some provocative questions about the mutual implication of race and class in one another. The culturally and economically circumscribed lives of Cynthia (Brenda Blethyn) and her daughter Roxanne (Claire Rushbrook) are nonetheless informed by a racist assumption that the family has not thought through until Hortense (Marianne Jean-Baptiste) appears on the scene. They might be poor, their horizons might be limited—but at least they are not black. In the moment that Cynthia reveals to Roxanne, to her brother Maurice (Timothy Spall), and to his wife Monica (Phyllis Logan) the identity of Hortense—that she is the daughter Cynthia had given up for adoption all those years ago—the horror registered on each of their faces tells its own story. What is so incomprehensible, so unacceptable? That Hortense is black, and therefore cannot be part of their family? That a transgression of racial boundaries has apparently taken place? That an adoption from long ago has come back to haunt the family? The return, not so much of the repressed, as of the real—that which has been excluded by Cynthia to make her life livable? That Cynthia has succeeded in rediscovering a daughter she had given up, while Monica has failed to give birth to the children she so desperately wants? That Hortense is not the person they took her to be, "a mate" of Cynthia's from work? What becomes all too visible is the invisibility, until this moment, of the whiteness cementing the family's relations.

Mike Leigh's *Secrets and Lies* confronts us with a world whose characters are hemmed in by the constrained horizons of a white working-class English family, whose aspirations to occupy the ranks of the lower middle classes are most keenly exhibited by Maurice and Monica. Hortense, more affluent, urbane, and genteel than the family that defensively asserts its boundaries in the face of the prospect that she might be one of them, is, most definitively, in a different class. Her black skin becomes a site of Cynthia's abjection, in the moment when Roxanne casts her mother to the ground like the fallen woman she is, calling her a whore not only because Hortense was born out of wedlock, but perhaps more significantly because her father must have been black. Ostensibly

Maurice in *Secrets and Lies.*
Courtesy of Photofest.

a way of designating Cynthia's alleged status as a fallen woman, the word "slag" is heavily burdened with racist overtones. If Cynthia is a whore according to conventional attitudes about the sanctity of marriage and female chastity, she is all the more so because Hortense is black. Cynthia is thrown to the ground because she is seen as having transgressed the racial boundaries between black and white. The unspoken racialized fantasy that informs the word "slag" is that which unites, perhaps unconsciously, Cynthia's extended family: to be a member of this collectivity, one has to be white. The unspoken myth of the black racist hovers in the background.

Race is precisely constitutive, here, of sexuality. If race functions to police the borders of sexuality, it also performs a constitutive function in the class identity of a white family, forced to confront its own assumption that to be white is, for them, a necessary part of what it means to be working class. Only when whiteness is challenged, only when it is made explicit by being called into question, does the pervasive constitutive role that race plays in white identities become available for critical analysis. When Cynthia's family is asked to accept a black person as one of them, the limits of what is tolerable and what is not come to the fore.

Kalpana Seshadri-Crooks reads the film in terms of the logic of suture and jokes, but in my view she does not acknowledge the extent to which the film consistently returns to the site of this "joke," which is performed repeatedly. While I think Seshadri-Crooks provides a brilliant and inspired analysis of race from a Lacanian point of view, I do not agree that *Secrets and Lies* sacrifices an "extended inquiry into the logic of racial knowledge and looking" by a limited mocking of our narrative compulsion.[11] This reading fails to capture the subtlety with which the film exposes the mundane working-class sensibility that functions as a horizon for the psychologically abusive relationship between Cynthia and Roxanne. If the similitude that Cynthia sees between herself and Hortense functions for us as a joke at all, the joke is reenacted in a different way when Hortense is nearly turned away on the doorstep by Monica, who assumes that her black skin signifies that she must have come to the wrong house, or when Roxanne pushes Cynthia to the floor, in a gesture that bespeaks her fallen status as miscegenator. The void around which Monica's assumption revolves, when she thinks that Hortense must have got the wrong address, or that she must be selling something, is not simply the absence of the father, but the impossibility of blacks entering a white neighborhood, the impossibility of Cynthia's mate from work being black, in short the impossibility of blackness that invisibly structures the imaginary of Monica's white social world. Cynthia has to assert her relation to Hortense no less than five times before the truth begins to sink in: "She's my daughter. . . . Maurice . . . it's me daughter . . . Hortense, sweet'eart . . . She's yer sister . . . That's 'er 'alf-sister, Paul," and finally, to Roxanne, "SHE'S YOUR SISTER!" This anxious reiteration of family ties underscores the disbelief with which her assertions of kinship are met, an anxiety that stems from the social taboo on race-mixing. When Cynthia reveals that Hortense is her daughter, she precipitates a family crisis, which results in Monica confessing her bitter disappointment at being childless, and her consequent envy of Cynthia. The impossibility of confronting a delayed sibling rivalry—an impossibility that is structured in complex ways—is at the heart of Roxanne's aggressive refusal to accept her mother's sudden introduction of Hortense as her daughter, as Roxanne's half-sister. Seshadri-Crooks overlooks this by insisting that the absent father is the site of impossibility around which the film's problematization of race functions.

When Seshadri-Crooks says, quoting Lacan (1978), that "the body must be understood in relation to the 'sexual reality' of the unconscious, which is the nodal point of desire [XI: 154]" (2000, 125), she subordinates the significance of her own reading of the trope of race in the film to the Lacanian scenario that relentlessly privileges sexual difference over race. By reading the film in terms of abjection I resist that privileging, and suggest that, if the body can only be "discerned . . . in time" and "only as a series of part objects" (Seshadri-Crooks 2000, 125), those part objects are not inevitably beholden to a phallic logic, but can be parsed out according to the unfixed and halting syntax of a maternal mapping, an excremental logic. The full force of this excremental, abject logic finds expression in the word "slag" that condemns Cynthia's symbolic transgression not only of sexual but also of racial taboos, a transgression underwritten by a white, masculinized, racial imaginary.

Hortense, the optometrist—whose job it is to help others see—provides a mirror for the various members of the family she claims as her own. She is the other who helps them break through their loneliness, their secrecy, and their lies.[12] In this sense she provides a counterweight to Maurice, the photographer, who frames people's lives according to the requirements of his commission—whether he is photographing a wedding or the scars of a victim of a car accident for insurance purposes. Yet the role Hortense plays is one that takes on transformative meaning only because her black skin has become the site of her white mother's abjection. While Cynthia, not Hortense, is pushed to the ground by Roxanne, Hortense is racialized by a series of gestures, from the time that Cynthia sees her black skin and assumes that this is a case of mistaken identity. At their first meeting, the color of Hortense's skin signals to Cynthia that there must have been a bureaucratic mistake. When Hortense arrives at the front door, Monica is unable to imagine that she might be Cynthia's invited guest. And when Roxanne casts her mother to the floor, Hortense looks on uneasily, aware that it is the color of her skin that accounts for the violence of Roxanne's reaction. Must racialized others be the ground on which those who have been able to assume the privilege of their white skin break through their racism? In the fantasized space of contemporary independent cinema, some directors are beginning to ask us to reflect on such questions, and are thereby returning us to the fantasized space of representation that enables our idealizations and identifications, asking us to rethink the ways in which some bodies are asked to carry the burden of racialization for the sake of others. If there is a sense in which Hortense could still be read in terms of the trope of fetishization that white culture resorts to in negotiating race, there is also a sense in which Mike Leigh examines the economy by which such a trope is produced. In his citation of racist myths, he explodes them.

In *Revolution in Poetic Language* Kristeva suggests that capitalist modes of production have created a situation in which linguistic theories tend to deal with the fetishized product of language, rather than the processes by which meaning is generated. "The capitalist mode of production has st[r]atified language into idiolects and divided it into self-contained,

Hortense attends Roxanne's birthday party in
Secrets and Lies. Cynthia has introduced her as a mate from work.
Courtesy of Photofest.

isolated islands—heteroclite spaces existing in different temporal modes
(as relics or projections), and oblivious of one another" (1984, 13–14). The
suggestion is that capitalist society has repressed the processes by which
meaning is generated, codifying our experience according to the motives
of the ruling classes, namely economic profit, and alienating us from other
possible meanings. Any activity that doesn't conform to the useful—
where the meaning of the term "useful" is restricted to the production of
surplus value—is counted as irrelevant, rendering useless (within these
terms) those forms of language that express any other values.

    There is a truth to the fetishized linguistic entities—heteroclite
islands—that have come to be the object of linguistic investigation. Yet
this truth is produced by the historical circumstance of capitalism. By
unfolding the process by which fetishization has occurred, we can loosen
the grip of the fetish that language has become, and see how both the
subject of capitalism and its objects have become reified. As Kristeva puts
it, "capitalism eliminates the free subject unified in his process, which
Hegel was the last philosopher to summon," rendering it "a hypostasized
subjectivity . . . cut off from the signifying and socio-historical process"
(1984, 129–30). At stake in both the Cartesian question, how can I know
that my ideas of the world conform to the reality of objects in the world,

and the Kantian question, what must the world be like in order to be knowable, is the purity and priority of the judging I, whose unity is transhistorical. Despite Kant's Copernican revolution, the "I think" of the transcendental unity of apperception remains too close to a solipsistic Cartesian cogito, one that does not take itself to be situated in a historical world. For Hegel, both object and subject are historically constituted, and their constitution is not given once and for all. Like Hegel, rather than assuming the subject and the object as preexisting, Kristeva provides an account of how the subject comes to be a subject, or how the subject comes into relation with objects. For Kristeva, the process by which a subject becomes a subject, and thereby becomes capable of having objects, and in particular, how subjects are able to have a desiring relation to others, is embedded in historical relations. Kristeva steers a course between positing the subject on the one hand as transcendental ego, as originator of meaning, and on the other hand as embracing the chaos, delirium, or nonsense that would result from opting out of the symbolic altogether. She contests the theologization of the thetic by seeing it as a product of drives and facilitations, mapping the ways in which poetry, by way of mimesis, contests this theologization. Refusing to posit with Kant or Husserl "the judging 'I' as origin," Kristeva asks, "How is the thetic, which is a *positing* of the subject, produced?" (1984, 36). To construe the subject solely as symbolic would be to "reduce the subject to one of understanding" (1984, 27), to neglect the role of the imaginary in the signifying process that constitutes meaning, to enclose the subject in the ideality of its status as a judging subject, and to acquiesce to the repression of the corporeal materiality of the desiring subject.

Between 1974, when *Revolution of Poetic Language* appeared, and when Kristeva was still working through the impact of the events of May 1968, and 1996, a good deal had changed. In the course of time, the revolutionary ferment of Kristeva's work has considerably altered. *Tel Quel* had disintegrated, the Maoist inspiration of the Chinese Revolution proved not to be nearly as hopeful or productive as it once seemed, and the transformative impulse of the semiotic that Kristeva had tracked through the 1980s in *Powers of Horror: An Essay on Abjection, Tales of Love.* and *Black Sun* had considerably weakened.[13] If I insist on the importance of some of the insights contained in *Powers of Horror*, it is because I read them as mapping out in a provisional way not so much an alternative logic to the fetish, as the conditions of its possibility—the logic of abjection. As such, abjection also constitutes a site for the possible reworking of fetishism.

The logic of the fetish is one of substitution, a reiterated reification, in which the emergence of meaning is dependent on the stability of the terms being substituted for one another. In order for terms to be substituted for one another these terms need to have acquired a permanence: they need to exist as significant within a certain economy of meaning. How the set of meanings that signify as meaningful within a given system of signification came to be meaningful is not necessarily at issue within this system. The economic laws of substitution are not interrogated, so long as the series of substitutions depends upon keeping in the background or holding at bay the values that are assumed by a fetishistic economy—the logic of which generally does not present itself as available for questioning. Symbolic forms appear as fixed and static, but also as isolated and independent of one another, and the social fabric that they constitute is reproduced as if one form could stand for another metonymically, without either feeding into or disrupting the stability and integrity of the social whole. It is as if the shared unity of meaning characteristic of the social whole, whether this meaning is produced under the rubric of nation, or some other imagined unity, could stand as inherent, as if emergent categories such as class or gender or race could function as autonomous and self-sustaining parts of that social unit without impinging on one another. In the process of cultural and intellectual exchange, guaranteed not so much by the phallus as the circulation of the fetish, such concepts appear to be autonomous and self-evident. Interrogation of the practices of exchange reveals that their absolute autonomy is not merely compromised but impossible as such. The coherence of each socially salient category is only achieved through a rhetorical referentiality that appeals to other socially salient categories, and is inscribed in a history of dependence, inheritance, and alienation. This dependence is often implicit, covert, unconscious, or indirect, but is no less powerful for it. Circuits of meaning have been set in play in which the possibility of asking about multiple aspects of identity as constitutive of one another has been closed down in favor of their analytic definition and separation. Yet at the same time these circuits of meaning only operate by providing for one another mutual confirmation.

In order to ask intelligible or meaningful questions about the imaginary that informs the values of a patriarchal, capitalist, and postcolonial world, in order to interrogate the myths that determine and set in place the values it takes for granted, we need to have an account of both how those values are established, and how they legitimate themselves. What myths of origin are mobilized in order to confer on these values the appearance of self-evidence, and how might new myths enable the contestation of such self-evidence? What are the conditions of possibility for the predominance of fetishistic theories, and how are they upheld by the marginalization and subordination of certain others who are not recognized as subjects? How are certain groups or identities abjected as insignificant, as non-subjects, whose claims are not registered as valuable, or not capable of signifying? How do these non-subjects function as the illegitimate, prohibited ground on which objects, signs, values, and desires can signify and circulate in an exchange economy that presents itself as closed, but which derives its impetus from an outside that is constitutive of it, while failing to acknowledge it as constitutive? In what way do social systems that present themselves as self-legitimating remain vulnerable to being called to account?

Has language tailored not so much our thoughts as our desires, channeling them according to the ends of capitalism, imposing on subjects a pseudo-rationality that makes it difficult to imagine what we want outside the terms that capitalism formulates for us? Or is there a more fundamental alienation effected by language than the appearance it takes on under capitalism that cuts us off from the process by which symbolization comes to represent our experience? Perhaps, as Kristeva suggests in *Powers of Horror,* language itself is the ultimate fetish (1982, 37), because it takes the sign for the thing. Even though we know that the sign is not the thing, we act, think, and feel as if it is. "Je sais bien mais quand même."[14] We substitute the name for the thing, and take this sign as determinative of it. Is it, then, a particular mode of production—capitalist—that represses that which is not captured by the sign, that fetishizes language, or is it language itself? Is it that language in and of itself stabilizes, atomizes, or commodifies the processes by which subjects signify to themselves and to others? And what would be the difference? If language has become fetishized under capitalism, how could it be otherwise as long as capitalism survives?

In *Powers of Horror* Kristeva suggests that in addition to neurosis and psychosis, and the respective modes of negativity that articulate them, denial (*dénégation*) and repudiation (*forclusion*), there is another form of rejection. Abjection is based not upon the repression of a desired object, nor upon the repudiation of desire itself, but upon "exclusion" (1982, 6). As such, it has a different relation to the unconscious, and a different relation to castration. Kristeva develops the notion of abjection as subjacent not only to denial and repudiation, but also to the fetishistic logic of disavowal (*déni/Verleugnung*), with its "perverse dodges" (1982, 5). At the same time, abjection is "related to perversion" (1982, 15) in the sense that "it neither gives up nor assumes a prohibition" (1982, 15). Concerned not merely with the "fetishized product" as "object of want [*manque*]," abjection is implicated in the more fundamental possibility of there being any object at all, with the "recognition of the *want* [*manque*] on which any being, meaning, language, or desire is founded" (5). As the revelation to the subject that "all its objects are based merely on the inaugural *loss* that laid the foundations of its own being" (5), abjection is related to the separation of the subject (who is not yet a subject) from the mother (who is not yet the mother). For we are dealing with a point at which there is as yet no "secure differentiation between subject and object" (7).

Abjection, says Kristeva, is, "above all, ambiguity" (1982, 7). It is ambiguous with regard to the self and other, with regard to passivity or activity, neurosis or psychosis, and with regard to the boundaries it sets up, which are permeable. Is abjection something that I do to the other or to myself? Is it an act I engage in, or is it a state I suffer? It is not clear who is abjected by what, who is doing the abjection, and who is affected by it. In emphasizing the ambiguity of abjection, Kristeva takes up the tension contained in the Freudian libido, the life-and-death struggle between Eros and Thanatos, or the need to think desire in tandem with destructive forces. Abjection concerns both the pleasurable and the fascinating, dangerous, or horrific—that which threatens. One can also say that central to Kristeva's psychoanalytic understanding of desire is the suggestion that it assumes, rather than following, prohibition. The object of desire is desirable precisely as forbidden.[15] At the same time, however, Kristeva is interested in the instability of the incest prohibition, and therefore in the ways in which the symbolic function that is set up in its wake is liable to revision and transformation. It is precisely because abjection does not operate at the level of desire, but rather constitutes the rejection that desire presupposes, that its relation to prohibition is not straightforward, but perverse.

If the abject signals a structuring lack of the subject, but one that is not at first specified in relation to sexual difference, since it predates castration anxiety and the recognition of sexual differentiation, a space is opened up for this fundamental lack to be articulated in racial, ethnic, or class codes, and in terms that are as yet unmarked by any heterosexual imperative. What happens when a fear of the unnameable occurs not just at the individual level, as it does when Little Hans metaphorically writes the horse as his phobic object because he cannot find the name for street sounds? What happens when a fear of the unnameable operates at the symbolic level to the point of a refusal to name what society finds impermissible? Or when the very paths along which desire is recognized as signaling an object are written in a symbolic whose imaginary forecloses the possibility of lesbian or gay or transgendered subjects of desire so as to make their objects unthinkable?

In *Hollow Reed*, according to Frank Donally (Jason Fleming), the only way to describe the sexuality of Martin and Tom is to cast it into

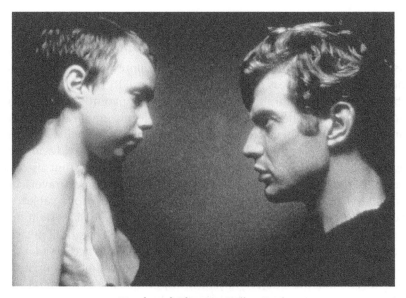

Frank and Oliver in *Hollow Reed*.
Courtesy of Photofest.

the realm of animality from which ostensibly civilized, decent society has progressed. Frank's condemnation of homosexuality as animality is a transparent attempt to prejudice Oliver against his father. What happens when the symbolic system that orders sexual relations, and establishes sexual propriety, setting up the rules of who is allowed to couple with whom, partakes of a racialized imagery that it does not own?

With the revolutionary potential of the semiotic, Kristeva has helped to uncover the sense in which language can be rethought from the ground up, as it were, or how we can uncover its constitutive elements. By emphasizing the affective ways in which language is produced, by returning to the moments that make language necessary, by rethinking the infant's separation from the maternal breast, Kristeva provides some access to the formative processes that give rise to language. Extending the purview of Kristeva's inquiry one can ask after not merely the devaluation of maternity, but also the dehumanization of racialized others, not merely after the fetishization of language, but also the fetishistic forms of cultural theories. Like the necrophilia of archival, archaeological linguistic theorists who take their objects to be fixed according to an economy that endows them with value that is always already sanctioned and as such unavailable for interrogation, theorists of gender, race, and even film are prone to take their objects as given. This condemns them to the fate of reproducing cultural theories that both present themselves as relatively autonomous, and feed off the oppression implied in but neglected by other areas of cultural interrogation. By failing to question the model of fetishism that gets reiterated by apparently autonomous areas of cultural theory—that are in fact deeply implicated in one another—cultural theory neglects its conditions of possibility.

Kristeva accepts the account of castration that Freud and Lacan give as putting the "finishing touches on separation" (1984, 47), but also distances herself from it in her examination of the thetic as a "traversable boundary" (1984, 51). That is, she accepts that in order for a subject to be capable of representation, to acquiesce to the symbolic system in a signifying capacity, that subject must accomplish a separation, detaching itself from its dependence on the mother. She also accepts that the subject's entry into language "presupposes a decisive imposition of the phallic" and that the "subject must be firmly posited by castration" (1984, 50). Yet she insists that the thetic is "clearly distinct . . . from a castration imposed once and for all, perpetuating the well-ordered signifier and positing it as sacred and unalterable within the enclosure of the Other" (1984, 51).

While Kristeva distances herself in *Revolution in Poetic Language* from the idea of castration as "decisive" (1984, 50), that it is "imposed once and for all" (51), and from fetishism (62–67), it is not until *Powers of Horror* that this criticism acquires more substance. She sees the literary or poetic text as allowing the subject to "delv[e] into" the "constitutive process" or the process by which the "human being constitutes himself as signifying and/or social" (67). Her entire project is fueled by thinking through the possibility of revolutionary change, and asking how that which has been excluded from apparently self-legitimating systems can become available for questioning in a way that transforms those systems. "Under what conditions," she asks, does "'esoterism,' in displacing the boundaries of socially established signifying practices, correspond to socioeconomic change, and, ultimately, even to revolution? And under what conditions does it remain a blind alley, a harmless bonus offered by a social order which uses this 'esoterism' to expand, become flexible, and thrive?" (16).

Not only is the imaginary in need of the symbolic, but just as crucially, the symbolic is sustained by the imaginary. So long as that imaginary is assumed to be phallic, so long as the symbols that cash out its value maintain the currency of an unexamined, monolithic fetishism that proves itself equally adaptable to race theory, feminist theory, class theory, and film theory, the possibilities of articulating radical challenges are limited. An imaginary that reinvents itself with apparently infinite malleability is supported by the incessant reproduction of the phallus as commodity. By interrogating the laws of the imaginary economy that sustain the symbolic production of the phallus as the only currency worthy of cultural accumulation, I have explored the repetitive and imitative gestures by which abjection is produced. It remains to be seen how capable the phallic economy proves to be in withstanding any investigation of the ways in which its imaginary shores up a symbolic system of exchange that depends on the unacknowledged production of dejects, a status that surreptitiously circulates between non-subjects, who overcome their own abjection by visiting it upon others.

Hollow Reed explores the hypocrisy of a society that is apparently willing to consider homosexuality, rather than child abuse, a sin. At the same time it explores the ramifications that Martyn's reluctance to admit his homosexuality have for those around him. Having gone through a divorce, his rejected ex-wife is in need of affirmation. Women are encouraged to believe that their worth is attested by their ability to find and keep a man, and Hannah (Joley Richardson) feels humiliated by her ex-husband's desertion of her for a gay partner, her sense of her femininity having been compromised. She is so desperate to avoid another failed relationship that she is willing to reconcile with her lover even after having discovered him abusing her child, wanting to believe that the abuse is over. In this context, Frank's violently abusive behavior represents a confirmation of his heteronormative manliness.

As he pins him up against the bathroom wall, Frank Donally (Jason Fleming), the abuser of nine-year-old Oliver (Sam Bould) in *Hollow Reed,* tells him that men like Oliver's father choose to be that way. Frank tells Oliver that the way gay men do it in bed is like dogs, like animals at the zoo. He tells him that he and Hannah, Oliver's mother, just want Oliver to be "normal," and assures him that he won't grow up homosexual like his father, that it can't be passed on through the genes. As Frank tries to poison Oliver's mind, ostensibly telling him that he doesn't have to worry about turning out like his father, but in fact warning him that he might do just that, Oliver stays mute, as he is throughout most of the film. By attempting to elicit Oliver's disgust at his father's gayness, Frank can represent himself as normal, safe, and conventional, while projecting on to Martyn (Martin Donovan), and thus denying, his own abjection of Oliver. Abusing or terrifying Oliver is a way of establishing control in a world in which he feels inadequate, a way of making him seem to himself a whole person, a way of venting his feelings of rage at his own abuse, without confronting them directly. He deflects them onto Oliver, continuing a chain of abjection. The social text of homophobia presents itself as available to him, and he draws upon it in order to facilitate his denial of his own aberrant behavior. I am not the one whose nature is excessive—it is you.

Desperate to remove his son from his abuser, Martyn determines to try to obtain legal custody of nine-year-old Oliver, despite the fact that he has no concrete evidence of the identity of the abuser. He might be aware that his ex-wife's lawyer will do all he can to parade his lifestyle as a gay man in front of the court, but nothing can prepare him for the humiliation he and his partner suffer, when it becomes all too obvious that, far from setting itself above abjection, the rhetoric of the legal system draws on its perverted logic. The court battle, as Martyn had anticipated when he asked his partner, Tom (Ian Hart), to move out temporarily, is played out on the terrain of homophobia. Martyn's alleged inability to sustain a "normal" sexual relationship with his ex-wife comes into play as the lawyer does everything in his power to abject Martyn and Tom for being gay. Disgust is elicited by an indirect appeal to, or a re-inscription, of boundaries that are assumed to be fixed, naturalized, and immovable, through the intimation that gay lifestyles are in excess of the norm, that they cross the boundary separating humanity from animality. Frank is able to disguise his own cruelty to Oliver, displacing his self-contempt onto Martyn, in what Kristeva calls a "sublimating elaboration" (1982, 7), which accompanies his refusal to recognize his child-abuse as out of bounds. Devising strategies designed to cleanse themselves of what otherwise might have to be acknowledged as dirty, disgusting, or repugnant, dejects—those "by whom the abject exists" (1982, 8)—persist in territorializing in order to remake the rules and absolve or purify themselves, thus requiring others to become impure receptacles (see 1982, 10–12). The law itself cashes in on the implied excesses of Tom and Martyn's behavior that Frank's displacement elaborates. The convoluted logic of abjection, its ritualistic, obsessive, re-drawing of imaginary boundaries in the service of defensive postures, and the ways in which institutions sanction and uphold such logics without drawing out their complex processes of sublimation, has been the subject of the preceding meditation.

There are phenomena that should disgust us, but which do not, inured as we are to fundamentally racist, homophobic, sexist, and classist fabrics that constitute our normative identifications. To elicit disgust can be a political function of art, just as much as art can elicit disgust in ways that confirm, reiterate, and reproduce the foundational fantasies that govern our realities. Art can subject us anew to such fantasies, or it can provide a space in which we take our distance from them. Abjection can thus help to reconstitute us, and we can help to reconstitute abjection, in a process that is ongoing—in a process that should remain contestable, available for scrutiny, and subject to revision. By drawing out the symbolic implications of what we find disgusting, or beautiful, and why we make such judgments of taste, we can rework the imaginaries that have drawn the boundaries of revolt: we can redraw the boundaries of abjection. I have focused in particular on our discovery of ourselves as having identified with characters in particular moments that might have momentarily disrupted identifications we normally take for granted, and which might open up the possibility of rethinking the ground of such identifications. I have also focused on moments of abjection with which some of us identify, moments in which such identification can be cathartic. Such moments can result in the revolution of symbolic norms, in their renewal. Alternatively, the result can be a restoration of the symbolic without its rebirth, in which case abjection amounts to a purging of negativity that allows the symbolic to continue unchallenged and uninterrupted.

Notes

INTRODUCTION

1. Kristeva says, "Laughing is a way of placing or displacing abjection" (1982, 8).

2. See, e.g., Robyn Ferrell's interesting discussion of terra nullius in the context of art. The judgment that the land was an empty was one, Ferrell argues, "did not say that it saw *nobody*, only that it did not see *law*." She goes on to ask, "What sort of blindness was this principle of settlement? It was aesthetically blind, in the most general sense, in that it didn't see what there was to see *as law, as order*" (2003, 42).

3. Antonio Gramsci suggests that "Subaltern groups are always subject to the activity of ruling groups, even when they rebel and rise up; only 'permanent' victory breaks their subordination, and that not immediately" (1971, 55).

4. As Raymond Williams puts it, hegemony "is not to be understood at the level of mere opinion or mere manipulation. It is a whole body of practices and expectations; our assignments or energy, our ordinary understanding of the nature of man and of his world. It is a set of meanings and values which as they are experienced as practices appear as reciprocally confirming. It thus constitutes a sense of reality for most people in society" (1997, 38).

5. The logic I am pointing to goes something like this. Gender (for example) is pulled from a nonconceptual background, which is the messy, indeterminate life of immediacy in all its confusion (what Levinas calls the "elemental") and is treated as if it made sense as a coherent, independent, abstract concept. Whether part of a patriarchal discourse or part of a feminist discourse, the apparent independence and integrity of the concept of gender needs to be resisted, because it repudiates its messy, material indeterminacy, and the impossibility of divorcing it from other terms that present themselves as if they too could be reduced to clearly definable concepts, such as race, class, or sexuality. In fact, however, while appearing to leave indeterminate a host of other notions, including race, class, and sexuality—as if they remained in some murky, nonconceptual, undefined, and indefinable flux—in order to be what it is, to have come to have the history that it has, the concept of gender constructs highly specific and determinable notions of race, class, etc. So, gender presents itself as independent, appears to leave as indeterminate all these other terms, but in an unacknowledged, covert way draws upon imaginary racist, classist, and heterosexist myths, the content of which are culturally specific and socially sanctioned. I owe a debt of gratitude to Mary Beth Mader, whose response to my paper at the

Central American Philosophical Association in December 2003 helped me clarify this logic.

6. I thank Rachel Jones, whose observations and conversation at a feminist conference, Phenomenological Reflections in Ethics, at Basel University in June 2003, helped me think about the mobility of this constitutive gesture.

7. As Mary Ann Doane puts it, "the logical consequence of the Lacanian alignment of the phallus with the symbolic order and the field of language is the exclusion of the woman or, at the very least, the assumption of her different or deficient relation to language and its assurance of subjectivity" (1987, 10).

8. Doane says, "Fetishism has been particularly important in the theorization of the film-spectator relation because its scenario turns on the 'glance' and on a reading of the image of the castrated woman. In the cinema, spectatorial fetishism is evidenced as a process of balancing knowledge and belief in relation to the reality status of the image. While the spectator knows that the image is merely an image and not the real (similarly, the fetishist knows that the fetish object is simply a substitute for the woman's lack), he simultaneously believes in the impression of reality produced by that image in order to follow the story (the fetishist believes in the substitute maternal phallus in order to attain sexual pleasure). Because it is so intimately articulated with castration anxiety and the desire to preserve the phallus, because it relies on the image of the mutilated female body, fetishism is not available to the woman—for she has nothing to lose" (1987, 15).

9. See Bhattacharjee 1997; Collins 1990; Carby 2000; Mohanty 1997a.

10. Civil rights have operated in largely liberatory ways for white, Western women, and in this Foucauldian sense power is not merely to be opposed but is that to which we seek access. Yet power has operated in negative and repressive ways for Native American women, whose forced assimilation to American, individualist, capitalist, and colonialist practices has all but obliterated the collective, tribal, traditional ways of life that existed prior to colonization. The effects of power tend to be variegated, often along racialized lines, so that both the Hegelian/Marxist model and the Foucauldian model are in operation at the same time for different groups. The classical model of the state as oppressive has more pertinence than Foucault's, depending on the color of your skin.

11. This point echoes, to some extent, Kelly Oliver's observations about recognition. She says, "Just as money has been the hard currency for which women and slaves have been exchanged (directly and indirectly), recognition is the soft currency with which oppressed people are exchanged within the global economy. In this way, recognition, like capital, is essential to the economy of domination, which is not to say that oppressed people should not fight for both capital and recognition" (2001, 23). Oliver is absolutely right to point out that "The internalization of stereotypes of inferiority and superiority leave the oppressed with the sense that they are lacking something that only their *superior* dominators have or can give them. The very notion of recognition as it is deployed in various contemporary theoretical contexts is, then, a symptom of the pathology of oppression itself. Implied in this diagnosis is the conclusion that struggles for recognition and theories that embrace those struggles may indeed presuppose and thereby perpetuate the very hierarchies, domination, and injustice that they attempt to overcome" (9). Oliver goes on, "An effective aspect of the pathology of oppression is that those who are dominant have the power to

create, confer, or withhold recognition, which operates as cultural currency" (26). The logic of disavowal circulates in a way that enables even those who use it to illuminate the conditions of oppression to benefit from its transference across discourses, so that its circulation either continues to abject the dejects of psychoanalytic or Marxist theory, or invents new dejects. Oliver says, "Even if oppressed people are making demands for recognition, insofar as those who are dominant are empowered to confer it, we are thrown back into the hierarchy of domination. This is to say that if the operations of recognition require a recognizer and a recognizee, then we have done no more than replicate the master-slave, subject-other/object hierarchy in this new form" (9). I agree, but by taking seriously the way in which the discourses of feminism and race theory, for example, create their own abjects, I also want to insist that this recognition is labile. That is, we create new hierarchies of domination, which have new imaginary configurations. Oliver is closer to this in one of her more recent books, co-authored with Trigo, where they say, "The fear of, or desire for, racial difference can be displaced onto a fear of, or desire for, sexual difference. The fear of maternal sexuality can be displaced onto or condensed into the threat of racial difference" (2003, xix)—and so on. Here she reads "the free-floating existential anxiety of film noir" as a "screen for concrete anxieties over arbitrary and blurred boundaries of racial, sexual, and national identity" (xv), and goes on to use abjection to illuminate the "lost boundaries of noir" (xxix).

12. Freud puts forward a similar set of observations in "The Dissolution of the Oedipus Complex" (1953d, 175).

13. Oliver uses the term "patriarchal imaginary" to describe the object of her criticism in her book *Family Values* (1997)

14. Beardsworth 2004, 234, 243, 247.

15. Beardsworth 2004, 232.

16. On abjection as a defense see Oliver and Trigo, 2003, xxxii; and Beardsworth 2004, 83, 241, 234–35. On abjection as a rewriting of the mirror stage, see Chase 1987, 67, 78; Jacobus 1995, 145.

17. This is not to say that Kristeva does not question Lacan at all, only that she does not elaborate her critique as far as I think it needs to go.

18. See Young 1990, 129.

19. See Freud 1953e, 26.

20. For various feminist responses to Fanon see Rey Chow (1999, 45); Kaja Silverman (1996, 30–31); Mary Ann Doane (1991, 225).

21. See Mary Douglas 1990, 148, for example.

22. See Kristeva 2001, 116 and Klein 1975, 197–98.

23. See hooks (1996a) and hooks (1996b).

24. Even the institution of gender and women's studies programs as discrete from lesbian, gay, bisexual, and transgender centers of study or centers that focus on race theory, ethnicity, or diasporic studies, which themselves are divided into African American, Asian American, Latina/Latino studies and so on reflect such logics. On the one hand, the need to rally around identities that are maligned produces such centers of organization, but on the other hand there is a danger of invisibly reproducing other hegemonic relations precisely insofar as such centers remain sufficient unto themselves.

25. I use the term "revolutionary" in the sense in which Kristeva employs it in her later work. See Kristeva 2000.

26. See Ewa Ziarek for an illuminating discussion of Lyotard (2001).

1. ABJECTION AS THE UNTHOUGHT GROUND OF FETISHISM

1. The complexity of Klein's "internal object" is that it includes bits and pieces of both the child's and the mother's bodies, that is, it does not yet correspond to the boundary between self and other that the skin fixes, or which corresponds to the ego conceived as that which is constituted in relation to the body's surface. As such, it forms the basis of projective identification, in which "I" expel from "myself" all that I do not like, while incorporating or introjecting all that I like. Lacan acknowledges that for Klein "objects become variegated . . . to the extent that they make their appearance within a process of expulsion linked to the instinct of primitive destruction," but considers Klein's "theory of the *ego*" to be "incomplete" (Lacan 1991, 68), rather than acknowledging that Klein is formulating a theory about the formation of the ego.

2. Arthur Danto cites Theophile Gautier, who writes in *Mademoiselle de Maupin:* "everything useful is ugly, for it is the expression of some need," cited in Danto 2000.

3. Danto 2000.

4. John Keats, "Ode on a Grecian Urn."

5. Marita Nadal suggests that Kristeva echoes Ann Radcliffe's view in "On the Supernatural in Poetry" (1826), that "the sublime produces the expansion of the soul, alluding also to the ambivalent feelings of pleasure and pain inherent in this phenomenon" (Nadal 2000, 375). Nadal also cites Ann Williams, who suggests that "the sources of the sublime primarily reside within the culturally 'female,' the other. The 'sublime' is, perhaps, a 'sublimation of the culturally female'" (Williams, *Art of Darkness: A Poetics of Gothic* [Chicago: University of Chicago Press, 1995, 78]; quoted by Nadal 2000, 375).

6. Referring to the unresolved relationship between Freud's "hysterical identification" and "narcissistic identification," Elizabeth Cowie, for example, says that this "dualism has been translated into film theory in the work of Christian Metz in his investigation of cinema as the imaginary signifier, where the spectator's identifications with characters in a film are called secondary, while the cinema's primary identification is found by Metz in what he describes as the spectator's identification with the camera . . . . It is the issue of sexual difference for the cinema spectator which Metz's account fails to address" (1997, 75). However, in her own Lacanian reading of Freud, rich though it is, Cowie does not pursue the ambiguity that sustains Freud's slippage from hysterical to narcissistic identification, a slippage I argue depends on the occlusion of maternal identification. Kristeva's elaboration of the abject mother and the imaginary father can be read as a response to this problematic. While she demurs when it comes to identifying either the mother or the father as the "absolute origin of . . . love as a psychic and symbolic capacity" (1987, 28), she nonetheless invokes the tyranny of phallic idealization: "Situating th[e] unifying guideline within an objectality in the process of being established rather than in the absolute of the reference to the Phallus as such has several advantages. It makes the transference relation dynamic, involves to the utmost the interpretative intervention of the analyst, and calls attention to countertransference as identification, this time of the analyst with the patient, along with the entire aura of imaginary formations germane to the analyst that all this entails. Without those conditions doesn't analysis run the risk of becoming set within the tyranny of idealization,

precisely? Of the Phallus or of the superego? A word to wise Lacanians should be enough!" (1987, 30).

7. As Andrew Edgar says, "in a short reflection on 'commodity music,' written in the 1930s," Adorno says even 'the most stupid people have long since ceased to be fooled by the belief that everyone will win the big prize.' The shop girl in the cinema audience does not therefore believe that the fictional secretary's good fortune could happen to her. Rather, only in the cinema can she admit to herself that this is true, and thus experience that 'most minimal degree of happiness, namely the knowledge that happiness is not for you,'" "Culture and Criticism: Adorno" (1999, 451). Edgar is quoting from Adorno (1992, 50).

8. See Copjec 2000, 292.

9. On feminine irony see Kristeva 2000, 153; see also Ziarek 2005. On feminist critiques influenced by fetishism see Emily Apter 1999. Exceptions to this include Doane, who sees very clearly that fetishism is inapplicable to the position classical psychoanalytic theory reserves for woman. "Because it is so intimately articulated with castration anxiety and the desire to preserve the phallus, because it relies on the image of the mutilated female body, fetishism is not available to the woman—for she has nothing to lose" (1987, 15). Yet Doane does not follow through the implications this has for the difficulty of transferring the trope of fetishism to the raced subject.

10. This threefold distinction is significant to Kristeva's reading of Freud, as she makes clear, in one of many references to it (1989, 43–45).

11. For Kristeva the "pure/impure opposition represents . . . the striving for identity, a difference. It appears instead of *sexual difference*" (1982, 82). Yet Douglas's exploration of purification rites could be read not only as a mapping of sexual difference but also of other socially salient differences, including those orchestrated by racial and class regimes.

12. As Kristeva says, Klein "does not speak of 'primal fantasies': no matter how diverse Kleinian phantasies may be as they respond to the various 'positions' that they reflect, they are intrinsically 'primal' and are brought about by an extremely early Oedipus conflict and by the permanence of the death drive" (2001, 243).

13. Freud points out that "someone else is invariably involved, as a model, as an object, as a helper, as an opponent" so that "from the very first individual psychology . . . is at the same time social psychology as well" (1953h, 69).

14. This, it seems to me, is the logical conclusion of Doane's own insight about Freud's apparently innocent employment of the phrase "dark continent" to describe femininity (1991, 210–12).

15. See also McClintock 1995, 193–94.

16. See Mannoni 1969.

17. The discourse of the uncanny is encoded with the theory of fetishistic disavowal, the centrality of which a theory of abjection displaces.

18. I use the language of enigma to describe how the problematic of race is inscribed into the texts of classical psychoanalysis only in order to echo the terms in which the enigma of woman has been posed, and not because I think it is particularly viable. At stake in refiguring the discourse of fetishism against the background of abjection is an attempt interrogate the adequacy of shrouding or veiling femininity and/or race in the mystery of the enigmatic, as unsayable or unthinkable—othering, abject maneuvers that only serve to code or fetishize as impenetrable important questions.

19. Rose says, "The fact that the subject's own body is not on the screen does not necessarily distinguish its experience from that of the mirror stage; the subject never specularises its own body as such, and the phenomenon of transitivism demonstrates that the subject's mirror identification can be with another child" (1986, 196). Citing this passage from Rose, Copjec adds, "What is most often forgotten, however, is the corollary of this fact: one always locates *the other in one's own image*" (2000, 304, n. 12). Copjec also says, "Whether that which is represented is specularized as an image of the subject's own body or as the subject's image of someone or something else, what remains crucial" for Lacan is that the subject sees "in any representation not only a reflection of itself, but a reflection of itself as master of all it surveys" (2000, 292).

20. Jean-Louis Baudry 1999a, 1999b. Christian Metz 1982.

21. See Beardsworth (2005) on maternal authority.

22. In mobilizing the discourse of abjection, I am emphasizing certain aspects of Kristeva's work that her own subsequent theoretical developments have put into question. I agree with Joan Brandt, who argues that a shift can be discerned between Kristeva's conception of the semiotic in *Powers of Horror* and her reworking of it in *Tales of Love*. Brandt suggests that the "tendency in *Powers of Horror* to pit the anobjectal mother-child symbiosis of archaic narcissism against the structuring, ternary relationship of the Oedipal and symbolic realm of identity undergoes a series of modifications in *Tales of Love*, due in part perhaps to Kristeva's abandonment of her revolutionary goals . . . she alters the distinction between the semiotic and the symbolic, giving the semiotic a more 'Oedipal' configuration" (1997, 130–31). While Brandt is right in suggesting that *Tales of Love* provides a more adequate account of the complexities of primary narcissism than *Powers of Horror*, I think it can be shown that in her more radical account of abjection in *Powers of Horror* there are at least the seeds of a more dramatic questioning of the Freudian paradigm than can be found in the resolution to the relation between primary and secondary narcissism that she provides in *Tales of Love*. In emphasizing Kristeva's understanding of abjection as presented in *Powers of Horror*, rather than its later, more oedipal configuration in *Tales of Love*, my attempt is to open out Kristeva's notion of abjection in a more politicized direction than Kristeva herself would be willing to go, particularly in her later work.

23. Parveen Adams argues that "the counter-celebration of other candidate organs as the model of female completeness is itself an act of phallic identification and is a defence against the emergence of desire" (1996, 50). Since Kristeva's analysis of abjection does not view the breast or the maternal body as a "model of female completeness" but rather as a part-object, her revisiting of the child's relation to the breast does not fall prey to this critique.

24. Adams says, "Only when the assumption of having or being the phallus is relinquished can the subject make the separation from the object with which it has made an identification. For Lacan, it is only at this point that desire can emerge from the identifications which the subject made to defend itself from castration" (1996, 50). This assumes that phallic identification operates as a model for object identification, which is precisely what Kristeva's account of abjection brings into question, by rethinking the child's separation from the mother in terms of abjection.

25. Jacobus 1995, 145. In fact, Kristeva asks, in *Tales of Love*, "Does the 'mirror stage emerge out of nowhere? What are the conditions of . . . [its] emergence?" (1987, 22). Insofar as the symbolic and the imaginary are irrevocably

implicated in one another, one might rephrase Jacobus, to suggest that Kristeva is asking about the conditions of both the imaginary and the symbolic. This would also take into account Kaja Silverman's understanding of the imaginary as "fundamentally reparative, and, hence, unthinkable prior to the subject's structuration" (1996, 46). Silverman adds, "if the imaginary cannot be thought apart from the symbolic, neither can the symbolic be 'entered' without imaginary mediation" (46).

26. Kelly Oliver suggests that the imaginary father could be understood "as a primary form of social support necessary for psychic development, creativity, and love" (2005, 82). I think the suggestion is an interesting one, but, given the way in which the logic of fetishism infects even ostensibly radical discourses such as feminism and anti-racism, I am worried about whether such support can be offered in ways that do not typically reinvent univocal meanings and sites of privilege as discrete from one another. Does a white imaginary father communicate the privileged invisibility of whiteness to the child in his loving support?

27. Picking up on the nonobjectal quality of abjection established in *Powers of Horror*, Kristeva focuses attention again in *Tales of Love* on the instability of the object relation, or what she describes as less "a partial object than . . . a nonobject. As magnet of identification constitutive of identity and condition for that unification, which insures the advent of a subject for an object, the object of Einfühlung is a *metaphorical* object" (1987, 29). The subject is thus no longer submerged in autoeroticism, but is set up through metaphorization as "an opposite One" (30). "The object of love is a metaphor for the subject—its constitutive metaphor, its 'unary feather,' which, by having it choose an adored part of the loved one, already locates it within the symbolic code of which this feature is a part. Nevertheless, situating this unifying guideline within an objectality in the process of being established rather than in the absolute of the reference to the Phallus as such has several advantages" (30). Kristeva goes on to enumerate these advantages: "It makes the transference relation dynamic, involves to the utmost the interpretative intervention of the analyst, and calls attention to countertransference as identification" (30). The identification at stake here is "not object-oriented" and "it is because identification is not object-oriented that the signifier's nonobject-oriented underlying layer of drives becomes activated during the treatment that is carried out without the *Einfühlung* being repressed. In such a case, therefore, it is possible for transference to gain a hold on nonobject-oriented psychic states such as 'false selves,' borderline cases, and even psychosomatic symptoms" (37). Yet, Kristeva also warns that again "since it is not object-oriented, identification reveals how the subject that ventures there can finally find himself a hypnotized slave of his master; how he can turn out to be a nonsubject, the shadow of a nonobject" (37).

Kristeva goes on to suggest that the discourse of analysis "complies with the dynamics of identification," that the analyst occupies both the "'maternal' position" and the "'paternal' position" and that the task of the analyst "is perhaps . . . to make use of identification and along with it . . . imaginal resources" (1987, 29).

28. Kristeva 2000, 53.

29. On the basis of such passages in Freud it is easy to conjecture how Melanie Klein's theories developed in the direction that they did, along the lines of distinguishing between the good and the bad mother on the basis of what is taken inside, and what is rejected as that which must remain outside.

The distinction between inside and outside is one that Freud revisits in his essay "Negation," and one that I discuss in chapter 2.

30. See also Freud 1953r, 222, n. 1.

31. The editors of the *Standard Edition* of Freud also comment on this. See 1953m, 242.

32. If the father is the one to whom destructive urges are directed, and the mother is the one to whom self-preservative instincts are directed, perhaps what is at stake here is the relative importance of the death drive and the pleasure principle.

33. Freud even understands cannibalism to be synonymous with the oral phase, such that the infant's incorporation of the breast is understood to be cannibalistic (see Freud 1953q, 198).

34. In "The Dissolution of the Oedipus Complex" (1924) Freud confirms the importance of his "discovery" of the phallic phase in "The Infantile Genital Organization" (1923). See Freud 1953d, 174–75.

35. Kristeva 2002, 87. See also 102. This is already in play in *Tales of Love*. Kristeva says, for example, "The whole symbolic matrix sheltering emptiness is thus set in place in an elaboration that precedes the Oedipus complex" (1987, 27).

2. Abjection as the Failure of Protection against Emptiness

1. On the maternal archaic, see Kristeva 2001, 156.

2. Kristeva 1987, 41.

3. See Cynthia Chase 1989, 80.

4. Melanie Klein, "Notes on Some Schizoid Mechanisms" (1986, 183 and 186).

5. See for example Isaacs 1989, 72–73 and 84. See also Heimann 1989, 124; Kristeva 2001, 169; Rose 1998, 137.

6. See Hyppolite 1991, 289–95.

7. For Klein, "the wholly undeveloped ego is faced with a task which at this stage is quite beyond it—the task of mastering the severest anxiety" (in "The Importance of Symbol Formation in the Development of the Ego" [1986, 97]). See also Jacqueline Rose, who says, "The problem for Klein's critics was that conflict was seen to arise before there was an ego there to manage it: 'According to the theory of the English school of analysis, introjection and projection, which in our view should be assigned to the period after the ego has been differentiated from the outside world, are the very processes by which the structure of the ego is developed'" (1998, 135). Rose is quoting Anna Freud, *The Ego and the Mechanism of Defence* (London: Hogarth Press and the Institute of Psycho-Analysis, 1937).

8. Freud says in "Group Psychology," "Identification with an object that is renounced or lost, as a substitute for that object—introjection of it into the ego—is indeed no longer a novelty to us" (1953h, 109). Freud gives as an example melancholia, in which there is an "introjection of the object" (109), a phenomenon that, as is well known, Freud explores in "Mourning and Melancholia" (1953m).

9. See Lacan 1991, 69. See also Isaacs 1989, 73.

10. In this respect, Klein's understanding of the paranoid-schizoid position prepares for abjection. Kristeva says of Klein that "as long as the infant is dominated by the paranoid-schizoid position, he is incapable of experiencing absence, with the result that he will experience the absence of the good object as an attack by the bad object. The infant will then proceed to split the object into a good part and a bad part while denying both frustration and persecution" (2001, 67–68).

11. Kristeva 2001, 68.

12. I owe this phrase to Sara Beardsworth.

13. Unlike Kristeva, for Klein object-relations exist from the start. Yet the "objects" that exist are fantasmatic—projections of the child's wants, fears, and frustrations, and do not conform to a stable differentiation between inner psychic life and the external world.

14. Kristeva does not introduce the term "imaginary father" until *Tales of Love*, although the role of castration is already in play in *Powers of Horror.*

15. In fact, as Kristeva will acknowledge in *Melanie Klein,* Klein's view is that the oedipal complex takes effect very early, so that the critique Kristeva makes in *Tales of Love* does not really apply.

16. However, Kristeva notes in *Melanie Klein* that Klein "attempts to distinguish" her idea of the "'mother with a penis' . . . from Freud's 'phallic mother' " (2001, 235). Also see Kristeva 2001, 243.

17. Kristeva only implicitly appeals to the loving or imaginary father in *Powers of Horror* (1982, 6; 13).

18. See Irigaray 1985a, 48; Rose 1986, 202.

19. Rose 1998, 131.

20. See Kristeva 1991 and 1993.

21. See the opening chapter of *Tales of Love.*

22. Klein 1986, 205. See also Jacobus 1995, 146.

23. Hyppolite 1991, 294–95.

24. Lacan 1977, 272; Jacobus 1995, 129.

25. See Kristeva 2001, chap. 8. See also Kristeva 1984, chap. 6.

26. See Rose 1998.

27. The breast, for Klein, functions metaphorically for the mother's body, which is figured as containing part of the father—the penis.

28. As Kristeva says, "The 'good breast,' which becomes the core of the ego and that guarantees its strength, is also laden with traps. The idealization of the breast, which is a counterpart to the splitting of the ego, encourages the exaggeration of its good qualities in order to counteract the fear of the persecutory 'bad breast' " (2001, 67). For Klein, although the good or gratifying breast forms the core of ego, it too may be subject to fragmentation. Klein says in "Notes on Some Schizoid Mechanisms," "In addition to the divorce between a good breast and a bad breast in the young infant's phantasy, the frustrating breast—attacked in oral-sadistic phantasies—is felt to be in fragments; the gratifying breast, taken in under the dominance of the sucking libido, is felt to be complete. This first internal good object acts as a focal point in the ego. It counteracts the processes of splitting and dispersal, makes for cohesiveness and integration, and is instrumental in building up the ego. The infant's feeling of having inside a good and complete breast may, however, be shaken by frustration and anxiety. As a result, the divorce between the good and bad breast may be difficult to maintain, and the infant may feel that the good breast too is in pieces" (1986, 181).

29. Kristeva says that in the paranoid-schizoid position the child is "afraid that he will be destroyed by the very bad objects that he has projected outside him" but in the depressive position he is more "ambivalent." There is "nostalgia" for the good object, that is "comparable to mourning" but there is also "guilt" since the loss of the good object is "buttressed by a feeling of . . . having destroyed it by assimilating it" (2001, 76).

30. This talk of "not until" is not quite accurate, since Klein is concerned not so much with developmental schemata as with "positions" or "states," as Kristeva makes clear when she says, "Once Klein's concepts were solidified into a 'paranoid-schizoid position' and a 'depressive position,' they began to connote a certain structure of emotional life—one that appears at a particular moment of history and that is susceptible to reappearing in the unconscious: 'the regular association of a series of anxiogenic situation with a series of determinate defense mechanisms'" (2001, 67). Kristeva is quoting J-M. Petot in *Melanie Klein*, vol. 2, trans. Christine Trollope (Madison, Conn.: International Universities Press, 1991), 106. This might also serve as a description of the mechanism of abjection, which is also susceptible of reappearing in the unconscious.

31. Following the same logic, for Klein it is also the breast (and the threat of its loss), as a precursor to castration anxiety, that gives rise to the superego. She says, in "The Origins of Transference," that "the introjection of the breast is the beginning of super-ego formation" (1986, 203).

32. Kristeva notes that the question of the role of the father is left open, and "must be left unanswered here" (2001, 176) but goes on to identify such questions as the "the most pressing problems of psychoanalytic study today" and refers her readers in a note to *Tales of Love*, 26–53 and *The Sense and Non-Sense of Revolt*, 94–106. For a discussion of this issue in *Tales of Love* see Jacobus, 148–49. I take up Kristeva's reading of the effect of castration on girls and their ironic stance to the symbolic in *The Sense and Non-Sense of Revolt* later in this chapter. See also Ziarek (2005) for a reading of this aspect of Kristeva.

33. As Kristeva says, for Klein, "The loss of the mother—which for the imaginary is tantamount to the death of the mother—becomes the organizing principle for the subject's symbolic capacity. . . . in order to think one must lose the mother" (2001, 129–30). "To rid oneself of the mother becomes the sine qua non for accessing the symbol" (2001, 134). On Klein's "combined parent figure" see "The Origins of Transference" (1986, 208). See also Klein 1975b, 132–33; 200.

34. Klein, "The Importance of Symbol Formation in the Development of the Ego" (1986, 96).

35. Ibid..

36. See Lacan 1991, 85. See also Kristeva 2001, 161; Jacobus 1995, 137.

37. See Kristeva 2001, 139. See also Kristeva's discussion of Melanie Klein's study of Dick, whom Klein believed "possessed two forms of linguistic competence: both a passive familiarity with language and a fantasy-like presymbolism, that is, an infralinguistic capacity to fantasize that accorded with the fantasies communicated by Melanie's speech" (2001, 162).

38. Hyppolite says that "Freud posits the intellectual as separated from the affective" (1991, 292), but he goes on to read Freud through the lens of Lacan, perhaps reneging on his earlier insight that the "construction" of Freud's text is "not at all that of a professor" (290). By interpreting Freud's analysis of intellect and affect by way of Lacan, who, as Hyppolite is only too aware, has taken up a somewhat Hegelian reading of Freud, Hyppolite produces a tension in his

reading of Freud's text on negation. He suggests that "the role that Freud has . . . primordial affectivity play, in so far as it is the progenitor of intelligence . . . should be understood in the way that Dr. Lacan teaches: that is to say that the primal form of relation known psychologically as the affective is itself situated within the distinctive field of the human situation, and that, if it engenders intelligence, it is because it already, from its beginnings, brings with it a fundamental historicity. There is no pure affective on the one hand, entirely engaged in the real, and the pure intellectual on the other, which detaches itself from it in order to grasp it once again" (293). My suggestion is that Kristeva's notion of abjection, as a rejection that is not at the level of intellectual negation, not a Hegelian determinate negation, but precisely at the level of affect, picks up on an insight Freud offers in his essay on Negation that neither Hyppolite nor Lacan do (although reading Hyppolite helped me see this). It is not that we as thinkers can ever access the real without imposing on it, and thus transforming it, the categories of thought—and in this sense Hyppolite is right to follow Lacan in claiming that even the affective is always already situated within historicity. It is rather that even the way in which the real is thought—when it is thought, when that margin of thought allows its retrieval—will be specific to the philosopher who thinks it, such that even the descriptions of its impossible, excluded status will be laden with grand myths that themselves have to be called into question, myths of feminine or racialized alterity that permeate the grandest of our philosophical systems. Like Hyppolite, Kristeva is sensitive to the difference to which Hyppolite points in Hegel between "genuine negativity" and "destructive appetite" (292).

Hyppolite points out that Freud is concerned with a negation that is "different from the ideal negation [*négation*] in which the intellectual is constituted" (292). He points out the "asymmetry between the emergence of affirmation staring off from the unifying drive [*tendance*] of love, and the genesis, starting off with the destructive drive [*tendance*], of that negation whose true function is that of giving rise to intelligence and the very starting point of thought" (292).

39. For a more extended discussion of authority see John Phillips (1998).

40. While Freud's claim that all presentations derive from perception does not amount to the empiricist claim that all knowledge arises from experience, it flirts dangerously with such a suggestion. Lacan comments on this observation (1991, 59), as does Kristeva (1984, 160). Freud's claim is not reducible to such an empiricism because it is not yet a claim about knowledge. It is however on the way to becoming one, and in this respect it is worth recalling the Hegelian point that Joseph C. Flay makes when he says that the "pursuit of a desire, no matter how casual or intense, always occurs as an act by a real individual in a specific historico-cultural context. It can be considered as essentially an act of perception . . . only by abstracting from the concrete conditions and circumstances within which it occurs" (1984, 171).

41. See Kristeva 1982, 10.

42. In Jacqueline Rose's words, "On Narcissism" was a "major reference point" for Lacan's concept of the imaginary as elaborated in the "The Mirror Stage" (1986, 170).

43. Cowie's gloss on this is useful. In "infantile autoeroticism . . . satisfaction is distinguished as an aim but the drives remain objectless. In narcissism, however, the sexual drives are organized in relation to an *object:* they are directed to an image of a unified body. Just like an external object, the ego is cathected,

charged with libido. Freud is thus led to speak of primary or infantile narcissism as a stage in which the ego becomes cathected with energy, and can pass itself off as the source of libido. But this is not simply a progression . . . Freud emphasizes that 'a new psychical action' is involved, enabling the taking of the body-image as an object, and thus indicating a clear disjunction between the two mechanisms. For Freud the ego, the human subject, is made and not born. The organizing effects of this disjunction are given articulation in Lacan's concept of the mirror phase" (1997, 78).

44. Kristeva 2000, 99.

45. This bears comparison with Kristeva's observations about Klein's "interpretive imaginary" or the "intrusion of the negative" that is "the negative of the drive, and then the negation of that first negation" (2001, 201).

46. Lacan says the "jubilant assumption of his specular image by the child at the *infans* stage, still sunk in his motor incapacity and nursling dependence, would seem to exhibit in an exemplary situation the symbolic matrix in which the *I* is precipitated in a primordial form, before it is objectified in the dialectic of identification with the other, and before language restores to it, in the universal, its function as subject" (1977, 2). Dylan Evans observes, "Symbolic identification is the identification with the father in the final stage of the OEDIPUS COMPLEX which gives rise to the formation of the EGO-IDEAL). It is by means of this secondary identification that the subject transcends the aggressivity inherent in primary identification [1977, 23], and thus can be said to represent a certain 'libidinal normalization' [1977 2]. Although this identification is called 'symbolic', it is still a 'secondary identification' [1977, 22] modeled on primary identification and thus, like all identification, partakes of the imaginary; it is only called 'symbolic' because it represents the completion of the subject's passage into the symbolic order" (1996, 81).

47. Isaacs 1989, 104–105.

48. See Klein 1986, 95–111; Lacan 1991, 83; Kristeva 1991, 165; Jacobus 1995, 137, 143.

49. See Kristeva 2001, 229–30.

50. See Kristeva 2001, 202.

51. Kristeva says, "On the face of it, Klein's writings include reports of 'case studies' that are exhaustive, even oversimplified, and that are accompanied with ready-made, almost forced, interpretations" but goes on to say "At the same time, however the artifice that she constructs crumbles without warning, and we are struck by the truths that shine through" (2001, 198). Kristeva comments on Klein's "courageous coexistence with the negative," on her "audacious" thinking (201) and the "respect" (197) she commands.

52. See Kristeva 1987, 34 and Freud 1953n.

3. ABJECT ART

1. One could, of course, proliferate the possibilities of how one identifies the inauguration of modernist art. T. J. Clark identifies Jacques-Louis David's *Death of Marat* as the first modernist work of art (*Farewell to an Idea: Episodes from a History of Modernism* [New Haven, Conn.: Yale University Press, 1999]). I owe the reference to Horowitz 2001, 1.

2. "For Greenberg, Manet became the Kant of modernist painting: 'Manet's became the first Modernist pictures by virtue of the frankness with which they declared the flat surfaces on which they were painted' " (Danto 1997, 7; quotation from Greenberg 1993, 86). Danto goes on: "Flatness, the consciousness of paint and brushstroke, the rectangular shape—all of them what Meyer Schapiro speaks of as 'nonmimetic features' of what may still have been residually mimetic paintings—displaced perspective, foreshortening, chiaroscuro as the progress points of a developmental sequence. The shift from 'premodernist' to modernist art, if we follow Greenberg, was the shift from mimetic to nonmimetic features of painting. . . . its representational features were secondary in modernism where they had been primary in premodernist art. . . . My sense is that modernism . . . is marked by an ascent to a new level of consciousness, which is reflected in painting as a kind of discontinuity, almost as if to emphasize that mimetic representation had become less important than some kind of reflection on the means and methods of representation. . . . Van Gogh and Gaugin . . . are the first modernist painters" (7–8).

3. Danto says, "Greenberg is typical of the period he tries to analyze in that he has his own definition of what the essence of painting must be. In this he belongs to the Age of Manifestos" (1997, 68).

4. See Horowitz 2001.

5. The association of poetry with the masculine ideal should not be over-played. After all, Antigone is the purest tragic hero for Hegel (even if he qualifies this by suggesting that she does not understand the ethical implications of her stance). In naming a play after Antigone (even if *Oedipus Rex* remains the undisputed centerpiece of psychoanalysis and Western culture, following Aristotle's privileging of it, and even if there is a debate about who is the true tragic hero, Creon, Antigone, or both), Sophocles opens up the question of the relative roles of women and men. Arguably, Aeschylus too is concerned with a similar issue, especially when he has Apollo and Athena confront one another at the end of the *Oresteia*, in a contest between the old order of female goddesses, the Furies, and the new order of male gods (even if Athena's vote acquits Orestes of matricide, while Clytemnestra, as murderer of her husband, a hero of the Trojan war, could be taken to embody the monstrous feminine).

6. This is a point made by Véronique Fóti, who admires Merleau-Ponty's innovative placing of painting at the center of philosophy—thereby contesting the priority that Heidegger accords to poetry (Fóti 2003, 3), which does not prevent her from marking her departure from Merleau-Ponty's privileging of painting over the other arts (Fóti 1996, 15).

7. See Kristeva 2002, 77.

8. See Mattick on Lessing (1995, 33–34). See also Burke, for whom "the images raised by poetry are always . . . obscure" whereas those of painting "are exactly similar to those in nature" (1987, 62).

9. Like Lyotard, Deleuze resists the tendency to resolve the meaning of the visual image into linguistic signification, arguing rather for an excess that disturbs the order of the linguistic sign. Like Kristeva, Lyotard endorses a semiotics that reserves a "density" not transliterated into signification. See Geller (2007) on Lyotard.

10. Among those whose work has a place in the Derridean returns to Freud that Caruth's (1996) interpretation of trauma and memory authorizes, I would include Elissa Marder, whose paper at Society for Phenomenological and

Existential Philosophy (2005) is a wonderful example of the brilliant work that can be done in this vein.

11. Arguably, Heidegger's emphasis on finitude merely renews that of Kant.

12. Deleuze and Guattari (1983) have of course produced an influential critique of the psychoanalytic oedipal machine as complicitous with capitalism, in which the infinite debt of consumer society is translated into the infinite debt to the name of the oedipal father (dead or not).

13. Alessia Ricciardi (2003) adheres to the trope of mourning in her interrogation of the aesthetic in the age of postmodernism, while also bringing into question reliance on the myth of castration.

14. Also see Jan-Ove Steihaug (2005).

15. Krauss is critical of an earlier version of the essay Mulvey published in a revised form in *Fetishism and Curiosity.*

16. Mulvey does not go as far as thinking through the decisive differentiation between the abject and the uncanny, a differentiation that would be logically entailed by a thorough confrontation of the logic of fetishism with that of abjection.

17. Silverman 1996, 224.

18. Kristeva says, "The functioning of writing [*écriture*], the trace, and the grammè, introduced by Derrida in his critique of phenomenology and its linguistic substitutes, points to an essential aspect of the semiotic: *Of Grammatology* specifies that which escapes *Bedeutung*" (1984, 40–41).

19. Deleuze says, "Hitchcock had begun the inversion of this point of view by including the viewer in the film. But it is now that the identification is actually inverted: the character has become a kind of viewer. He shifts, runs, and becomes animated in vain, the situation he is in outstrips his motor capacities on all sides, and makes him see and hear what is no longer subject to the rules of a response or an action. He records rather than reacts. He is prey to a vision, pursued by it or pursuing it, rather than engaged in an action" (1997, 3).

20. To read in the repetition of the scream a reminder of the artifice of filmic production is to respond to a fetishistic reading of the film.

21. The logic here is reminiscent of Derrida's explication of the pharmakon (see Derrida 1981). Some of the rituals Douglas describes involve taboo objects that take on a curative, purifying function (1999).

22. See Chase 1989.

23. See Schiebinger 1993, 163.

24. For Danto, Duchamp challenged the idea that beauty was a "defining attribute of art," bringing to our attention the aesthetic nondescriptness of ready-made objects. Danto notes, however that Walter Arensberg "thought Duchamp was drawing attention to the "white gleaming beauty of the urinal" (1997, 84). See also Danto's discussion of Duchamp in *The Abuse of Beauty* (2003).

25. See Taylor 1993, 71.

26. See Mohanty 1997b.

27. Deleuze's acumen deserts him, however, when it comes to providing incisive critical analysis of the politics of sexual difference.

28. See Beardsworth 2004, 160.

29. See Cowie 1990, and Geller, 2007.

30. Walter Benjamin has famously argued that in the age of mechanical reproduction politics takes the place of ritual (1968). By suggesting that art reenacts the setting up of the boundary between nature and culture whereby

humans discriminate themselves from animals, Kristeva can be read as giving one more twist to Benjamin's thesis. In miming the entry into a symbolic economy, we can also rework the terms of that entry.

31. Associated with the Hegelian aesthetic (see Kristeva 1984, 110), for Kristeva, "Negativity . . . splits and prevents the closing up of Being. . . . It points to an outside that Hegel could only think of as something inherent in belief. . . . Hegelian negativity prevents the immobilization of the thetic . . . lets in all the semiotic motility that prepares and exceeds it . . . this negativity is the fourth term of the dialectic" (113). Ultimately, however, Kristeva comments on what she sees as an "Hegelian closure" that amounts to the "Inability to posit negativity as anything but a representation of ideational unity in itself" (159).

32. On preventing the "theologization" of the thetic, Kristeva points out that poetic language can be both "complicitous with dogma" and "may also set in motion what dogma represses" (1984, 61), thereby protesting it.

33. Colette Guillaumin says, "Negations are not recognized as such by our unconscious mental processes. From this point of view, a fact affirmed and a fact denied exist to exactly the same degree, and remain equally present in our affective and intellectual associative networks. Just talking about race means that it will always be there in residue" (1999, 44).

34. See Cowie 1990.

35. See Freud 19563j.

36. See Chase 1989 and Lacan 1991.

37. A number of theorists have made a similar point with regard to Freud's "A Child is Being Beaten." See Freud 1953c.

38. hooks, 1996b.

39. Kaja Silverman acknowledges both the normative force of "dominant cultural values" (1996, 45), and the importance of circulating "alternative images and words" which can provide access to "new identificatory coordinates" (81). Focusing on the importance of idealization, Silverman suggests that "visual texts have the power to reeducate the look" (5). She challenges the assumption that "only a cinema which thwarts identification can be truly transformative" and suggests that the "identificatory 'lure' " of cinema, far from being a limitation to the capacity of film to participate in transformative political projects, might be "one of its greatest political assets, since it represents the potential vehicle for a spectatorial self-estrangement" (85).

4. Fantasy at a Distance

1. As Dolores Burdick, the translator of "Ellipsis" observes, "Deriving from the verb *frayer* (to trace out, open out, make way, beat a track, etc.), the noun *frayage* is often used in this essay in juxtaposition with *frayeur* (terror, dread)" (Kristeva 1986, 242, n.3).

2. Kristeva 1986a, 236–43.

3. It is perhaps worthy of note that Kristeva's "Ellipsis" appeared directly following an essay by Baudry in *Communications.*

4. Referring to Lacan's emphasis in placing the "*mirror* at the core of the Ego's formation," Kristeva stresses that "specular fascination is a belated phenomenon in the genesis of the Ego" (1987, 40). While there must be a "visual" or

"speculative cathexis," this can be hallucinatory—"elusive, fleeting, and baffling" (1982, 46). That is, there must be a "sign," a "representation, hence a seeing" that holds together even a "visual hallucination" of a "non-object" (1982, 46). At the same time, for Kristeva the image "should not be conceived as simply visual but as a representation activating various facilitations corresponding to the entire gamut of perceptions, especially the *sonorous* ones; this because of their precocious appearance in the domain of neuropsychological maturation, but also because of their dominant function in speech" (40). Distancing herself from the innatism of Chomsky as well as from "Lacanian notions of an always-already-there of language that would be revealed as such in the subject of the unconscious" Kristeva thinks "with respect to the *infans,* that the symbolic function preexists" but also maintains "an evolutionary postulate that leads me to seek to elaborate *various dispositions* giving access to that function, and this corresponds as well to various psychic structures" (44). Kristeva distances herself from "the dominant place of language in the constitution of *being*" and to the "resurgence of monotheism" and wonders whether the assumption of language as dominant amounts to a monotheistic outlook: "is there really a difference?" (27).

5. As Mary Jacobus says in "Revising 'The Mirror-Phase,'" Kristeva posits narcissism as an already ternary, 'complex' structure prior even to the complex structure of oedipalization" (1995, 145). Cynthia Chase also refers to Kristeva's "retheorization of the mirror stage as 'primary narcissism' involving an 'immediate identification' with the imaginary father and 'abjection' of the mother" (1989, 67). Quoting *Tales of Love* Joan Brandt says, "Kristeva . . . establishes even before the structuring relations of the Oedipal triangle and preceding the subjective, representational structurations of the mirror stage an even earlier instance of subjectivity, what she calls a 'position of symbolicity' located within the semiotic itself and constituting 'a fragile inscription of subjecthood'" ([Kristeva, 1987, 46] 1997, 131).

6. Silverman (1996, 14). Silverman draws on Paul Schilder, and on Henri Wallon's "proprioceptive ego," in her corrective to Lacan's emphasis of the specular ego, an account of the "body's sensation of occupying a point in space" which "involves a nonvisual mapping of the body's form" (16). She suggests that "the subject comes to have a body that is sensationally marked by gender, race, and sexual preference" (16–17). Silverman adds in a footnote, "The way in which a body is touched (or, for that matter, not touched) can also communicate love for, or revulsion against, its color" (231, n.21). This last observation, especially, marks the proximity between Silverman and Kristeva, although Silverman does not cite Kristeva in this book.

7. Kristeva says that "the cinema is not really our subject: we have arrived here through the intermediary of intimacy in revolt and the imaginary that constitutes it, in order to examine the imaginary of demystification" (2002, 80).

8. Lacan uses the term abjection very rarely, and without developing it. See for example Lacan 1990.

9. See Cowie 1990.

10. See Freud, "The Uncanny" (1953v). The primal fantasies are seduction, the primal scene, castration, and that of intrauterine existence. Is abjection the revival of just another primal Freudian fantasy, that of intrauterine existence?

11. Kaja Silverman argues along more Lacanian lines that there is a "nonvisual mapping of the body's form" (1996, 16). "At the heart of Lacan's theory

of the mirror stage there would seem to be something which has gone largely unremarked, something which calls into question the currently fashionable notion of a perpetually mobile subject, capable of a wide range of contradictory bodily identifications: the principle of the self-same body" (1996, 11). This, I suggest, is precisely the idea that that Kristeva takes up in terms of the clean and proper body in *Powers of Horror*, and in terms of the being particular in *Tales of Love*. Kristeva attributes the fact that we are prone to "crises" in love to a lack of differentiation, or being particular: the fact that "today we lack being particular (propre), covered as we are with so much abjection, because the guideposts that insured our ascent toward the good have proven questionable, we have crises of love" (1987, 7). To fail to have separated from the mother is to have difficulty in sustaining love relationships, not least because one lacks autonomy, or one's own clean and proper body. To be autoerotic is to be "undifferentiated" (35); it is "Oedipal rivalry" that "creates mediations" (47). Identification "causes the subject to exist within the signifier of the Other" (37); "primary identification endows the mother with existence" (52). The work that the mother does in encouraging the child to identify with the imaginary father in Kristeva's account could be read as similar to Silverman's reading of Lacan's "active gift of love" (1996, 105). For Kristeva, the immediacy with which the child is able to identify with the loving father is facilitated by the mother's gift, which is to elaborate her desiring relation to the phallus for the child. "If there is an immediacy of the child's identification with *that desire* (of the Father's phallus), it probably comes from the child's not having to elaborate it; rather he receives it, mimics it, or even sustains it through the mother who offers it to him (or refuses it) as a gift. In a way, such an identification with the father-mother conglomerate, as Freud would have it, or with . . . the maternal desire for the Phallus, comes as a godsend. And for a very good reason, since without that disposition of the psyche, the child and the mother do not yet constitute 'two' . . . " (1987, 40). It is worth noting that in *Powers of Horror*, it is the loving father who helps the child sever its dependence on the mother (see 1982, 13), while in *Tales of Love*, the mother's gift of love to the child effects the separation.

12. See Terry Eagleton (1990a, 64). See also Susan Buck-Morss (1992, 7–10).

13. One can see why Eagleton says, "like the maternal body, the thing-in-itself is posited and prohibited at a stroke, so utterly self-identical that language falters and swerves off from it, leaving behind it the sheer trace of a silence. Kant's epistemology mixes concept and intuition, masculine form and feminine content, but this marriage is unstable from the outset, neither fish nor fowl. Form is external to content in the realm of understanding, left without content in practical reason, and elevated to an end in itself in aesthetic judgement. Hegel, by contrast, will have the courage of his idealist virility, penetrating to the very essence of the object and delivering up its inmost secret. He will carry the contradictions of thought right into the thing itself, into the veiled and tabooed, and so will risk fissuring the reality which for Kant must remain chastely intact, dividing it against itself by the labour of the negative. But this is only possible because he already knows, in some Kleinian fantasy of reparation, that this violated being will finally be restored to itself whole and entire" (1990a, 121).

14. See also Kristeva 1995a.

15. See also Elizabeth Cowie (1997, 155). Cowie refers to the same passage in Freud, but puts the reference to mixed race under erasure. Using ellipses

does not eradicate the problem, but rather partakes in a strategy of disavowal—I see this, but I refuse to register it. One wonders what kind of anxiety fuels the decision to write a problematic reference to race out of the text.

16. Likewise, Laplanche and Pontalis do not comment on the racial phantasmatics of this passage. See also Laplanche and Pontalis (1963:1).

17. Levinas's the-more-I-do-the-more-I-am-obligated philosophy is as critical of an ethics of good intentions as it is of a philosophy of sameness, in which I grasp otherness through my ideas, reducing alterity to me, and refusing the alterity of a future by reeling it back in, assimilating it to a now—just as the hand grasps hold of objects, or eats food in a way that leaves nothing but me.

18. For a nuanced discussion of the role music plays in Kristeva, see Robin James (2002).

19. Kaja Silverman suggests that *Psycho* refuses to let the viewer "off the hook" and "obliges us to understand . . . that we want suture so badly that we'll take it at any price" (1983, 212).

20. Kristeva also appears to be concerned with this self-referential quality, as is clear when she stipulates two extremes that need to be avoided: "stereotypical, soap opera images reduce the viewer to a passive consumer, or, on the contrary, when so-called auteur cinema pulverizes fantasy and invents a veritable cinematic *écriture* with ambitions of conceptualizing the specular" (2002, 69).

21. Neil Jordan's *The Crying Game* not only encourages us to shift our allegiance to a new "hero" halfway through the film, but also puts into question the heteronormative codes in terms of which even Hitchcock's heroes are constructed. Norman's mother might be a phantom of his mind, but in presenting her as such, Hitchcock does not manage to go beyond the pathologizing of transgendered sexuality.

22. Kaja Silverman's *The Threshold of the Visible World* is helpful in unpacking the complex political logic of conscious and unconscious identifications. See especially her discussion of Brecht and Benjamin in chapter 3, "Political Ecstasy" and her consideration of the relation between classical, Renaissance perspective in relation to identification, suture, and Comolli at the beginning of chapter 4 on "The Gaze" (1996).

23. *Ma vie en rose* (Belgium, 1997). Alain Berliner, 89 min. Sony Pictures. Ludovic's fantasy of Pam and Ben figures as a kind of counter-phobic fantasy, one that is akin to Klein's good object, invoked to counteract the bad object—in this case the world's negative response to Ludovic's identification as a girl.

24. Quoted by Paul Willemen in Pines and Willemen (1989, 9).

25. For a detailed analysis of third cinema, with which the films I discuss here have some affinity, see Pick, 1993.

26. As Solanas and Gettino say, "Until recently, film had been synonymous with show or amusement: in a word, it was one more *consumer good*. At best, films succeeded in bearing witness to the decay of bourgeois values and testifying to social injustice. As a rule, films only dealt with effect, never with cause; it was a cinema of mystification or anti-historicism. It was *surplus value* cinema. Caught up in these conditions, films, the most valuable tool of communication of our times, were destined to satisfy the ideological and economic interests of the owner of the film industry, the lords of the world film market, the great majority of whom were from the United States" (2000, 265).

27. See Buck-Morss 1992, 18.

28. For Laplanche and Pontalis, repression is the operation by which "the subject attempts to repel, or to confine to the unconscious, representations (thoughts, images, memories) which are bound to an instinct. Repression occurs when to satisfy an instinct—though likely to be pleasurable in itself—would incur the risk of provoking unpleasure because of other requirements" (1973, 390). Freud says in his 1915 essay "Repression": "*the essence of repression lies simply in turning something away, and keeping it at a distance, from the conscious*" ([1953q, 147]; quoted in Laplanche and Pontalis 1973, 392). Like much of Freud's terminology, the distinction of repression and defense, and the relationship between them, does not remain constant throughout his works. According to Laplanche and Pontalis, Freud "subsum[es] repression under the category of the mechanisms of defence," so that (contra the editors of the Standard Edition of Freud who claim that defense and repression are synonymous) for Laplanche and Pontalis repression is "one moment of the defensive operation—and this in its precise sense of repression into the unconscious," although they go on to concede that repression "does constitute" for Freud "a sort of prototype of other defensive operations" (1973, 392). In "Repression" Freud distinguishes three phases of repression, which Laplanche and Pontalis summarize as follows:

1. Primal repression "directed not against the instinct as such but . . . its signs or 'representatives', which are denied entrance to the consciousness and to which the instinct remains fixated" (393).
2. Repression proper (*eigentliche Verdrängung*) or 'after-pressure' (*Nachdrängen*) is therefore a dual process, in that it adds to this attraction a repulsion (*Abstossung*).
3. The third phase is the "'return of the repressed' in the guise of symptoms, dreams, parapraxes, etc. What does repression act upon? It must be emphasized that it acts neither upon the instinct which, in so far as it is organic, escapes the split between conscious and unconscious, nor upon the affect. . . . It is only the ideational representatives of the instinct (ideas, images, etc.) that are repressed" (393).

The term repression is sometimes used to refer to all three phases, and sometimes used "in a more restrictive sense which refers to the second phase taken alone" (1973, 393). Hence, when Kristeva uses the term "primal repression," with which she associates abjection, she is referring to the first phase. Alan Bass's gloss is useful: "Freud explained the clinical manifestations of repression in terms of a theory of primal repression. His most general conception is that representatives of mental processes may either never enter consciousness at all (primal repression) or can be withdrawn from it (secondary, or clinical repression). Interpretation works to reverse the process of secondary repression; primal repression creates the possibility that what is most meaningful may never have been conscious" (2000; 3).

29. One thinks of Aquinas's notion of intellection, in which the thing conforms to the idea of it, and of Levinas's objection both to rationalism and empiricism, in so far as both involve the reduction of alterity to sameness. Whether the object conforms to the mind, or the intellect submits to the thing, in both cases, to comprehend is to eliminate otherness. As Koerner says, "By disputing the

fixity of object, and of the human subjects rendered homologous to objects (in the symmetry of viewer to viewed), abject art exposes the mechanism whereby some subjects are expelled in order to objectify the sovereignty of others" (1997, 6).

30. Kristeva notes the limitations of the term "negativity," finding it "too closely associated with negation" (1984, 117), and suggesting that "Expenditure or rejection are better terms for the movement of material contradictions that generate the semiotic function" (119). Kristeva uses the term negativity to name that which is in excess of the symbolic order, or signification, but also cautions that it is "an inappropriate term for semiotic movement, which moves through the symbolic, produces it, and continues to work on it from within" (117). "It registers a conflictual state which stresses the heterogeneity of the semiotic function and its determination" (118). Or again, "*The sole function of our use of the term 'negativity' is to designate the process that exceeds the signifying subject, binding him to the laws of objective struggles in nature and society*" (119).

31. See Kristeva 1984, 58, 68–69.

32. The idea of borderline cases, which is used "to designate psychopathological troubles lying on the frontier between neurosis and psychosis" (Laplanche and Pontalis 1973, 54), is not unique to Kristeva.

33. It does, however bear some relationship to perversion.

34. Kristeva says, even "if our borderlander is, like any speaking being, subject to castration to the extent that he must deal with the symbolic, he in fact runs a far greater risk than others do. It is not a part of himself, vital though it may be, that he is threatened with losing, but his whole life" (1982, 55). This is because the "jouissance" of abjection is one in which "identity becomes absent" (54). The "body's inside . . . shows up in order to compensate for the collapse of the border between inside and outside" and those "flows from within suddenly become the sole 'object' of sexual desire—a true 'ab-ject' where man, frightened, crosses over the horrors of maternal bowels, and, in an immersion that enables him to avoid coming face to face with an other, spares himself the risk of castration. But at the same time that immersion gives him the full power of possessing, if not being, the bad object that inhabits the maternal body" (53–54).

35. Kristeva elaborates the relief provided by the father in the following way in *Tales of Love*, putting the emphasis both on the fact that the father is a "godsend," and on the sense in which the distance that the mother offers the child is a "gift": the father signals to the child that the mother's desire is elsewhere, and in this sense "he is simple virtuality, a potential presence" (1987, 43). "If there is an immediacy of the child's identification with *that desire* (of the Father's phallus), it probably comes from the child's not having to elaborate it; rather he receives it, mimics it, or even sustains it through the mother who offers it to him (or refuses it) as a gift. In a way, such an identification with the father-mother conglomerate, as Freud would have it, or with . . . the maternal desire for the Phallus, comes as a godsend. And for a very good reason, since without that disposition of the psyche, the child and the mother do not yet constitute 'two' . . . " (40). It is this failure that haunts Matthew: "*Appended to his mother, described as the key figure in the family, Matthew has not ceased being her phallus. Within their dual economy, which the father did not broach, it seemed apparently inconceivable that she might have a desire other than her child. The voracity of the dual symbiosis, accompanied by denial of the imaginary father . . . came back to Matthew from outside, projected*" (55). In contrast to Matthew's mother, the

"loving mother, different from the caring and clinging mother, is someone who has an object of desire; beyond that, she has an Other with relation to whom the child will serve as go-between. She will love her child with respect to that Other, and it is through a discourse aimed at that Third party that the child will be set up as 'loved' for the mother. 'Isn't he beautiful,' or 'I am proud of you,' and so forth, are statements of maternal love because they involve a Third Party: it is in the eyes of a Third party that the baby the mother speaks to becomes a *he*, it is with respect to others that 'I am proud of you,' and so forth. . . . without the maternal 'diversion' toward a Third Party, the bodily exchange [of maternal fondness] is abjection or devouring . . . Any borderline person ends up finding a mother who is 'loving' for her own sake, but he cannot accept her as loving himself, for she did not love any *other* one" (34).

36. For Freud, phobia is a subdivision of hysteria. See Freud 1953a, and Laplanche and Pontalis (1973, 92).

37. Kristeva asks the rhetorical question: "is desire ever anything else but desire for an idealized norm, the norm of the Other?" (1982, 47).

38. Heather Rakes' unpublished paper "Me and a Gun," helped me to think about the significance of how idiolect functions.

39. Contra Lacan, Kristeva emphasizes the "heterogeneity" of the Freudian sign (1982, 51), as distinct from the "overly philosophical" or "Kantian" reading, pointing to the "very heterogeneous (involving both drive and thought) importance of the symbol of negation" in Freud (52). "When Lacan posits the Name of the Father as the keystone to all sign, meaning, and discourse, he points to the *necessary condition* of one and only one process of the signifying unit, albeit a constitute one: the process of condensing one heterogeneous set (that of word presentation) with another (that of thing presentation), releasing the one into the other, and insuring its 'unitary bent' " (53). Kristeva, on the other hand, emphasizes the collapse of the sign, which is also "a collapse of the Oedipal triangulation that supports it" (53), and thus allows for the possibility for new meanings to emerge.

40. Spivak herself is suspicious of Kristeva. She rightly points out that Kristeva's work sometimes falls prey to Eurocentrism. No doubt Kristeva, along with many other intellectuals in France, would fall prey to similar criticisms to those Spivak makes of Deleuze and Foucault in "Can the Subaltern Speak?" They ignore "the international division of labor" and "global capitalism" (1988, 272). They belong to "the exploiters' side of the international division of labor" (280). They "align themselves with bourgeois socialists" (274). They are implicated in the project "to constitute the colonial subject as Other" (281). Foucault undertakes "an unquestioned valorization of the oppressed subject" (274). Deleuze and Foucault ignore both the epistemic violence of imperialism and the international division of labor" (289). Nonetheless, I think certain structural parallels obtain between the work of Kristeva and Spivak.

41. Koerner 1997, 7. Also see Hamburger (1997).

42. Hegel 1975, 872. Also cited by Danto (2003, 56).

43. Sara Beardsworth's discussion of Kristeva's reading of Holbein's painting—which Kristeva discusses in the context of the depressive experience—is illuminating, as is her juxtaposition of it with Kristeva's response to Duras's film *Hiroshima mon amour*. If ultimately my reading departs from that of Beardsworth, it is because her reading, despite the nods to Adorno and Nietzsche, appeals to a muted or veiled Hegelianism. In the end Beardsworth's analysis of Kristeva

betrays an allegiance to a view of politics that is more indebted to Hegel than to Beardsworth's own delineation of the art work as situated historically would seem to allow. At one level, a Hegelian reading of Kristeva is certainly justified, since, from *Revolution in Poetic Language* on, Kristeva explicitly evinces the need to evoke Hegel, even as she finds it necessary to supplement the Hegelian subject with the Freudian subject, a subject of the unconscious. Yet, as is clear as early as *Revolution in Poetic Language,* while finding resources in Hegel, Kristeva also sees the need to move beyond what she finally sees as his submission to ideality. At one point Kristeva affirms the Hegelian notion of negativity, when she says "Although negativity is a concept and therefore belongs to a contemplative (theoretical) system [see 95–9], it reformulates the static *terms* of pure abstraction as a process, dissolving and binding them within a mobile law. . . . negativity recasts . . . all categories used in the contemplative system. . . . Negativity constitutes the logical impetus beneath the thesis of negation and that of the negation of negation, but is identical to neither since it is, instead, the logical functioning of the movement that produces these theses. . . . It is the liquefying and dissolving agent that does not destroy but rather reactivates new organizations and, in this sense affirms" (1984, 109). We begin to see Kristeva's distancing of her own position from that of Hegel's, her radicalization of negativity, when she says, "Negativity . . . splits and prevents the closing up of Being . . . It points to an outside that Hegel could only think of as something inherent in belief. . . . Hegelian negativity prevents the immobilization of the thetic . . . lets in all the semiotic motility that prepares and exceeds it . . . this negativity is the fourth term of the dialectic" (113). Yet ultimately, however, Kristeva comments on what she sees as an "Hegelian closure" that amounts to the "Inability to posit negativity as anything but a representation of ideational unity in itself" (159).

In Beardsworth's reading of Kristeva, the "artwork that confronts the need to give form to melancholia survives the aesthetic test in and through a new painterly vision that imparts a new vision of mankind in respect, precisely, of loss and death" (2004, 146–7). On my reading, the suggestion that art must "give form" to the semiotic only tells part of the story. To be sure, the semiotic must be raised to the level of the signifier, the semiotic must be made to signify, and in this sense, Beardsworth is correct to say that art gives form to melancholia. Yet it cannot only be a question of giving symbolic form to the semiotic; at the same time, it is a question of transforming what constitutes symbolic meaning. Indeed, Beardsworth acknowledges this at a different moment of her analysis, when she points out that what is at stake is a crisis not just in rationality, but in legitimacy, (see 9). The incursion of semiotic residues is not merely dependent on the emergence of a new historical "vision," which would subordinate the semiotic to the forces driving history. In the materialization of the abject, the bearers of those forces that sustain yet are excluded from the symbolic are identifiable. Whether or not their cries are heard, whether or not we read into them significance, whether or not we allow interpret the signification of abjection, is up to us.

Despite these hesitations, Beardsworth's reading of Kristeva remains valuable in its emphasis on the need to understand that it becomes possible to distinguish the semiotic from the symbolic only under conditions that lead to their "tendential severance." Beardsworth's reading of Kristeva underscores that it is only under conditions that lead to the "tendential severance" of the semiotic and the symbolic that it becomes possible to distinguish the two from one another. Only "in the conditions of tendential severance of the semiotic and the symbolic" (14), only as they "fall apart" (18) that the distinction between the two becomes possible (14). "The categorical distinction can appear only in conditions where modern institutions and discourses have failed to provide the semiotic and symbolic sites or practices for the adequate connection of the semiotic and symbolic. Psychoanalytic insights into suffering subjectivity discover these conditions" (14).

44. Kristeva 1995b, 22.

45. Danto 2003, 60.

46. As Foster suggests, Sherman's centerfolds evoke "the subject under the gaze" (1996a, 148). See also Foster 1996b.

47. In addition to de Sade's Justine, the film was inspired by a children's picture book, *Golden Hearted*. See Stevenson 2002, 89.

48. Benjamin 1968, 238.

49. See Kristeva 1982, 64.

50. Bataille 1970, 219.

51. Bataille, 1970, 219.

52. Both Kristeva and Douglas make the point that filth, in Kristeva's words, is not a "quality in itself" (1982, 69) but concerns the disruption of identity and order.

53. Kristeva, "Pouvoirs de l'horreur," *Visions capitales* (Paris: Réunion des Musées Nationaux, 1998), 111–139.

54. See Laplanche and Pontalis 1973.

55. Kristeva 1995b, 25.

56. Kristeva, "Fetishizing the Abject," undated, 29.

57. Kristeva says this in an undated interview with Lotringer.

58. Kristeva says, "The spectacle is heir to all the weakness of the project of Western philosophy, which was an attempt to understand activity by means of the categories of vision. Indeed the spectacle reposes on an incessant deployment of the very technical rationality to which that philosophical tradition gave rise. So far from realizing philosophy, the spectacle philosophizes reality, and turns the material life of everyone into a universe of speculation" (1994, 17).

5. THE *EXOTICA*-IZATION AND UNIVERSALIZATION OF THE FETISH, AND THE NATURALIZATION OF THE PHALLUS

1. Recall the exasperated claim that Judith Butler associates with Lacanians: "'But it is the law!' "—an "utterance that performatively attributes the very force to the law that the law itself is said to exercise. . . . Thus the status given to the law is precisely the status given to the phallus, the symbolic place of the father, the indisputable and incontestable" (2000, 21).

2. See Rubin 1975, 157–210; Irigaray 1985b, 170–91; De Lauretis 1984, 20; Rose 1986, 69; Cowie 1997, 20–26; Butler 2000, 15–20.

3. William Pietz traces the development of the Latin *facticius*, to the Portuguese *feitiço* and the pidgin *fetisso*, as precedents for the word *fétichisme*, coined by Charles de Brosses in 1757, in a text that Marx read, *Du Culte des dieux fétiches, ou parallele de l'ancienne religion de l'Egypte avec la religion actuelle de Nigritie* (Geneva, 1760). Pietz argues that "the fetish, as an idea and a problem . . . originated in the cross-cultural spaces of the coast of West Africa

during the sixteenth and seventeenth centuries." He goes on to trace the roots of the "initial application of *feitiço* on the African coast." The "Portuguese word feitiço . . . in the late Middle Ages meant 'magical practice' or 'witchcraft' performed, often innocently, by the simple, ignorant classes. Feitiço, in turn derives from the Latin adjective facticius, which originally meant 'manufactured' " (1985, 5). Pietz locates the "emergence of the distinct notion of the fetish" in the "intercultural spaces along the West African coast" which "were triangulated among Christian feudal, African lineage, and merchant capitalist social systems" and suggests that "the fetish must be viewed as proper to no historical field other than that of the history of the word itself, and to no discrete society or culture, but to a cross-cultural situation formed by the ongoing encounter of the value codes of radically different social orders" (6–11). Emily Apter notes that the concept of fetish has also been related to "*fatum,* signifying both fate and charm" while Giorgio Agamben "deduced from the Latin facere neither charm nor beauty but rather the degraded simulacrum or false representation of things sacred, beautiful, or enchanting" (1991, 4; 1981, 69–71). Apter is quoting Agamben.

4. For a related argument, see Anne McClintock, *Imperial Leather: Race, Gender and Sexuality in the Colonial Contest* (1995). McClintock argues, and I agree, that "race, gender and class are not distinct realms of experience," rather "they come into existence in and through relation to each other—if in contradictory and conflictual ways" (5). Like McClintock, I also "wish to avoid privileging one category over the others as the organizing trope" (8), but my focus is less on refusing the theoretical reduction of the trope of fetishism to the phallic scene of castration (see 67), and more on using abjection strategically as a way of detailing the tendency of fetishism to reinvent itself in a way that is complicit with a univocal assertion of valence. Whereas McClintock's focus is on multiplying the signification of fetishes beyond their phallic reference (see 183), I am interested in the ways in which phallic discourse tends to close down the proliferating references of fetishism. While McClintock discusses abjection to some extent, she does not clarify its theoretical status in relation to castration and fetishism. By doing so, I hope to establish the sense in which discourses of race, gender, and class, precisely because of the tendency of discourses toward reification, can in turn come to abject one another. I am grateful to Namita Goswami for bringing McClintock's *Imperial Leather* to my attention.

5. Commenting on the ambiguous status of the incest prohibition, Lévi-Strauss says it is "the link between" the biological and the social: "Before it, culture is still non-existent; with it, nature's sovereignty over man is ended. The prohibition of incest is where nature transcends itself. . . . It brings about and is in itself the advent of a new order" (1969, 25).

6. As Rai says, in a related point, "Lacanian psychoanalysis has ridden on the coat-tails of a discipline (Western anthropology) that is complicit with the colonial project of producing the Orient as pure alterity. This symbiotic relationship between psychoanalysis and anthropology has been crucial to the history and conceptual possibility of both fields" (Rai 1998, 97–98).

7. As Irigaray says, "Given women's social and cultural role, the commodities that women *are forced to exchange would be their children,* along with the actions and words *related to the children.* Women trade children . . . in exchange for a market status *for themselves* . . . . In motherhood, women become socially valuable and . . . phallic, according to Freud" ("Women, the Sacred, Money," 1993, 84).

8. Lacan 1977a, 65–66.

9. See Lévi-Strauss 1969, 496. As De Lauretis says, "Lévi-Strauss over-looks or does not see a contradiction that lies at the base of his model: for women to have (or to be) exchange value, a previous symbolization of biolog-ical sexual difference must have taken place. . . . The assimilation of the notion of sign (which Lévi-Strauss takes from Saussure and transposes to the ethno-logical domain) with the notion of exchange (which he takes from Marx, col-lapsing use-value and exchange-value) is not a chance one . . . the universalizing project of Lévi-Strauss—to collapse the economic and the semiotic orders into a unified theory of culture—depends on his positing woman as the functional opposite of subject (man), which logically excludes the possibility—the theo-retical possibility—of women ever being subjects and producers of culture. . . . It is in his theory, in his conceptualization of the social, in the very terms of his discourse that women are doubly negated as subjects: first, because they are defined as vehicles of men's communication—signs of their language, carriers of their children; second, because women's sexuality is reduced to the 'natural' function of childbearing, somewhere in between the fertility of nature and the productivity of a machine. Desire, like symbolization, is a property of men, property in both senses of the word: something men own, possess, and some-thing that inheres in men, like a quality" (1984, 20). Or as Elizabeth Cowie puts it, "The image/meaning of woman in social discourse, in representation, is explained by reference to a structure—here exchange in kinship—which is itself dependent on appropriating pre-given terms, woman, as a value already recognised in the society. This original 'valuing' has, however, remained unex-amined. This contradiction is at the heart of Lévi-Strauss's own arguments, for he assumes woman as the valuable available and waiting in kinship exchange while at the same time he argues that kinship structures inaugurate social rela-tions, in which case there can be no prior social valuing of women. The con-tradiction arises from the way Lévi-Strauss uses the notion of 'sign' which he draws from structural linguistics. . . . In drawing upon the prestige of Lévi-Strauss's account of kinship to support his concept of the symbolic law, Lacan has also introduced the contradictions of Lévi-Strauss's theory of woman as sign. . . . 'Woman' is not given, biologically or psychologically, but is a category produced in signifiying practices. These practices, whether kinship structures, or the processes of signification in the unconscious, or the signifying systems of public and published forms of representation, do not produce a unified identity equivalent to biological women. . . . The power of images is not that they 'dupe' us, but that they are encountered at both a cognitive level as significa-tions and at the level of identification in all its complex forms" (1997, 20–26).

10. Gayle Rubin says: "If it is women who are being transacted, then it is the men who give and take them who are linked, the woman being a conduit of a relationship rather than a partner to it. . . . If women are the gifts, then it is men who are the exchange partners. And it is the partners, not the presents upon whom reciprocal exchange confers its quasi-mystical power of social linkage. The relations of such a system are such that women are in no position to realize the benefits of their own circulation. As long as the relations specify that men exchange women, it is men who are the beneficiaries of the product of such exchanges—social organization" (1975, 174).

11. Castoriadis 1987, 136.

12. Rose does, however, address this issue in her discussion of Metz (1986, 200–13).

13. For Rose a crucial shift takes place in Lacan's conception of language, such that language is no longer thought as mediation, but in terms of "its fundamental division" (1986, 69), a division which is however "persistently disavowed" (70). The mechanism of disavowal is the "sexual relation" itself, which sets up a "unity" that disavows unconscious division in favor of "oneness" and "completion" (70). The persistent disavowal that Rose invokes already operates within language, and as such it assumes the moment of symbolization, or mediation. Woman, as the site of loss, remains the absence that stabilizes language as a system, represented within the system as division, splitting, or the unconscious. One could make the same point about Lacan's view of language as division that Rose herself makes in relation to Kristeva, when she says, "even the one who plays with language through writing has of course come through to the other side: 'The writer: a phobic who succeeds at metaphor so as not to die of fear but to resuscitate through signs'" (162). Rose is quoting Kristeva (1982, 38) in a modified translation. It is striking that Rose employs the language of disavowal, thereby implicitly invoking a discourse of fetishism, in accounting for the role that woman plays in Lacan's later texts: "As the place onto which lack is projected, and through which it is simultaneously disavowed, woman is a 'symptom' for the man" (1986, 72). This raises the question of how far Lacan has in fact moved away from the naturalizing imaginary that posits women's value as both somehow outside discourse, and as guaranteeing a phallic fantasy of completion, albeit false. Women's use value as reproductive vessels remains determinative of their status as objects of exchange in a way that is not theorized by the system of signs that they legitimate. To emphasize that the status of the father is "normative," rather than given, in Lacan's psychoanalysis (63) does nothing to address the fact that women continue to play the role of a constitutive outside. To do this the series of questions Rose poses to Metz and Comolli, prompted by the question of disavowal, would have to be followed through (211). One would have to address in detail Rose's reading of narcissism (174–79) and identification (180–84) to show what I suspect to be a problematic appeal to a fetishistic splitting of the ego (see 194) that remains dependent on castration theory, confirming Freud and Lacan's relegation of women to the constitutive outside, as enabling of discourse, yet excluded from its creativity.

14. Rather than questioning the conceptual foundations of fetishism as such, the move that is often made is to accept the logic of fetishism and expand its reference. See for example, McClintock's argument, "that female fetishism dislodges the centrality of the phallus and parades the presence and legitimacy of a multiplicity of pleasures, needs and contradictions that cannot be reduced to the 'desire to preserve the phallus'" (1995, 183). McClintock is quoting Lacan, *Feminine Sexuality* (1983, 96). See also most of the essays in Apter and Pietz 1993. For a notable exception see the essay by Charles Bernheimer in the same volume, "Fetishism and Decadence: Salome's Severed Heads" (62–83).

15. See Freud, "Three Essays on the Theory of Sexuality" (1953r, 195).

16. Ibid.

17. See Freud, "Jokes and their Relation to the Unconscious" (1953l, 72 and 254).

18. For Adorno and Horkheimer, if "Bourgeois society is ruled by equivalence," if it "makes the dissimilar comparable by reducing it to abstract quantities," enlightenment thinking imposes its own peculiar form of uniformity. "Abstraction, the tool of enlightenment, treats its objects as did fate, the notion of

which it rejects: it liquidates them. . . . Before, the fetishes were subject to the law of equivalence. Now equivalence itself has become a fetish" (1979, 7, 13, and 17).

19. My point here, of course, is not to single out Adorno—or Freud, for that matter. Many philosophers suffer from, to adopt Irigaray's term, "blindspots." Yet some manage to overcome these earlier than others. I think we continue patterns of injustice if we agree to merely read over them.

20. I use the term resignification in deference to Klein's understanding of the preverbal symbolism she identifies in fantasy—what she calls "primary symbolism."

21. As Caroline Williams points out, Lacan's notion of the real remains resistant to signification. It is "an absolute which resists recuperation on all fronts" (1994, 177). Žižek also points out that "we must not obliterate the distance separating the Real from its symbolization: it is this surplus of the Real over every symbolization that functions as the object-cause of desire. To come to terms with this surplus (or, more precisely, leftover) means to acknowledge integration-dissolution" (1992, 3). I am suggesting that this movement of "integration-dissolution" be thought as circulating, for example, from the feminine to the racialized other. At stake is the way in which the real as unsymbolizable anchors the system of signification from which it is excluded. The impossibility of signifying the real is bound up with the forms of authority that the real, as excluded, legitimates precisely by its exclusion. To contest the authority of the symbolic is also to contest the impossibility of signifying the real in its terms.

22. See Kristeva 1982.

23. See Kristeva 1987.

24. See Catherine Clément and Kristeva 2001, 59. Kristeva says, "Without that pulsating, active, phallic share of maternal love, where would the call of language come from, the thrill of breaking free, that erection (yes, I say the word and insist upon it), which allow the mother and baby to stand up, to move beyond each other toward third parties?

In short, the woman and the Phallus: here we are again, with the scandal our feminist friends have condemned so, leaving old Freud behind!" (2001, 57–58).

25. A tension in Kristeva's view emerges here. "'Nothing is more sacred, for a woman, than the life of her child.' . . . If all love of the other is rooted in that archaic and fundamental, unique and universal, experience of maternal love, if maternal love is the least ambivalent kind then, the *caritas* of Christians and the human rights of secular people . . . are built on maternal love (Kristeva and Clément, 2001, 57). At the same time Kristeva says that she only can "only half-believe" the "serenity of the mother-baby" relation, a serenity she relates to Winnicott and Heidegger. She goes on, "the mother is never short on the tendency to annex the cherished other, to project herself onto it, to monopolize it, to dominate it, to suffocate it" (57). Again, "The desire to devour and murder remain, however, underlying every baby and every mother in their coexcitation, even if it is serene. . . . But, via a strong cathexis of the breast . . . the aggressiveness inherent in that archaic link is obliterated, and we are saturated solely with the being of serenity" (77). Clément responds, "There is an omnipotence of maternal attachment, I grant you, but, infanticide exists" (83). See also 16.

26. See Clément and Kristeva 2001, 95. This aspect of Kristeva's account of abjection is emphasized in her earlier work.

27. Here Kristeva is following Douglas, but compare her earlier remark (1995b).

28. See Kristeva 2000. See also Freud 1953s.

29. Marx 1977, 165.

30. See Freud 1953t.

31. See Freud 1953f.

32. The fetish can either be "some part of the body (such as the foot or hair) . . . or some inanimate object which bears an assignable relation to the person whom it replaces and preferably to that person's sexuality (e.g. a piece of clothing underlinen)" (1953r, 153). (In a passage to which I will return Freud adds, "Such substitutes are with some justice likened to the fetishes in which savages believe that their gods are embodied" ([1953r, 153.]) Freud adds that in other cases "the sexual object is required to fulfil a fetishistic condition—such as the possession of some particular hair-colouring or clothing, or even some bodily defect—if the sexual aim is to be attained" (1953r, 153). What determines the "choice of a fetish" Freud goes on is "an after-effect of some sexual impression, received as a rule in early childhood (this may be brought into line with the proverbial durability of first loves: *on revient toujours à ses premiers amours*" (1953r, 154). In a footnote added in 1920, Freud writes that "behind the first recollection of the fetish's appearance there lies a submerged and forgotten phase of sexual development. The fetish, like a 'screen-memory', represents this phase and is thus a remnant and precipitate of it" (1953r, 154, n. 2). Alternatively, Freud suggests, although he will proceed to claim that even this alternative "is not always unrelated to sexual experiences in childhood" (1953r, 155), "the replacement of the object by a fetish is determined by a symbolic connection of thought" (1953r, 155) so that the foot is symbolic of the genitals, while fur is symbolic of pubic hair. In another footnote, added in 1910, Freud adds that "the foot represents a woman's penis, the absence of which is deeply felt" and then extends the note further: "the scopophilic instinct, seeking to reach its object (originally the genitals) from underneath, was brought to a halt in its pathway by prohibition and repression. For that reason it became attached to a fetish in the form of a foot or shoe, the female genitals (in accordance with the expectations of childhood) being imagined as male ones" (1953r, 155, n. 2). See also "Fetishism" (1953f, 155), where Freud summarizes this account.

33. Cf. Freud, "Splitting of the Ego," where the "memory of the perception" of female genitals in the girl is said to be "harmless" except as a "dreaded confirmation" of the threat of castration (1953u, 276).

34. Cf. Freud 1953p, 189–90.

35. See Freud 1953p, 190.

36. Freud goes on to talk about regression to an oral phase, and the fear of "being eaten by his father" (1953u, 278).

37. See Freud, "On the Sexual Theories of Children" (1953t, 216).

38. Freud says, "the normal prototype of fetishes is a man's penis," "Fetishism," (1953f, 157).

39. See Freud, "Fetishism" (1953f, 154).

40. I cannot help but think here of Jody's quip to Fergus in *The Crying Game* that "women are trouble"—a problem Jody circumvents, in accordance to the logic in Freud to which I am pointing—through his relationship with Dil.

41. Freud, "Three Essays" (1953r 154).

42. As Amanda Lipman puts it, "Francis turns his mourning for his dead daughter into a fetishistic, psychosexual relationship through Christina's striptease character" (1995, 45).

43. bell hooks reads the film as putting forward an inclusive agenda (1996a, 27–33). Following this logic it could be added that Egoyan not only presents an inclusive analysis of gender, race, and class, but also a positive representation of disability or differently abled bodies, in the figure of Harold (Victor Garber), who is wheelchair-bound. At the same time, Egoyan could be read as playing with the idea of disability as fetish.

44. hooks, "The Oppositional Gaze: Black Female Spectators" (1996b, 197–213).

45. That Christina knows the window was built for voyeuristic purposes, that she knows its history, does not prevent its voyeuristic use, but neither does it put her in the position of a hapless victim, as might be suggested by Laura Mulvey's celebrated analysis of fetishism and voyeurism, which hooks is by no means the only one to bring into question. See Laura Mulvey (1990). See also Christian Metz (1982).

46. hooks comments on the protective gesture that Lisa makes in holding up her hand to block the camera, a gesture that takes on a peculiar pertinence in relation to the voyeuristic and murderous events thematized in the film (1996a).

47. The role of film as capable of documenting history is one that Egoyan revisits in *Ararat*, a film about the making of a documentary about the Turkish genocide of Armenians (1915–1918). Given the disputed status of the genocide, and the fact that it took place without any video archive, the status of such a documentary as establishing the "reality" of the genocide is of particular interest. Like *Exotica*, *Ararat* is also concerned with the issue of crossing international boundaries. The narrative is structured around the interrogation of Raffi (David Alpay) by customs officer David (Christopher Plummer), who suspects that the film cans Raffi carries contain drugs.

48. This question bears affinity to those Foucault engages when he asks questions of the order: what kind of reality is represented by the seventeenth century's confinement of a diverse and heterogeneous group of people linked together by the ostensible idleness of its members? (1973, 19–20 and 45). Such questions are part of his attempt to characterize the ways in which objects of knowledge come to be constructed by subjects in particular historical eras, whose allegiance to certain imaginary ideals, the contours of which he seeks delineate, contribute to a more general social imaginary specific to the West.

6. Prohibiting Miscegenation and Homosexuality

1. See, for example, Leif Furhammar and Folke Isaksson 1971, 234–35. See also Robert Ray, 1985, 92.

2. Robert Ray's interesting reading of *Casablanca* sees it as resolving a conflict between Victor Laszlo and Rick, and even develops the connection between *Huckleberry Finn* and Rick, but does not go on to comment on the theme of miscegenation that I want to trace. Ray says, "Having transposed American anxiety regarding the intervention decision into Rick's reluctance to help Victor Laszlo, *Casablanca* set itself the task of demonstrating how Rick could act without sacrificing his separateness. The movie's solution involved moving Rick and Laszlo closer together until, if only for a moment, they could act in concert. Thus, the film progressed from one set of attitudes (isolation, independence, autonomy,

self-sufficiency) to another (participation, interdependence, responsibility, collectivity). . . . *Casablanca* not only made Rick a reincarnation of the renegade Huck; it also imitated basic elements of Twain's plot. The opening map sequence of *Casablanca*, with its dark, moving line representing 'a tortuous, roundabout refugee trail,' simulated a river, in the midst of which the city of Casablanca, and Rick's café, lay like a raft. Like Huck, Rick lived on this 'raft' with a black companion (Sam), and this 'river' (like the Mississippi) provided an escape route from oppression. *Casablanca* divided the character of Jim, the runaway slave, into two figures: the black friend, Sam, and the white man, Laszlo, who assumed Jim's problem, the need to escape," (1985, 105–109). Ray's suggestion that Jim's blackness was parceled out between Sam and Laszlo is symptomatic of his failure to push his reading as far as it could go, or his blindness to the racism that, as Gooding-Williams insists (1995), re-inscribes itself in *Casablanca*. Donald Bogle has commented on what he calls *Casablanca*'s "*huckfinn fixation*" (1997, 140).

3. Bush's illegal spying on American citizens is only the most extreme example of the undermining of freedom that followed in the wake of the war against Iraq.

4. Mark Twain, *Adventures of Huckleberry Finn* (New York: Harper and Row, 1959).

5. Robert Gooding-Williams (1995), "Black Cupids, White Desires: Reading the Representation of Racial Difference in *Casablanca* and *Ghost*," in *Philosophy and Film*, ed. and with an introduction by Cynthia A. Freeland and Thomas E. Wartenberg (London: Routledge), 143–60. Gooding-Williams implicitly appeals to the trope of fetishism in his reading of Sam. The essay is reprinted in Gooding-Williams (2006), where he distances himself from the trope of fetishism (having, however, read an earlier version of the argument I make in this chapter).

6. Donald Bogle, *Toms, Coons, Mulattoes, Mammies, and Bucks: An Interpretive History of Blacks in American Films* (New York: Continuum, 1997).

7. Referring to Sam (Dooley Wilson), Thomas Cripps says, "It is clear that he is to be taken for an equal," (1977, 371–72). For Aljean Harmetz, Sam endows the representation of African Americans with "dignity" (1992, 141).

8. See Cripps 1977, 373.

9. As part of a Department of Philosophy Faculty Research Seminar at DePaul University in March 2003, Claire Pirkle commented on my suggestion that Sam can be read as figuring abjection. I am grateful to her for her illuminating response, and for pushing me to clarify my reading, by raising some excellent points that I had not taken on. By stressing his effeminization at the hands of Rick, my suggestion is, as Pirkle points out, that the homoerotic undertones of Sam's relationship with Rick is actually a product of his abjection. His maternal aspect resides in the refuge he provides for Rick, and as Pirkle says, the safe place he represents is well demonstrated by the fact that Rick chooses to hide the letters of transit in the piano. As Pirkle says, Sam "provides Rick with a psychological space to realize his full subjectivity and, simultaneously, for the US/America to redefine its borders outside its history of slavery." As Pirkle also points out, "Sam's maternal role" is highlighted when Ilsa fails to meet him at the station. Sam puts an arm around him, takes care of Rick, and helps him live through the "trauma of rejection." Yet, to quote Pirkle again, "he must eventually detach from Sam" and the "threat to his subjectivity" that Sam poses to

Rick when he tries to persuade him to "drive all night . . . get drunk . . . go fishin' "
is the impetus that Rick needs to finally enable him to "detach from" Sam.

10. It is striking that Ilsa is figured as threatening through her relationship
to Laszlo, since her unavailability to Rick is a function of her marriage to Laszlo.
What matters here is that Ilsa functions as an object of exchange, a commodity,
whose value derives from Laszlo's marital ownership of her. Her desirability is
enhanced by her unattainable status. She is not for sale. At the same time, Rick's
attraction for Ilsa derives from his association with, and ownership of, Sam.

11. Ray quotes all these lines, but does not read into them the possibility of
a homosexual undertone, just as he quotes the line that Gooding-Williams makes
central to his analysis, without drawing from it the meaning Gooding-Williams
draws out of it: "We'll take the car and drive all night. We'll get drunk. We'll go
fishin' and stay away until she's gone." Ray has, however, read Leslie Fiedler's
interpretation of *Huckleberry Finn*, to which he refers, although he invokes Molly
Haskell to distance himself from the interpretation that his own analysis and, in
particular, the relationship he establishes between Huck Finn and *Casablanca*,
would suggest.

12. At the end of the film Renault offers to get tickets for both himself and
Rick to a Free French Garrison, Brazzaville. I am grateful to Darrell Moore for
reminding me of this point. There are other points at which this chapter has
benefited from his response.

13. Critics have noted "*Casablanca*'s extreme cosmopolitanism" (Ray 1985,
27), but in fact the staging of *Casablanca* carefully contains the foreign elements
in the limbo of a place that is neither quite Europe, nor quite Africa, and is certainly not America.

14. One could follow Kristeva who focuses attention on *Oedipus at Colonus*
rather than *Oedipus Rex*. Robin James gives an elegant reading of Oedipus's self-
imposed exile as a spatial exclusion that is also symbolic, a refusal or rejection
that is also a "spacing between proper and improper," an abjection that is also a
founding of society (2005, 256).

15. That psychoanalytic theory, and in particular the privileging of the motif
of fetishism, continues to inform race theory is evident both in film theory, but
also in the wider field of race theory and cultural theory. See, for example,
Homi K. Bhabha (1994 and Henry Krips (1999).

16. Not only do both Taylor and Gooding-Williams employ the notion of
fetishism, but they also appeal to the idea of an Edenic time of innocence or flaw-
lessness. By using abjection as a resource, I suggest that the appeal to a mythical lost past that is cast as innocent can be recast as a struggle for identity that
shows how gender and sexuality are implicated in one another.

17. See Gooding-Williams 1995, 145. Gooding-Williams cites Eve Sedgwick
(1985) as exemplary of the tendency to thematize gender and sexuality, but
not race.

18. As Homi K. Bhabha observes, Fanon "does not simply make the question of ontology inappropriate for black identity, but somehow *impossible* for
the very understanding of humanity in the world of modernity" (2000, 355).

19. Taylor says, "As a probationary branch of the aesthetic, cinema studies
can only be legitimated through the exercise of the fundamental act of the aesthetic: the establishment of its discourse as autonomous. Were the discussion
of the social implications of Griffith's racist movie to intrude to the fullest

impact possible, then the discipline of film studies might lose its status, might enact its own 'undisciplining' " (1996, 16).

20. Tommy Lott questions the tendency to treat "aesthetics and politics" as "inseparable in the critical assessment of a black film's strengths and weaknesses" (1999). Also see Lott 1995, 50–51. Such an argument brings him into critical dialogue with Taylor, whose concern is precisely to establish that the aesthetic canon is infused with a whiteness that it takes pains to disguise. The difference, of course, between Taylor's and Lott's arguments is that while Taylor wants to establish a connection between the genius of Griffith, and his whiteness, Lott wants to develop a notion of black aesthetics. Such an enterprise needs to be developed in a way that does not tie it to the political in a way that would either confine it to a simplistic rejection of a white aesthetic, or bind it according to essentialist notions of a black audience.

21. Scott Renshaw, http://reviews/imdb.com/Reviews/152/15207. Access date November 3, 2006.

22. James Berardinelli, http://movie-reviews.colossus.net/movies/a/americanx.html. Access date November 3, 2006.

23. One could read here a revival of the insistence that the male head of the household be paid a family wage, a practice that not only discriminated against women, by not granting them equal pay for equal work, but also effectively prevented women from seeking work outside the home.

24. It is worth noting in this context an observation by Freud, especially since Kristeva privileges milk as a substance in relation to which one might feel disgust in *Powers of Horror* (although, to my knowledge, Kristeva does not cite this passage by Freud). Freud says, "The same child who once eagerly sucked the milk from his mother's breast is likely a few years later to display a strong dislike to drinking milk, which his upbringing has difficulties in overcoming. This dislike increases to disgust if a skin forms on the milk or the drink containing it. We cannot exclude the possibility, perhaps, that the skin conjures up a memory of the mother's breast, once so ardently desired. Between the two situations, however, there lies the experience of weaning, with its traumatic effects" ("General Theory of the Neuroses," *Introductory Lectures on Psychoanalysis* [1953k 366]).

25. See Guerrero 1997, 103.

26. Roger Ebert, http://www.suntimes.com/ebert/ebert_reviews/1998/10/103004.html. Access date November 3, 2006.

27. Alexander Walker, http://www.thisislondon.co.uk.html/hottx/side_nav.html. Access date April 2006.

28. Kristeva 2000, 171.

29. Richard Wright (1998).

30. Derek says, "We're so hung up on this notion that we have some obligation to help the struggling black man, you know, cut him some slack until he can overcome his historical injustice. It's crap. This stuff you guys are saying just perpetuates it, all this liberal nonsense. Everyone's turning and looking the other way, while our country rots from the inside out. I mean, Christ, Lincoln freed the slaves a hundred and thirty years ago. How long does it take to get your act together?"

31. This is a phrase used by Tom Hayden at a public lecture celebrating the publication of his book, *Irish on the Inside* (New York: Verso, 2003), held at DePaul University, November 7, 2002.

32. See Judith Butler, "Imitation and Gender Insubordination," in *The Second Wave: A Reader in Feminist Theory*, ed. Linda Nicholson (New York: Routledge, 1997), 300–315, esp. 305.

33. One of the more vociferous proponents of the idea that race is an illusion that we must get rid of in order to combat racism, at least in his early work, is Kwame Anthony Appiah, *In My Father's House: Africa in the Philosophy of Culture* (New York: Oxford University Press), 1992.

34. In one sense, abjection must always be named from within the symbolic, but in another sense, as that which constitutes the separation of the infant from the mother, the abject is the founding moment of the symbolic, at least for the infant. The abject establishes at least one subject in its subjectivity, a subject that sets itself up as a subject in its rejection of the mother. I say at least one subject, both because there is some question as to the mother's subjectivity too, in that Western culture has tended to designate motherhood as the only viable path for women, and because the mother is abjected. For Kristeva, as Oliver and Benigno say, "the mother or the maternal body becomes an object for the infant, it is an abject" (2003, xxxii). Because motherhood consists essentially in putting someone else's needs and desires before one's own, the institution of motherhood tends to undermine women's subjectivity—unless subjectivity is figured as an infinite obligation to the other, as Levinas has suggested.

7. ABJECT IDENTIFICATIONS IN *THE CRYING GAME*

1. As Zilliax says, "This figuration can be seen to describe race as both radically external to the subject—literally a deposit on the skin, rather than the psyche—and, in that way, as analogous to gender: like Dil, Fergus is just 'a bit heavy on the powder'" (1997, 33). In *Secrets and Lies,* Hortense is shown with a face mask when she receives a telephone call from Cynthia, in an image that foreshadows the difficulty her new family will have in getting past the color of her skin, while it also represents a play on the practice of blackface, in a way that is reminiscent of Jordan's image of Fergus's "face mask."

2. Patrick McGee draws on Eve Sedgwick's distinction between homosocial and homosexual desire to suggest that Jody "deconstruct[s] male homosexuality," even as McGee recognizes that "the fact that [Jody] must conceal his sexual identity dramatizes the subordination of homosexuality to the heterosexual norm" (1997, 140). If we read Dil as a woman, and not as the "biological male" so that her anatomy, according to hegemonic conventions, dictates her gender, Jody's relation to her is not homosexual, and Sedgwick's point that "modern homosocial desire is characterized by homophobia" (140) must be developed differently in relation to Jody and Fergus. If it is the "repressed homoeroticism within homosocial desire that compels Fergus to leave Ireland and seek out the object of Jody's desire" (140), it also the case that, according to McGee's own reading, the "sexual Real" in terms of which he reads Dil explodes the binary oppositions "man/woman, heterosexual/homosexual, white/black, British/Irish" (148). Curiously, McGee stabilizes the opposition man/woman by insisting that Jude is the "only *real* woman in the film" (104).

3. I have decided to use the term "transgendered" identity to refer to Dil, an umbrella term that includes both the term "transvestite" and "transsexual."

Jordan refers to Dil as a "transvestite" (Falsetto 2000, 239) and as a "man" (237), and to Jody as "a black solider who is gay" (237). While Dil at no point identifies herself as transsexual, she does refer to herself as a "girl."

4. Just as he could not bring himself to kill Jody, so he cannot reconcile himself to the love he feels for Dil.

5. As Giles points out, "glasshouse" is a slang term for prison (1997, 74, n. 25).

6. See, for example Seamus Heaney's "Act of Union," a poem in which the imagery of England as a masculine, conquering force of a feminine Ireland is quite explicit, as Ireland is represented as a woman's body. "Your back is a firm line of eastern coast / And arms and legs are thrown Beyond your gradual hills. I caress / The heaving province where our past has grown. . . . And I am still imperially / Male, leaving you with the pain/ The rending process in the colony / The battering ram, the boom burst from within" (1990, 87). I want to thank Paul Catterson for bringing this poem to my attention. For further discussion of "the symbolic representation of Ireland as female," see Nash 1994, 229.

7. As Helen Hanson notes, Jordan "shows that an interrogation of gender precipitates a questioning and crisis of other categories. This ultimately leads to an examination of social, racial, national and political identities," so that the "crisis is initially instituted in the realm of gender, but then proves uncontainable and takes in the realms of the sexual, political, social and national" (1999, 53–56).

8. Darrell Moore's fine, multidimensional analysis eschews the oversimplifications that tend to inhibit most approaches to The Crying Game (1993, 63–67).

9. Some theorists maintain that Jude's character is in some respects a more radical site of instability than Dil's. See Lloyd 1999.

10. See also Bruzzi 1997; Handler 1994; Simpson 1994.

11. Frank O'Connor (1979); see esp. 5–19. The reference to Jody as a "guest" in The Crying Game functions as a reference to O'Connor's short story.

12. Brendan Behan (1959). Emer Rockett and Kevin Rockett write that Behan "discards the limited concerns of O'Connor's story with national allegiances in favour of an exploration of male sexuality" (2003, 128) Neil Jordan cites both Behan and O'Connor in his preface to A Neil Jordan Reader (1993, xii).

13. Thus Mark Simpson regards "Northern Ireland" as "merely a plot device" (1994, 166). Sarah Edge insists that "of course, Dil is not a woman—she is a man," thereby repudiating even as she recognizes the challenge Dil issues to essentialist categories of gender (1995, 180). bell hooks, for all the nuances of her reading, asserts that "Dil is really a black man" (1994, 61).

14. Lloyd suggests that "it is Jude rather than Dil who represents the film's locus of maximum instability" (1999, 73). Lloyd's suggestion occurs in the context of a sophisticated discussion of the "aberrational figure" cut by Jude, whose status as a woman terrorist manages to at once upset conventional masculine stereotypes of terrorists as pathological while at the same time confirming the problematic feminization of Ireland in Anglo representations (see 73–74). In its own terms Lloyd's argument is compelling. Of interest is the residual need that apparently drives even interpretations that are sensitive to the way in which conservative sexual politics function in the service of nationalist and antinationalist imaginaries to play off Dil's transgendered identity against the challenge the figure of Jude issues to such conservative narratives. My suggestion is that rather than construing Jude as the more radical site of instability— which suggests that the film is really about the Anglo-Ireland conflict—we

understand the crisis that Fergus sets in motion when he abjects Dil because she overturns his gendered, heterosexual assumptions as a crisis that permeates the symbolic dimensions of gender that allot to women the function of preserving domestic harmony and stability while reserving for men the role of pathological terrorist.

15. Patrick McGee reflects on the ways in which *The Crying Game* operates as a commodity while at the same time, insofar as it encourages self-reflection, undercutting its status as commodity (see 1997, 80–94).

16. Consider for example Dudley Andrew's claim that the penis is the "absolute signifier" of *The Crying Game*, a claim that I would say recuperates the diverse treatment of difference in terms of race, class, and nationalism under the rubric of a phallic reading, reducing the political differences explored by Jordan to the monological phallic signifier in accordance with the tendency that I am trying to uncover in this book, namely the insistent reemergence of the monistic discourse of fetishism. Andrew says, "For difference is scandalously real in this film, the penis—unveiled and completely undisguised—its absolute signifier" (2002, 44).

17. As Frann Michel points out, "To describe Dil as a transvestite, crossdresser, or drag queen is implicitly to describe her as 'really' a man, and thus effectively to preempt the audience's experience of watching and reading a character as a woman, only to have that reading challenged by a piece of information that is not part of our culture's definition of 'woman.' The surprise of the experience is presumably greatest for those who (like Fergus) walk into the film believing that there are always only two genders and that one can always tell them apart. Indeed, this epistemological certainty is recuperated by those viewers who insist that Jaye Davidson is 'really' a woman wearing a prosthetic penis, or by those who insist that they could tell from the beginning (by the hands, or the jaw, or some other purported telltale feature) that Dil was 'really' a man. Either response by viewers asserts that there is a single, clear gender boundary, and that they cannot be deceived about where it lies. By avowing that gender is a stable and legible essence, such viewers disavow the film's demonstration that gender is a performance, and they refuse the conceptual reframings that the film provides" (1994, 32). While I agree with Michel's analysis for the most part, I would stress that gender is performative, rather than a performance—which makes it sound much too voluntaristic, and depart from the judgment she reaches that "the only good woman is a man" (1994, 34). Michel reaches this disappointing conclusion after having effectively pointed out the contrast that *The Crying Game* presents between Jude and Dil. Jude is a "a heartless, selfish, unattractive bitch"—or, as Handler puts it even more directly "Jude doesn't have to have a dick, she *is* a dick" (1994, 36)—who is not interested in "the conventionally feminine concerns of appearance and romance," and who "dresses according to the needs of her politics, devoting herself to the public pursuit of violent nationalism," while Dil is "indifferent to politics . . . wears sequined miniskirts . . . decorates her apartment as a shrine to lost love" and "displays an undemanding goodness compounded of the most painful elements of masochistic femininity" (Michel 1994, 34). The conclusion that the only good woman in the film is a man belies Michel's earlier rejection of those who appeal to gender as if it were a stable essence, with a reliable and causal bodily referent.

With surprising regularity, even those critics of *The Crying Game*, who, like Michel, exhibit for the most part a sophisticated approach to the gender issues

dealt with throughout the film, lapse into the predictable and ultimately conservative conclusion that after all, Jude is the only real woman. See, for example, Kristin Handler, who, while providing a nuanced critique of the politics of
homosexuality engaged by Jordan, undercuts this critique by insisting that
"the sole woman, Jude, is as her name suggests a Judas figure, and winds up a
dead *femme fatale*. . . . It's not accidental that the sole woman in the film becomes
the representative scorpion and that the untroublesome kind of woman turns
out not to be one after all" (1994, 35–37). See also Patrick McGee, whose very
interesting reading of *The Crying Game* intersects in some ways with my own.
He reads Dil's sexuality in terms of the Lacanian notion of the "Real" (1997, 114),
or as "the Thing itself, das Ding" (139), that is, in terms of "the excess or remainder of signification that marks each subject with a radical difference that cannot
be entered into the account of an absolute identity" (144), but who nonetheless
invokes a problematic metaphysics of gender in seeing Jude as the "only *real*
woman in the film" (1997, 104). This gesture implicitly reverts to appealing to
Dil's male body as the transcendental ground that prevents her from being identified as a real woman, thereby abjecting her transgender identity in order to
preserve a stable conventional ground of sexual identity from which to launch a
critique of the film's homo-social politics. See also James, whose parallel of *The
Crying Game* with *Mona Lisa* reduces the radical edge of Dil's transgender status,
and who says, quoting Michel, "*The Crying Game*'s misogyny demonizes the only
biological female in a movie where the 'good woman is a man' and the 'really
gay man is a woman'" (1995, 38–39). Boozer Jr., while acknowledging at one
moment Dil as a "male transsexual" then goes on to assert that "Jody and Dil
are both black and gay" (1995, 175), a comment that elides Dil's identification
as a woman—if we read Dil as a woman then she is not gay—at the same time
as occluding as significant Dil's comparatively light skin in relation to Jody.
Examples of readers who have seen fit to describe Dil as a "transvestite" include
Hennessy (2000, 154). I am grateful to Mary Bloodsworth-Lugo for providing
me with this reference.

18. Edge 1995; hooks 1994.

19. In contrast, see bell hooks's excellent discussion of *Exotica* (1996).

20. Edge echoes hooks when she says, "But, of course, Dil is not a woman—
she is a man" (180). Both hooks and Edge thereby discount Dil's transgender
identity. Other critics echo this sentiment, for example, Patrick McGee, who says
"Jude is the only *real* woman in the film" (1997, 104).

21. It is worth noting that the more recent and much acclaimed (at least in
the United States) film *Boys Don't Cry* was based on a true event, but entirely
neglected the fact that at the same time that Teena Brandon was murdered for her
transgendered sexuality, a black disabled man was also murdered. The director
decided to focus on the murder of Teena Brandon and did not want to distract
from this focus. By contrast, *The Crying Game* succeeds in questioning identity in a
number of interrelated ways, even if its critical reception often proceeds by abjecting one form of identity in order to highlight the marginalization of another.

22. Lugowski 1994, 35.

23. Eagleton says, for example, "Sexual politics, like class or nationalist
struggle, will . . . necessarily be caught up in the very metaphysical categories it
hopes finally to abolish; and any such movement will demand a difficult, perhaps ultimately impossible double optic, at once fighting on a terrain already
mapped out by its antagonists and seeking even now to prefigure within that

mundane strategy styles of being and identity for which we have as yet no proper names" (1990b, 24).

24. Eagleton says, "Subjects, national or otherwise, do indeed experience needs that are repressed but demand realization; it is just that one ironic effect of such repression is to render us radically uncertain of what our needs really are. The very repressive conditions that make it necessary for the subject to express itself freely also tend to render it partially opaque to itself" (1990b, 29). One need that subjects have is "to know what one's needs are" but "The metaphysics of nationalism tend to obscure this point, by assuming a subject somehow intuitively present to itself; in privileging the concept of self-realization, it elevates a subject-object relation over a subject-subject one, forgetting that the expression and formulation of needs are always in some sense received back from an 'other.' . . . A radical politics can prescribe what must be done for this to occur; but it cannot prescribe the content of what will then be lived" (29). In Ireland, the poetic is "still being counterposed to the political" and is thus "historically constructed to carry out just that business of suppressing political conflict. . . . The political left is . . . doubly disabled: if it seeks to evolve its own discourse of place, body, inheritance, sensuous need, it will find itself miming the cultural forms of its opponents, if it does not do so it will appear bereft of a body, marooned with a purely rationalist politics that has cut loose from the intimate affective depths of the poetic. The feminist analogy is exact: if women speak the discourse of the body, the unconscious, the dark underside of formal speech . . . they merely confirm their aberrant status; if they appropriate . . . the language of radial rationalism, they are no different from men." The choice is cast as one between Habermasian universal rationalism and poststructuralist anarchism (see 33–34). "The paradox or aporia of any transformative politics is that it demands, to be successful, a 'centered,' resolute, self-confident agent, but would not be necessary in the first place if such self-confidence were genuinely possible" (37).

25. See Lloyd 1999, 73.

26. Lloyd says "In the relatively long history of the current Irish Troubles (1969–1995), the IRA has not resorted to taking hostages, an act which precipitates the narrative of *The Crying Game*. . . . But supposing a hostage were to be taken, the likelihood of the IRA's choosing to kidnap a *black* British soldier is infinitesimal. As Jody himself intimates, the presence of black people is sufficiently uncommon in Ireland that nothing would be more likely to attract attention at a small rural fairground than an Irish lass in the company of an Afro-Caribbean man" (1999, 64).

27. Lloyd points to the "exceptionally violent assault" by the British army on the IRA safe house as flying in the face of the "Low Intensity Operations" that have in fact characterized British military strategies in an effort to avoid "scandalizing domestic public opinion by conducting . . . high-powered raids and thereby highlighting the violence of the state" (1999, 64–65). Lloyd also points out the improbability of Fergus "finding work in the building trade without the company of other 'Paddies'" (65). These improbabilities are, Lloyd argues, "organized around certain ideological givens: that terrorists and the Irish are by *nature* fanatical, pathological, atavistic and, by virtue of these characteristics, lack full humanity. . . . Insurgency is severed from any articulate, however contestable, programme for social transformation, and, above all, from any relation to subordinated communities" (67). Lloyd reads this in terms of *The Crying Game*'s correspondence to "the strategies of the British and Irish states in those

military and censorship policies that have attempted to cut off the insurgents from any base in the community, to transform political violence into 'mere' crime by the policy of criminalization, to restrict Sinn Féin and the IRA's capacity to articulate their rationales and policies by strict media censorship, and thereby to depict the armed struggle as the 'irrational' and 'mindless' malevolence of 'men of violence' " (67). *The Crying Game,* Lloyd suggests, pathologizes terrorism as violent, wild, and irrational, and individualistic as it participates in and colludes with an "unstated erasure of any communities, whether the army, the Catholic 'ghetto,' or the émigré community in London" (68).Yet, crucially, he also acknowledges that "*The Crying Game,* in keeping with its mobilization of the figure of drag and, indeed, of performance at every other level, at once displaces and reinscribes the borders of ideological and generic modes of representation, but does so in ways that produce an excess of possible signification that the film can neither control nor elaborate" (68).

28. After quoting an observation by John Hill, who, characterizing essentialist readings of insurgent communities, says, "It is only metaphysics or race, not history and politics, which offer an explanation of Irish violence" (Hill 1988), Lloyd goes on to say "But the distinction between a racial and a metaphysical explanation is hard to sustain once it is recognized that a metaphysics which speaks in the name of an essential human subject underwrites the racializing process which speaks to the 'in-adequacy' of certain groups or cultures in relation to the end embodied in the human archetype" (1999, 66).

29. When Fergus fails to appear for the suicidal mission of killing "some judge" Peter does not question Jude, when she tells him to "drive around again."

30. Jordan's portrayal of Jude as a femme fatale *extraordinaire* is surely tongue is cheek. As Handler points out, "Jude has acquired an inhumanly lacquered glamour. The visual tropes of film noir so thoroughly permeate the scene in which she materializes in Fergus's apartment that I assume Jordan is playing her transformation partly as a joke" (1994, 38).

31. While the clothes that Jude wore to entice Jody into a hostage situation are readily forgettable details for Fergus, the fact that Dil is not, anatomically, the "girl" that Fergus took her for is dismissed as "Details, details" by Dil.

32. Mary Bloodsworth-Lugo's response to this chapter helped to underline the importance of this point.

33. Lloyd says, "Jude performs in succession a working-class and somewhat slatternly Irish lass, Fergus's movement girlfriend in an ethnically marked aran sweater, a hardened and heartless terrorist, an executive off the pages of *Vogue,* the jealous and jilted lover and, again, the hardened terrorist" (1999, 71). Handler says, "When the film begins, Jude looks like a woman trying to look girlishly 'sexy': to pick up Jody, she wears, somewhat awkwardly, a tarty, lower-class version of the uniform of conventional femininity—short skirt, high heels, make-up, jewelry, coifed hair. Her appearance after Jody's capture reveals this outfit to be a costume. For the remainder of the 'Irish' part of the film she is conspicuously and emphatically deglamorized: the unkempt hair, shapeless clothing, flat boots, no make-up, no jewelry, no nonsense. This look isn't any more 'natural' than the first, but it appears to be so because Jude is no longer wearing her gender as a sexual lure. Far from being the phallic female terrorist she is in London, here she seems subordinate to the men" (1994, 37). Giles points out that in London Jude has "transformed herself into a sleek urban *femme fatale*" and

that she "dresses for the assassination in front of a three-piece mirror, recalling *The Lady from Shanghai* (Orson Welles, 1948)" (1997, 61–62). Also see Edge 1995 and Bruzzi 1997.

34. My point here is not that Lloyd ignores the difference between Dil's transgression of gender and Jude's upsetting of conventional femininity because he simply does not see it. Rather, by privileging the way in which the film over-turns stereotypes of terrorists over the way in which it overturns gender stereotypes—a privilege, Lloyd deprives himself of the conceptual vocabulary with which to acknowledge both that Jude adheres to traditional conventions of femininity, even as she upsets them at another level. If the myths of nation-alist identity that the film both trades in and questions are seen as operating as metaphorically mirroring those of gender identity, *and vice versa,* it seems to me that such privileging becomes superfluous.

35. Hanson suggests, and I concur, that "Dil might be passing to the audience through passing to Fergus" (1999, 50). Although Hanson adheres to the discourse of fetishism from which I want to distance myself, her very interesting reading of the film helped me formulate my own reading, in which I think Dil func-tions not "as a symbol of what the child originally hoped to see—the 'woman' in possession of the maternal phallus" (Hanson 1999, 60), but rather underwrites the mythic impossibility of such a figure.

36. Dil becomes a killer only when she is dressed in Jody's male clothes, and after Fergus has cut her hair. Boozer Jr. observes that "While Fergus's dramatic shearing of Dil's hair is a literal effort to disguise and protect her, it is also a metaphorical awakening of her assertive capabilities" (1995, 174.) The fact that Dil murders Jude at the one point in the film that she is dressed not only as a man but in Jody's cricket whites complicates the relationship between her mur-derous aspect and her femininity. Dressed as Jody—in the garb of his favorite sport—Dil takes revenge on Jude for Jody's death who is the film's most stal-wart symbol of the IRA. That she does so dressed in Jody's cricket whites solidi-fies her connection to Fergus, with whom Jody had exchanged pleasantries about Jody's love of cricket and Fergus's fondness for hurling. Their respective sports, which also underline Fergus's antipathy to England, and England's colo-nial relationship to West Indian Antigua, not only proffer a language of accept-able male bonding, but also provide the terms of the final exchange between Fergus and Jody. When Jody runs from Fergus, and Fergus lets him go, Jody refers back to their conversation about sport in order to consolidate their friendly bond, in order to prevent Fergus from forgetting their intimacy.

37. Althusser 1971, 182.

38. In this paragraph I draw on points suggested to me in conversation with Darrell Moore and in an exchange with Mary Bloodsworth-Lugo.

39. Dil has unwittingly prevented Fergus from killing the judge who Peter kills in his stead. In this sense, Dil saves Fergus from a murder that he would have performed, in part to keep Dil safe from the IRA, and which would have led to his certain death.

40. James says "*Mona Lisa* and *The Crying Game* embody the 'deviancy' of the black, the female, the prostitute, and the lesbian/transgender through the fetishization of black female sexuality. . . . The sexual gaze of Jordan's camera fetishizes the black character's body as 'female,' establishing the black woman's femininity as the sexual antithesis of the white hero" (1995, 36–38).

41. James says "That white male cinematographers would elevate black 'females' as the ideal subject-objects of their sexual interests seems, at first glance, another challenge to racism," yet as she goes on to observe, "Jordan reserves the most brutal behavior for his black women . . . . Only black female characters actually fire guns—that they obtained from the white heroes—to slaughter (bad) people" (1995, 39). James goes on to suggest that Jordan's black femme fatales "are packaged and sold as the objects of white/male fantasy in voyeuristic violence" (44–45).

42. See, e.g., DuttaAhmed, who says, "as the film progresses it becomes clear that the politics of the IRA is not invoked as a matter for serious examination but rather for narrative juxtaposition: as Fergus flees Ireland and goes into hiding in London the film shifts its already marginal concern with the political to the domestic sphere" (1998, 61–73). This assumes that what is narratively juxtaposed cannot be intended seriously, and that what happens in the domestic sphere is apolitical. Kristin Handler also suggests that *The Crying Game* "dodges the political issues it raises in its rush to issues of sex and gender" and "puts Jody's parable in the place of a substantive treatment of the armed conflict in Northern Ireland" (1994, 41). In a reference to Pat O'Connor's 1984 film—in which a member of the IRA falls in love with the widow he helped murder—Jane Giles says that "Jordan felt liberated by the fact that the film of *Cal* has prioritised politics and realism rather than the personal odyssey of its protagonist" (1997, 25). Yet to see the first part of *The Crying Game* as political and the second part as personal is, in my view, to underestimate the complexity of both. In an interview Neil Jordan says of *The Crying Game*, "The first part seems to be about politics, and the second part seems to be about something else, but, if anybody thinks politics in not about something else, they're insane. The second part is a mirror of the first part, and everything that happens in the first part happens again in the second part, but in a different way" (Falsetto 2000, 239).

43. Handler says, e.g., "The film could . . . be said to substitute 'libidinal politics' for racial and national politics" (1994, 32). Merely to celebrate the film for its elevation of the personal over the political, as Jack Boozer (1995) does, partly in response to Handler, is no more satisfactory. The strengths of the film can be found, rather, in the extent to which it shows how the personal is constructed through the political, and vice versa. When Fergus discovers that Dil has a penis he is challenged by his personal belief about his own sexual identity, but that identity is constructed in relation to signifiers that are always already political. The idea that a man should love a woman, and that only men should have penises, are beliefs that emanate from ideologically privileged positions.

44. From the opening lines of the film, when Jody metaphorically employs the term to designate his success at winning the teddy bear at the fairground, the upper-class connotations with which cricket is traditionally associated are aired. When Jody runs from Fergus he refers back to their earlier conversation about cricket and hurling, in an effort to establish who can run faster.

45. hooks reads Jody as "childlike, innocent, a neoprimitive" (1994, 59). One could add that he also occupies a spiritual, mystical mastery over both Fergus and Dil. His image intervenes in moments of sexual intimacy between Dil and Fergus, and his memory is enough to prevent Dil from shooting Fergus. When she tries to, she finds she can't. "He won't let me," says Dil to Fergus, indicating Jody's picture.

46. As part of a series of parallels and echoes that the film exploits, and as several critics comment upon, the scene in which Fergus must hold Jody's penis while he urinates because his hands are tied echoes that in which Jude holds Jody's hand while he urinates, because Jody does not want her to run off.

47. Other critics have commented on the homoerotic bond that springs up between Fergus and Jody, and the way in which it anticipates the bond that will be forged between Fergus and Dil, who becomes a substitute for Jody. See Bruzzi 1997, 191 and Simpson 1994. I would add that the fact that Dil is of mixed race is crucial to Fergus's identification of Jody and Dil, and that it echoes her gender ambiguity. Fergus cannot confront his homoerotic attraction to Jody, whose masculinity gets in the way, but Dil's overt femininity offers Fergus an appearance that conforms to the conventional fabric of heterosexuality with which he feels at home. The fact that Dil and Jody are both racially coded "others" creates a bond not only between them, but also a triangular bond between Dil, Jody, and Fergus, who transfers his unexpressed affections toward, and guilt over, Jody, onto Dil. According to Frann Michel, "Certainly the relation between the two men is eroticized: Jody persuades Fergus to remove his blindfold by insisting he has already seen Fergus's face; 'You're the handsome one,' Jody tells him. Jody also persuades Fergus to help him urinate, and smiles at Fergus's embarrassment at handling the prisoner's penis. The conceptual reframing effected by the frontal view of Dil's genitals seems to narrow the interpretive boundaries available to some critics, who read the kinship between Jody and Fergus solely as indicative of their sexual affinity. The film, in the final analysis, is not merely preoccupied with erotic quandaries, but demonstrates the way in which sexual politics reflect broader political concerns" (Michel, 1994, 34).

48. As Bruzzi points out, this scene is recalled when Fergus cuts Dil's hair later in the film (1997, 191), a scene, however in which he wants to disguise her in order to protect her from the IRA, and not only to change her appearance in an attempt to redirect his desire.

49. Scottish and Northern Irish accents can be similar, but Dil's elision of Scotland and Ireland also signifies the parochialism of Londoners. As far as the average, working-class English person on the street is concerned, the film seems to be saying, there is not much difference between Scotland, Ireland, or any other of those peripheral outlying territories—part of the amorphous, one "great," colonial United Kingdom. Dil thinks Fergus is American before she settles on Scottish, and then with a Welsh twang, tells him his accent is "like treacle." One could also see Dil's mistake as representative of a depoliticized, somewhat self-absorbed member of the working class.

50. As Bruzzi says, "Dil is consistently presented against a backdrop of shifting identities. . . . Fergus, in hiding after the botched kidnap of Jody, goes by the name of Jimmy when in London; Jude, the female IRA member, changes disguise or look three times; Jody (the soldier who is kidnapped and dies) confides to Fergus about Dil, but never reveals she is a transvestite" (1997, 187).

51. Bruzzi also notices "the detached, choric figure of Carl [*sic*] the barman who performs the role of interpretative go-between. On a superficial level this extremely self-conscious exchange is an exclusory game at Fergus's expense, as Dil and Carl absent Fergus (whilst simultaneously engaging him) by referring to him in the third person as if he is not there ('D'you see that Carl? He gave me a look'; 'That was a look'). The conversation also, however functions as a metaphor for Dil: the insistence on performative naming procedures (the

substitution by Carl of the indirect 'she' and 'he' for any direct forms of address) paralleling the citationality of Dil's androgyny" (1997, 187–89).

52. Kate Robbins sings the version of "The Crying Game" that Dil lip-synchs. The song, for which the film (having had the original title "The Soldier's Wife") was eventually named, is played twice more, sung once by Dave Berry, and at the end of the film by Boy George.

53. Toward the beginning of the film Jody says to Jude that "Jody's never offended" while Dil says to Fergus "You're not having me on, are you? 'Cause Dil can't stand that. . . . And she does get very upset." Even when Dil, who is just as capable of hiding the truth from herself as anyone else, admits that she might have been to blame for the fact that Fergus did not know she was passing as a woman, she distances herself from this responsibility, by again referring to herself indirectly, when she says that "it was basically the fault of yours truly."

54. It is worth noting that Mr. Deveroux adopts a similar conversation pattern with his foreman, repeating to him what he knows he heard when he says that Fergus wants to know if he means it when he tells Fergus that the cost of the window pane will be deducted from his wages.

55. Zilliax suggests that Dil must be seen to be understood (1997).

56. The threat of castration, of course, plays a key role in Mulvey's analysis (1990). See Hanson's discussion of Mulvey (1999, 57).

57. As Helen Hanson says, "*The Crying Game* suggests that the presence of the penis has the potential to institute crisis rather than to stand for the socio-symbolic order. . . . Dil retains her/his sexual and gender ambiguity and it is the phallus as a signifying figure that is called into question" (1999 64). Rather than reading this in terms of fetishism, as Hanson does—even as she suggests that the film "complicates rather than explicates the fantasy of disavowal" (60)—I suggest that abjection provides a way of following through the complication to which Hanson points.

58. Thus, while I agree with Hanson that "*The Crying Game* suggests that the *presence* of the penis has the potential to institute crisis rather than to stand for the socio-symbolic order" and that the "phallus as signifying figure that is called into question" (1999, 64), I do not think the disruption of the function of the phallus effected by the film can be contained by the trope of fetishism in terms of which she reads the film. Although Hanson acknowledges that the "sight of Dil's penis . . . complicates rather than explicates the fantasy of disavowal" (60) she does not follow through the implications of this claim. She suggests that "Dil could be seen as a symbol of what the child originally hoped to see—the 'woman' in possession of the maternal phallus; the penis is there 'after all' and has been all along" (60). In my view, on the contrary, what Dil suggests is the impossibility of embodying the maternal phallus within the Freudian theory of fetishism.

59. Of course, for Freud, female genitals provoke horror too. I have suggested that this must be understood in terms of the failure of the masculine imaginary to come to terms with the fact that women are not men.

60. In his interesting and exhaustive reading of *The Crying Game*, McGee suggests that "it is not gender as a social construction that constitutes Jody's other but the Real of sexual difference" (1997, 114). My reading of Dil as abject, rather than in terms of the Lacanian Real, attempts both to question the imaginary commitments informing the logic of disavowal (a trope to which McGee appeals throughout his discussion), and to read Dil as a figure of abjection in the sense that she occupies an abject position in relation to Lacanian theory. The Lacanian registers

of the symbolic, imaginary, and real operate in the shadow of Freud's oedipal triangle, taking for granted that the symbolic law is the law of the father, and the forbidden desire for the mother (or her substitutes) is a desire for the phallic mother. As I am using it here, the abject occupies a position that is in some ways similar to Lacan's real, as excluded, or foreclosed, but in other ways the abject calls into question the imaginary that informs Freudian and Lacanian psychoanalysis. (See Penley, quoting Clément, 1989, 187, n. 7.) In this sense, abjection functions as a term that is productive of a new imaginary, one that is elaborated in order to avoid a repetition of the assumptions that demand of certain figures that they play the role of what Butler calls "structuring absences" (103, 1993) of the binary, masculinized, heteronormative imaginary. At the same time, I distance myself from the language of disavowal and fetishism, which Butler continues to use even when discussing Brandon Teena (2004, 142–43). By pointing out the cultural baggage of this imaginary, and suggesting that the usefulness of abjection resides partly in its naming a process of separation that cannot be unproblematically recuperated by the language of castration, except in theories that continue to privilege the masculine imaginary of psychoanalysis, my aim is not of course to outlaw the term "disavowal," but rather to increase awareness of its imaginary commitments.

61. Dil's bloodied lips call up the earlier image of Jody's bloodied lips, after Jude has hit him with a gun, continuing the chain of reversals and echoes around which the film is meticulously structured.

62. Robin James makes a similar point in a different context in her dissertation (2005).

63. For an interesting reading of the film that organizes itself around this motif see Zilliax 1997.

64. In an interview Stephen Rea responds to Luke Gibbons's question "Can you talk about the role of the black British soldier in *The Crying Game*?" in the following way: "Neil wanted something ambiguous about the hostage. He wanted him black because it would make him part of another minority, part of an oppressed minority. He did not want him to be a straightforward Brit. It made it more confusing for the IRA man to feel that he was brutalizing someone like that: it wasn't quite as straightforward as it might have been. So he was much more open to be seduced by the soldier, which is what happened. The soldier seduced Fergus into not killing him. That's how he keeps himself alive. That was a potent force in the film" (Gibbons and Whelan 2002, 14).

65. Rockett and Rockett point out that Orson Welles first used the fable of the Scorpion and the Frog in *Mr. Arkadin* (2003, 135). Lloyd points out that Dil follows up Fergus's quotation from Corinthians 1:13, when she says, "No greater love, as the man said" (71). It is also worth noting that in the next chapter of the same book, we read, "Brethren, do not be children in your thinking; be babes in evil, but in thinking be mature." That in his maturity Fergus ends the film by quoting Jody's fable confirms that the moral authority of the film belongs to Jody, who uses the fable to disrupt the idea of "natural" morality. While some critics have traced the fable back to Aesop, there is little similarity between Aesop's fable and Jody's.

66. For some highly suggestive connections between Sophocles' Oedipus cycle and Jordan's *The Crying Game* see Lloyd 1999, 63–76.

67. Simpson suggests that the hood that "is placed over his head" is symbolic of Jody's "impotence," reminding us that "loss of sight symbolizes castration: Oedipus is blinded after he sleeps with his mother" (1994, 166). Zilliax sees the black hood as figuring Jody's race (1997, 33). That Jody had told Fergus the fable

while his face was covered with a black mask might also mark the continuity between Jody and Tiresias, the blind soothsayer of Greek tragedy, who divined the future. Molly Nesbit says, "Politics sets up the violent destruction of the face, here the soldier's face hooded in a black sack through which he speaks, smokes, sobs, bleeds. And still, through all this, a man makes a friend of his enemy. Nothing rational can bound this face. From its bloodied and fabric blackness come sweet and devilish prodding, a parable about a scorpion and a frog, and an escape. For the soldier does escape his captor's narratives. Then by the hand of fate he dies" (1993, 94). I read the film more politically than does Nesbit, and so resist the idea that Jody dies at the hand of "fate." The political irony—which in my view underscores the extent to which the IRA's violent methods mimic those of British imperialism in terms of which the myth of nationalism was constructed—is that it is the British army who kills the hostage they are presumably on their way to save. In other words, politics is the death of Jody, even as his spirit refuses to die, and the film refuses to let him die.

68. The parallels critics have drawn between the role Cathy Tyson plays as Simone in Jordan's *Mona Lisa,* and the role Jaye Davidson plays in "The Crying Game," are instructive here. See in particular hooks (1994), James (1995), and Moore (1993).

69. Jude's racist epithet is elicited when Jody lunges at her, but he does so from a position of powerlessness, bound up and imprisoned, and only after the provocation of Jude's taunting. Jude's response is to brush herself down, as if cleansing herself of the animal contamination that Jody's blackness represents. That Jude has duplicitously used her feminine sexuality to render Jody vulnerable to capture puts on the agenda from the outset of the film one of the themes the film will interrogate, namely, the way in which masculinity is typically bound up with the reduction of women to sexual objects. As Dil puts it before she kills Jude, "You used those tits and that ass to get him, didn't you?" At the same time, the sexual encounter between Jude and Jody foregrounds the issue of race-mixing, thus introducing another structuring theme of the film. As Lugowski says, "it is Jody's willingness to break . . . racial boundar[ies] which enables his kidnapping" (1994, 35). Again, as Lugowski points out, the names of both Jude and Peter carry a religious resonance that will not be lost on a Christian audience, and which signal their characters (31). Jude's loyalty to the IRA is coupled with her deception first of Jody, then of Fergus—with whom she bestows the kiss of Judas, before warning him, in a gesture that draws on Christian authority to underwrite that of the IRA, to "keep the faith." When Fergus fails to show up to assassinate a British judge as he leaves a prostitute, Peter proves himself willing to die for the cause, as he substitutes for Fergus, at the cost of his life. The compromising circumstances in which the judge is killed not only provide a commentary on the ideology of the Catholic church that informs the position of the IRA—the judge is a sinner and deserves to die—but also constitute one of the echoes of *The Hostage,* which takes place in a brothel, that we find reverberating in Jordan's film (Behan 1959).

70. At one point, as Rockett and Rockett point out, Jordan nods explicitly toward O'Connor's short story, invoking its title when he has Peter ironically refer to Jody as their "guest" (2003, 127).

71. I owe this point to Darrell Moore.

72. Both Lloyd and Hanson suggest in different ways that the film demands a kind of rereading (see Lloyd 1999, 68), or a "reading back" (1999, 62) as Hanson calls it, although neither of them develop it in the direction I pursue here.

73. Heaney writes, in "The Betrothal of Cavehill," "Adam untouched, before the shock of gender" (1980, 206).

74. Silverman says that cuts divide "one shot from the next. The cut guarantees that both the preceding and the subsequent shots will function as structuring absences to the present shot" (1983, 205). Or, in Dayan's words, "no shot can constitute by itself a complete statement. The absent-one stands for that which any shot necessarily lacks in order to attain meaning: another shot" (Dayan 1999, 128). As Silverman puts it, "Each image is defined through its differences from those that surround it . . . . Each positive cinematic assertion represents an imaginary conversion of a whole series of negative ones. This castrating coherence, this definition of a discursive position for the viewing subject which necessitates not only its loss of being, but the repudiation of alternative discourses, is one of the chief aims of the system of suture" (1983, 205).

75. Leighton Grist is one of the few critics to have taken on the challenge presented by Dil's transgendering, although only at the expense of relegating race to the sidelines. Race, says Grist is "not a particular concern of this article" (2003, 25, n. 14). Grist thereby refuses to follow through the radical implications raised by Dil's transgendered identity as fully as they need to be followed through. In order to comprehend the challenge Dil presents, it is necessary to think it through not only in terms of gender but also in terms of race, nationality, and class, questions that Grist's interesting reading of the film ultimately foreclose on account of its Lacanian, fetishistic commitments. Having said that, this is certainly one of the more sophisticated articles to have been published on the gendered aspects of *The Crying Game* to date, despite the fact that at key moments it avoids the most difficult aspects of *The Crying Game* by having recourse to *M. Butterfly*. While there are undoubted similarities between the two films, and it may well be the case, as Grist suggests, that Jordan's final version of the screenplay for *The Crying Game* was influenced by *M. Butterfly*, Grist's oscillation between these two film texts allows for equivocation on a key point. Grist relies on the lack at the heart of Freudian and Lacanian castration theory, when in fact one of the greatest challenges of *The Crying Game* is its subversion of this trope.

76. At the same time I agree with Zilliax that "while the film's preoccupation with who knows and who doesn't is clearly part of Fergus's anxiety that he will be 'known' . . . it also indicates the degree to which Dil, though she may maintain, even cling to a very feminine look, and while a racial 'passing' clearly plays a part in her filmic construction, *doesn't* aspire to 'pass' in a number of other ways" (1997, 47).

77. Žižek says, "this is an 'impossible' love which will never be consummated" and in this sense, "far from denouncing heterosexual love as a product of male repression, it renders the precise circumstances in which this love can retain its absolute, unconditional character" (1994, 105). Yet, as McGee, who also quotes this passage, says, "heterosexual love can maintain its normative force only by deconstructing itself and thus displacing the binary system that constitutes its identity in the first place. Heterosexual love redeems itself by puncturing the illusion of its self-identity as the norm of a relation that does not exist" (1997, 158–59).

78. In the original ending of the film Dil gives Fergus a copy of Freud's *Interpretation of Dreams* when she visits him in prison. See Giles 1997, 37.

79. This confirms, rather than contradicting, Lloyd's observation that the plot is constituted by multiple narrative improbabilities (1999).

8. THE FETISHISTIC TEMPORALITY OF HEGEMONIC POSTCOLONIAL NATIONALIST NARRATIVES AND THE TRAUMATIC REAL OF ABJECTION

1. Lloyd 1999, 3. According to Lloyd, S. B. Cooke discusses Charles Trevelyan, who "transferred the logic of subject transformation from Indian schools" in the 1830s "to the administration of the Famine in Ireland"; cited by Lloyd 1999, 15. Lloyd says, "Each imperial system, within the larger global structures of colonialism, furnishes a complex space of incorporation and localization, all of which demand of the analyst an attentive differential practice" (1999, 15).

2. In fact, I think that the logic of atavism that Lloyd describes as implicating hegemonic discourses of nationalism confirms that these discourses abject feminist movements, and that the language of abjection would be more appropriate for Lloyd's own argument than that of conjuncture.

3. It should be noted that the intellectual's point of view is not the same as the people's point of view. In a nuanced account of the way in which class politics works itself out in a colonial context, Fanon shows in *The Wretched of the Earth* how the national bourgeoisie of the colonized culture discovers its historic mission in the role of intermediary (see 152). An internal division between a decadent urban bourgeoisie and a recalcitrant rural population is set up (see 153–55). Because the "birth of nationalist parties in the colonized countries is contemporary with the formation of an intellectual elite engaged in trade" (108), and because the "rank and file of a nationalist party is urban" and "have begun to profit . . . from the colonial setup" (60), they are quite willing to compromise with the colonial powers. Unlike the peasants of colonial countries who "alone are revolutionary, for they have nothing to lose and everything to gain" (61), the national middle class suffers from an "incapacity to think in terms of all the problems of the nation as seen from the point of view of the whole of that nation" and has "nothing better to do than to take on the role of manager for Western enterprise (154). For the peasant, "the enemy is not at all the occupying power with which they get along on the whole very well, but these people with modern ideas who mean to dislocate the aboriginal society, and who in doing so will take the bread out of their mouths" (110).

4. Amit S. Rai makes a similar point when he says that there is a "desire for totality" in Bhabha's "uncanny chain of difference" and that "Bhabha's postcolonialism seems unable to tolerate [a] surplus of meaning" (1998, 95).

5. Ranajit Guha and Gayatri Chakravorty Spivak (1988). Ranajit Guha (1997).

6. Benjamin 1969, 261–62. After quoting Benjamin, Benedict Anderson (1991, 24) goes on to say that the "novel and the newspaper . . . provided the technical means for 're-presenting' the *kind* of imagined community that is the nation" (25) and that "print-capitalism" thus made it "possible for rapidly growing numbers of people to think about themselves, and to relate themselves to others, in profoundly new ways" (36). It is perhaps worth noting that while Bhabha is critical of Anderson for not taking on board Benjamin's Messianic time, he himself is not entirely faithful to Benjamin's notion of time, in so far as he collapses clock time with calendrical time.

7. See Fanon 1967b, 38.

8. See E. Ann Kaplan's discussion of Fanon, which links the notion of the black as "cripple" to the film *The Home of the Brave* (1999, 150).

9. See Fanon 1968, 222. Also see Fanon 1967b, 38. For a useful discussion of how successful Fanon's distinction between the elite and the masses see Neil Lazarus (1990, 174).

10. Both Dipesh Chakrabarty (2000) and Partha Chatterjee (1993) point to this paradox in different ways.

11. My point here is not that Lloyd fails to see the importance of social movements such as feminism as distinct from, as both contributing to and diverging from, the more general discourses of anticolonial nationalism. Rather, in his adherence to the discourse of fetishism—even while he directs his efforts to complicating the usual narratives of nationalism that remain beholden to the state—he fails to see the masculine bias of the theoretical tools he uses to make his argument.

12. Narayan published a revised version of this essay in her book *Dislocating Cultures.* I have preferred to adhere to the earlier version.

13. T. J. Jackson Lears (1985, 573–74).

14. I owe the formulation of "constant deviation" to Eagleton 1990, 25.

15. Lears is referring to Gramsci.

16. See Gairola 2003 for a reading of *Fire* in relation to Gayatri Spivak's "Can the Subaltern Speak?"

9. Concluding Reflections on the Necrophilia of Fetishism

1. See Freud, "Mourning and Melancholia" (1953m).

2. See Fanon 1967a and Weate 2001.

3. Cowie says, "The camera's look is not always or simply a look which is powerful, which knows and thus can control. It is sometimes a character's look, and it is this play of looks and the spectator's movement of identification between these looks which is one of the pleasures of cinema" (1997, 101). To be fair, Metz recognizes this formally by discussing not just the identification (which he calls primary in the context of cinema) with the camera, but also identification with characters (which he calls secondary).

4. Rose has suggested that "sexual difference functions as the vanishing point" in the theories of Metz and Comolli (1986, 200). See also Lacan 1983, 47; Chase 1989, 82.

5. As Kaja Silverman puts it, we are "far from being liberated of [the] assumption . . . that the pleasure of identifying with a fictional character always turns on the spectator's rediscovery of his or her preordained place within gender, class, and race. Secondary identification, in other words, is frequently equated with interpellation into the dominant fiction. . . . It logically follows . . . that only a cinema which thwarts identification can be truly transformative" (1996, 85).

6. W. J. T. Mitchell also comments, in the context of a discussion of Marxist criticism, commodity fetishism, and ideology, on the tendency to make "a fetish out of the concept of fetishism" (1986, 163).

7. As Kristeva says, Lacan "emphasizes language and verbalization" and focuses on "the symbol" (2001, 174).

8. See Kristeva 2001, 140–41. Also see Klein et al. 1989, 75.

9. Constance Penley says: "'Small object o' in Lacanian algebra stands not for the object of desire itself, but for the experience of separation, separation from all the things that have been lost from the body (for example, the mother's breast, which was once experienced as part of the infant's body" (1989, 24).

10. The actors whose photographs are taken in the stills appear in Mike Leigh's previous films. See Watson 2004, 130–31.

11. Kalpana Seshadri-Crooks (2000, 124). I would like to thank Kalpana Seshadri-Crooks for taking the time to respond to an earlier version of my discussion of *Secrets and Lies*. Seshadri-Crooks says that the impossibility of knowing the identity of Hortense's father "functions as a point where our suture as subjects of race is produced symptomatically even as we navigate between the secret and the lie. Any attempt to manufacture a narrative to cover over that lacuna becomes a lethal exposure of the effect of the signifier upon our unconscious. . . . However, this strategy is rather limited in that it questions our suturing to race through what is essentially a mockery of our narrative compulsion, rather than an extended inquiry into the logic of racial knowledge and looking" (124). She describes the scene in which Cynthia "referring to her other (white) daughter Roxanne, who is mostly rude or indifferent towards her, says that she believes that she shares more of a resemblance with Hortense than with Roxanne. She says: 'I'm more like you really,' etc. At this the audience invariably bursts into laughter." Seshadri-Crooks suggests that this scene is "coded for comic effect. This scene is 'too much' for the film, and thus the possibility of similitude 'across races' is turned into a joke. There is something anxiety-producing in the notion that this mother and her daughter may share certain similarities. . . . It is not so much similitude itself that is uncanny as the discovery of one's own surprise in encountering similitude. The unconscious logic of the joke can be stated thus: The subject of race runs into his/her own splitness with regard to race. We are surprised by ourselves. We thought we knew that people across races could bear similarities. Then why are we surprised into recognizing it? To encounter something about ourselves that we knew but hadn't recognized is uncanny" (124–25).

12. Castoriadis 1987, 127. Also see 140–41. If for Fanon "the real Other for the white man . . . is the black man" (1967a, 161), Hortense's blackness serves to reflect the identity of this white family back to them.

13. See Kristeva, *About Chinese Women*. See also Sara Beardsworth (2004) on what she calls the "1980s trilogy."

14. It is worth noting that following this invocation of Mannoni, Kristeva adds an example that for some reason is missed out of the English translation (1992, 49).

15. In this way desire is structured in a way that parallels Foucault's discussion of sexuality, wherein the prohibition of sexuality contained in the repressive hypothesis functions as an incitement to discourse. Discourses of sexuality proliferate, far from being contained by their repression.

Bibliography

Adams, Parveen. 1996. *The Emptiness of the Signifier: Psychoanalysis and Sexual Differences.* New York: Routledge.

Adorno, Theodor. 1982. "On the Fetish-Character in Music and the Regression of Listening." In *The Essential Frankfurt School Reader,* ed. Andrew Arato and Eike Gebhardt. New York: Continuum.

————. 1992. *Quasi una fantasia: Essays on Modern Music.* Trans. Rodney Livingstone. London: Verso.

Adorno, Theodor, and Max Horkheimer. 1979. *Dialectic of Enlightenment.* London: Verso.

Agamben, Giorgio. 1981. *Stanze.* Trans. Yves Hersant. Paris: Christian Bourgeois.

Ahmed, Sarah. 2005. "The Skin of the Community: Affect and Boundary Formation." In *Revolt, Affect, Collectivity: The Unstable Boundaries of Kristeva's Polis,* ed. T. Chanter and E. Ziarek. Albany: State University of New York.

Allen, Richard, and Murray Smith. 1997. *Film Theory and Philosophy.* Oxford: Oxford University Press.

Althusser, Louis. 1971. "Ideology and Ideological State Apparatuses (Notes Towards an Investigation)." In *Lenin and Philosophy and Other Essays.* New York: Monthly Review Press.

American History X (United States, 1998). Tony Kaye, 119 min., New Line Cinema.

Anderson, Benedict. 1991. *Imagined Communities: Reflections on the Origin and Spread of Nationalism.* New York: Verso.

Andrew, Dudley. 2002. "The Theater of Irish Cinema," ed. Dudley Andrew and Luke Gibbons. Special issue. *Yale Journal of Criticism* 15, no. 1: 23–58.

Appiah, Kwame Anthony. 1992. *In My Father's House: Africa in the Philosophy of Culture.* New York: Oxford University Press.

Apter, Emily. 1999. *Feminizing the Fetish: Psychoanalysis and Narrative Obsession in Turn-of-the-Century France.* Ithaca, N.Y.: Cornell University Press.

Apter, Emily, and William Pietz, eds. 1993. *Fetishism as Cultural Discourse.* Ithaca, N.Y.: Cornell University Press.

Bass, Alan. 2000. *Difference and Disavowal: The Trauma of Eros.* Stanford: Stanford University Press.

Bataille, Georges. 1970. "L'abjection et les formes misérables." In *Œuvres complètes de G. Bataille.* Vol. 2. *Ecrits posthumes 1922–1940.* Paris: Gallimard.

————. 1985. *Visions of Excess: Selected Writings, 1927–1939.* Ed. with an introduction by Allan Stoekl. Trans. Allan Stoekl, with Carl R. Lovitt and Donald M. Leslie Jr.Theory and History of Literature series, vol. 14. Minneapolis: University of Minnesota Press.

Baudry, Jean-Louis. 1999a. "Ideological Effects of the Basic Cinematographic Apparatus." In *Film Theory and Criticism*, ed. Leo Braudy and Marshall Cohen. 5th ed. New York: Oxford University Press.

———. 1999b. "The Apparatus: Metapsychological Approaches to the Impression of Reality in Cinema." In *Film Theory and Criticism*, ed. Leo Braudy and Marshall Cohen. 5th ed. New York: Oxford University Press.

Beardsworth, Sara. 2004. *Julia Kristeva: Psychoanalysis and Modernity.*Ed. T. Chanter. Gender Theory Series. Albany: State University of New York.

———. 2005. "From Revolution to Revolt Culture." In *Revolt, Affect, Collectivity: The Unstable Boundaries of Kristeva's Polis*, ed. Tina Chanter and Ewa Ziarek. Gender Theory Series. Albany: State University of New York.

Behan, Brendan. 1959. *The Hostage.* London: Methuen.

Benjamin, Walter. 1968a. "Theses on the Philosophy of History." In *Illuminations: Essays and Reflections*, ed. Hannah Arendt. Trans. Harry Zohn. New York: Schocken Books.

———. 1968b. "The Work of Art in the Age of Mechanical Reproduction." In *Illuminations: Essays and reflections*, ed. Hannah Arendt. New York: Schocken Books.

Bennington, Geoffrey. 1990. "Postal politics and the institution of the nation." In *Nation and Narration*, ed. Homi K. Bhabha. New York: Routledge.

Berardinelli, James. Review of *American History X*. http://movie-reviews.colossus.net/master.html. Access date November 3, 2006.

Bernardi, Daniel. 1996. "The Voice of Whiteness: D. W. Griffith's Biograph Films (1908–1913)." In *The Birth of Whiteness: Race and the Emergence of U.S. Cinema*, ed. Daniel Bernardi. New Brunswick, N.J.: Rutgers University Press.

Bernheimer, Charles. 1992. "Penile Reference in Phallic Theory." *Differences* 4, no. 1: 116–32.

———. 1993. "Fetishism and Decadence: Salome's Severed Heads." In *Fetishism as Cultural Discourse*, ed. Emily Apter and William Pietz. Ithaca, N.Y.: Cornell University Press.

Bhabha, Homi K. 1990. "DissemiNation: Time, Narrative and the Margins of the Modern Nation." In *Nation and Narration*, ed. Homi K. Bhabha. New York: Routledge.

———. 1994. *The Location of Culture.* London: Routledge.

———. 2000. " 'Race,' Time and the Revision of Modernity." In *Theories of Race and Racism*, ed. Les Back and John Solomos. London: Routledge.

Bhattacharjee, Anannya. 1997. "The Public/Private Mirage: Mapping Homes and Undomesticating Violence Work in the South Asian Immigrant Community." In *Feminist Genealogies, Colonial Legacies, Democratic Futures*, ed. M. Jacqui Alexander and Chandra Talpade Mohanty. New York: Routledge.

The Birth of a Nation (United States, 1915). D. W. Griffith. 159 min. Allied Artists Classic Library.

Bogle, Donald. 1997. *Toms, Coons, Mulattoes, Mammies, and Bucks: An Interpretive History of Blacks in American Films.* New York: Continuum.

Boozer, Jack, Jr. 1995. "Bending Phallic Patriarchy in *The Crying Game*." *Journal of Popular Film and Television* 22: 172–79.

Boyarin, Daniel. 1998. "What Does a Jew Want? or, The Political Meaning of the Phallus." In *The Psychoanalysis of Race*, ed. Christopher Lane. New York: Columbia University Press.

Brandt, Joan. 1997. *Geopoetics: The Politics of Mimesis in Postructuralist French Poetry and Theory.* Stanford: Stanford University Press.

———. 2005. "Julia Kristeva and the Revolutionary Politics of *Tel Quel.*" In *Revolt, Affect, Collectivity: The Unstable Boundaries of Kristeva's Polis,* ed. T. Chanter and E. Ziarek. Albany: State University of New York.

Breaking the Waves (Denmark, 1996). Lars von Trier. 159 min. October Films.

Bruzzi, Stella. 1997. *Undressing Cinema: Clothing and Identity in the Movies.* New York: Routledge.

Buck-Morss, Susan. 1992. "Aesthetics and Anaesthetic: Walter Benjamin's Artwork Essay Reconsidered." *October* 62, nos. 3–4 (autumn): 3–41.

Burke, Edmund. 1987. *A Philosophical Enquiry into the Origin of Our Ideas of the Sublime and Beautiful,* ed. James T. Boulton. Oxford: Basil Blackwell.

Butler, Judith. 1993. *Bodies That matter. On the Discursive Limits of "Sex."* New York: Routledge.

———. 1997. *The Psychic Life of Power: Theories in Subjection.* Stanford: Stanford University Press.

———. 2000. *Antigone's Claim: Kinship between Life and Death.* New York: Columbia University Press.

Carby, Hazel V. 2000. "White Woman Listen! Black Feminism and the Boundaries of Sisterhood." In *Theories of Race and Racism,* ed. Les Back and John Solomos. London: Routledge.

Caruth, Cathy. 1996. *Unclaimed Experience: Trauma, Narrative, and History.* Baltimore: Johns Hopkins University Press.

Casablanca (United States, 1942). Michael Curtiz. 102 min. Warner Brothers.

Castoriadis, Cornelius. 1987. *The Imaginary Institution of Society.* Trans. Kathleen Blamey Cambridge, Mass.: MIT Press.

The Celebration (Denmark, 1998). Thomas Vinterberg. 106 min. October Film, Nimbus Film.

Chakrabarty, Dipesh. 2002. "A Small History of Subaltern Studies." In *Habitations of Modernity: Essays in the Wake of Subaltern Studies.* Chicago: University of Chicago Press.

Chase, Cynthia. 1989. "Desire and Identification in Lacan and Kristeva." In *Feminism and psychoanalysis,* ed. Richard Feldstein and Judith Roof. Ithaca, N.Y.: Cornell University Press.

Chatterjee, Partha. 1993. "Whose Imagined Community?" In *The Nation and Its Fragments: Colonial and Postcolonial Histories.* Princeton, N.J.: Princeton University Press.

Chow, Rey. 1999. "The Politics of Admittance: Female Sexual Agency, Miscegenation, and the Formation of Community in Frantz Fanon." In *Frantz Fanon: Critical Perspectives,* ed. Anthony C. Alessandrini. 34–56. New York: Routledge.

Clément, Catherine, and Julia Kristeva. 2001. *The Feminine and the Sacred.* Trans. Jane Marie Todd. New York: Columbia University Press.

Cole, Merrill. 1998. "Nat Turner's Thing." In *The Psychoanalysis of Race,* ed. Christopher Lane. New York: Columbia University Press.

Collins, Patricia Hill. 1990. *Black Feminist Thought: Knowledge, Consciousness, and the Politics of Empowerment.* New York: Routledge.

Copjec, Joan. 2000. "The Orthopsychic Subject: Film Theory and the Reception of Lacan." In *Oxford Readings in Feminism,* ed. E. Ann Kaplan. Oxford: Oxford University Press.

Cowie, Elizabeth. 1990. "Fantasia." In *M/F: The Woman in Question*, ed. Parveen Adams and Elizabeth Cowie. Cambridge, Mass.: MIT Press/October Books.

———. 1997. *Representing the Woman: Cinema and Psychoanalysis*. Minneapolis: University of Minnesota Press.

Creed, Barbara. 1993. *The Monstrous-Feminine: Film, Feminism, Psychoanalysis*. New York: Routledge.

Cripps, Thomas. 1977. *Slow Fade to Black: The Negro in American Film, 1900–1942*. London: Oxford University Press.

———. 1996. "The Making of *The Birth of a Race:* The Emerging Politics of Identity in Silent Movies." In *The Birth of Whiteness: Race and the Emergence of U.S. Cinema*, ed. Daniel Bernardi. New Brunswick, N.J.: Rutgers University Press.

The Crying Game (Ireland, 1992). Neil Jordan. 112 min. Miramax Films Release, Palace and Channel Four Films.

Danto, Arthur C. 1997. *After the End of Art: Contemporary Art and the Pale of History*. The A. W. Mellon Lectures in the Fine Arts, 1995, National Gallery of Art, Washington D.C. Bollingen Series 35, no. 44. Princeton, N.J.: Princeton University Press.

———. 2000. "Marcel Duchamp and the End of Taste: A Defense of Contemporary Art." In *Tout-fait: The Marcel Duchamp Studies Online Journal*, vol. 3. http://www.toutfait.com/duchamp.jsp?postid=846&keyword=. Accessed November 9, 2006.

———. 2003. *The Abuse of Beauty: Aesthetics and the Concept of Art*. The Paul Carus Lecture Series, no. 21. Chicago and La Salle, Ill.: Open Court.

Dayan, Daniel. 1999. "The Tutor-Code of Classical Cinema." In *Film Theory and Criticism*, 5th ed., ed. Leo Braudy and Marshall Cohen. Oxford and New York: Oxford University Press.

Debord, Guy. 1994. *The Society of the Spectacle*. Trans. Donald Nicholson-Smith. New York: Zone Books.

De Lauretis, Teresa. 1984. *Alice Doesn't: Feminism, Semiotics, Cinema*. Bloomington: Indiana University Press.

Deleuze, Gilles. 1986. *Cinema 1: The Movement-Image*. Trans. Hugh Tomlinson and Barbara Habberjam. Minneapolis: University of Minnesota Press.

———. 1989. *Cinema 2: The Time-Image*. Trans. Hugh Tomlinson and Robert Galeta. Minneapolis: University of Minnesota Press.

———. 1995. *Negotiations, 1972–1990*. Trans. Marin Joughin. New York: Columbia University Press.

Deleuze, Gilles, and Félix Guattari. 1983. *Anti-Oedipus: Capitalism and Schizophrenia*. Trans. Robert Hurley, Mark Seem, and Helen R. Lane. Minneapolis: University of Minnesota Press.

Derrida, Jacques. 1974. *Of Grammatology*. Trans. Gayatri Spivak. Baltimore, Md.: Johns Hopkins University Press.

———. 1981. *Dissemination*. Trans. Barbara Johnson. Chicago: University of Chicago Press.

———. 2002. "The Right to Philosophy from a Cosmopolitan Point of View." *Negotiations: Interventions and Interviews*, ed. and trans. Elizabeth Rottenberg. Stanford: Stanford University Press.

Diawara, Manthia, ed. 1993. "Black American Cinema: The New Realism." In *Black American Cinema*. New York: Routledge.

Doane, Mary Ann. 1987. *The Desire the Desire: The Woman's Film of the 1940s*. Bloomington: Indiana University Press.

———. 1991. *Femmes Fatales: Feminism, Film Theory, Psychoanalysis.* New York: Routledge.

Doane, Mary Ann, Patricia Mellencamp, and Linda Williams, eds. 1984. *Re-Vision.* Los Angeles: American Film Institute.

Donovan, Miyasaki. 2002. "The Confusion of Marxian and Freudian Fetishism in Adorno and Benjamin." *Philosophy Today* 46, no. 4 (winter): 429–43.

Douglas, Mary. 1999. *Purity and Danger: An Analysis of the Concepts of Pollution and Taboo.* New York: Routledge.

DuttaAhmed, Shantanu. 1998. " 'I thought you knew!': Performing the Penis, the Phallus, and Otherness in Neil Jordan's *The Crying Game.*" *Film Criticism* 23, no. 1:: 61–73.

Dyer, Richard. 1997. *White.* New York: Routledge.

Eagleton, Terry. 1990a. *The Ideology of the Aesthetic.* Oxford: Basil Blackwell.

———. 1990b. "Nationalism: Irony and Commitment." In *Nationalism, Colonialism and Literature,* ed. Terry Eagleton, Frederic Jameson, and Edward W. Said. London: Minneapolis Press.

Ebert, Roger. Review of *American History X.* http://rogerebert.suntimes .com/apps/pbcs.dll/article?AID=/19981030/REVIEWS/810300301/1023. Accessed November 9, 2006.

Edgar, Andrew. 1999. "Culture and Criticism: Adorno." *The Encyclopedia of Continental Philosophy,* ed. Simon Glendinning. Edinburgh: Edinburgh University Press.

Edge, Sarah. 1995. " 'Women are trouble, did you know that Fergus?' Neil Jordan's *The Crying Game.*" *Feminist Review* 50: 173–86.

Evans, Dylan. 1996. *An Introductory Dictionary of Lacanian Psychoanalysis.* London: Routledge.

Exotica. (Canada, 1994). Atom Egoyan, 103 min. Miramax Films.

Falsetto, Mario, ed. 2000. *Personal Visions: Conversations with Contemporary Film Directors.* Los Angeles: Silman-James Press.

Fanon, Frantz. 1967a. *Black Skin, White Masks.* Trans. Charles Lam Markmann. New York: Grove Press.

———. 1967b. "Racism and Culture." In *Toward the African Revolution,* ed. Haakon Chevalier. New York: Grove Press.

———. 1968. *The Wretched of the Earth.* Trans. Constance Farrington. New York: Grove Press.

Ferrell, Robyn. 2003. "Untitled: Art as Law." In *Studies in Practical Philosophy: A Journal of Ethical and Political Thought* 3, no. 1: 38–52.

Fire (Canada/India, 1996). Deepa Mehta. 104 min. Trial by Fire Films.

Flay, Joseph C. 1984. *Quest for Certainty.* Albany: State University of New York.

Foster, Hal. 1991. "Convulsive Identity." *October* 57 (summer): 18–54.

———. 1996a. *The Return of the Real: The Avant-Garde at the End of the Century: An October Book.* Cambridge, MA: MIT.

———. 1996b. "Obscene, Abject, Traumatic." *October* 78 (autumn): 106–24.

Fóti, Véronique. 1996. "Bound Transcendence and the Invisible: On Merleau-Ponty on Painting." *Symplokē* 4, nos. 1–2: 7–20.

———. 2003. *Vision's Invisibles: Philosophical Explorations.* Albany: State University of New York Press.

Foucault, Michel. 1973. *Madness and Civilization: A History of Insanity in the Age of Reason.* Trans. Richard Howard. New York: Vintage Books.

350   BIBLIOGRAPHY

Freud, Sigmund. 1953a. "Analysis of a Phobia in a Five-year-old Boy." In *The Standard Edition of the Complete Psychological Works*. Trans. James Strachey. Vol. 10. London: Hogarth Press and the Institute of Psycho-analysis.

———. 1953b. "Beyond the Pleasure Principle." In *The Standard Edition*. Vol. 18.

———. 1953c. " 'A Child is being Beaten': A Contribution to the Study of the Origin of Sexual Perversions." In *The Standard Edition*. Vol. 17.

———. 1953d. "Dissolution of the Oedipus Complex." In *The Standard Edition*. Vol. 19.

———. 1953e. "The Ego and the Id." In *The Standard Edition*. Vol. 19.

———. 1953f. "Fetishism." In *The Standard Edition*. Vol. 21.

———. 1953g. "Female Sexuality." In *The Standard Edition*. Vol. 21.

———. 1953h. "Group Psychology and the Analysis of the Ego." In *The Standard Edition*. Vol. 18.

———. 1953i. "The Infantile Genital Organization: An Interpolation into the Theory of Sexuality." In *The Standard Edition*. Vol. 19.

———. 1953j. *The Interpretation of Dreams*. In *The Standard Edition*. Vol. 4.

———. 1953k. "Introductory Lectures on Psycho-Analysis." In *The Standard Edition*. Vol. 16.

———. 1953l. "Jokes and Their Relation to the Unconscious." In *The Standard Edition*. Vol. 8.

———. 1953m. "Mourning and Melancholia." In *The Standard Edition*. Vol. 14.

———. 1953n. "Narcissism, On: An Introduction." In *The Standard Edition*. Vol. 14.

———. 1953o. "Negation." In *The Standard Edition*. Vol. 19.

———. 1953p. "Outline of Psycho-analysis, An." In *The Standard Edition*. Vol. 23.

———. 1953q. "Repression." In *The Standard Edition*. Vol. 14.

———. 1953r. "Three Essays on the Theory of Sexuality." In *The Standard Edition*. Vol. 7, 130–243.

———. 1953s. "Totem and Taboo." In *The Standard Edition*. Vol. 13.

———. 1953t. "Sexual Theories of Children, On the.." In *The Standard Edition*. Vol. 9.

———. 1953u. "Splitting of the Ego in the Process of Defence." In *The Standard Edition*. Vol. 23.

———. 1953v. "The Uncanny." In *The Standard Edition*. Vol. 17.

———. 1953w. "The Unconscious." In *The Standard Edition*. Vol. 14.

Furhammar, Leif, and Folke Isaksson. 1971. *Politics and Film*. Trans. Kersti French. New York: Prager.

Gairola, Rahul. 2002. "Burning with Shame: Desire and South Asian Patriarchy." In Gayatri Spivak, "Can the subaltern speak?" to Deepa Mehta's *Fire*. *Comparative Literature* 54, no. 1 (fall): 307–24.

Geller, Teresa. 2007. " 'The Film-Work Does Not Think': Refiguring Lyotard for Feminist Film Theory." In *Gender after Lyotard*, ed. Margret Grebowiz. Gender Theory Series. Albany: State University of New York Press.

Gibbons, Luke, and Kevin Whelan. 2002. "In Conversation with Stephen Rea: 2 February 2001, Yale University." *Yale Journal of Criticism* 15, no. 1: 5–21.

Giles, Jane. 1997. *The Crying Game*. BFI Modern Classics. London: British Film Institute.

Gooding-Williams, Robert. 1995. "Black Cupids, White Desires: Reading the Representation of Racial Difference in *Casablanca* and *Ghost*." In *Philosophy and Film*, ed. with an introduction by Cynthia A. Freeland and Thomas E. Wartenberg. London: Routledge.

————. 2006. *Look, A Negro! Philosophical Essays on Race, Culture and Politics.* New York: Routledge.

Gordon, Lewis. 1966. "The Black and the Body Politic: Fanon's Existential Phenomenological Critique of Psychoanalysis." In *Fanon: A Critical Reader,* ed. Lewis R. Gordon, T. Denean Sharpley-Whiting, and Renée T. White. Oxford: Blackwell.

Gould, Timothy. 1995. Intensity and Its Audiences: Toward a Feminist Perspective on the Kantian Sublime. In *Feminism and Tradition in Aesthetics,* ed. Peggy Zeglin Brand and Carolyn Korsmeyer. University Park: Pennsylvania State University Press.

Gramsci, Antonio. 1971. *Selections from Prison Notebooks,* ed. and trans. Quinton Hoare and Geoffrey Nowell Smith. New York: International Publishers.

Greenberg, Clement. 1993. "Modernist Painting." In *Clement Greenberg: The Collected Essays and Criticism,* ed. John O'Brian. Vol. 4: Modernism with a Vengeance: 1957–1969. Chicago and London: University of Chicago Press, 85–93.

Grist, Leighton. 2003. " 'It's Only a Piece of Meat': Gender Ambiguity, Sexuality, and Politics in *The Crying Game* and *M. Butterfly.*" *Cinema Journal* 42, no. 4: 3–28.

Guha, Ranajit, ed. 1997. *A Subaltern Studies Reader 1986–1995.* Minneapolis: University of Minneapolis.

Guha, Ranajit, and Gayatri Chakravorty Spivak, ed. 1988. *Selected Subaltern Studies.* New York: Oxford University Press.

Guerrero, Marie Anna Jaimes. 1997. "Civil Rights versus Sovereignty: Native American Women in Life and Land Struggles." In *Feminist Genealogies, Colonial Legacies, Democratic Futures,* ed. M. Jacqui Alexander and Chandra Mohanty. New York: Routledge.

Guillaumin, Colette. 1999. " 'I know it's not nice, but . . .': The changing face of 'Race.' " In *Race, Identity, and Citizenship: A Reader,* ed. Rodolfo D. Torres, Louis F. Mirón, and Jonathan Xavier Inda, 39–46. Oxford: Basil Blackwell.

Hamburger, Jeffrey F. 1997. " 'To Make Women Weep': Ugly Art as 'Feminine' and the Origins of Modern Aesthetics." *Res* 31 (spring): 9–33.

Handler, Kristin. 1994. "Sexing *The Crying Game:* Difference, Identity, Ethics." *Film Quarterly* 47, no. 3: 31–42.

Hanson, Helen. 1999. "The Figure in Question: The Transvestite Character as a Narrative Strategy in *The Crying Game.*" In *The Body's Perilous Pleasures: Dangerous Desires and Contemporary Culture,* ed. Michele Aaron. Edinburgh: Edinburgh University Press.

Harmetz, Aljean. 1992. *Round Up the Usual Suspects.* New York: Hyperion.

Heaney, Seamus. 1980. *Poems: 1965–1975.* New York: Farrar, Straus and Giroux.

————. 1990. *Selected Poems 1966–1987.* New York: Farrar, Straus and Giroux.

Hegel, G. W. F. 1975. *Aesthetics: Lectures on Fine Art.* Trans. T. M. Knox. Vol. 2. Oxford: Oxford University Press.

Heimann, Paula. 1989. "Certain Functions of Introjection and Projection in Early Infancy." In *Developments in Psychoanalysis,* ed. Melanie Klein, Paula Heimann, Susan Isaacs, and Joan Riviere. London: Karnac Books and the Institute of Psycho-analysis.

Hennessy, Rosemary. 2000. *Profit and Pleasure: Sexual Identities in Late Capitalism.* New York: Routledge.

Higson, Andrew. 1998. "British Cinema." In *Oxford Guide to Film Studies,* ed. John Hill and Pamela Church Gibson. Oxford: Oxford University Press.

hooks, bell. 1994. "Seduction and Betrayal: *The Crying Game* Meets *The Bodyguard*." In *Outlaw Culture: Resisting Representations*. New York: Routledge.

———. 1996a. "*Exotica:* Breaking Down to Break Through." In *Reel to Real: Race, Sex and Class at the Movies*. New York: Routledge.

———. 1996b. "The Oppositional Gaze: Black Female Spectators." In *Reel to Real: Race, Sex and Class at the Movies*, 197–213. New York: Routledge..

Horowitz, Gregg M. 2001. "Sustaining Loss: Art and Mournful Life." In *Atopia: Philosophy, Political Theory, Aesthetics*. Stanford: Stanford University Press.

Hyppolite, Jean. 1991. "A Spoken Commentary on Freud's *Verneinung*." In *The Seminar of Jacques Lacan, Book 1: Freud's Papers on Technique 1953–1954*, ed. Jacques-Alain Miller. Trans. John Forrester. New York: W. W. Norton.

Irigaray, Luce. 1985a. *Speculum of the Other Woman*. Trans. Gillian C. Gill. Ithaca, N.Y.: Cornell University Press; *Speculum de l'autre femme*, Paris: Minuit, 1974.

———. 1985b. *This Sex Which Is Not One*. Trans. Catherine Porter with Carolyn Burke. Ithaca, N.Y.: Cornell University Press.

———. 1991. The Poverty of Psychoanalysis. Trans. David Macey. In *The Irigaray Reader*, ed. Margaret Whitford. Oxford: Basil Blackwell.

———. 1993. *Sexes and Genealogies*. Trans. Gillian C. Gill. New York: Columbia University Press.

Isaacs, Susan. 1989. "The Nature and Function of Phantasy." In *Developments in Psychoanalysis*, ed. Melanie Klein, Paula Heimann, Susan Isaacs, and Joan Riviere. London: Karnac Books and the Institute of Psycho-analysis.

Jacobus, Mary. 1995. *First Things: The Maternal Imaginary in Literature, Art, and Psychoanalysis*. New York: Routledge.

James, Joy. 1995. "Black Femmes Fatales and Sexual Abuse in Progressive 'White' Cinema: Neil Jordan's *Mona Lisa* and *The Crying Game*." *Camera Obscura* 36: 33–45.

James, Robin. 2002. "The Musical Semiotic: Kristeva, *Don Giovanni*, and Feminist Revolt." *Philosophy Today*, SPEP supp. (2002): 113–19.

———. 2005. "The Conjectural Body." Ph.D. diss. in Philosophy, DePaul University.

Jordan, Neil. 1993. *A Neil Jordan Reader*. New York: Vintage Books, 1993.

Kant, Immanuel. 1951. *Critique of Judgment*. Trans. J. H. Bernard. New York: Hafner.

———. 1983. "Idea for a Universal History with a Cosmopolitan Intent." In *Perpetual Peace and Other Essays on Politics, History, and Morals*. Trans. Ted Humphrey. Indianapolis: Hackett.

Kaplan, E. Ann. 1983. *Women and Film: Both Sides of the Camera*. New York: Routledge.

———. 1999. "Fanon, Trauma and Cinema." In *Frantz Fanon: Critical Perspectives*, ed. Anthony C. Alessandrini. New York: Routledge.

Klein, Melanie. 1975a. *Envy and Gratitude and Other Works 1946–1963*. New York: Free Press.

———. 1975b. *The Psycho-analysis of Children*. Trans. Alix Strachey. New York: Dell Publishing.

———. 1986. *The Selected Melanie Klein*, ed. Juliet Mitchell. New York: Free Press.

Koerner, Joseph Leo. 1977. Editorial: The abject of art history. *Res* 31. Spring: 5–8.

Kofman, Sarah. 1980. *The Enigma of Woman: Woman in Freud's Writings*. Trans. Catherine Porter. Ithaca, N.Y.: Cornell University Press.

Krauss, Rosalind. 1996. "*Informe* without Conclusion." *October* 78 (autumn): 88–105.

Krips, Henry. 1999. *Fetish: An Erotics of Culture.* Ithaca, N.Y.: Cornell University Press.

Kristeva, Julia. (n.d.). "Fetishizing the Abject, interview with Sylvere Lotringer." *More & Less,* ed. Sylvere Lotringer. Produced by The Fine Arts Graduate Studies Program and the Theory, Criticism and Curatorial Studies and Practice Graduate Programs, Art Center College of Design, Pasadena, Calif. Brooklyn, N.Y.: Semiotext(e)/Autonomedia.

———. 1982. *Powers of Horror: An Essay on Abjection.* Trans. Leon S. Roudiez. New York: Columbia University Press.

———. 1984. *Revolution in Poetic Language.* Trans Margaret Waller. New York: Columbia University Press.

———. 1986a. "Ellipsis on Dread and the Specular Seduction," In *Narrative, Apparatus, Ideology,* ed. Philip Rosen. New York: Columbia University Press.

———. 1986b. "Women's Time." In *The Kristeva reader,* ed. Toril Moi. Oxford: Basil Blackwell.

———. 1987. *Tales of Love.* Trans. Leon S. Roudiez. New York: Columbia University Press.

———. 1989. *Black Sun: Depression and Melancholia,* Trans. Leon S. Roudiez, New York: Columbia University Press.

———. 1991. *Strangers to Ourselves.* Trans. Leon S. Roudiez. New York: Columbia University Press.

———. 1993. *Nations without Nationalism.* Trans. Leon S. Roudiez. New York: Columbia University Press.

———. 1995a. *New Maladies of the Soul.* Trans. Ross Guberman. New York: Columbia University Press.

———. 1995b. "Of Word and Flesh: An Interview with Julia Kristeva by Charles Penwarden." In *Rites of Passage: Art for the End of the Century,* ed. Stuart Morgan and Frances Morris. London: Tate Gallery.

———. 1998. "Pouvoirs de l'horreur." In *Visions capitales,* 111–39. Paris: Réunion des Musées Nationaux.

———. 2000. *The Sense and Non-Sense of Revolt: The Powers and Limits of Psychoanalysis.* Vol. 1. Trans. Jeanine Herman. New York: Columbia University Press.

———. 2001. *Melanie Klein.* Trans. Ross Guberman. Vol. 2, *Female Genius.* New York: Columbia University Press.

———. 2002. *Intimate Revolt.* Vol., 2, *The Powers and Limits of Psychoanalysis.* Trans. Jeanine Herman. New York: Columbia University Press.

Lacan, Jacques. 1977a. *Ecrits: A Selection.* Trans. Alan Sheridan. London: Tavistock Publications.

———. 1977b. *The Four Fundamental Concepts of Psycho-analysis,* ed. Jacques-Alain Miller. Trans. Alan Sheridan. Harmondsworth, Middlesex: Penguin Books.

———. 1983. *Feminine Sexuality,* ed. Juliette Mitchell and Jacqueline Rose. New York: W. W. Norton.

———. 1990. "A Challenge to the "Psychoanalytic Establishment." Trans. Jeffrey Mehlman, ed. Joan Copjec. In *Television,* trans. Denis Hollier, Rosalind Krauss, and Annette Michelson. New York: W. W. Norton.

———. 1991. *The Seminar of Jacques Lacan. Book I: Freud's Papers on Technique, 1953–1954.* Trans. John Forrester, ed. Jacques-Alain Miller. New York: W. W. Norton.

Laplanche, Jean, and J.-B. Pontalis. 1973. *The Language of Psychoanalysis*, trans. Donald Nicholson-Smith. New York: W. W. Norton.

———. 1986. "Fantasy and the Origins of Sexuality." In *Formations of Fantasy*, ed. Victor Burgin, James Donald, and Cora Kaplan. London: Methuen. 1968. Reprinted from *The International Journal of Psychoanalysis* 49: 1–11.

Lazarus, Neil. 1999. "Disavowing Decolonization: Fanon, Nationalism, and the Question of Representation in Postcolonial Theory." In *Frantz Fanon: Critical Perspectives*, ed. Anthony C. Alessandrini. 161–94. New York: Routledge.

Lears, T. J. Jackson. 1985. "The Concept of Cultural Hegemony: Problems and Possibilities." *American Historical Review* 90, no. 3: 567–92.

Lessing, Gotthold Ephram. 1984. *Laocoön: An Essay on The Limits of Painting and Poetry*. Trans. Edward Allen McCormick. Baltimore: Johns Hopkins University Press.

Lévi-Strauss. 1969. *The Elementary Structures of Kinship*. Trans. James Harle Bell, John Richard von Sturmer, and Rodney Needham. Boston: Beacon Press.

Lipman, Amanda. 1995. *Exotica. Sight and Sound* 5 (May): 45.

Lloyd, David. 1999. "Critical Conditions: Field Day Essays." In *Ireland After History*. Notre Dame, Ind., and Cork: University of Notre Dame Press in association with Field Day.

Lott, Tommy L. 1995. "A No-Theory of Contemporary Black Cinema." In *Cinema of the Black Diaspora: Diversity, Dependence, and Oppositionality*, ed. Michael T. Martin. Detroit: Wayne State University.

———. 1999. Aesthetics and Politics in Contemporary Black Film Theory. In *Film Theory and Philosophy*, ed. Richard Allen and Murray Smith. Oxford: Oxford University Press.

Lugowski, David. 1994. "Genre Conventions and Visual Style in *The Crying Game*." *Cineaste* 20, no. 1: 31–35.

Lyon, Elizabeth. 1988. "The Cinema of Lol V. Stein." In *Feminism and Film Theory*, ed. Consance Penley. New York: Routledge.

Lyotard, Jean-François. 1983. "Fiscourse, digure: The Utopia behind the Scenes of the Phantasy." *Theatre Journal* 35: 3.

Mannoni, Octave. 1969. *Clefs pour l'imaginaire ou l'autre scène*. Paris: Editions du Seuil.

Marder, Elissa 2005. Presentation on panel, "Futures of Psychoanalysis," Society for Phenomenology and Existential Philosophy Conference, Salt lake City, Utah, 2005.

Margaret's Museum (Canada, 1995). Mort Ransen. 118 min. Cinépix Film Properties.

Marx, Karl. 1977. Capital: *A Critique of Political Economy*. Vol. 1. Introduced by Ernest Mandel and trans. Ben Fowkes. New York: Vintage Books.

Mattick, Paul. 1995. "Beautiful and Sublime: 'Gender Totemism' in the Constitution of Art." In *Feminism and Tradition in Aesthetics*, ed. Peggy Zeglin Brand and Carolyn Korsmeyer. University Park: Pennsylvania State University Press.

Ma vie en rose (My life in pink) (Belgium, 1997). Alain Berliner. 89 min. Sony Pictures.

McClintock, Anne. 1995. *Imperial Leather: Race, Gender and Sexuality in the Colonial Contest*. New York: Routledge.

McGee, Patrick. 1997. *Cinema, Theory and Political Responsibility in Contemporary Culture*. Cambridge: Cambridge University Press.

Merleau-Ponty, Maurice. 1993. "Cézanne's Doubt." In *The Merleau-Ponty Aesthetics Reader: Philosophy and Painting,* ed. Galen A. Johnson. Trans. Michael B. Smith. Evanston, Ill.: Northwestern University Press.

Metz, Christian. 1982. *The Imaginary Signifier: Psychoanalysis and the Cinema.* Trans. Celia Britton, Annwyl Williams, Ben Brewster, and Alfred Guzzetti. Bloomington: Indiana University Press.

Michel, Frann. 1994. "Racial and Sexual Politics in *The Crying Game.*" *Cineaste,* 20, no. 1: 32–34.

Mitchell, W. J. T. 1986. *Iconology: Image, Text, Ideology.* Chicago: University of Chicago Press.

Mohanty, Chandra Talpade. 1997a. "Under Western Eyes: Feminist Scholarship and Colonial Discourses." In *Third World Women and the Politics of Feminism,* ed. Chandra Talpade Mohanty, Ann Russo, and Lourdes Torres. Bloomington: Indiana University Press.

———. 1997b. :Women Workers and Capitalist Scripts: Ideologies of Domination, Common Interests, and the Politics of Solidarity." In *Feminist Genealogies, Colonial Legacies, Democratic futures,* ed. Jacqui Alexander and Chandra Talpade Mohanty. New York: Routledge.

Moore, Darrell. 1993. "Now You Can See It: The Liberal Aesthetic and Racial Representation in *The Crying Game.*" *Cineaction* 32: 63–67.

Mulvey, Laura. 1990. "Visual Pleasure and Narrative Cinema." In *Issues in Feminist Film Criticism,* ed. Patricia Erens. Bloomington: Indiana University Press.

———. 1996. *Fetishism and Curiosity.* Bloomington: Indiana University Press with the British Film Institute.

Nadal, Marita. 2000. "Beyond the Gothic Sublime: Poe's Pym or the Journey of Equivocal (E)motions." *Mississippi Quarterly* 53, no. 3: 373–87.

Narayan, Uma. 1997a. "Contesting Cultures: 'Westernization,'Respect for Cultures, and Third-World Feminists." In *The Second Wave: A Reader in Feminist Theory,* ed. Linda Nicholson. New York: Routledge.

———. 1997b. *Dislocating Cultures: Identities, Traditions and Third World Feminism.* New York: Routledge.

Nash, Catherine. 1994. "Remapping the Body/Land: New Cartographies of Identity, Gender, and Landscape in Ireland." In *Writing Women and Space: Colonial and Postcolonial Geographies,* ed. Allison Blunt and Gillian Rose. New York: Guildford Press.

Nesbit, Molly. 1993. "Apart without a Face: *Orlando* and *The Crying Game.*" *Artforum International Magazine* 31.

O'Connor, Frank. 1979. *Guests of the Nation.* Dublin: Poolberg Press.

Oliver, Kelly. 1997. *Family Values: Subjects between Nature and Culture.* New York: Routledge.

———. 2001. *Witnessing: Beyond Recognition.* Minnesota: University of Minnesota Press.

———. 2005. "Revolt and Forgiveness." In *Revolt, Affect, Collectivity: The Unstable Boundaries of Kristeva's Polis,* ed. T. Chanter and E. Ziarek. Albany: State University of New York.

Oliver, Kelly, and Benigno Trigo. 2003. *Noir Anxiety.* Minneapolis: University of Minnesota Press.

Penley, Constance. 1989. *The Future of an Illusion: Film, Feminism and Psychoanalysis.* Minneapolis: University of Minnesota Press.

Phillips, John. 1998. "The Tissue of Authority: Violence and the Acquisition of Knowledge." In *Reading Melanie Klein*, ed. Lyndsey Stonebridge and John Phillips. New York: Routledge.

Pick, Zuzana M. 1993. *The New Latin American Cinema: A Continental Project.* Austin: University of Texas Press.

Pietz, William. 1985. "The Problem of the Fetish, I." *Res.* 9: 5–17.

Rai, Amit S. 1998. " 'Thus Spake the Subaltern . . .': Postcolonial Criticism and the Scene of Desire." In *The Psychoanalysis of Race*, ed. Christopher Lane. New York: Columbia University Press.

Ray, Robert. 1985. *A Certain Tendency of the Hollywood Cinema 1930–1980.* Princeton, N.J.: Princeton University Press.

Renshaw, Scott. http://reviews/imdb.com/Reviews/152/15207. Access date: November 9, 2006.

Ricciardi, Alessia. 2003. "Cultural Memory in the Present." In *The Ends of Mourning: Psychoanalysis, Literature, Film.* Stanford, Cal.: Stanford University Press.

Rockett, Emer, and Kevin Rockett. 2003. *Neil Jordan: Exploring Boundaries.* Contemporary Irish Filmmakers Series. Dublin: Liffey Press.

Rose, Jacqueline. 1986. *Sexuality in the Field of Vision.* London: Verso.

———. 1998. "Negativity in the Work of Melanie Klein." In *Reading Melanie Klein*, ed. John Phillips and Lyndsey Stonebridge. London and New York: Routledge.

Rubin, Gayle. 1975. "The Traffic in Women: Notes on the 'Political Economy' of Sex." In *Toward an Anthropology of Women*, ed. RaynaR. Reiter. New York: Monthly Review Press.

Schiebinger, Londa. 1993. *Nature's Body: Gender in the Making of Modern Science.* Boston: Beacon Press.

Secrets and Lies (England, 1996). Mike Leigh. 142 min. October Films.

Sedgwick, Eve. 1985. *Between Men: English Literature and Male Homosocial Desire.* New York: Columbia University Press.

Seshadri-Crooks, Kalpana. 2000. *Desiring Whiteness: A Lacanian Analysis of Race.* New York: Routledge.

Silverman, Kaja. 1983. *The Subject of Semiotics.* New York: Oxford University Press.

———. 1988. *The Acoustic Mirror: The Female Voice in Psychoanalysis and Cinema.* Bloomington: Indiana University Press.

———. 1996. *The Threshold of the Visible World.* New York: Routledge.

Simpson, Mark. 1994. *Male Impersonators: Men Performing Masculinity.* New York: Routledge.

Solanas, Fernando, and Octavio Gettino. 2000. "Towards a Third Cinema." In *Film and Theory: An Anthology*, ed. Robert Stam and Toby Miller. Oxford: Blackwell.

Spivak, Gayatri Chakravorty. 1988. "Can the Subaltern Speak?" In *Marxism and the Interpretation of Culture*, ed. Cary Nelson and Lawrence Grossberg. Urbana: University of Illinois Press.

———. 1999. *A Critique of Postcolonial Reason: Toward a History of the Vanishing Present.* Cambridge, Mass.: Harvard University Press.

Steihaug, Jan-Ove. 2005. "Abject/*informe*/trauma: Discourses on the Body in American Art of the Nineties." http://www.forart.no/steihaug/introduction. html. Access date: December 13, 2005.

Stevenson, Jack. 2002. *Lars von Trier.* World Directors Series. London: British Film Institute.

Taylor, Clyde. 1996. "The Re-birth of the Aesthetic in Cinema." In *The Birth of Whiteness: Race and the Emergence of U.S. Cinema,* ed. Daniel Bernardi. New Brunswick, N.J.: Rutgers University Press.

Taylor, Simon. 1993. "The Phobic Object: Abjection in Contemporary Art." *Abject art: Repulsion and Desire in American Art: Selections from the Permanent Collection.* June 23–August 29, 1993. New York: Whitney Museum of American Art.

Walker, Alexander. http://www.thisislondon.co.uk.html/hottx/side_nav.html. Access date: November 9, 2006.

Wallace, Michele. 1993. "Race, Gender and Psychoanalysis in Forties Film: *Lost Boundaries, Home of the Brave,* and *The Quiet One.*" In *Black American Cinema,* ed. Diawara, Manthia. New York: Routledge.

Watson, Garry. 2004. *The Cinema of Mike Leigh: A Sense of the Real.* London: Wallflower Press.

Weate, Jeremy. 2001. "Fanon, Merleau-Ponty and the Difference of Phenomenology." In *Race: Blackwell Readings in Continental Philosophy,* ed. Robert Bernasconi. Oxford: Blackwell.

Willemen, Paul. 1989. *Questions of Third Cinema,* ed. Jim Pines and Paul Willemen. London: British Film Institute.

Williams, Caroline. 1994. "Feminism, Subjectivity and Psychoanalysis: Towards a (Corpo)real Knowledge." In *Knowing the Difference: Feminist Perspectives in Epistemology,* ed. Kathleen Lennon and Margaret Whitford. London: Routledge.

Williams, Linda, ed. 1997. *Viewing Positions: Ways of Seeing Film.* New Brunswick, N.J.: Rutgers University Press.

Williams, Raymond. 1997. *Problems in Materialism and Culture: Selected Essays.* New York: Routledge. Verso.

Wright, Richard. 1998. *Native Son.* New York: HarperCollins.

Young, Iris Marion. 1990. *Justice and the Politics of Difference.* Princeton, N.J.: Princeton University Press.

Young, Lola. 2000. "Imperial Culture: The Primitive, the Savage and White Civilization." In *Theories of Race and Racism,* ed. Les Back and John Solomos. London: Routledge.

Young, Robert J. C. 1995. *Colonial Desire: Hybridity in Theory, Culture and Race.* New York: Routledge.

Ziarek, Ewa. 2001. *An Ethics of Dissensus: Postmodernity, Feminism, and the Politics of Radical Democracy.* Stanford: Stanford University Press.

———. 2005. "Fanon and Kristeva: Revolutionary Violence and Ironic Articulation." In *Revolt, Affect, Collectivity: The Unstable Boundaries of Kristeva's Polis,* ed. T. Chanter and E. Ziarek. Albany: State University of New York.

Zilliax, Amy. 1997. "The Scorpion and the Frog: Agency and Identity in Neil Jordan's *The Crying Game.*" *Camera Obscura.* 35: 25–51.

Žižek, Slavoj. 1994. *The Metastases of Enjoyment: Six Essays on Women and Causality.* London: Verso.

———. 1992. *The Sublime Object of Ideology.* New York: Verso.

———. 2000. *Everything You Always Wanted to Know About Hitchcock but Were Afraid to Ask.* London: Verso.

Index

seeing, 310n19; and Jordan, 235; Kristeva on, 78, 113, 124; and sexuality, 314n21; and spectators, 121–122; and transgendered identity, 314n21

Holbein, Hans, 137, 313n43

Hollow Reed (Pope), 290–294

Hollywood, 182, 200

holocaust, 88, 94, 116

homoeroticism/homosexuality, 15–16, 136, 166, 167, 326n9. *See also under specific films*

hooks, bell: and *The Crying Game,* 219, 221, 244, 336n45; and *Exotica,* 325n43, 325n46; and gazes, 23, 108; and gender, 330n13

Horkheimer, Max, 158, 322n18

Horowitz, Gregg M., 308n1

horror. *See also Powers of Horror* (Kristeva): and abjection, 122, 125; context of, 90–91; in *The Crying Game,* 232; of female genitalia, 32, 58–59, 81, 82, 338n59; at identificatory regimes, 139; Kristeva on, 124; origins of, 123; power of, 145

horror film, 17, 79, 83, 213. *See also* Hitchcock, Alfred

The Hostage (Behan), 219

"Hottentot Venus," 92

Hyppolite, Jean: on Freud, 62, 63–64, 66–67; on intellect, 306n38; and negation, 21, 54

identification: and abjection, 23, 46, 303n27; with camera, 276, 300n6; compulsory, 108–109; in *The Crying Game,* 236; disruption of, 43, 235–236; and dominant systems, 45, 51; and fantasy, 97, 126; with father, 47; in feminist film theory, 113; Freud on, 46–47; Freudo-Lacanian, 30; hysterical, 106–108, 109, 113–114, 300n6; and the imaginary, 16–17, 75; in Kristeva, 54; and language, 75; maternal, 21, 51, 75; in modern film, 86; and object-choice, 46; primary, 45, 48, 54, 70, 71, 308n46; process of, 313n11;

projective, 21, 54; by protagonists, 89, 95; and psychoanalytic theory, 33, 35, 106–108; by spectators, 34–35, 96, 99; and the symbolic, 43, 308n46; unconscious, 314n22; unfamiliar, 42

identificatory regimes: complicity of, 274; destabilizing, 122; disrupting, 273; heterosexist, 109; and identification, 108; and imaginaries, 1; redefinition of, 43–44

identities. *See also specific identities:* and abjection, 7, 9, 46, 303n27, 316n34; complicity of, 2, 219, 228–229, 320n4, 341n75; disruption of, 319n52; instability of, 102, 248; multiple, 288–289, 299n24; and sexual difference, 274

ideology, 100, 108, 263

idiolect, 317n38

images, 145–146, 150, 312n4. *See also* thought specular

imaginaries. *See also* third, imaginary: and abjection, 17; emergence of, 45; in film, 35; logic of, 18; male/psychoanalytic, 56, 338n59; in *Margaret's Museum,* 89; nationalist, 24, 25, 62, 73–74; political, 19, 21; postcolonial, 27; of psychoanalytic theory, 40; racist, 19; and the real, 95; and the symbolic, 43, 113, 152–153, 292–293, 302n25; various, 24, 25; Western, 30, 325n47

imagination: lack of, 117

Imagined Communities (Anderson), 259

immigrants, 207

Imperial Leather: Race, Gender and Sexuality in the Colonial Contest (McClintock), 320n4

imperialist theory. *See* discourses, progressive

impurity, 20

incest, 101, 320n5

Indian culture, 262, 263, 264, 266

indiscernibility, 88, 89, 95

individuation, 31

"The Infantile Genital Organization" (Freud), 13, 48, 304n34

TINA CHANTER is Professor of Philosophy at DePaul University, Chicago. She is author of *Ethics of Eros: Irigaray's Re-writing of the Philosophers*, *Time, Death and the Feminine: Levinas with Heidegger*, and *Gender* and editor of *Feminist Interpretations of Emmanuel Levinas*. She is co-editor of *Revolt, Affect, Collectivity: The Unstable Boundaries of Kristeva's Polis*, and editor of the Gender Theory series at the State University of New York Press.

Printed and bound by CPI Group (UK) Ltd, Croydon, CR0 4YY

09/06/2025

14685942-0001